More maps & texts

Parrish
Towne & Castle
Slygoe Harbour
Slygoe
Castle
Abie
Fort
Snt Johns Parrish
Catt
rie

More maps & texts

Sources and the Irish Historic Towns Atlas

Edited by H.B. Clarke and Sarah Gearty

First published in 2018 by the
Royal Irish Academy,
Irish Historic Towns Atlas,
19 Dawson Street,
Dublin 2.

www.ria.ie

Copyright © The Royal Irish Academy

ISBN 978-1-908997-73-9

British Library Cataloguing-in-Publication Data. A catalogue record is available from
the British Library.

The Royal Irish Academy is grateful to the Marc Fitch Fund for a grant towards
production.

MARC FITCH FUND

Design: Fidelma Slattery
Index: Angela Byrne
Printed in Poland by L&C Printing Group

Contents

Part I: Introduction

Part II: Monastic proto-towns and Viking towns

Part III: Anglo-Norman, gaelicised and plantation towns

Part IV: Georgian and Victorian towns

Preface

The exploration of the urban past has a long and venerable history but from the 1970s a new interest in the history of towns began to develop, exemplified by the 1972 collective volume edited by Peter Clark and Paul Slack, *Crisis and order in English towns*. In Ireland the decision to devote the biennial Irish Conference of Historians in 1979 to the theme of 'The town in Ireland' demonstrates that interest here too was growing. Those involved in the practice of this sort of urban history had no agenda or complex theoretical underpinning. What they emphasised was the diversity of urban life in the past, from the physical world of topography and archaeology through urban government to economics and urban sociability, a diverse approach clearly revealed in the multi-volume, multi-authored Mercier Press Irish Country Towns/Irish Cities series (1994–5) and the Cambridge Urban History of Britain (2000). The study of towns was, therefore, a good way of drawing together, in a particular social, legal and topographical context, themes usually treated by a wide range of people who studied the past.

It was into this context that the Irish Historic Towns Atlas was born, with the first fascicles appearing in 1986. As the preface to each atlas states, fascicles were not conceived of as a complete piece of urban history but rather as a contribution to this very widely defined exploration of the entire range of the urban past. Some authors of fascicles, notably Anthony Wilson (Downpatrick), Harman Murtagh (Athlone), Stephen Royle and Raymond Gillespie (Belfast) and Brian Ó Dálaigh (Ennis), have written more developed urban histories of their own places but that was not their task when compiling the atlas. Fascicles were intended to contribute to a particular aspect of the Irish urban past — the topographical evolution of towns. In this it was inspired by the wider European project, of which it is part, that has created over 520 atlases to date.

As with the wider European project the aim of the Irish atlas has been twofold. First, each fascicle provides the evidence for, and some analysis of, the morphological development of a particular place with an interaction of maps depicting points in time and the textual topographical information that records the development of urban sites over time. In this it has been remarkably successful with twenty-eight fascicles across the entire country published to date, each one making a contribution to local urban studies. Nevertheless, studies of particular places in the model of nineteenth-century town histories can tend towards the simple anti-quarian accumulation of information unless the more complex problem of context is introduced.

This volume, and its predecessor *Maps and texts: exploring the Irish Historic Towns Atlas* (2013), develop the second strand to the atlas project — the question of providing a comparative context for the existing work. With twenty-eight published fascicles, it should be possible to consider whether there are general morphological similarities or differences (or perhaps, over time, both) between towns and types of site and to reflect on the processes that created difference or similarity over time. Deploying morphological evidence in this way is an attempt to grapple with what Estyn Evans described, in another context, as the question of 'personality'. This volume is concerned particularly with the written, cartographical and archaeological sources for the Irish Historic Towns Atlas, but also with making comparisons to discover what is unique about urban places and what is generic, how those categories of urban life interacted and changed over time and why that might be so. In that this volume tries to broaden the ways in which the historic towns atlas and its sources might be used, to consider morphology as a social process in the making of urban Ireland. These reflections, necessarily, will engage with some of the criticisms of the project that have been made to date and the result will be a more exciting and expansive approach to Irish urban history that will find many imitators.

Raymond Gillespie, H.B. Clarke, Jacinta Prunty, Michael Potterton
February 2018

Irish Historic Towns Atlas

Editorial team, authors and publications, 2018

IHTA series editors: H.B. Clarke, Raymond Gillespie, Jacinta Prunty, Michael Potterton; consultant editors: J.H. Andrews, Anngret Simms; cartographic editor: Sarah Gearty; editorial assistants: Jennifer Moore, Frank Cullen.

Bound volumes

Nos 1–6 *Volume I* (1996)
Nos 7–10, 13, 14 *Volume II* (2005)
Nos 15, 16, 18, 20, 21 *Volume III* (2012)

Individual fascicles

No. 1 *Kildare* (1986) by J.H. Andrews
No. 2 *Carrickfergus* (1986) by Philip Robinson
No. 3 *Bandon* (1988) by Patrick O'Flanagan
No. 4 *Kells* (1990) by Anngret Simms with Katharine Simms
No. 5 *Mullingar* (1992) by J.H. Andrews with K.M. Davies
No. 6 *Athlone* (1994) by Harman Murtagh
No. 7 *Maynooth* (1995) by Arnold Horner
No. 8 *Downpatrick* (1997) by R.H. Buchanan and Anthony Wilson
No. 9 *Bray* (1998) by K.M. Davies
No. 10 *Kilkenny* (2000) by John Bradley
No. 11 *Dublin, part I, to 1610* (2002) by H.B. Clarke
No. 12 *Belfast, part I, to 1840* (2003) by Raymond Gillespie and Stephen A. Royle
No. 13 *Fethard* (2003) by Tadhg O'Keeffe
No. 14 *Trim* (2004) by Mark Hennessy
No. 15 *Derry-Londonderry* (2005) by Avril Thomas
No. 16 *Dundalk* (2006) by Harold O'Sullivan
No. 17 *Belfast, part II, 1840 to 1900* (2007) by Stephen A. Royle
No. 18 *Armagh* (2007) by Catherine McCullough and W.H. Crawford
No. 19 *Dublin, part II, 1610 to 1756* (2008) by Colm Lennon

No. 20 *Tuam* (2009) by J.A. Claffey
No. 21 *Limerick* (2010) by Eamon O'Flaherty
No. 22 *Longford* (2010) by Sarah Gearty, Martin Morris and Fergus O'Ferrall
No. 23 *Carlingford* (2011) by Harold O'Sullivan and Raymond Gillespie
No. 24 *Sligo* (2011) by Fióna Gallagher and Marie-Louise Legg
No. 25 *Ennis* (2012) by Brian Ó Dálaigh
No. 26 *Dublin, part III, 1756 to 1847* (2014) by Rob Goodbody
No. 27 *Youghal* (2015) by David Kelly and Tadhg O'Keeffe
No. 28 *Galway/Gaillimh* (2016) by Jacinta Prunty and Paul Walsh

POCKET MAPS

Dublin c. 840 to c. 1540: the medieval town in the modern city (2002) by H.B. Clarke
Belfast c. 1600 to c. 1900: the making of the modern city (2007) by Raymond Gillespie and
    Stephen A. Royle
New Ross c. 1200 to c. 1900: seven hundred years in the making (2007) by Linda Doran
Dublin 1610 to 1756: the making of the early modern city (2009) by Colm Lennon
Limerick c. 840 to c. 1900: Viking longphort *to Victorian city* (2010) by Eamon O'Flaherty
    and Jennifer Moore
Galway c. 1200 to c. 1900: from medieval borough to modern city (2015) by Jacinta Prunty
    and Paul Walsh

ANCILLARY PUBLICATIONS

Georgian Belfast, 1750–1850: maps, buildings and trades (2004) by C.E.B. Brett with
    contributions by Raymond Gillespie and W.A. Maguire
Maps and views of Derry 1600–1914: a catalogue (2005) by W.S. Ferguson
John Rocque's Dublin: a guide to the Georgian city (2010) by Colm Lennon and John
    Montague
Reading the maps: a guide to the Irish Historic Towns Atlas (2011) by Jacinta Prunty and
    H.B. Clarke
Maps and texts: exploring the Irish Historic Towns Atlas (2013), edited by H.B. Clarke and
    Sarah Gearty
More maps and texts: sources and the Irish Historic Towns Atlas (2018), edited by H.B.
    Clarke and Sarah Gearty

DUBLIN SUBURBS
Series editors: Colm Lennon and Jacinta Prunty

No. 1 *Clontarf* (2018) by Colm Lennon

Figures

Captions to figures include brief details of the relevant IHTA fascicle from which the illustration is drawn followed by the source of the original material. Full bibliographical references and further details may be found in the respective atlas. For map extracts, the scale bar has been moved for inclusion. Quality of images reflects that of original source material. Figures are placed as close as possible to where they are referred to in the text, except where an image has been already used and referred to in a previous essay.

Tables

General abbreviations

The following is the list of general abbreviations that is included in the IHTA fascicles and has been used in this volume.

AAI   *Art and architecture of Ireland.* Ed. Andrew Carpenter and others. 5 vols. Dublin, New Haven and London, 2014.

AFM   *Annála ríoghachta Éireann: Annals of the kingdom of Ireland by the Four Masters, from the earliest period to the year 1616.* Ed. John O'Donovan. 7 vols. Dublin, 1851.

ALC   *The Annals of Loch Cé: a chronicle of Irish affairs from A.D. 1014 to A.D. 1590.* Ed. W.M. Hennessy. 2 vols. London, 1871.

Ann. Clon.   *The Annals of Clonmacnoise, being annals of Ireland from the earliest period to A.D. 1408, translated into English, A.D. 1627, by Conell Mageoghagan.* Ed. Denis Murphy. Dublin, 1896.

Ann. Conn.   *Annála Connacht: the Annals of Connacht (A.D. 1224–1544).* Ed. A.M. Freeman. Dublin, 1944.

Ann. Inisf.   *The Annals of Inisfallen (MS Rawlinson B 503).* Ed. Seán Mac Airt. Dublin, 1951.

Ann. Tig.   *The Annals of Tigernach.* Ed. Whitley Stokes. Facsimile reprint from *Revue Celtique*, xvi–xviii (1895–7). 2 vols. Lampeter, 1993.

AU 1, 2   (1) *Annála Uladh, Annals of Ulster … : a chronicle of Irish affairs, 431 to 1541.* Ed. W.M. Hennessy and Bartholomew MacCarthy. 4 vols. 2nd ed. Dublin, 1998; (2) *The Annals of Ulster (to A.D. 1131),* pt 1, *Text and translation.* Ed. Seán Mac Airt and Gearóid Mac Niocaill. Dublin, 1983.

BL	British Library, London.
Bodl.	Bodleian Library, Oxford.
Boundary com. rept	*Municipal boundaries commission (Ireland)*, pt III, *Report and evidence*. HC 1881 [C.3089], 1.
Cal. Carew MSS	*Calendar of the Carew manuscripts preserved in the archiepiscopal library at Lambeth, 1515–74* [etc.]. 6 vols. London, 1867–73.
Cal. chart. rolls	*Calendar of the charter rolls, 1226–57* [etc]. 6 vols. London, 1903–27.
Cal. doc. Ire.	*Calendar of documents relating to Ireland, 1171–1251* [etc.]. 5 vols. London, 1875–86.
Cal. justic. rolls Ire.	*Calendar of the justiciary rolls or proceedings in the court of the justiciar of Ireland, 1295–1303* [etc.]. 3 vols. Dublin, 1905–56.
Cal. papal letters	*Calendar of entries in the papal registers relating to Great Britain and Ireland: papal letters, 1198–1304* [etc.]. London and Dublin, 1893–.
Cal. pat. rolls	*Calendar of the patent rolls, 1216–25* [etc]. London, 1901–.
Cal. pat. rolls Ire.	*Calendar of the patent and close rolls of chancery in Ireland*. 3 vols. Dublin, 1861–3.
Cal. pat. rolls Ire., Jas I	*Irish patent rolls of James I: facsimile of the Irish record commissioners' calendar prepared prior to 1830*. IMC, Dublin, 1966.
Cal. S.P. Ire.	*Calendar of the state papers relating to Ireland, 1509–73* [etc.]. 24 vols. London, 1860–1910.
Cal. treas. bks	*Calendar of treasury books*. 32 vols. London, 1904–62.
Census, 1659	*A census of Ireland circa 1659*. Ed. Séamus Pender. IMC, Dublin, 1939; reprinted, 2002.
Census, 1821 [etc.]	Printed census reports (for full references see W.E. Vaughan and A.J. Fitzpatrick, *Irish historical statistics 1821–1971* (Dublin, 1978), pp 355–61).

Census returns, 1901 [etc.]	Unpublished census returns, NAI.
Chartae	*Chartae, privilegia et immunitates, being transcripts of charters and privileges to cities, towns, abbeys, and other bodies corporate … .* Dublin, 1829–30.
Chron. Scot.	*Chronicum Scotorum: a chronicle of Irish affairs … to A.D. 1135, with a supplement … from 1141 to 1150.* Ed. W.M. Hennessy. London, 1866.
C. of I.	Church of Ireland.
Commons' jn. Ire.	*Journals of the house of commons of the kingdom of Ireland.* Printed in four series (for full lists see H.D. Gribbon, 'Journals of the Irish house of commons', *An Leabharlann: the Irish Library*, 2nd ser., ii (1985), pp 52–5).
CS	*The civil survey, A.D. 1654–56.* Ed. R.C. Simington. 10 vols. IMC, Dublin, 1931–61.
DIB	*Dictionary of Irish biography: from the earliest times to the year 2002.* Ed. James McGuire and James Quinn. 9 vols. Cambridge, 2009. Available at dib.cambridge.org (last accessed 5 Mar. 2018).
Education repts	*Reports from the commissioners of the board of education in Ireland.* HC 1813 (47), v.
Endowed schools rept	*Report of the commissioners for enquiring into the endowed schools in Ireland.* HC 1857–8 [2336], xxii, pt iv; 1881 [2831], xxxv, pt i.
Excavations	*Excavations 1969: summary accounts of archaeological excavations in Ireland* [etc.]. Dublin and Bray, 1969–76, 1985–. Available at www.excavations.ie (last accessed 5 Mar. 2018).
Extents Ir. mon. possessions	*Extents of Irish monastic possessions, 1540–41, from manuscripts in the Public Record Office, London.* Ed. N.B. White. IMC, Dublin, 1943.

Fairs and markets rept	*Report of the commissioners appointed to inquire into the state of the fairs and markets in Ireland.* HC 1852–3 [1674], xli.
Fiants	'Calendar of fiants of Henry VIII … Elizabeth'. In *PRI repts D.K. 7–22.* Dublin, 1875–90. Reprinted as *The Irish fiants of the Tudor sovereigns … .* 4 vols. Dublin, 1994.
Gwynn and Hadcock	Gwynn, Aubrey and Hadcock, R.N. *Medieval religious houses: Ireland.* London, 1970.
HC	House of commons sessional paper.
IAA	Irish Architectural Archive, Dublin.
IHS	*Irish Historical Studies.* Dublin, 1938–.
IHTA	*Irish historic towns atlas.* Ed. J.H. Andrews, Anngret Simms, H.B. Clarke, Raymond Gillespie, Jacinta Prunty and Michael Potterton. Dublin, 1986–.
IMC	Irish Manuscripts Commission.
Ir. Builder	*The Irish Builder and Engineer.* Dublin, 1867–. Formerly *The Dublin Builder.* Dublin, 1859–66.
Lewis	Lewis, Samuel. *A topographical dictionary of Ireland.* 2 vols with atlas. London, 1837.
Logainm	Logainm. Bunachar logainmneacha na hÉireann — Placenames database of Ireland. Available at www.logainm.ie (last accessed 5 Mar. 2018).
Lucas	Lucas, Richard. *A general directory of the kingdom of Ireland … .* Dublin, 1788.
Mac Niocaill	Mac Niocaill, Gearóid. *Na buirgéisí, xii–xv aois.* 2 vols. Dublin, 1964.
Mun. boundary repts	*Municipal corporation boundaries (Ireland) reports and plans.* HC 1837 (301), xxix.
Mun. corp. Ire. rept	*Municipal corporations (Ireland), appendices to the first report of the commissioners.* HC 1835, xxvii, xxviii; 1836, xxiv.

NAI   National Archives of Ireland, Dublin.
                             Formerly Public Record Office of
                             Ireland.

*NIAH intro./*survey   *National Inventory of Architectural*
                             Heritage. An introduction to the
                             architectural heritage of County Meath
                             [etc.]. Dublin, 2002–. Survey available at
                             www.buildingsofireland.com (last
                             accessed 5 Mar. 2018).

NHI   *A new history of Ireland.* Ed. T.W. Moody,
                             F.X. Martin, F.J. Byrne, and others. 9
                             vols. Oxford, 1976–2005.

NLI   National Library of Ireland, Dublin.
OSM   Ordnance Survey memoirs, RIA.
Parl. boundary repts   *Parliamentary representation: boundary*
                             reports, Ireland. HC 1831–2 (519), xliii.

Parl. gaz.   *The parliamentary gazetteer of Ireland.* 3
                             vols. London, 1846.

Petty   Petty, William. *Hiberniae delineatio*
                             quoad hactenus licuit perfectissima … .
                             [London], 1685.

Pigot   *Pigot's national commercial directory of*
                             Ireland. Dublin, 1824.

Pratt   Pratt, Henry. *A map of the kingdom of*
                             Ireland newly corrected and improved …
                             with plans of the citys and fortified towns
                             … . London, [1708]. Reprinted Dublin,
                             [1732].

Primary educ. returns   *Royal commission of inquiry, primary edu-*
                             cation (Ireland), vi, Educational census.
                             Returns showing the number of children
                             actually present in each primary school on
                             25th June 1868 … . HC 1870 [C.6.v],
                             xxviii, pt V.

PRI rept D.K. 1 [etc.]   *First [etc.] report of the deputy keeper of the*
                             public records in Ireland. Dublin, 1869–.

PRONI   Public Record Office of Northern
                             Ireland, Belfast.

Publ. instr. rept 1   *First report of the commissioners on public*
                             instruction, Ireland. HC 1835 [45, 46],
                             xxxiii.

Publ. instr. rept 2	*Second report of the commissioners on public instruction, Ireland.* HC 1835 [47], xxxiv.
RC	Roman Catholic.
RCB	Representative Church Body Library, Dublin.
RD	Registry of Deeds, Dublin, memorials of deeds.
RIA/*RIA Proc.*	Royal Irish Academy, Dublin (*Proceedings of*). Dublin, 1836–.
RSAI Jn.	*Journal of the Royal Society of Antiquaries of Ireland.* Dublin, 1850–.
Slater	*Slater's national commercial directory of Ireland.* Manchester, 1846, etc.
Stat. Ire.	*The statutes at large passed in the parliaments held in Ireland … .* 22 vols. Dublin, 1786–1801.
Taylor and Skinner	Taylor, George and Skinner, Andrew. *Maps of the roads of Ireland, surveyed in 1777.* London and Dublin, 1778.
TCD	Trinity College, Dublin.
Thom	*Thom's Irish almanac and official directory.* Dublin, 1844, etc.
Thomas	Thomas, Avril. *The walled towns of Ireland.* 2 vols. Dublin, 1992.
TNA: PRO	The National Archives: Public Record Office, Kew.
UJA	*Ulster Journal of Archaeology.* Belfast, 1853–.
Urb. Arch. Survey	Urban Archaeology Survey, National Monuments Service, Department of the Environment, Heritage and Local Government.
Watson	Watson, John, and others. *The gentleman and citizen's almanack.* Dublin, 1729–1844.

Part I
Introduction

I. Sources for town atlases

H.B. Clarke and Sarah Gearty

In 1982, around the time when the IHTA was being established as a project of the Royal Irish Academy, the geographer William Nolan published a valuable survey of historical (including cartographical) sources for Irish local history.[1] Its contents are arranged in broadly chronological order, with most attention being paid to the period after the middle of the sixteenth century. The opening chapter deals with the administrative framework extending from county down to townland, while the closing one reviews the national repositories of archival resources as they were at that time. There is useful bibliographical material, including an appendix listing maps for local studies. Towns (and cities) are not singled out for special treatment, but here and there pertinent observations are made.[2] At the very beginning we are told that 'It would appear that the process of urbanisation, which is rapidly changing the intimate and familiar rural landscape where the linkages between past and present were more clearly discernible, is in some way responsible for the vitalisation of interest in localised places'. As a result, there was a 'need to document and record the items and lore which provide a connecting link between ourselves and those who have gone before us'.[3] In past urban contexts in Ireland, mainly down to 1900, this is what the IHTA was set up to achieve. The source-base is both primary in the form of printed and (less commonly) manuscript records and secondary in the form of compendia, monographs, journal articles, book chapters and essays, and newspapers, all of which need to be treated critically. Maps constitute a category on their own, while archaeology and placenames have their own contributions to make. In a modest way this particular collection of essays seeks to convey some sense of the range and quality of the sources available to a typical IHTA contributor and, by extension, to the typical reader as well.[4]

MEDIEVAL PRIMARY SOURCES

The inside back cover of every IHTA fascicle bears a list entitled 'general abbreviations'.[5] In bound volumes the same list is printed among the prefatory material and it is also accessible as part of IHTA Online.[6] The contents are miscellaneous in character and include items that are not discussed here, such as the names of cultural institutions and libraries. The earliest primary sources on the list are a selection of the principal annalistic compilations of the medieval and early modern periods.[7] One such collection that does not have the word 'annals' in its title, *Chronicum Scotorum*, belongs to this category.[8] Two other sets of annals do not appear in the list, for reasons of space, and are distinguished by the adjectives 'fragmentary' and 'miscellaneous'.[9] The first of these contains a good deal of chronicle material and should be used with particular care, though at least it is available in a modern edition. Most of the rest are available only in nineteenth-century editions and stand in need of re-editing. Exceptionally, the *Annals of Ulster* down to the year 1131 have been so treated, though not all of the experts regard the English translation as an improvement on the earlier one.[10] It should always be borne in mind that most of the extant manuscripts are late or post-medieval in date, with the attendant risks of errors and interpolations. Another standard problem is that, in varying ways and at various times, these year-by-year compilations are out of step with true chronology: the correct year has always to be ascertained. A case in point is that of the first recorded Dubliner, Abbot Bearaidh, whose corrected date of death is A.D. 656 assuming, that is, that he ever existed at all.[11] The most problematic set of annals is also the most famous, being the *Annals of the Four Masters*. This is a compilation undertaken, heroically, in Co. Donegal in the 1630s, in the age of enforced Gaelic exile, confiscation and plantation. Understandably, some of the interpolations reflect those painful circumstances, though at least we now have two invaluable modern guides to the precise nature and utility of these annals as an historical source.[12] For IHTA purposes, these annals have been used in two ways: as an early seventeenth-century record of placenames in section **1** Name and in all other sections as in effect a 'contemporary' source of information. This inconsistency is open to criticism and may not be adhered to in the future.[13]

Whereas Irish and Latin were the languages of historical recording in the annals, the Viking or Scandinavian contribution in Old Norse resides in a small number of runic inscriptions and in the largely fictional sagas.[14] The inscriptions amount mainly to personal names, while the sagas, replete with both names and stories about their bearers, have to be interpreted with great care. Quite the opposite is true of the governmental records begun by the 'new foreigners' or Anglo-Normans in *c.* 1171. The Angevin kings of England, or at least their administrative elite, were nothing if not inventive in matters such as the common law, financial accounting, sheriffs and shiring, taxation and town governance. Governmental record-keeping became ever more elaborate and thorough, especially from the reign of John onwards (1199–1216). During the nineteenth century it became customary for the guardians of these voluminous public records to commission 'calendars' or English summaries of the Latin originals. In the case of Ireland, these were not only convenient for researchers but, fatefully, prescient in view of the calamitous destruction of the Irish public record office in 1922.[15] For so many classes of recording, these summaries are now all that we have following the loss of the Latin originals. For the period down to the early fourteenth century two sources are specific to Ireland, the first being H.S. Sweetman's calendar of miscellaneous documents extending from 1171 to 1307 (the death of King Edward I).[16] Where he has been tested, Sweetman's workmanship has been found generally to be accurate and this collection is invaluable in the circumstances.[17] A shorter run of a particular type of roll contains detailed accounts of legal cases that mention incidentally town-related facts for the period 1295–1314.[18] In 2012 a new online resource became available: known as CIRCLE, this is a calendar of all known letters enrolled in the Irish chancery during the middle ages, drawing on surviving originals, facsimiles, transcripts and calendars.[19]

Parallel to these specifically Irish records are those of the English government, in which the more important Irish towns are mentioned in various historical contexts.[20] English sources tend to reflect royal or official interest in things Irish, in relation to section **2** Legal status and section **12** Defence in the shape of castles and other types of fortification. These, of course, reflect the colonial status of parts of the island during the middle ages, a point that has often been overestimated by modern historians.[21] Even more imperial in the context of Latin Christendom was the papacy and another non-Irish resource becomes available in the pontificate of Innocent III, an exact contemporary (and indeed formidable opponent) of King John, in the form of a calendar of papal letters starting in 1198.[22]

For those who are able to read medieval Latin there are two important collections of charters, which are useful in various ways such as indicating the legal status of towns and cities. An early nineteenth-century collection relating to corporate bodies in general, including towns and cities, extends from 1171, at the time of King Henry II's expedition to Ireland, to 1399 at the beginning of the reign of Henry IV.[23] The first document is the well-known charter granting the *civitas* of Dublin to the men of Bristol, marking the start of the colonisation of the Hiberno-Norse town by the new foreigners. Throughout this collection a special 'record' type was used in order to replicate the system of Latin abbreviations and contractions. More conventional, though even more selective, is the collection of town charters assembled by Gearóid Mac Niocaill and published in 1964.[24] Best served are Dublin with eleven charters, Drogheda with ten and Waterford with seven. The first volume also contains the by-laws, in Norman-French, of Dublin and Waterford in parallel and of Cork as a single entity. The second volume analyses the content of the charters under various headings such as offices and officials, finances, property and trade. Regrettably this has been seldom used on account of its being written in Irish. Not listed in the general abbreviations for each fascicle is an excellent edition of the Irish exchequer records held in The National Archives in London, covering the period 1270–1446 and indeed in an admirably comprehensive manner.[25] Similar exchequer material can be accessed in some of the volumes of the reports of the deputy keeper of public records in Ireland.[26] In much of both Britain and Ireland, the middle ages came to a dramatic end with the dissolution of monasteries, friaries and hospitals near the beginning of the Henrician Reformation. Surveys with valuations, known as 'extents' from Latin *extenta*, survive now in London and were edited by Newport White for the Irish Manuscripts Commission.[27] These contain material relating to 172 religious houses, many of them based in towns and cities, across twelve of the modern counties that in 1540–41 were then under governmental control.[28]

EARLY MODERN PRIMARY SOURCES

The Tudor age, generally regarded as the beginning of modern times in both Britain and Ireland, witnessed renewed attempts to establish greater governmental control by Ireland's colonial masters, including only partially successful plantation programmes in Laois–Offaly and in Munster.[29] The supreme new source is the series of fiants starting in 1522, 'fiants' being shorthand for the Latin *fiant litterae patentes*, 'let letters patent be made'.[30] Again miraculously, the originals were calendared in reports of the deputy keeper of public records prior to their destruction in 1922. There is a degree of overlap with the calendar of patent and close rolls of the same period.[31] Their contents range widely, but material relating to towns and cities can be accessed readily with the aid of comprehensive indexes. Another vast governmental source starts at the beginning of the reign of Henry VIII in the form of correspondence issued by official lay and ecclesiastical personages.[32] The inadequate Victorian editions of 1860 (for the years 1509–73) and 1867 (for the years 1574–85), whose summaries are too brief, are in the process of being replaced by superlative new versions by the Irish Manuscripts Commission and these should now be used by IHTA authors.[33] The third great series of sources to start in the same reign was preserved not by the state but by a single family — that of Sir George Carew, the earl of Totnes (1555–1629).[34]

The end of the Nine Years War and the exile of the northern earls inaugurated a tragic century of destruction, dispossession and disruption, combined with further colonisation and consolidation, that is reflected in many of the historical sources. Unfortunately the early Stuart kings (James I, 1603–25 and Charles I, 1625–49) are less well served than their Tudor predecessors in terms of calendaring.[35] The Irish Record Commissioners' calendar of the patent rolls covers the whole reign of James I, but only a partial index has yet been published.[36] Another illustration of the unsatisfactory nature of nineteenth-century calendaring, J.C. Erck's *Repertory*, is not listed in the general abbreviations.[37] The amount of detail is impressive, but the work comes to an end at 1609 and only the first part (1603–7) includes an index of places as distinct from persons.[38] As it happens, the following years (1608–13) were the time of the Ulster plantation, a complex process involving the development of existing towns and the creation of new ones.[39] One technique was the formal incorporation of boroughs and by the end of 1613 fourteen towns in the plantation counties had received their charter.[40] This process was essentially political at that time, for the king was anxious to obtain a Protestant majority in the house of commons.

The year 1613 marks the beginning of a new and long-running series of parliamentary records.[41] These are potentially useful for section **3** Parliamentary status in the topographical information, as was demonstrated in the fascicle for Mullingar.[42] Yet another incomplete nineteenth-century exercise in calendaring patent and close rolls is the single volume, headed no. I, for the reign of Charles I covering the years from 1625 to early 1633.[43] Very recently, however, a quite different type of primary source for a little later in this dramatic period has become available electronically, namely the depositions or statements of those who witnessed the course and consequences of the insurrection of 1641, just prior to the descent of England itself into civil war.[44] These contain incidental evidence for the development of towns, especially in the north of Ireland, and for industrial activities such as glass-making, iron-working and tanning. Online access makes this source readily available.

One widespread consequence of the disturbed 1640s was land confiscation and reorganisation. This necessitated surveys of land and its ownership and thus the so-called Civil Survey of Ireland was conducted in 1654–6. What survives now extends to parts of the provinces of Leinster, Munster and Ulster.[45] Among the omissions are the cities of Cork and Waterford, for which slightly later surveys with valuations of a similar type and dating from *c.* 1663–4 are available.[46] A pocket at the back of vol. x contains a large map of Ireland showing the areas covered by the great survey by county and by barony. The information was supplied locally, in the case of corporate towns and cities by juries composed of the mayor, aldermen and burgesses, together with representatives of business and professional interests. This unprecedented amount of detail has been used creatively for two published cities in the IHTA programme. For Kilkenny a special text map shows land use in 1654, the symbols representing the distribution of houses, malt houses, outhouses, yards, gardens and orchards. The information is incomplete, but over two hundred residential buildings range from stone-built structures to ones made of wattles and clay with thatched roofs.[47] Similar maps were made for Limerick's Englishtown and Irishtown. These have a wider range of symbols, distinguishing house types, and in addition others for 'castles', mills, bake houses, forges, 'kill houses' (slaughter houses) and tan houses. Altogether 404 houses were recorded, the superiority of those in Englishtown being made abundantly clear.[48]

Another comprehensive survey of Ireland was made at the end of the same decade.[49] This is now to be understood as an abstract of poll-tax returns for 1660–61, with a 'central' date of 1660. For the towns the number of taxpayers is listed by street and by parish. No returns have survived for Cos Cavan, Galway, Mayo, Tyrone and Wicklow or for parts of other counties. Some towns are missing altogether: for example, Carrick-on-Suir, Cashel, Clonmel and Fethard in Co. Tipperary. As with poll taxes in general, there was a high incidence of evasion and the cities presented particular difficulties for the collectors. Nevertheless, in the opinion of the more recent editor, 'we can place far more reliance on the 1660 returns than some commentators have suggested'.[50] The full population of many towns can be estimated by using a multiplier of 2.8–3.0.[51] Among the text maps is one showing the distribution and ethnic composition of all nucleated settlements with an adult population of seventy-five or more, the planters commanding possession of much urban property and controlling local administration and external trade.[52] The seventeenth century had seen enormous changes in Ireland and its townscapes were no exception.[53] The end result can be seen in a map, compiled by J.H. Andrews, of the towns and main roads of the country in *c.* 1692, about two years after the battle of the Boyne and based on the contents of journals of the house of commons.[54] As the author notes, 'separate parliamentary representation is the only test of urban status that can be uniformly applied to the whole country at this period, though the parliamentary boroughs included a number of places that were too small to be classed as towns in a socio-economic sense'.

Modern primary sources

The eighteenth century in Ireland was the age of the Big House. This theme has already been dealt with in another IHTA publication, the examples chosen being Dundalk and Maynooth.[55] Kells in Co. Meath provides a small-scale, suburban instance with the creation of a compact 'ascendancy quarter' focused on Headford Place. Sources for this are a combination of estate papers and maps.[56] A view from the east dating from *c.* 1800 was chosen for the cover illustration of the first bound volume of the IHTA. Whereas the Big House at Kells was located well outside the town on the same side, a much earlier example was built on the northern frontage of the triangular market place at Fethard. This was the Mansion House of the Everard family, whose story is told in outline in section **22 Residence**. First constructed in 1623, the great house went into decline in the mid-eighteenth century but was then rebuilt. This in turn was demolished and replaced by a cavalry barracks, which itself was destroyed by fire in 1922. Again a combination of estate papers and maps provides the evidence.[57] Private records of this sort start to be complemented by those in the official repository in Dublin's Henrietta Street in 1708 — the Registry of Deeds, whose documents are held in a combination of manual, microfilm and electronic formats.

Another type of source, somewhat improbably, starts to become useful for the history of towns in the eighteenth century — the almanac. These appear to have begun life focused on matters to do with the calendar, feast days and holidays, astronomical phenomena and the like, but were extended to include details about towns. The example listed in the general abbreviations seems to have started in 1724 without a printer's or publisher's name before the main series commenced in 1729.[58] It was authored jointly by 'a Protestant clergyman and [a] popish priest', as they claimed 5,686 years from the creation of the world![59] In a preface signed Vulgar (intended presumably to be understood in the Latin sense of 'of the people'), we are informed that 'this almanack [*sic*] will be useful to the native Irish, who have had such education that they can read and write English, because it will teach them to write their own language also, which as yet, to their discredit be it spoken, they cannot do'. Fortunately later issues of John Watson's work and those of his successors contain useful information about fairs (by calendar days and concentrated in the months of summer), markets and post towns.

The late eighteenth century saw the publication of the first national directory for Ireland.[60] Others on the list are those of Pigot (1824), Thom (1844 and later) and Slater (1846 and later). They are of particular use in section **15** Manufacturing, though their categorisation of trades and occupations is not always consistent. The same caution applies to the bigger towns and cities for which local directories were produced in the nineteenth century. The analytical potential of these sources is illustrated in some fascicles by listing in an appendix the total number of manufactories at specific dates. This was done, for example, for Belfast in 1841–3, 1870 and 1890–94 on the basis of one local directory and Slater.[61] Belfast, of course, was the greatest of Ireland's industrialising cities in the nineteenth century, but a similar experiment for Limerick yielded telling results for the years 1769, 1824, 1838 and 1870, based on two local and two national directories, when 'the urban landscape was altered by the impact of industrialisation'.[62] More lists of this sort could reveal much about changing patterns of manufacturing both within the same town and on a comparative basis.

The era of direct rule ushered in on 1 January 1801 by the Act of Union eventually brought with it a veritable rash of governmental reports. The most obviously relevant deal with municipal reform (1835–6) and related matters such as fairs and markets (1852–3).[63] The first of these has information on section **2** Legal status; the second on section **15** Trades and services. Even earlier, parliament had been concerned with the irregular and often hazy question of municipal boundaries and this continued until much later in the century.[64] A standard feature of IHTA fascicles is a text map showing the changing official boundary of each town pertaining to section **5** Municipal boundary. The other big area of governmental concern and action during the nineteenth century was education, providing at intervals vast amounts of information for section **20**.[65] Some IHTA authors have researched more widely still, a notable example being those of the Galway fascicle.[66] In terms of Foucault's concept of governmentality, the establishment of state institutions, including barracks and prisons, led to the creation of a 'state quarter' in some towns, a well-studied Irish example being Trim.[67]

The central decades of the nineteenth century saw the production of two major sources for urban history that have a strong cartographical identity and an equally strong textual one, these being the Ordnance Survey and what is known as the 'General tenement valuation' or as 'Griffith's valuation'. The textual aspect of the former is a set of written descriptions, called 'memoirs', intended to accompany the maps and containing information that could not be fitted onto them.[68] Unfortunately the scheme was discontinued in 1839–40, by which time only the northern half of the island had been covered. The memoirs document the landscape and situation, buildings and antiquities, land-holdings and population, and employment and livelihood in what has been described as a nineteenth-century Domesday Book. For the six counties of Northern Ireland, these have been published in admirable editions.[69] The textual parts of the valuation records comprise a number of components. For the tenement valuation there are house books giving detailed descriptions of the function of each building and a 'quality letter', now preserved in the National Archives of Ireland and accessible online.[70] The later printed tenement valuation of the 1850s is similarly accessible (normally denoted as Val. 2).[71] Finally what are known as revision or cancel books that carry the history of property to the twentieth century can be consulted in the Valuation Office in Dublin (normally denoted as Val. 3). Using this material in combination can be a complicated procedure, though helpful summaries are available.[72]

SECONDARY COMPILATIONS AS SOURCES

For various periods of urban history there are a number of secondary works compiled by individuals or by teams of scholars. The great pioneer was Samuel Lewis, whose *Topographical dictionary of Ireland* was published in 1837. Here it is worth continuing with the enormously long title:

comprising the several counties, cities, boroughs, corporate, market, and post towns, parishes, and villages, with historical and statistical descriptions; embellished with engravings of the arms of the cities, bishopricks [*sic*], corporate towns, and boroughs; and of the seals of the several municipal corporations; with an appendix, describing the electoral boundaries of the several boroughs, as defined by the act of the 2d & 3d of William IV.

Lewis announced that his chief aim was 'to give, in a condensed form, a faithful and impartial description of each place'.[73] The work was difficult. Major sources of information were what he termed 'resident gentlemen' together with the census of 1831 for population (then nearing its maximum) and houses. The boundaries of a selection of towns are described in words at the very end.[74]

An even more ambitious survey of Ireland, the *Parliamentary gazetteer*, was conducted on the eve of the Great Famine by a team of enquirers.[75] Again the title's continuation is informative:

adapted to the new poor-law, franchise, municipal and ecclesiastical arrangements, and compiled with a special reference to the lines of railroad and canal communication, as existing in 1844–45; illustrated by a series of maps, and other plates; and presenting the results, in detail, of the census of 1841, compared with that of 1831.

The gazetteer 'aspires to be the informant and the guide, on all Irish affairs, of alike the Protestant and the Roman Catholic, the landlord and the tenant, the farmer, the merchant, and the tradesman, the statist and the political economist, the tourist, the antiquarian, the historian, and the general scholar'.[76] As all IHTA contributors have discovered, 'difficulties in securing accuracy, and risks of giving offence, incumber every work of a minutely topographical character'.[77] In another interesting observation, 'the Ordnance Survey has afforded invaluable aid in settling differences; yet it is sometimes silent, and at other times indiscriminating, when other high authorities are at variance, and hence is very far from being, in every case, a final appeal'.[78]

Published in London in the same year as the first of a series of measures (23 January 1846) intended to relieve distress caused by the arrival of potato blight in the previous September, the gazetteer contains an astonishing amount of information, place by place. Its lengthy introduction comments on a number of relevant topics, such as manufacturing, commerce, banks, fisheries, prisons, the constabulary, education and medical charities. A particular section deals with the recently reformed municipal corporations.[79] There is a useful table listing the number of MPs sent to the house of commons by towns as well as by counties, with their population in 1841.[80] Scattered at intervals are maps of Ireland, including the provinces; that for Leinster shows amongst other things Dublin's then existing railway links, north to Drogheda, south to Dalkey, south-south-west to Carlow and south-west to Cashel.[81] A brave new world of communications was just dawning. For all three volumes there is a comprehensive index.[82]

Six years later, after a very long period of gestation, a vast undertaking dealing with public offices in Ireland was published.[83] Work on this project had been initiated back in 1812 and a seven-part version had been published in 1824. Even in 1852 its defects had been recognised and this edition contained notes to that effect by F.S. Thomas. The story is told in some detail by James Morrin in the preface to his calendar of patent rolls, with the observation that 'it is to be regretted, as Mr Lascelles himself acknowledged, various portions are given in an imperfect and unmethodical form … yet, with every defect and irregularity, the collection constitutes a storehouse of information relating to the official history of Ireland'.[84] What makes it usable by IHTA contributors is the index published later by the indefatigable J.T. Gilbert.[85] Many of the documents in question are calendared elsewhere, but others did not survive the disaster of 1922. The *Liber munerum publicorum* should therefore be consulted as a matter of course.

The late twentieth and early twenty-first centuries have produced a number of valuable secondary compilations. Virtually every IHTA fascicle features material derived from *Medieval religious houses: Ireland* (1970).[86] It relates mainly to section **11** Religion, but also to section **19** Health for medieval hospitals and hospices. It has been used frequently for dates of foundation, for summaries of monastic possessions at their dissolution and for the names of favoured grantees of the Tudor age. Each category of religious institution has an informative introduction and the main index of places is cross-referenced to the accompanying *Map of monastic Ireland.* Likewise section **12** Defence is well served by Avril Thomas's *The walled towns of Ireland* (1992).[87] The first volume provides a comparative study of Irish walled towns and discusses problems of evidence and aspects of distribution. There is an instructive table of murage grants for the period 1220–1485.[88] The second volume is a gazetteer of walled towns, equipped with clearly drawn maps and very full bibliographical references. There are a summary location map and three listings at the end.[89]

Other compilations have been sponsored by the Royal Irish Academy itself. In addition to seven volumes of historical narrative, *A new history of Ireland* has two valuable service volumes.[90] Both are essential tools for accessing generally accepted forms of personal names, whether Gaelic or Anglo-Norman, as well as dates. The final volume begins with a carto-graphical section comprising 121 maps and explanatory notes. Two are maps of the island's towns, though that for *c.* 1300 is disappointing in that it employs the same symbol for (rural) manors.[91] Many others have implications for the evolution of town life, while Dublin and Belfast are given special treatment.[92] A few years earlier the Royal Irish Academy had published an atlas of Ireland, a work of enduring value.[93] Of particular relevance to the initiation of the IHTA itself is a map of the origins of the principal towns compiled by Anngret Simms and Katharine Simms.[94] This features distinctive symbols to represent different types of town foun-dation, ranging from Gaelic ecclesiastical sites to twentieth-century new towns and satellite towns. Towns had founders, manorial lords, leading families and famous inhabitants, with the result that the *Dictionary of Irish biography* (2009) is an essential source of reliable information of a personal nature. Finally in this category comes the five-volume *Art and architecture of Ireland* (2014), many of whose illustrations are town-based or town-re-lated.[95] The fourth volume, focused on architecture, is complemented by a continuing, long-term government project called the National Inventory of Architectural Heritage.[96]

CARTOGRAPHICAL SOURCES

One of the defining traits of an atlas is the dominance of the graphic, in particular maps, over the textual. Like that of its predecessor, the main title of this volume is (more) *Maps and texts*, reflecting the nature of its source material (the IHTA).[97] Underlying the simplified 'half map and half book'[98] character of the atlas lies a process of interrogation and inter-action between maps and texts as two distinct forms of communication. The cartographical aspect is most visible in the published fascicles through the variety of maps that are included, which can be broadly character-ised as core comparative maps (relating to the wider European historic towns atlas project), thematic and text maps, and most significantly in this context, the facsimiles that present the original cartographical source material. Less obvious are the multiple ways in which early maps and plans are used in the creation of the IHTA. They are unpicked and translated into text for the topographical information; provide the basis for descriptions of the town in the essay; and are overlaid and traced to be reshaped into new thematic maps.[99]

The inclusion of large-format facsimiles is, for some, the greatest service the IHTA offers as it provides access to a cartographical record that would otherwise be widely dispersed.[100] Presented in chronological order on loose sheets in a range of sizes, the facsimiles allow the user to experience, in their own way, the cartographical source material that was available to the authors for their research. Although the general format of the atlas has remained the same since the project's inception, the process of map reproduction has been an evolving one. It was ten years before pages were printed in colour and quality improved considerably over the years following developments in photographic and scanning techniques and the associated facilities in the relevant repositories. The number and type of maps included have also increased, a change only partly associated with more affordable printing costs.[101] The early atlases presented between four and six reproductions of town plans or detailed map views, a pattern that changed significantly as the project progressed and editorial policy loosened. *Carrickfergus* (1986), for example, contains six facsimile maps from a possible list of nineteen that are detailed in the text.[102] The *Maynooth* (1995) 'six' excludes the Noble and Keenan map of *c.* 1750, which is heavily referenced throughout the topographical information.[103] A change may be identified with the production of important medieval towns such as *Kilkenny* (2000) and *Trim* (2004) – places that despite complex topographical histories remain cartographically poor as they were without a dominant landlord or plantation to provide the impetus to repeatedly 'town plan'. From this point, we see more flexibility in the types and scales of maps reproduced and an increase in the number of pages allocated to the cartographical record.[104] By the time *Carlingford* was published in 2011, the existence of six dedicated town plans (1793–1833) did not preclude the inclusion of extracts from coastal charts and county surveys in a selection of fifteen maps reproduced, with several of these extending to double pages.[105] The twenty-eight IHTA fascicles published to date include 270 facsimile maps. The originals are held in over forty different locations, with fifty-five in repositories in England and sixteen in private collections.[106] A study of the IHTA's published sample allows for observations on cartographical sources for Irish towns and how they have been used in the atlas.

The cartographical record in Ireland starts with the early military surveys of the sixteenth century. From the 1520s there are maps of Ireland displaying cities and towns under crown control. Regional maps from the period offer depictions of towns. Despite their small scale, these documents can provide key topographical references, as in Sligo where maps of the area from 1589 and *c.* 1600 were used to tease out the complex relationship between the Green Fort, Stone Fort and Sligo Castle sites.[107] Maps dedicated to towns appear in manuscript from the mid-sixteenth century and not surprisingly the strategically placed and well-established centres of Carrickfergus, Galway, Limerick and Youghal provide the earliest IHTA examples from 1560 onwards.[108] Taken from the 'bird's eye' perspective, the three-dimensional character of these views reveals a sense of urban form in addition to detail on the nature of mural defences, building types and landownership.[109] This visual information is joined with documentary and archaeological references in the creation of thematic maps in the IHTA that aim to reconstruct the medieval town or record the first phases of development.[110]

The pictorial style of mapping continued into the seventeenth century, when the first printed town maps appear, often in contemporary atlases and books such as John Speed's *Theatre of the empire of Great Britaine* (1611 [1612]) and Thomas Stafford's *Pacata Hibernia* (1633). Though generally referenced in the IHTA text according to their publication date, the question of when and how the original content of these maps was surveyed remains open.[111] The spectacular pictorial map of Galway was printed on one page and is a uniquely complex example in this category.[112]

Maps associated with the plantations of the seventeenth century raise deeper issues for the topographical historian in deciphering what was 'present' in the townscape. Richard Bartlett's map of Armagh depicts what one commentator described as a 'portrait of the toponomy of one old world going down and a new world in embryo'.[113] A seemingly derelict place on the eve of plantation in 1602, its value is the view it provides of the past. As the source for the reconstruction of medieval Armagh and its monastic inheritance, its influence is clear in the text map that illustrates the atlas essay, in the accompanying topographical information and in the associated literature on the early evolution of towns in Ireland.[114] Meanwhile, plantation maps associated with Bandon represent 'a future that never materialised'.[115] In that case, the only details extracted from the maps that have been classed as topographical information are those that have been verified from later sources.[116]

The practice of mapping urban features pictorially continued as the seventeenth century progressed.[117] The work of Thomas Phillips marked a new era in military mapping, his two-dimensional town plans offering a degree of accuracy that was difficult to achieve when combining oblique views of buildings. He is the most prolific single cartographer in the IHTA sample, having mapped Athlone, Belfast, Carrickfergus, Derry-Londonderry, Dublin, Galway and Limerick, with several versions or drafts and accompanying perspectives in some cases.[118] The order of originality and the mapping of intention (rather than what existed) are issues dealt with in atlas appendices dedicated to pre-1700 maps.[119] As town plans, they are often the first view of the town or city from the vertical perspective and have informed discussions that range from the form of early street patterns to the nature of port activities.[120]

The mapping of property for the purposes of landownership and management dominates the record from the early eighteenth century until the establishment of the Ordnance Survey in 1824. Within this category of 'estate mapping', two distinct phases have been distinguished – roughly before and after the arrival in Ireland of the influential Anglo-French cartographer John Rocque in mid-century,[121] who introduced a new style of map-making that combined artistic flare with topographical precision. Before 1750, there are eight estate maps reproduced in the IHTA, a sample that suggests some difficulty and reluctance in the surveying of complex town properties. Early examples by Simon Garstin (Dundalk, 1655) and Redmond Grace (Fethard, 1703, 1708) 'sketch' the towns in the old style within their wider network of field plots. The detail is rudimentary but these maps have proved to be valuable links to the medieval past and thought-provoking documents in the conceptualisation of urban space.[122] A series of dedicated plans of Downpatrick from the early eighteenth century hint at the alternative style that was to follow.[123] The thirty-one facsimile maps for the period 1750 to 1800 portray a new confidence in urban mapping where the challenge of density and detail provided an opportunity to elaborate a topographically rich map, usually presented on its own page in a volume of estate maps or as a dramatic item for display.[124] Typical topographical characteristics are: buildings drawn in plan; plot boundaries outlined, numbered and linked to an accompanying reference table; streets and significant buildings named; gardens symbolised and pathways depicted. Intentions for future development often feature, from new street proposals to grand plans, such as Christopher Colles's map of Limerick that provided the blueprint for the new suburb of Newtown Pery.[125] Commissioned by landowners, a feature of estate maps is that they can exclude detail on property owned by others and sometimes key topographical features.[126] Absence of detail can have other meanings. The author of *Kildare* has an impression of decline from John

Rocque's map (1757) showing 'numerous almost empty peripheral streets and lanes which played no essential part in the local road system ... [and the] absence of buildings on all sides of the churchyard except the south-east'.[127] Accompanying reference tables have the advantage of providing additional detail that has been repurposed in the form of text maps that illustrate features such as building types and landownership.[128]

The eighteenth century also witnessed developments in cartography outside the realm of the developer. Maps became recognised as having a certain value and purpose beyond military and estate utility. One amateur admits on his map of Limerick that his purpose for drawing it was for his 'own amusement' and that he has 'not been very exact'.[129] John Rocque's spectacular and influential printed 'exact plan' of Dublin was primarily a commercial venture,[130] as were the contemporary county atlases and road maps that include informative town depictions.[131]

This diversity continued into the nineteenth century. Towns are mapped as a consequence of broader surveys carried out by governmental agencies in planning associated with bogs, roads and boundaries, providing useful insights into urban developments in the early part of the century.[132] As the art of town planning progressed, so did the sophistication of what could be managed via a map if the scale was sufficiently large. A set of drainage maps for Derry~Londonderry and insurance plans by C.E. Goad for Belfast, Derry~Londonderry and Limerick provide an unprecedented level of detail, showing uses of buildings to the rear of the street frontage such as outhouses and warehouses.[133] From the mid-nineteenth century, the comprehensive primary or Griffith's valuation produced town plans that provided the locational information (property boundaries and numbers) for the published valuation listings and their manuscript updates. The topographical utility of this source is exemplified in the 'valuation maps' that are specially drawn for the majority of IHTAs.[134] The practice of printing street directories with inset maps became popular and the city IHTAs illustrate the utility of these generalised but informative town plans, particularly in tracing the development of streets.[135]

The Ordnance Survey started surveying towns as part of their countrywide endeavour in 1827, having recognised the necessity for a much larger scale for urban areas. The resulting town plans are the core cartographical source used in the IHTA, both in the topographical information and as the basis for the creation of what is known as map 2 — the key map produced at the scale of 1:2500 that facilitates comparisons with other European historic town atlases.[136] The Ordnance Survey is also the basis for the other comparative maps (maps 1, 3 and more recently 4).[137]

In thematic mapping, it is usual that an Ordnance Survey map is used as a base, either in its original form or redrawn and simplified. As a source for the IHTA, Ordnance Survey maps are not without their difficulties and one recurring issue is their treatment of historical sites. The recording of tradition has proved useful, as in Kildare where the location of the early Christian Fire House of St Brigid is indicated.[138] In Mullingar, however, the depiction of medieval sites in plan using a mix of solid and broken lines as representations of the original building and the treatment of antiquities on the maps have raised issues about the Survey's historical judgement.[139] The real value of the Ordnance Survey town plans lies in the accuracy, detail and consistency they deliver about the nineteenth-century townscape — cartographical prerequisites for the production of an historic towns atlas within the wider European scheme. From the Irish perspective, they provide the key cartographical source material for a project that expresses the belief that 'large-scale plans constitute the best kind of source material for a comparative analysis of the topography of European towns, whether as a starting point for retrospective topographical research or as a basis for studying the changes associated with modern urban expansion'.[140]

ARCHAEOLOGICAL SOURCES

For the medieval period in particular as well as for the post-medieval one in principle, archaeology has provided a certain amount of topographical information relating to Irish towns, some of it of decisive importance. As we have already seen, for Dublin a limited amount of textual material has been recovered in the form of runic inscriptions, but Ireland has nothing to compare with Novgorod's birch-bark deeds.[141] Most of what has been found takes the shape of major features and small artefacts. Archaeology takes us into the world of material culture, which is not easily reconciled with that derived from documentary sources. It is a world largely without words, to which textual expression has to be supplied by the excavator(s). In terms of interpretation, archaeology deals with trends whereas history deals with events. One of the greatest difficulties is simply that of dating features and artefacts with the sort of precision that written records often offer. A site or an object labelled, say, 'late medieval' is not readily combined with a succession of exact dates in the fourteenth and fifteenth centuries. One theoretical advantage of archaeological methodology is that it is site-specific, which should lend itself to the creation of grid references. Unfortunately not all of archaeological reportage is sufficiently detailed topographically to make this possible.

For most Irish towns the natural starting point is the survey directed by the late John Bradley during the 1980s and 1990s.[142] These volumes have never been published, but can be accessed in some libraries. They are based on a skilful admixture of archaeological and documentary sources. More purely archaeological are the summary reports published annually since 1985.[143] These notices are brief in nature and are not a substitute for full-scale site reports, generally lacking maps or plans and often giving inadequate indications of the precise location of the excavation in question. For many counties, on the other hand, there is an archaeological inventory produced to a very high standard. To take a specific example, one of the volumes covering the large county of Cork includes the main city together with Youghal and Kinsale.[144] A prefatory note signals a qualification: 'The major sites within and about these walled towns are listed here in the fashion of other sites, for the sake of consistency, but their accounts are taken from available published sources and do not represent a survey of the towns as such'. Nevertheless the arrangement is clear and systematic, and bibliographically useful. Location maps for each of these three towns are tied in with site reference numbers.[145]

Several already published IHTA fascicles have demonstrated the utility of archaeology. The investigations on Cathedral Hill at Downpatrick have yielded mixed results archaeologically, but at least there was affirmation of the existence of a major monastic site.[146] For a later period two sections of town wall confirmed the alignment of the medieval defences.[147] A rare find, completely undocumented historically, was a pottery kiln on English Street.[148] Excavations at Armagh have tended to reinforce the tradition that the earliest Christian site was Tempul na Ferta (Church of the Repository) on the eastern slope of the drumlin, whose summit had been occupied by a pagan sanctuary prior to its takeover by the new religion.[149] At Toberjarlath south-east of Tuam there is archaeological evidence for a church and an early ecclesiastical enclosure, yet little is known of this site from the written record and almost nothing of the local saint from whom it took its name.[150] On the other hand, the excavation of a 'thick cashel-like wall' south of St Mary's Cathedral provides us with valuable evidence for the sheer scale of the enormous outer enclosure of what would in 1152 become the chief church of the provincial kingdom of Connacht.[151] Archaeology has provided vital clues to the history of Viking Limerick, including the D-shaped enclosure of the original *longphort* or ship harbour and the admittedly conjectural layout of the later King's Island town site.[152]

Archaeologically no Irish town or city can compare with Dublin.[153] By normal European standards, a significant proportion of the medieval city, both inside and outside the defensive walls, has been investigated archaeologically and scientifically over the last half-century or so.[154] An enormous archaeological literature has been generated, most notably the magnificent series edited by Seán Duffy.[155] Many of the city's archaeological sites reported on here have not otherwise been published more fully. The first Dublin fascicle of the IHTA pre-dated most of these volumes and now stands in need of updating archaeologically, at least in detail for the basic historical outline has not changed radically.[156] In the years before 2002 a fair amount of archaeological material was available, including the inventory compiled by Dúchas (the Heritage Service) in an admirable governmental initiative. The large-scale map of medieval Dublin shows the results of some of the excavations, notably features discovered at Wood Quay and Viking-Age defensive alignments towards the east and the south.[157] Whereas our textual sources are unlikely ever to be increased in quantity, urban archaeology has unlimited potential for the future.

CONCLUSION

The IHTA is primarily an exercise in local history, albeit with a strong international and pan-European dimension.[158] In principle the main map in each fascicle, at the scale of 1:2500, represents the built-up area of each town as closely as possible to 1840. In the case of the very largest cities, this is not always the case, since page dimensions and cost factors determine the size and precise positioning of the urban 'box' for which the topographical information is compiled. The most obvious exception is Dublin, for which the main atlas series was limited to the area between the two canals. This necessary restriction is now being remedied by a new ancillary series dealing with a selection of suburban districts.[159] The study of local history goes back a long way and has become more sophisticated over recent decades. The preparation of IHTA fascicles is a challenging undertaking, partly because the range of cartographical and textual sources is so wide, especially for towns with very long histories. We hope, therefore, that this essay will prove to be of some assistance both to atlas contributors and to users of the final product.

By their nature, towns and cities serve in varied and complex ways the multifarious needs of the inhabitants of the district or region in which they are located. The hinterland and sometimes the hinterlands of a town, whether entirely rural or containing other urban centres, have to become part of the story.[160] A superlative demonstration of this point has been made for medieval Dublin.[161] At the other end of the chronological spectrum sits a volume of essays with a strong regional identity on the city of

Belfast,[162] while covering the entire history of Cork is another impressive map-based volume.[163] For smaller places there is an invaluable resource – the county series energised and masterminded by William Nolan. This began in 1985 and is now nearing completion.[164] Many of these volumes are very substantial in size and coverage and all contain material of an urban nature. Depending on the precise location of a town, one or more of these should be consulted by IHTA contributors. Thereby the IHTA will continue to make its own distinctive contribution to Irish local and regional history based on both primary and secondary sources.

NOTES

[1] William Nolan, *Tracing the past: sources for local studies in the Republic of Ireland* (Dublin, 1982). A shorter but still valuable booklet had already been published privately by the same author as *Sources for local studies* (Dublin, [1977]).

[2] This gap was later filled in William Nolan and Anngret Simms (eds), *Irish towns: a guide to sources* (Dublin, 1998).

[3] Nolan, *Tracing the past*, p. 1.

[4] By the same token this introductory essay merely skims the surface of what could be a subject requiring book-length treatment. Nevertheless we hope that it will prove useful for all researchers into the history of Irish towns.

[5] In the current Dublin suburban fascicles the list of general abbreviations is specific to requirements. See, for example, Colm Lennon, IHTA, Dublin suburbs, no. 1, *Clontarf* (Dublin, 2017), pp 135–9.

[6] www.ria.ie/irish-historic-towns-atlas-online (last accessed 8 Feb. 2018). IHTA Online includes the text sections and core maps for IHTA, nos 1–25.

[7] For a still useful survey, see Gearóid Mac Niocaill, *The medieval Irish annals* (Dublin, 1975). Sources in the Irish language, including the annals, can be accessed at www.ucc.ie/celt/ (last accessed 5 Feb. 2018).

[8] *Chron. Scot.* For keys to abbreviations, see the list at pp xvi–xxi.

[9] *The Fragmentary Annals of Ireland*, ed. J.N. Radner (Dublin, 1978); *Miscellaneous Irish annals, A.D. 1114–1437*, ed. Seamus Ó hInnse (Dublin, 1947).

[10] *AU* 1, 2.

[11] Clarke, IHTA, no. 11, *Dublin, part I, to 1610*, p. 17, misdated 650; Seán Duffy, 'The saint's tale', in Sparky Booker and C.W. Peters (eds), *Tales of medieval Dublin* (Dublin, 2014), pp 7–17.

[12] Bernadette Cunningham, *The Annals of the Four Masters: Irish history, kingship and society in the early seventeenth century* (Dublin, 2010); P.A. Breatnach, *The Four Masters and their manuscripts: studies in palaeography and text* (Dublin, 2013).

[13] See Nollaig Ó Muraíle below, p. 56 The established source for Irish placenames is accessible at www.logainm.ie (last accessed 5 Feb. 2018).

[14] M.P. Barnes, J.R. Hagland and R.I. Page, *The runic inscriptions of Viking Age Dublin* (Dublin, 1997). For references to Dublin and the Scandinavian kingdom in Old Norse, see H.B. Clarke, '"Go then south to Dublin; that is now the most praiseworthy voyage." What would Brynjólfr's son have found there?', in Andras Mortensen and S.V. Arge (eds), *Viking and Norse in the north Atlantic: select papers from the proceedings of the Fourteenth Viking Congress, Tórshavn, 19–30 July 2001* (Tórshavn, 2005), pp 441–5. Dublin became and to some extent remained a city-state during the middle ages (H.B. Clarke, 'From

Dyflinnarskíri to the Pale: defining and defending a medieval city-state, 1000–1500', in Jenifer Ní Ghrádaigh and Emmett O'Byrne (eds), *The march in the islands of the medieval west* (Leiden and Boston, 2012), pp 35–52.

[15] For the medieval period down to *c.* 1540, see H.B. Clarke, 'Making up for lost time: the impact of the destruction in 1922 of the Irish Public Record Office', in Igor Filippov and Flocel Sabaté (eds), *Identity and loss of historical memory: the destruction of archives* (Bern, 2017), pp 289–302.

[16] *Cal. doc. Ire.*

[17] But see Philomena Connolly (ed.), *Irish exchequer payments, 1270–1446* (2 vols, Dublin, 1998), p. xv, n. 3.

[18] *Cal. justic. rolls Ire.*

[19] CIRCLE – a calendar of Irish chancery letters *c.* 1244–1509, at chancery.tcd.ie/ (last accessed 5 Feb. 2018).

[20] Listed are *Cal. chart. rolls, Cal. pat. rolls* and *Cal. treas. bks.*

[21] H.B. Clarke, 'Decolonization and the dynamics of urban decline in Ireland, 1300–1550', in T.R. Slater (ed.), *Towns in decline, AD 100–1600* (Aldershot and Burlington, VT, 2000), pp 163–73 and fig. 8.2.

[22] *Cal. papal letters.*

[23] *Chartae*, pp 1–100.

[24] Mac Niocaill, vol. i.

[25] Connolly, *Irish exchequer payments.*

[26] Ibid., p. xv, n. 1; also Clarke, *Dublin, part I, to 1610*, p. 35 for pipe rolls.

[27] *Extents Ir. mon. possessions*, a regular source for section **11** Religion.

[28] The details of All Saints' Priory at Dublin are not given since it had already been granted to the mayor and commonalty by way of compensation for damage caused to the city in the course of Silken Thomas's rebellion (ibid., p. 122).

[29] For a recent discussion with extensive referencing, see H.B. Clarke, 'Planning and regulation in the formation of new towns and new quarters in Ireland, 1170–1641', in Anngret Simms and H.B. Clarke (eds), *Lords and towns in medieval Europe: the European historic towns atlas project* (Farnham and Burlington, VT, 2015), pp 332–8.

[30] *Fiants.* For the background, see the introduction to vol. i, pp v–xi by Kenneth Nicholls. Like the Christ Church deeds, they are cited in IHTA fascicles by number and in this instance by monarch.

[31] *Cal. pat. rolls Ire.*, vols i–ii. The preface to the first volume contains a valuable survey of the public records of Ireland and their publication to date, that is, seven years before the opening of the Public Record Office of Ireland behind the Four Courts complex in 1868.

[32] *Cal. S.P. Ire.* In addition to Tudor material there is an extraordinary preface to vol. i composed by Hans Claude Hamilton, the assistant keeper of public records, which reveals much about mid-Victorian (1860) attitudes to the Irish and their benighted history. We are informed, for example, that 'most of the wild Irish led a nomad life, tending cattle, sowing little corn, and rarely building houses, but sheltered alike from heat and cold, and moist and dry, by the Irish cloak' (*Cal. S.P. Ire., 1509–73*, p. iii).

[33] S.G. Ellis and James Murray (eds), *Calendar of state papers Ireland, Tudor period, 1509–1547* (revised edn, IMC, Dublin, 2017); Colm Lennon (ed.), *Calendar of state papers Ireland, Tudor period, 1547–1553* (IMC, Dublin, 2015); Bernadette Cunningham (ed.), *Calendar of state papers Ireland, Tudor period, 1566–1567* (IMC, Dublin, 2009); Bernadette Cunningham (ed.), *Calendar of state papers Ireland, Tudor period, 1568–1571* (IMC, Dublin, 2010); Mary O'Dowd (ed.), *Calendar of state papers Ireland, Tudor period, 1571–1575* (revised edn, IMC, Dublin, 2017). Two more volumes will complete the series.

[34] *Cal. Carew MSS.* For George Carew's varied career, see *DIB*, ii, pp 326–33. He bequeathed his vast manuscript collection to his illegitimate son and only child, Sir Thomas Stafford, whose widow sold the bulk of the papers to a private bookseller in London. Miraculously they had found their way by 1677 into Lambeth Palace library (*DIB*, viii, p. 1113).

[35] A rare copy of *Cal. pat. rolls Ire.*, vol. iii, ceasing at the year 1610, is generally disregarded, having been replaced by Erck's *Repertory* (see below).

[36] *Cal. pat. rolls Ire., Jas I.* For background information, see the foreword by M.C. Griffith to the Irish Manuscripts Commission's facsimile edition of 1966.

[37] *A repertory of the inrolments on the patent rolls of chancery, in Ireland; commencing with the reign of King James I*, ed. J.C. Erck (2 pts, Dublin, 1846–52).

[38] Ibid., pt 1, p. 303. Both parts, however, contain marginal citations of places.

[39] For a summary based on the key primary and secondary sources, see Clarke, 'Planning and regulation', pp 338–52. See also Annaleigh Margey below, pp 199–219.

[40] Clarke, 'Planning and regulation', p. 341 and n. 121.

[41] *Commons' jn. Ire.*

[42] Andrews with Davies, IHTA, no. 5, *Mullingar*, p. 7 referring to the town's unique status in Irish parliamentary records as a manor.

[43] That is, the first to the eighth regnal years. This is generally treated as the third volume of *Cal. pat. rolls Ire.* (*NHI*, iii, p. 650).

[44] Accessible at 1641.tcd.ie (last accessed 5 Feb. 2018).

[45] *CS.*

[46] Ibid., vi, pp 215–85 (Waterford), 397–497 (Cork).

[47] Bradley, IHTA, no. 10, *Kilkenny*, p. 5, fig. 2.

[48] O'Flaherty, IHTA, no. 21, *Limerick*, p. 6, figs 5 and 6.

[49] *Census, 1659.* The reprint of 2002 contains an extremely informative introduction by W.J. Smyth at pp v–lxii.

[50] Ibid., p. xxviii.

[51] Ibid., p. xiv.

[52] Ibid., p. lix, fig. 11.

[53] For a sense of Ireland *c.* 1685, see the magisterial survey by J.H. Andrews in *NHI*, iii, pp 454–77.

[54] Ibid., p. 470, map 13.

[55] Jacinta Prunty and H.B. Clarke, *Reading the maps: a guide to the Irish Historic Towns Atlas* (Dublin, 2011), pp 202–13. See also Toby Barnard below, pp 239–52.

[56] Simms with Simms, IHTA, no. 4, *Kells*, pp 4, 12.

[57] O'Keeffe, IHTA, no. 13, *Fethard*, pp 4–5, 11–12. A cattle mart now occupies part of the site.

[58] Watson.

[59] Ibid. The 1724 volume is largely unpaginated, though at pp 23–8 the same text is reproduced in English on the left and in Irish on the right.

[60] Lucas. A separate version was produced for Cork and this was reissued in a slightly modified form in the *Journal of the Cork Historical and Archaeological Society*, 2nd ser., lxxii (1967), pp 135–57.

[61] Royle, IHTA, no. 17, *Belfast, part II, 1840 to 1900*, pp 88–9.

[62] O'Flaherty, *Limerick*, pp 9, 59.

[63] *Mun. corp. Ire. rept*; *Fairs and markets rept.* These are accessible online in the NLI. Not listed as standard sources are town council minute books of the pre-reform period. Some of these have been published, an outstanding example being Brian Ó Dálaigh (ed.), *Corporation book of Ennis, 1660–1810* (Dublin, 1990). The editor is also the author of IHTA, no. 25, *Ennis.*

[64] *Parl. boundary repts*; *Mun. boundary repts*; *Boundary com. rept*, accessible online in the NLI.

[65] Listed are *Education repts*; *Publ. instr. rept 1* and *Publ. instr. rept 2*; *Endowed schools rept*; *Primary educ. returns*, accessible online in the NLI.

[66] Prunty and Walsh, IHTA, no. 28, *Galway/Gaillimh*, including the archives of the Mercy order.

[67] Hennessy, IHTA, no. 14, *Trim*; Mark Hennessy, 'Adapting a medieval urban landscape in nineteenth-century Ireland: the example of Trim, Co. Meath', in Simms and Clarke, *Lords and towns*, pp 483–92.

[68] OSM.

[69] Angélique Day and Patrick McWilliams (eds), *Ordnance Survey memoirs of Ireland* (20 vols, Belfast, 1990–93).

[70] At census.nationalarchives.ie/search/vob/house_books.jsp (last accessed 5 Feb. 2018).

[71] At askaboutireland.ie/griffith-valuation or at search.findmypast.com/search-world-records/griffiths-valuation-1847-1864 (last accessed 5 Feb. 2018).

[72] Prunty and Clarke, *Reading the maps*, pp 220–23; Hélène Bradley-Davies and Marie Taylor below, pp 281–305.

[73] Lewis, i, p. iv.

[74] Ibid., ii, pp 731–7.

[75] *Parl. gaz.*

[76] Ibid., i, pp iii–iv.

[77] Ibid., p. iv.

[78] Ibid.

[79] Ibid., pp cxxiii–cxxv.

[80] Ibid., pp cxxii–cxxiii.

[81] Ibid., ii, facing p. 602.

[82] Ibid., iii, pp 583–715.

[83] Rowley Lascelles, *Liber munerum publicorum Hiberniæ, ab an. 1152 usque ad 1827; or the establishments of Ireland …* (2 vols, London, 1852).

[84] *Cal. pat. rolls Ire.*, i, pp xxv–xxvi.

[85] *PRI rept D.K. 9*, appendix III, pp 21–58. The tortuous story of how this work ever saw the light of day is retold ibid., pp 6–7.

[86] Listed as Gwynn and Hadcock.

[87] In 2005 the same author produced IHTA, no. 15, *Derry-Londonderry*, on which see also Brian Lacey below, pp 87–102.

[88] Thomas, i, p. 155, fig. 5.3.

[89] Ibid., ii, pp 256–7.

[90] *NHI*, viii and ix.

[91] Ibid., ix, nos 37 and 102.

[92] Ibid., nos 38–42 (Dublin), 59–62 (Belfast).

[93] J.P. Haughton (ed.), *Atlas of Ireland* (Dublin, 1979).

[94] Ibid., no. 43. A modified version can be found in Prunty and Clarke, *Reading the maps*, p. 160, fig. 126.

[95] In the IHTA's topographical information, freestanding monuments are entered in section **21** Entertainment, memorials and societies.

[96] Available at buildingsofireland.com (last accessed 5 Feb. 2018).

[97] H.B. Clarke and Sarah Gearty (eds), *Maps and texts: exploring the Irish Historic Towns Atlas* (Dublin, 2013). This collection contains much of a complementary nature to the present one.

[98] J.R. Akerman, 'From books with maps to books as maps: the editor in the creation of the atlas idea', in Joan Winearls (ed.), *Editing early and historical atlases* (Toronto and London, 1995), p. 7.

[99] Some examples of how documentary source material has been cartographically represented in text maps in the IHTA have already been mentioned. The subject of thematic mapping in the atlas is referred to briefly below, but the main discussion is focused on the use of historical maps as a source for the IHTA.

[100] Arnold Horner, 'Of atlases and Irish towns', in *Studia Hibernica*, no. 39 (2013), p. 173.

[101] In addition to maps, the IHTA includes a number of plates – topographical paintings

and prints, photographs – on loose sheets and these have also increased. O'Flaherty, *Limerick*, for example, includes views by Thomas Phillips (1685), J. Jones (*c.* 1835), James Henry and Samuel Frederick Brocas (*c.* 1820) and Turner de Lond (1821).

[102] Fifteen of these are recorded in the appendix on 'Pre-1700 plans and views of Carrickfergus' and all are listed in the bibliography (Robinson, IHTA, no. 2, *Carrickfergus*, pp 13–16).

[103] Five of the thirty entries in section **10** Streets give Noble and Keenan's map as the first reference (Horner, IHTA, no. 7, *Maynooth*, p. 8).

[104] An extract from a Down Survey barony map features for the first time in Bradley, *Kilkenny*, map 4, providing an example of a detail from a more regionally focused map, while Hennessy, *Trim*, map 5 presents the first example of a lease map limited to one plot (Trim parsonage, 1747).

[105] Maps 4–10 are all depictions of Carlingford in its wider setting (down to 1777); maps 11 and 12 are limited to parts of the town (1793 and 1805); and map 13 (McCary, 1793) is the first reproduction in the sequence that may be classed as a full 'town plan' (O'Sullivan and Gillespie, IHTA, no. 23, *Carlingford*).

[106] The Irish maps are spread between eleven different English repositories, the main ones being the British Library and The National Archives, Kew. In Ireland, the largest number of IHTA map reproductions come from originals held in the National Library of Ireland and Trinity College Dublin, where fifteen facsimiles maps emanate from one single collection known as the Hardiman Atlas (MS 1209).

[107] Gallagher and Legg, IHTA, no. 24, *Sligo*, pp 2, 14; maps 4 and 5.

[108] Robinson, *Carrickfergus*, map 4 (1560), map 5 (1567); Prunty and Walsh, *Galway/Gaillimh*, maps 6 and 7 (1583); Kelly and O'Keeffe, IHTA, no. 27, Youghal, maps 4 and 6 (1585); O'Flaherty, *Limerick*, map 5 (1587).

[109] See, for example, Robinson, *Carrickfergus*, p. 3.

[110] See Prunty and Walsh, *Galway/Gaillimh*, p. 3, fig. 2 (Medieval Galway), map 5 (Galway *c.* 1200–*c.* 1900) and map 28 (Growth, to 1895) for examples of thematic maps that draw heavily on the early cartographical record (maps 6–8, appendix A), particularly in their depiction of the walled town.

[111] See Clarke, *Dublin, part I, to 1610*, map 6; O'Flaherty, *Limerick*, maps 8 and 9, with appendix on p. 59; Kelly and O'Keeffe, Youghal, map 9, with appendix on p. 29; Prunty and Walsh, *Galway/Gaillimh*, maps 9 and 10, with appendix on p. 45.

[112] Prunty and Walsh, *Galway/Gaillimh*, map 12, with appendix on p. 45.

[113] W.J. Smyth, *Map-making, landscapes and memory: a geography of colonial and early modern Ireland c. 1530–1750* (Cork, 2006), p. 50.

[114] McCullough and Crawford, IHTA, no. 18, *Armagh*, p. 2, fig. 1 and entries in section **11** Religion, pp 12–13. For comparisons with other towns, see Catherine Swift below, pp 67–86; P.J. Duffy, 'Armagh and Kells', in Clarke and Gearty, *Maps and texts*, p. 22; Prunty and Clarke, *Reading the maps*, p. 163.

[115] O'Flanagan, IHTA, no. 3, *Bandon*, p. 15.

[116] Ibid. For a fuller discussion on plantation maps with reference to Armagh, Bandon and Derry, see Annaleigh Margey below, pp 199–219.

[117] There are examples of the pictorial style continuing on maps in the IHTA down to 1763 (see O'Keeffe, *Fethard*, map 9).

[118] Murtagh, IHTA, no. 6, *Athlone*, map 4; Gillespie and Royle, IHTA, no. 12, *Belfast, part I, to 1840*, maps 4 and 5; Robinson, *Carrickfergus*, map 6; Thomas, IHTA, no. 15, *Derry-Londonderry*, maps 12 and 13, plate 1; Lennon, IHTA, no. 19, *Dublin, part II, 1610 to 1756*, map 10; Prunty and Walsh, *Galway/Gaillimh*, map 13, plate 1; O'Flaherty, *Limerick*, map 12, plate 2. Gallagher and Legg, *Sligo* includes Phillips's prospect as plate 1.

[119] See the map appendices in Gillespie and Royle, *Belfast, part I, to 1840*, p. 13; Robinson, *Carrickfergus*, pp 13–14; Prunty and Walsh, *Galway/Gaillimh*, p. 45; O'Flaherty, *Limerick*, p. 59.

[120] Gillespie and Royle, *Belfast, part I, to 1840*, pp 2–4, 6.

[121] J.H. Andrews, *Plantation acres: an historical study of the Irish land surveyor* (Omagh, 1985), p. 150.

[122] The author (Tadhg O'Keeffe) redrew Grace's maps in Fethard to highlight the architectural detail and used the cartographical evidence to discuss the late medieval social architecture of the town in the essay (O'Keeffe, *Fethard*, maps 4 and 5, pp 3–4). See Ó Dálaigh, *Ennis*, p. 5 for a narrative account of Thomas Moland's map of 1703, reproduced in that fascicle as map 5.

[123] Buchanan and Wilson, IHTA, no. 8, *Downpatrick*, maps 4–6.

[124] See, for example, Bernard Scalé's town plans from larger estate volumes: Horner, *Maynooth*, map 6 (1773); O'Flanagan, *Bandon*, map 7 (1775); Kelly and O'Keeffe, *Youghal*, maps 10 and 11 (1776); and O'Sullivan, IHTA, no. 16, *Dundalk*, map 7 (1777).

[125] O'Flaherty, *Limerick*, p. 8, map 18.

[126] John Rocque's map of Kildare does not reveal the location of the tholsel (recorded in 1674), but then 'the only estate he professed to be surveying in detail was Lord Kildare's' (Andrews, IHTA, no. 1, *Kildare*, p. 5).

[127] Ibid.

[128] See, for example, Kelly and O'Keeffe, *Youghal*, pp 7–8, figs 5 and 6.

[129] O'Flaherty, *Limerick*, map 11.

[130] Lennon, *Dublin, part II, 1610 to 1756*, map 16.

[131] For an example of a county map, see the extracts from Matthew Wren's *A topographical map of the county of Louth* (London, 1766) that are reproduced in O'Sullivan, *Dundalk*, map 9; also O'Sullivan and Gillespie, *Carlingford*, map 9. Extracts from Taylor and Skinner's *Maps of the roads of Ireland* are reproduced in Gearty, Morris and O'Ferrall, IHTA, no. 22, *Longford*, map 8; Gallagher and Legg, *Sligo*, map 9; Claffey, IHTA, no. 20, *Tuam*, map 7; and O'Sullivan and Gillespie, *Carlingford*, map 10.

[132] See, for example, Claffey, *Tuam*, map 8 (roads), map 9 (bogs).

[133] For the drainage maps, see Thomas, *Derry-Londonderry*, p. 9, map 18, and for an example of a Goad plan in the same fascicle see map 23.

[134] These maps are the subject of the essay by Bradley-Davies and Taylor below, pp 281–305.

[135] See particularly the use of directory references in section **10** Streets in S.A. Royle, *Belfast, part II, to 1840–1900*, pp 7–41 (also map 11); and Goodbody, IHTA, no. 26, *Dublin, part III, 1756 to 1847*, pp 10–44 (also maps 6 and 12).

[136] Anngret Simms, 'The European historic towns atlas project: origin and potential', in Simms and Clarke, *Lords and towns*, pp 13–32.

[137] The use of the Ordnance Survey town plans in the compilation of the atlas is described in more detail in H.B. Clarke and Sarah Gearty, 'Multi-dimensionality', in Clarke and Gearty, *Maps and texts*, pp 9–11, 12–13.

[138] Andrews, *Kildare*, p. 1.

[139] Andrews with Davies, *Mullingar*, p. 13.

[140] In the 'Introduction' from the cover of the published IHTA fascicles.

[141] See, for example, Valentine Yanin, 'Medieval Novgorod: fifty years' experience of digging up the past', in H.B. Clarke and Anngret Simms (eds), *The comparative urban origins in non-Roman Europe* (2 pts, Oxford, 1985), pp 660, 662–6 and figs 24.I, 24.XII, 24.XIII.

[142] Urb. Arch. Survey. John Bradley went on to become the author of *Kilkenny* (2000) and of a pioneering essay linked thematically to the present volume: 'The Irish Historic Towns Atlas as a source for urban history', in H.B. Clarke, Jacinta Prunty and Mark Hennessy (eds), *Surveying Ireland's past: multidisciplinary essays in honour of Anngret Simms* (Dublin, 2004), pp 727–46.

[143] *Excavations*.

[144] Denis Power *et al.*, *Archaeological inventory of County Cork, volume 2: east and south Cork* (Dublin, 1994), pp 275–86. Another section deals with post-medieval urban sites (ibid., pp 296–311).

[145] Ibid., pp 431, map 22 (Cork city), 432, map 23 (Kinsale and Youghal).

[146] Buchanan and Wilson, *Downpatrick*, pp 2–3.

[147] Ibid., p. 3 and fig. 1. Compare Thomas, ii, pp 70–72, published five years earlier.

[148] Buchanan and Wilson, *Downpatrick*, pp 3, 11.

[149] McCullough and Crawford, *Armagh*, pp 1, 12.

[150] Claffey, *Tuam*, pp 1, 11.

[151] Ibid., pp 2, 12 and fig. 1.

[152] O'Flaherty, *Limerick*, pp 1–2 and figs 1 and 2. See further Brian Hodkinson below, pp 103–12.

[153] The next best-served city archaeologically after Dublin is Waterford, for which see especially M.F. Hurley, O.M.B. Scully with S.W.J. McCutcheon, *Late Viking Age and medieval Waterford: excavations 1986–1992* (Waterford, 1997), an enormous volume with 935 pages and numerous maps, plans and illustrations.

[154] Linzi Simpson, 'Fifty years a-digging: a synthesis of medieval archaeological investigations in Dublin city and suburbs', in Seán Duffy (ed.), *Medieval Dublin XI: proceedings of the Friends of Medieval Dublin symposium 2009* (Dublin, 2011), pp 9–112.

[155] Seán Duffy (ed.), *Medieval Dublin I: proceedings of the Friends of Medieval Dublin symposium 1999* (Dublin, 2000) and continuing to date (2017) with a sixteenth volume.

[156] The first two volumes were then available (Clarke, *Dublin, part I, to 1610*, p. 34).

[157] Ibid., map 4. Plate 1 is part of an artist's impression of Viking Dublin *c.* 1000 and is based on archaeological content provided by P.F. Wallace, one of the site directors at Wood Quay. For further observations, see Andy Halpin below, pp 156–60.

[158] H.B. Clarke, 'Joining the club: a Spanish historic towns atlas?', in *Imago temporis. Medium Aevum*, ii (2008), pp 27–43; Simms and Clarke, *Lords and towns*. For examples of comparative studies based on the European towns atlas project, see Ferdinand Opll, 'Colonia e Vienna nel medioevo: un confronto', in Francesca Bocchi (ed.), *Medieval metropolises: proceedings of the congress of the atlas working group, International Commission for the History of Towns, Bologna 8–10 maggio 1997* (Bologna, 1999), pp 71–102; H.B. Clarke, 'London and Dublin', ibid., pp 103–25; Anngret Simms, 'Interlocking spaces: the relative location of medieval parish churches, churchyards, marketplaces and town halls', in H.B. Clarke and J.R.S. Phillips (eds), *Ireland, England and the Continent in the Middle Ages and beyond: essays in memory of a turbulent friar, F.X. Martin, O.S.A.* (Dublin, 2006), pp 222–34 and plates 14.1–14.8; Anngret Simms, 'Unity in diversity: a comparative analysis of thirteenth-century Kilkenny, Kalkar and Sopron', in Seán Duffy (ed.), *Princes, prelates and poets in medieval Ireland: essays in honour of Katharine Simms* (Dublin, 2013), pp 107–23.

[159] See above, n. 5.

[160] Towns with long histories could have a whole succession of different hinterlands, as in the case of Dublin (H.B. Clarke, 'Cities and their spaces. The hinterlands of medieval Dublin', in Michel Pauly and Martin Scheutz (eds), *Cities and their spaces. Concepts and their use in Europe* (Cologne, Weimar and Vienna, 2014), pp 197–215).

[161] Margaret Murphy and Michael Potterton, *The Dublin region in the middle ages: settlement, land-use and economy* (Dublin, 2010). Michael Potterton has recently become one of the IHTA's general editors.

[162] F.W. Boal and S.A. Royle (eds), *Enduring city: Belfast in the twentieth century* (Belfast, 2006). This was published in association with the IHTA and Stephen Royle is the co-author of *Belfast, part I, to 1840* and the sole author of *Belfast, part II, 1840 to 1900*.

[163] John Crowley *et al.* (eds), *Atlas of Cork city* (Cork, 2005).

[164] William Nolan and T.G. McGrath (eds), *Tipperary: history and society: interdisciplinary essays on the history of an Irish county* (Dublin, 1985). Still to come are volumes for Cos Antrim, Leitrim, Louth, Roscommon, Sligo and Westmeath.

Part II
Monastic proto-towns
and Viking towns

2. Environment

H.B. Clarke

A standard feature of all IHTA fascicles is map 1, a black-and-white regional map dating broadly from the third quarter of the nineteenth century and occasionally later. The town or city is normally positioned centrally, giving some idea of the environment at that time. Relief is indicated by hachuring (rather than by contour lines) and the Ordnance Survey employed various experts in that technique. It had first been made familiar in some regions of Ireland by John Rocque's county maps, while Daniel Augustus Beaufort was the first Anglo-Irish cartographer to publish hachures on a national map, in 1792. Ironically, by the second half of the nineteenth century public taste was turning against this technique.[1] For towns atlas purposes, the scale of reproduction is 1:50,000.

Such a map was prescribed by the originators of the atlas project of the International Commission for the History of Towns, especially by the highly influential Heinz Stoob. He recommended that such maps should show lines of communication, the configuration of the ground, the vegetation and drainage of the surrounding area, sometimes individual fields, plus neighbouring settlements. He also prescribed that ideally this map should date from the same period as the reconstruction (cadastral) map (no. 2 in the IHTA) and recommended reproduction at the scale of 1:25,000.[2] Thus the IHTA is broadly in line with the prescribed formula, though not entirely so.

These Ordnance Survey maps show variations arising from different draughtsmen and levels of wear on the plates. They can be hard to read even with a magnifying glass in some cases. For those fascicles with a CD component, the zoom facility can be very helpful at around 400%. In addition to what can be deduced from map 1 for each town, every essay starts off with observations of a general geographical and geological nature regarding relief, drainage, soil conditions and other relevant factors. In combination these sources alert the reader to a selection of factors that could be deemed favourable to successful urbanisation at some point in the historical past. With varying degrees of exactitude the essay-head illustration also conveys something of the essence of the site.

These towns (and cities) have here been divided into three groups to suit the historical theme of this volume. Group 1 comprises those towns that did not have a monastic or Viking background and may be thought to serve as a non-specific 'control' group. Group 2 comprises those towns that had, or are thought to have had, some sort of monastic background. Group 3 comprises those towns that had a Viking background. In each case they are presented, very briefly, in alphabetical (neutral) order. I shall focus in particular on immediate location, lines of communication and the basic street pattern. Special points of interest are mentioned on occasion.

It should be borne in mind that these maps, ranging from 1860 (Dublin) to 1894–1900 (Kilkenny), were drawn in the post-famine decades; many towns had lost population, some a great number of inhabitants, but in those cases the basic core shows up all the better. For each group a table of the relevant population data is provided, the pre-famine census being that of 1841 and the post-famine one nearest to the date of map 1 and thus varying between 1861 and 1901.

GROUP 1 ('CONTROL', 14 TOWNS)

We start with the most centrally located town on the island of Ireland, Athlone, Co. Westmeath. It is situated at a crossing of the country's biggest river, the Shannon, with a largely waterlogged hinterland of glacial and

TABLE 2.1 POPULATION DATA FOR GROUP 1

Town or city	Date of map 1	Pre-famine (1841)	Post-famine	% change
Athlone	1871–5	6,393	6,565 (1871)	+ 2.7
Bandon	1880	9,049	3,997 (1881)	- 55.6
Belfast	1864–5	71,447	121,602 (1861)	+ 70.2
Bray	1865	3,209	6,087 (1871)	+ 89.7
Carrickfergus	1864	3,885	4,028 (1861)	+ 3.7
Dundalk	1874	10,782	11,616 (1871)	+ 7.7
Ennis	1885–7	9,318	5,460 (1891)	- 41.4
Fethard	1893–5	3,915	1,607 (1891)	- 59.0
Galway	1877–80	17,275	15,471 (1881)	- 10.4
Longford	1870–3	4,966	4,375 (1871)	- 11.9
Maynooth	1860–2	2,029	1,497 (1861)	- 26.2
Mullingar	1868–71	4,569	5,103 (1871)	+ 11.7
Sligo	1868–78	14,318	10,670 (1871)	- 25.5
Youghal	1879	9,939	5,396 (1881)	- 45.7

later deposits and a wide flood-plain known as the callows. There were, and to some extent still are, numerous peat bogs towards both east and west. The great river was bypassed by a canal in 1757 to avoid the shallows, but later (1849) the Shannon navigation works caused it to become disused. Athlone came to be well served by railways with the convergence of four lines. The street pattern is linear east–west at right-angles to the main river on both sides, reflecting the sinuous esker ridges of sand and gravel that led to the original fording place.

Next, Bandon in Co. Cork is situated at the lowest crossing of a small river of the same name, where two tributaries join it, forming a marshy flood-plain surrounded by hilly terrain. Mixed farming was practised in both lowland and upland soils. The main river would serve as a fishery and industrial power supply, but not for navigation. Like Athlone, Bandon was in effect two towns, though in this case with differing street patterns: on the north side it was curvilinear leading down towards the river crossing; on the south side linear and parallel to the river. The single railway line was more favourable to southsiders, with a junction serving the Clonakilty branch 5.5 km west of Bandon.

Belfast is situated at the lowest crossing of the River Lagan, the original ford being probably near the Long Bridge, necessitating a causeway in alignment with present-day Ann Street. The River Blackstaff is an important tributary flowing down from the dramatic hills to the west and would have been used for fresh water in historic times. With a poorly drained flood-plain, the early town was built on estuarine clays or 'sleech'. Belfast's map 1 is one of those that is less easy to decipher and, exceptionally, a special isometric text map was provided as an aid to understanding (Fig. 2.1). A vital environmental feature of Belfast's location was the banks and shallows of the headwaters of Belfast Lough. By the mid-1860s a new channel for shipping had been dredged, resulting in the formation of Queen's Island

Fig. 2.1 *Belfast, part I*, fig. 1, site of Belfast.

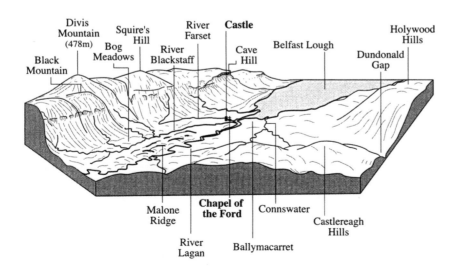

as we see on the map drawn at a time when it was a recreational facility.[3] By then, too, this fast-growing city was served by four railway lines leading to three termini. The street pattern was already complex, but the original east–west alignment was at right-angles to the main river.

Nineteenth-century Belfast grew at a phenomenal rate, of course, but perhaps surprisingly this rate of growth was outstipped by that of Bray in Co. Wicklow. Unfortunately a badly worn map 1 makes this difficult to discern. Situated at the lowest crossing of the River Dargle, a short distance inland, the original settlement occupied firm ground in a narrow flood-plain leading to a marshy estuary. The northside subsidiary settlement of Little Bray is marked clearly and the street pattern, essentially north–south and at right-angles to the river, stands out prominently as well. Much less clear is the nineteenth-century grid towards the seaside, whose growth was stimulated to some degree by the attractiveness of the mountainous backdrop, including the sharply hachured Powerscourt waterfall. The single railway line, going along the sea front and around Bray Head, had been extended northwards six years earlier than the date of the map to the Harcourt Street terminus in the city of Dublin.

On the northern shore of Belfast Lough, focused on a prominent rocky outcrop and a small and at least partly natural harbour, stands Carrickfergus in Co. Antrim. Its hinterland comprises a coastal plain up to 4 km wide, overlooked by a basalt escarpment. Sea-based communication, both locally within the confines of the lough and farther afield, was the norm for most of the town's history until the nineteenth century, for which map 1 shows a single railway line with a spur to the harbour and a branch line to Ballymena through a gap in the hills. The street pattern is linear, parallel to coast and influenced by the great medieval castle, which is depicted so dramatically in the early nineteenth-century essay-head engraving.

Dundalk in Co. Louth is situated at the lowest crossing of the Castletown River, which flows across a low-lying plain towards a shallow bay and silty harbour. Commanding the gap of the north, the early stronghold (*dún*) at Castletown Mount (unnamed on map 1) was located 1.25 km west of later town. A text map makes the relationship between the two settlement sites clear (Fig. 2.2). Estuarine gravel ridges built up by the interaction of flood waters from the river and storm waters of the inner bay, visibly hachured on the map, were utilised by medieval town builders, the South Marsh being reclaimed in the eighteenth century. By 1874 Dundalk was a significant transport hub, with north–south and east–west railway lines and a substantial railway works south-west of the town. The

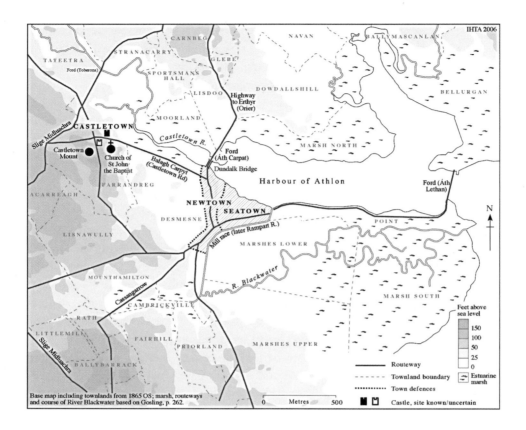

Base map including townlands from 1865 OS; marsh, routeways
and course of River Blackwater based on Gosling, p. 262.

0   Metres   500

Routeway
Townland boundary
Town defences
Castle, site known/uncertain
Estuarine marsh

Feet above
sea level

150
100
50
25
0

principal street pattern is forked-linear north–south at right-angles to the
river, with a pronounced spur towards the harbour.

Situated at a crossing of the Inch or Claureen River, which contained
islands amid a highly fractured landscape with flood-plains here and
there, stands Ennis, the county town of Clare. The village of that name lay
3.5 km downstream to the south. The medieval settlement of Ennis was
divided between the O'Brien castle site and the Franciscan friary, the latter
becoming the focus of the market area and the most prominent feature of
Thomas Dineley's prospect of 1681 (shown in the essay-head illustration
partially reroofed for Protestant parishioners). There was still only one
main railway line in the mid-1880s, the famous West Clare Railway being
opened slightly later. The street pattern is forked-linear east–west parallel
to and following the curvature of the River Fergus in the case of the Mill
Street, High Street and Church Street alignment.

Fethard in Co. Tipperary is situated at a crossing of the Clashawley
River in a narrow flood-plain serving fertile, generally well-drained soils.
The placename suggests the presence of woodland on the site or at least in

Fig. 2.2 *Dundalk*, fig. 1, site of
medieval Dundalk.

the vicinity. There was no major medieval castle, but the whole town was walled, in contrast to Ennis for example, and the defences remain one of the best-preserved circuits in the country. As a result, a metrological map of medieval Fethard is included in the text.[4] To the west of what was still a small town in the nineteenth century there was a single railway line, while the single linear east–west street alignment first laid out in the thirteenth century ran parallel to the river.

The city of Galway occupies one of the most complex, diverse and transformed urban sites in Ireland. Both land form and water courses have contributed to this. Map 1 shows the principal medieval axis running from north-east to south-west along present-day Bohermore, Prospect Hill, one side of Eyre Square, William Street, Shop Street, Mainguard Street and Bridge Street to William O'Brien Bridge. The latter stands on or near the site of an early ford across the fearsome and fast-flowing River Corrib. An important branch inside the town represented nowadays by High Street and Quay Street led down to the Anglo-Norman castle, the strand and the medieval docks. In both directions on either side of this axial fork an irregular chequer of streets developed, all of which constitutes the commercial core of the modern city. The main railway connection to Dublin terminated on the opposite side of Eyre Square, while map 1 also shows the Clifden branch line opened in 1895 and crossing the Corrib by means of an impressive steel viaduct.

Situated at a crossing of the Camlin River, Longford lay on a major early east–west highway (the Slige Assail) running from Meath to Rathcroghan in Co. Roscommon. Indeed, the essay begins by stressing Longford's position in a frontier region 'between distinctive geographical, cultural, social and political spaces'.[5] Its medieval nucleus was north of the river with a castle in one direction and a Dominican friary in the other, somewhat reminiscent of the duality at Ennis. Newtown started in the mid-seventeenth century on gently sloping ground on the south side. The link to the Royal Canal from near Killashee had been built in 1830, drawing further urban development in that direction as can be seen on map 1. The Dublin to Sligo railway line passed over the canal terminus and would supersede it for long-distance traffic. The town's street pattern is linear north–south, at right-angles to the river and with a zigzag round the castle/barracks site at Church Street.

Until the eighteenth century Maynooth was a village in Co. Kildare situated at a crossing of the Lyreen River, a tributary of the Rye Water and itself a tributary of the Liffey. The Lyreen and another small tributary provided an opportunity for moating the castle, which came to acquire major political significance in the late Middle Ages. Ecclesiastical significance came with the opening of the Royal College of St Patrick as a Roman Catholic seminary at Stoyte House in 1795: a view of the ruined castle and the burgeoning college *c.* 1800 was chosen as the essay-head illustration. Maynooth was then favoured in succession by both the Royal Canal (1796) and a major railway line in and out of Dublin (1847). The linear street layout was planned for an estate town linking the Royal College to Carton House, with only minor regard to the river.

Mullingar, the county town of Westmeath, is situated at a crossing of the River Brosna on an east–west routeway. The first element of the placename refers to a watermill and map 1 shows (rather faintly) an early church site at Lynn to the south-south-west, whose mill this presumably was. The modern town came to be dominated by the great curve of the Royal Canal, which reached Mullingar from Dublin in 1806. Like Maynooth, the town was located on the main east–west railway line from Dublin to Galway, with an important branch line to Sligo. The basic street pattern is linear east–west and at right-angles to the river.

The town in this group with the most picturesque and unmistakable backdrop is Sligo, so often viewed with the brooding prow of Ben Bulben in the near distance. A good example was chosen in this case for the front cover of the fascicle, a pen and ink wash by Thomas Phillips dating from *c.* 1685 (reproduced naturally as plate 1). Situated at the lowest crossing of the River Garvoge, which links Lough Gill to the bay and the open sea, the town's site takes the form of a hollow dominated by steep hills and ridges, shown with admirable clarity on map 1 (Fig. 2.3). When it came to Sligo and opened in 1862, the railway stopped short of crossing the river, though a spur led down to the quayside. In a southerly direction there was an important junction serving what is now called the (partially reinstated) western rail corridor at Collooney. Sligo's street pattern was probably originally linear to start with, but later became rectilinear both parallel to and at right-angles to the river, which has a pronounced bend at that point.

Finally in this group we come to Youghal in Co. Cork. Like Bandon on the other side of the main city, Youghal had suffered serious population loss since the Great Famine. Reminiscent of Carlingford, it occupied a steep slope on the western shore of a major estuary, here called Prospect Hill. No bridge was ever built across the River Blackwater directly opposite the town, though the wooden predecessor of the modern structure 2.5 km to the north is indicated on map 1. For a time Youghal benefited from a branch railway link to Cork city, one result of which was the extraordinary popularity of The Strand for day-trippers and holiday-makers, as

Fig. 2.3 *Sligo*, map 1, 1868–78. Ordnance Survey Ireland, extract.

Carney

Milltown

Castle

Drumcliff Br.

Glebe Ho.

Church

R.C. Chapel

Tober Columbhille

Doonweelin Lough

Barnasrahy

Springfield West

Tully Ho.

Wynnesfort Ho.

Cregg Ho.

Cregg Cottage

Springfield East

290

Washington Ho.

Millbrook Ho.

Old Seal Bank

Middle Bank

Millport Lodge

Ballinear Castle

Doonally Ho.

Willowbrook Ho.

New Seal Bank

Rath Lodge

Summerhill

Wellsborough Ho.

n Strand

Lisnalarry Ho.

Belview Hill

Mount Shannon

Rathbraghan Cott.

Auburn Cott.

Marlbrook Ho.

Vaughis Cott.

R.C. Chap

Standalone Pt.

Ballytivnan Ho.

Gibraltar

Finisklin Ho.

Cartron Pt.

C

A

L

R

Cranneen Ho.

Marino Cott.

Union Work Ho.

Ballyglass Ho.

Colgagh

Farmhill

Forthill Ho.

Bellanode

Colgagh Lough

Woodville Ho.

SLIGO

Terminus

Newtown Anderson

Kevinsfort

Ellenville

Perry Mount

Lark Hill

Gaol

Abbey View

Macheraboy

Cairnsfoot

Innagh Bay

Lugnafella Br.

Peterville

Hazelwood Ho.

Castle Pt.

Fairy Is.

Oakfield Ho.

L

Caltragh

Church I.

Prospect Ho.

392

G

ST. JOHNS

Wolf Is.

Listoghil

Stony Pt.

Cottage Is.

Cloverhill Ho.

Flat Is.

Goats Is.

Toberanalt

Aghamore Bay

Bunower

M. A. COWEN

L. Naminbrack

1   0   1   2   3   Kilometres

0   1   2 Miles

shown on plate 7 (*c.* 1900). Youghal's street pattern is linear and parallel to the river.

An analysis of the basic environmental attributes of towns in this group leads to six conclusions. First, all but one town (Carrickfergus) were located at a river crossing, usually a ford succeeded by a bridge with the exception of Youghal. The rivers range in size from the Blackwater at Youghal, the Corrib at Galway and the Shannon at Athlone to the Clashawley at Fethard, the Camlin at Longford, the Lyreen at Maynooth and the Brosna at Mullingar. Non-tidal rivers were used extensively for fresh water and for tanning as well as for powering mills. Secondly, seven towns were situated at the lowest crossing place of their respective principal river (Bandon, Belfast, Bray, Dundalk, Galway, Sligo and Youghal). Thirdly, street patterns comprised three types: (a) linear at right-angles to the main river (Athlone, Belfast, Bray, Dundalk plus a spur to harbour, Longford with a pronounced zigzag and Mullingar); (b) linear parallel to the main river (Bandon south side, Ennis, Fethard and Youghal); and a miscellaneous sub-group consisting of Carrickfergus (linear parallel to the coast plus a spur to the castle), Galway (forked linear and chequer), Maynooth (an estate town and essentially linear) and Sligo (linear/recti-linear). Fourthly, three towns in low-lying locations were suited to canal access (Longford, Maynooth and Mullingar). Fifthly, all of the towns in Group 1 had railway access, in one of three ways: (a) at a junction of lines (Athlone, Dundalk, Ennis and Mullingar); (b) on a single line (Bandon, Bray, Carrickfergus, Fethard, Longford and Maynooth); (c) at one or more termini (Belfast, Galway, Sligo and Youghal). Sixthly, the hinterlands in this group varied enormously, including the size of the local flood-plain. Map 1 provides some indication of the geographical environment and further information can be gleaned from the first part of the essay in all cases as well as from certain sections of the topographical information.

GROUP 2 ('MONASTIC', 9 TOWNS)

Arguably the island's most important ecclesiastical site, the early monastery at Armagh was situated on a drumlin east of the Callan River and west of a minor tributary, in the middle of classic drumlin territory clearly delineated in map 1 by extensive hachuring (Fig. 2.4). Thus the next drumlin to the north, supporting a Roman Catholic chapel in 1877, would become the site of the cathedral completed in 1904. The double enclosure of the early medieval monastery was almost perfectly circular, influencing the concentric and radial street pattern down to the present day, with the Protestant cathedral in the centre. It is possible to discern the market space to the east

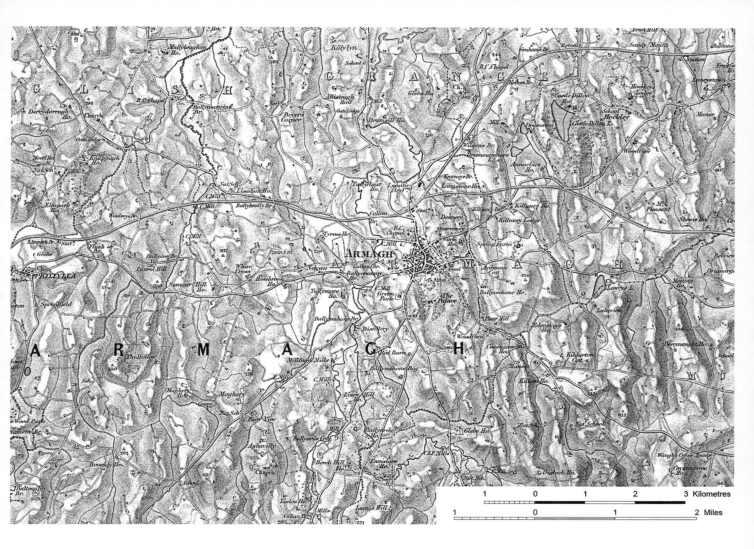

Fig. 2.4 *Armagh*, map 1, 1877.
Ordnance Survey Ireland, extract.

of the enclosure system plus the *aonach* ('assembly') site (The Mall) beyond that again. The railway lay some distance to the north of the town, with a junction to the east for the branch line to Newry.

The monastery at Derry was sited quite differently at the lowest crossing of the Foyle, on an island about 80 hectares in area at a bend in the fast-flowing river. Hence no enclosure system had been deemed necessary and the Bogside offered natural protection towards the west. The town was, as is well known, a plantation of the early seventeenth century on the same island, but with no obvious relation to the monastic layout. The street pattern takes the form of a chequer focused on The Diamond. The Foyle was not bridged at Derry until 1789–91, then by a wooden structure founded on sixteen piers; hitherto the town's more accessible hinterland was Co. Donegal rather than the county to which it had given its (colonial) name. By the date of map 1 (1862–9) there were three railway termini in the vicinity of the bridge, a matching fourth being provided at the very end of the century.

TABLE 2.2 POPULATION DATA FOR GROUP 2

Town or city	Date of map 1	Pre-famine (1841)	Post-famine	% change
Armagh	1877	1,774	1,588 (1881)	- 10.5
Derry	1862–9	15,196	25,242 (1871)	+ 66.1
Downpatrick	1865	4,651	3,621 (1871)	- 22.1
Dublin	1860	232,726	254,808 (1861)	+ 9.5
Kells (Meath)	1860–5	4,205	3,225 (1861)	- 23.3
Kildare	1862–7	1,629	1,426 (1861)	- 12.5
Kilkenny	1894–1900	19,071	10,609 (1901)	- 44.4
Trim	1860–8	2,269	2,058 (1861)	- 9.3
Tuam	1871	6.034	4,223 (1871)	- 30.0

Downpatrick came to have another drumlin-based monastery, situated on the largest of three drumlins adjacent to the River Quoile, on Cathedral Hill. The latter's peripheral location relative to the town is still apparent on map 1, dating from 1865. More akin to monastic Derry, however, it was surrounded by tidal waters and marshland, since drained, although some sort of enclosure system was installed. As the essay informs us, down to the mid-eighteenth century the Quoile marshes formed a shallow bay as an extension of Strangford Lough.[6] The medieval town evolved towards the east along English Street, to a junction with other principal streets where the market space lay some distance from the cathedral and parish church. The basic street pattern is forked-linear. The inhabitants of Downpatrick in the nineteenth century were able to access the Belfast and Down Railway via a terminus of their own, from which they could also reach Newcastle on a branch line.

As in so many other ways, Dublin defies easy classification; here it has been placed in two groups. Its early medieval monastery was situated on gently rising ground between the River Poddle and the River Steine, due south of the tidal pool from which town and later city took its English name. The key indicator is the large single enclosure still defined by streets and, as at Armagh, there may have been an assembly place to the east of that (the remote ancestor of St Stephen's Green). The principal river crossing was overlooked by an even older settlement called Áth Cliath, the probable meeting-point of a number of long-distance overland routes. The Viking takeover in A.D. 841 resulted both in the destruction of monastic life and in the creation of a third pre-urban nucleus in the Castle Street area, as will be seen in the next section. Monastic life would eventually be restored in the twelfth century, but in the very different circumstances of church reform and the importation of continental monastic orders. Other major features that stand out clearly on map 1 include, of course, the magnificent bay and a hint of the Dublin Mountains towards the south.

Associated inescapably with the Book of Kells (made essentially on the island of Iona in the Inner Hebrides of Scotland), the monastery of that name was situated on rising ground at a remove from the River Blackwater, on an early historic long-distance route (the Slige Assail) from the east coast of Ireland and the fertile lowlands of north Leinster to the poorer lands of the kingdom of Connacht (via the later site of another 'frontier' town, Longford). The Columban monastery, founded in the very early ninth century, had a double enclosure, the outer one of which is visible on map 1. Like that of Armagh the street pattern was concentric, being most pronounced on the eastern side of the monastic site where later on the medieval castle became the focus of urban life, creating a crossroads effect. The single railway line was a minor one terminating at Oldcastle and with a station at some distance from Kells itself.

The early monastery at Kildare, a great rival of Armagh, was situated on the gently rising ground shown by hachuring on map 1 as a ridge (carrying the expressive Irish name Druim Criaig) with no significant watercourse nearby. A prominent feature is the Curragh, a spread of rolling pasture devoid of permanent habitation. Like Kells it was a double-enclosure site, less strongly reflected in the later street pattern that was essentially linear and focused on an irregular crossroads leading to and from the triangular Market Square. In the nineteenth century Kildare found itself on the main Dublin to Cork railway, though with a rather distant station from the town as it then was towards the north-east and Carlow junction for the Waterford line 4 km westwards.

Kilkenny would evolve in multiple ways from its early monastic phase. The general location is a small plain with the name Mag Roigne, forming the fertile heartland of the later county. The monastery itself was situated on rising ground west of the River Nore, near an early crossing represented later by Green's Bridge. Like Dublin it had only a single enclosure,[7] but by surviving the Viking experience this evolved eventually into the medieval Irishtown focused on the cathedral and the adjoining round tower. Running into the Nore from the west is a small stream, the Breagagh, and to the south of this the Anglo-Norman Hightown was centred on a north–south main street, leading to the castle, plus another crossing of the Nore at John's Bridge. Hightown's linear street pattern was quite different from Irishtown's concentric one, reflecting the original monastic enclosure north of the Breagagh. The single railway line ran at a distance from the main town on the left bank of the Nore, with a junction to a line serving Waterford 4 km away to the south-east.

Another complex example is provided by Trim in Co. Meath. Here the monastery was situated on rising ground north of the River Boyne, where the single enclosure was poorly preserved in the later streetscape, hence alternative theories as to where it actually had been sited.[8] The Anglo-Norman town came to be located on the opposite side of the Boyne, focused on the great baronial castle and Market Street leading to the river crossing. Somewhat reminiscent of Kilkenny, the street pattern on one side (the northern one) includes curvilinear Main Street, in contrast to the linear layout of the south side. The single railway line was a minor one on the branch connection to Athboy with the station rather inconveniently distant from the town centre.

Finally in this group comes Tuam in Co. Galway, which was chosen as the chief church in the kingdom of Connacht and the eventual archbishopric. The monastery (a successor to an earlier ecclesiastical site to the south) was situated on gently rising ground mainly south of the River Nanny, which apparently passed through the enormous outer enclosure. The double enclosure had Temple Jarlath in the centre and later St Mary's Cathedral on the south-western edge, its exceptionally large size reflecting Ua Conchobair patronage. There was also a subsidiary enclosure to the north-east at Templenascreen, linked by what became Bishop Street to the main town. The street pattern was based partly on the outer enclosure at Shop Street and Vicar Street, with a market space containing the famous cross (now preserved in the Protestant cathedral) in the middle due east of the early church. The single railway line from Athenry terminated at Tuam some distance from the town centre in 1871, but was extended northwards to Claremorris in 1894.

Again an analysis of the 'vital statistics' of this group leads to some broad generalisations. First, the river crossings were usually of less importance than those in Group 1, the exceptions being Kilkenny, Trim and

Tuam. Derry, located on an island beside a powerful river, was accessible from the east only by ferry until the late eighteenth century. Secondly, rising ground relative to the average is a common feature, most obviously at Armagh, Derry and Downpatrick, but also visible on map 1 at all of the other sites. Thirdly, with the exception of Derry and Downpatrick, some part of the medieval and later streetscape followed the trajectory of the monastic enclosure system, especially at double-enclosure sites. The latter are Armagh, Kells, Kildare and Tuam, the single enclosures being at Dublin, Kilkenny and Trim. Fourthly, none of these places came to have canal access, apart from Dublin. Fifthly, on the other hand, all of these towns would have railway access, though the station was sometimes located some distance away, again in one of three ways: (a) at a junction of lines (Armagh, Downpatrick); (b) on a single line, sometimes with a junction at a distance (Kells, Kildare, Kilkenny, Trim and Tuam); (c) at more than one termini in two of the cities (Derry and Dublin). Sixthly, apart from the large cities of Derry and Dublin, all of the towns suffered loss of population over the course of the famine, ranging from 9.3% at Trim to a catastrophic 44.4% at Kilkenny.[9] Seventhly, as in the first group the hinterlands varied enormously, including the size of the local flood-plain. Again map 1 in each case provides some indication of the geographical environment and further information can be gleaned from the first part of the essay as well as from certain sections of the topographical information.

To declare an interest, I am not a believer in the validity of the concept of a monastic town. Instead I have argued elsewhere, on the basis of IHTA material, that none of these places became *primarily* urban in their monastic phase.[10] In this particular sample, the four relevant phases of meaningful initial urbanisation are as follows: Viking (Dublin); (b) Gaelic Irish (Tuam); (c) Anglo-Norman (Downpatrick, Kells, Kildare, Kilkenny and Trim); (d) plantation (Armagh and Derry). No doubt this topic will continue to be debated.[11]

Group 3 (Viking, 3 towns)

The Viking site at Carlingford in Co. Louth is unknown, but presumably on the shore of Carlingford Lough and possibly on the site of the later town, hence the *fjörðr* element in the placename. Small streams come down from the steep slopes of Slieve Foy, which were channelled for milling and for the town's water supply; one of these is reflected in the names Spout Gate at the western end of River Street. Turf from the uplands would traditionally provide fuel for heating and eventually for urban industrial processes

Table 2.3 Population data for Group 3

Town or city	Date of map 1	Pre-famine (1841)	Post-famine	% change
Carlingford	1874	1,110	971 (1871)	- 12.5
Dublin	1860	232,726	254,808 (1861)	+ 9.5
Limerick	1886	48,391	37,155 (1891)	- 23.2

such as brewing and salt manufacture. The single railway line came from Newry to Greenore, via which it was possible to access Dundalk. The street pattern is double-linear, parallel to the shore and with a principal link at Market Street.

Its monastic component having been forcibly replaced, the first Viking site (*longphort*) at Dublin was probably near the pool in the River Poddle, now represented by the Dubh Linn garden. A second site was selected, apparently nearer to Áth Cliath, hence the association of these foreigners with that name in Irish (but not in Icelandic) sources. Map 1 does not clarify much of this, though the large bay and the Norse placenames of Howth and Dalkey do, while a text map illustrates the relationship to the earlier monastic site.[12] Somewhat reminiscent of Mullingar, Dublin came much later to be surrounded by two canals, while railway termini became five in number and were already linked partially by the Phoenix Park tunnel in 1860. The original street pattern had a dominant east–west axis parallel to the Liffey on the south side down to the mid-eighteenth century, until it was refocused north–south on new bridges, moving progressively downstream from the medieval ford and bridge. In practice there were many other components, including suburban ones such as the chequer in Oxmantown on the north bank of the Liffey. As always, Dublin defies simple description.

Finally the first Viking site (*longphort*) at Limerick was near Athlunkard, on a great bend in the River Shannon. Then, following the pattern at Dublin (and elsewhere) a second site was chosen at the southern end of King's Island, whose northern end came to be linked to the opposite bank by a major bridge, first documented in 1199. Much later the great loop

Fig. 2.5 *Limerick*, map 1, 1886. Ordnance Survey Ireland, extract.

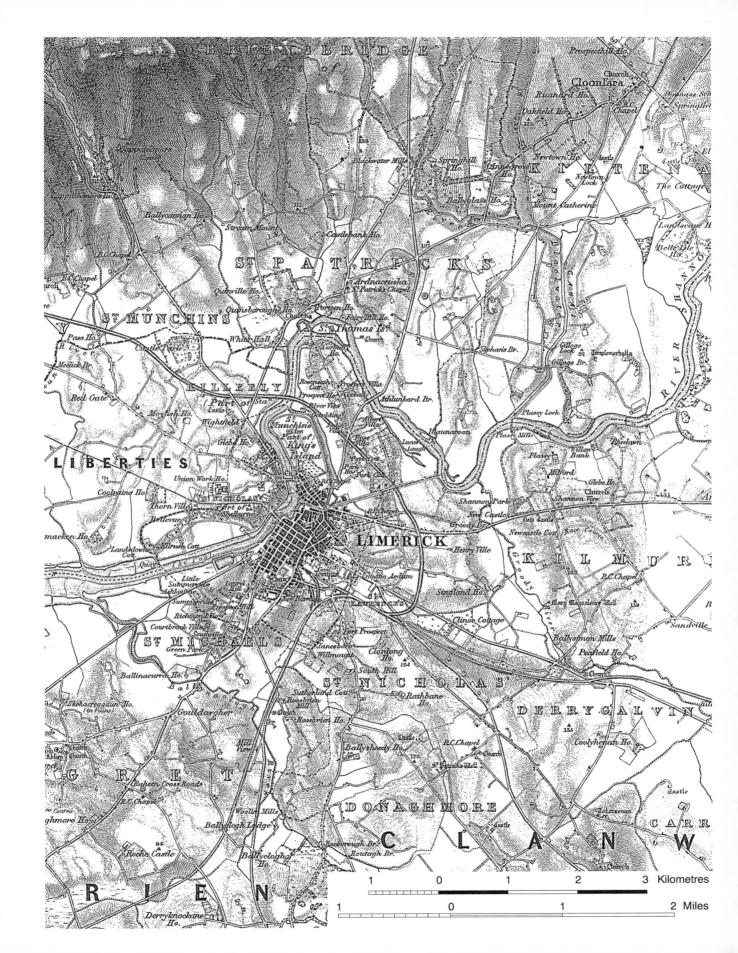

in the Shannon would be bypassed by a canal completed in *c.* 1760. The railway terminus was positioned adjacent to Newtown Pery for the main line to Waterford (and via Limerick Junction to Cork and Dublin), with junctions for lines leading both to the north-west (Co. Clare) and to the south-west (Co. Kerry). A special branch railway from the main line was built to serve the New Markets on the northern side of Mulgrave Street. Limerick evolved over the centuries into three towns in one city, each with a distinct street pattern: partial chequer with the main axis parallel to the river in Englishtown, forked linear in Irishtown, and full chequer again with the main axis parallel to the river in Newtown Pery. All of this is still clearly visible as late as 1886 on map 1 (Fig. 2.5).

Three other candidates for this group are Cork, Waterford and Wexford, but some tentative generalisations can still be suggested at this stage of the programme. First, and most obviously, access to the open sea and to harbour facilities was standard, though it should be borne in mind that much Viking raiding in Ireland was conducted over land and on horseback. Secondly, at both Dublin and Limerick there was a change of site, as we now know to have been true of the shift from Woodstown in the ninth century to Waterford in the early tenth. Thirdly, Dublin and Limerick were also near the lowest, bridgeable crossings of navigable rivers, which constituted political boundaries. Fourthly, urbanisation at the two major sites began with the Vikings, or more particularly with the Hiberno-Norse at some point in the tenth century. After the arrival of the Anglo-Normans both Dublin and Limerick became royal towns with important castles. Fifthly, the essential street axes were linear and parallel to the river, with quayside facilities to one side. And sixthly, as in Groups 1 and 2, hinterlands varied enormously, including the size of the flood-plain at Dublin and at Limerick. These are counted among the major cities of Ireland and further information can be gleaned both from the map 1 and from the first part of the essay in each case.

Conclusions

The sample in Group 2 is fairly substantial, though of course not complete,[13] with the result that some tentative conclusions can be reached. There are two main differences between the control group and the monastic one: (a) the former tended to relate almost universally to significant river crossings, the latter rarely; (b) the street pattern in the former tended towards a principal axis either at right-angles to or parallel to the river, in the latter towards a more curvilinear arrangement influenced in part by the monastic enclosure and/or its natural site. Few of the towns with a pre-urban monastic identity came to have canal access, but all came to have some sort of railway connection. For obvious reasons the Viking sites were always accessible to the open sea, although control of overland routes was particularly important at Dublin, which was the focus of a pre-existing network of highways (*slighte*). We have commented in each group that hinterlands varied enormously, including the size of the flood-plain where there was one, and that further information can be gleaned both from the map 1 and from the first part of the essay. Accordingly the IHTA can be regarded as a valuable resource for understanding and analysing the environment in which Irish towns and cities originated and developed.

Notes

[1] J.H. Andrews, *Shapes of Ireland: maps and their makers 1564–1839* (Dublin, 1997), pp 237–8, 313.

[2] Heinz Stoob, 'The historic town atlas: problems and working methods', in H.B. Clarke and Anngret Simms (eds), *The comparative history of urban origins in non-Roman Europe* (2 pts, Oxford, 1985), pp 594–601, including plates.

[3] Royle, IHTA, no. 17, *Belfast, part II, 1840–1900*, pp 3, 68, 78.

[4] O'Keeffe, IHTA, no. 13, *Fethard*, p. 2, fig. 1.

[5] Gearty, Morris and O'Ferrall, IHTA, no. 22, *Longford*, p. 1.

[6] Buchanan and Wilson, IHTA, no. 8, *Downpatrick*, p. 1.

[7] Following the interpretation in Bradley, IHTA, no. 10, *Kilkenny*, p. 1. More recent archaeological excavations have shown that the ditch of an inner enclosure was backfilled in the late ninth century, on which see the contribution by Cóilín Ó Drisceoil below.

[8] Shown in Hennessy, IHTA, no. 14, *Trim*, p. 2, fig. 1.

[9] Kilkenny had been raised to the dignity of a city in 1609: Bradley, *Kilkenny*, pp 6, 9.

[10] H.B. Clarke, '*Quo vadis?* Mapping the Irish "monastic town"', in Seán Duffy (ed.), *Princes, prelates and poets in medieval Ireland: essays in honour of Katharine Simms* (Dublin, 2013), pp 261–78.

[11] Most recently in John Soderberg, 'Anthropological *civitas* and the possibility of monastic towns', in *RSAI Jn.*, cxliv–cxlv (2014–15), pp 45–59, which ignores completely my own argument based on the IHTA.

[12] Clarke, IHTA, no. 11, *Dublin, part I, to 1610*, p. 3, fig. 2.

[13] The Cashel fascicle will complete the coverage of archiepiscopal towns.

3. Placenames

Nollaig Ó Muraíle

In this brief survey I propose to assess the treatment of placenames in the twenty-eight published fascicles of the IHTA — relating to twenty-five different towns and cities — that have appeared to date. I should mention that I have had some (slightly peripheral) connection with this project for the past quarter of a century or so. Kells was the first town for which my opinion was sought as to the treatment of the name — that was in 1990, when I worked in the Placenames Branch of the Ordnance Survey, based in the Phoenix Park.[1] I was next asked about Maynooth, which appeared in 1995. Then there was a gap of more than a decade before my advice was sought in relation to Dundalk, which was published in 2006. Over the past decade I have had some input in relation to Tuam, Limerick, Longford, Carlingford, Sligo, Ennis, Youghal and the most recent fascicle, Galway (nos 20–25, 27, 28).

General Observations

I shall begin with some general observations on placenames and their importance in the context of a project such as the IHTA and then shall proceed to look in some detail at the placename entries in relation to each of the twenty-five towns and cities covered in the IHTA. I should emphasise that if, in what follows, I sometimes appear rather critical of certain aspects of the IHTA, this should be taken in the spirit of friendly criticism. I am not trying to score points — merely seeking to improve what is already a very impressive and helpful piece of work.

My first observation is a general one. It is that, although section **1** Name is given prime position in the topographical information of the atlas — and I readily concede that space is at a premium — the treatment of placenames in the work must strike the disinterested observer as being somewhat parsimonious. For, I would argue, the name of a town or city is one of its most important and essential distinguishing features. It is, after all, one of the principal things that serve to distinguish that particular town from any other place or settlement, whether contiguous or otherwise.

It is perhaps stating the obvious to say that the name is the very first thing one sees on looking at the cover of the atlas — it is, after all, what decides one to look at *this* number rather than *that* one. When choosing to look at a particular fascicle of the work, one does not look primarily at the population or the area or its height above sea-level. One looks at the name, that which distinguishes it from any other place, large or small! Those other factors I have mentioned may then be taken account of.

It may be suggested that I am making rather a fuss about this pretty obvious fact, but my reason for doing so is to emphasise the overwhelming importance of a place's name. Of course, in the case of the IHTA the name in question would generally be considered to be the one *currently* in general use — and in English (or, more correctly) in anglicised form, I may add. (This is another issue to which I shall return presently.) But the name in which we are primarily interested here is the town's historically attested name (or, rather, name-*forms*). By that I mean the series of various names that have identified a particular town down through history. In fact, when one lays out these name-forms in chronological order, the result is like a skeletal history of the town; and indeed the documents from which the name-forms are abstracted are more or less the very same sources one would use to write a general history of the town.

Now when we look at the names of the twenty-five towns and cities covered so far by the atlas, what quickly becomes apparent is that the name-forms of all of them reflect a number of linguistic backgrounds

(Table 3.1, Fig. 3.1; for full publication details, see list on pp ix–x). But the primary one is Irish. In fact, it is striking that all but one of the twenty-five towns and cities and the further seventeen on which work is currently progressing (including those with a strong Viking heritage) bear a name that is linguistically Irish, or Gaelic, in origin (Table 3.2).[2] Indeed one can go so far as to assert that all the name-forms assembled in the IHTA, other than those from Irish-language sources, are simply corrupt or garbled versions of the original Gaelic forms.

When saying this, I am not seeking to be derogatory of other linguistic forms. And I am certainly not going down the road of linguistic bigotry — where, for example, the great seventeenth-century Munster poet Dáibhí Ó Bruadair mocked English as a 'babbling, messy, treacherous, dry-lipped, spluttering and stuttering' language ('gliogarnach Gall, Béarla

TABLE 3.1 ANGLICISED AND IRISH NAME-FORMS OF IHTA FASCICLES

1. Kildare	Cill Dara	14. Trim	Baile Átha Troim
2. Carrickfergus	Carraig Fhearghais	15. Derry-Londonderry	Doire
3. Bandon	Droichead na Bandan	16. Dundalk	Dún Dealgan
4. Kells	Ceanannas	18. Armagh	Ard Mhacha
5. Mullingar	An Muileann gCearr	20. Tuam	Tuaim
6. Athlone	Baile Átha Luain	21. Limerick	Luimneach
7. Maynooth	Maigh Nuad	22. Longford	An Longfort
8. Downpatrick	Dún Phádraig	23. Carlingford	Cairlinn
9. Bray	Bré	24. Sligo	Sligeach
10. Kilkenny	Cill Chainnigh	25. Ennis	Inis
11, 19, 26. Dublin	Baile Átha Cliath	27. Youghal	Eochaill
12, 17. Belfast	Béal Feirste	28. Galway	Gaillimh
13. Fethard	Fiodh Ard		

TABLE 3.2 FORTHCOMING IHTA TOWNS AND CITIES, ARRANGED BY PROVINCE

Connacht	Loughrea, Roscommon, Westport
Leinster	Carlow, Drogheda, Naas, New Ross, Tullamore
Munster	Caher, Cashel, Clonmel, Cork, Dungarvan, Tralee, Waterford
Ulster	Ballyshannon, Cavan

Fig. 3.1 Anglicised and Irish name-
forms of IHTA published towns and
cities, 2018.

prasamálta, Béarla bréaganta beoiltirim, truidireacht Bhéarla pléascadh is plubaireacht pluc').[3] J.R.R. Tolkien, author of *The Hobbit* and *The lord of the rings*, as well as being a professor of Anglo-Saxon, said equally uncomplimentary things about Irish.[4] In linguistic as in other matters, beauty is in the eye of the beholder — or in this case, the ear of the listener.

No! What I mean is that, in the case of the aforementioned twenty-five towns and cities, the placenames are all meaningful — in the linguistic sense *transparent*, that is, comprehensible — in the original Irish. In other words, they consist of elements that have meaning, whereas in Latin, Norse, Welsh, Norman-French or English forms the names are essentially meaningless ciphers that originated as attempts (often not very successful) to represent the sounds of the original Irish. This, of course, does not automatically confer superior status on the Irish form, for we know that people can operate perfectly comfortably with names of whose precise meaning they are wholly ignorant.[5] For example, we must not imagine people in say, Paris, London, Rome, Berlin, Madrid, etc. being in a state of existential angst because, for the most part, they do not know what those names mean. Likewise, most people probably have little or no understanding of the precise origin and meaning of the names they bear themselves, whether first names or surnames.

On the other hand, the majority of people who daily walk down Dawson Street or Grafton Street are almost certainly not thinking too deeply either about the precise population of the area under the jurisdiction of Dublin City Council, or the height of the city centre above sea-level — as long as there is no immediate danger of flooding — or the length of the River Liffey, or the date of earliest human habitation in this general area. Only strange, obsessive people — perhaps like some of us who contribute to the IHTA — are concerned about such things. And yet, seriously, if we are concerned about what may be broadly classified as the historical geography of our towns and cities, we must take such things into consideration. So back to placenames!

As indicated already, the attested name-forms of the twenty-five towns being considered in the present volume come to us in a number of linguistic guises. Strictly speaking, most of the forms taken by the various names could be classified as misspellings. In other words, only the original Irish name-forms can be considered to be spelt correctly — and even then there is the question of *which* Irish form is the most correct. Suppose the earliest occurrence of a name is in an Old or Middle Irish form, and there are other forms in Early Modern Irish and in present-day Irish, which of those various forms is the most 'correct'? Or is this even a meaningful question?

In relation to anglicised — or, earlier still, latinised — forms, these usually came about because the external language gained supremacy, either cultural or political, over the native one at some period. In this context, one is tempted to venture into the realm of contrafactual history — the 'what if' school of history, which can make for an entertaining parlour game, but of which several semi-serious volumes may be found on the shelves of the larger bookshops.[6] What if Cleopatra had had a longer nose? What if Hitler had been killed while running messages in the trenches on the western front during the First World War? What if the guns from the Aud had been landed in Kerry in 1916 and Roger Casement had not been captured? What if Michael Collins had not been shot? And so on, and so on. In this context, we might consider what might conceivably be the situation in linguistic terms had Anglo-Irish relations been somewhat different over the past millennium. What if some centuries ago there had been a Gaelic takeover of what is now England? Suppose English people were now obliged to spell well-known English placenames as follows: Bhast Mionstar, Faight Thál, Sabhat Theamptan, Cafantraí, Seifíold, Beirminn Theam, etc.[7] On one level, this may be considered merely a suitable subject for a Myles na Gopaleen-style parlour game.[8] But there is another more serious, and particularly thought-provoking, side to it. It shows what can happen when one language is forced into the straitjacket of another, very different, language. There is inevitably a problem about rendering words (and more particularly names) in one language with the orthography of a different language. And this is what has happened with a large proportion of Irish placenames. I do not mention this to pick at old sores, but merely to point it out as a fact, and one that needs to be taken account of when dealing with names such as those of the twenty-five towns being considered here.

And before going any further, it should be emphasised that many of the anglicised (or latinised) forms of Irish placenames are of considerable merit, and of great assistance to anyone studying Irish toponymy. For example, the medial consonant, written 'th' in the anglicised form Fethard — representing the Irish form Fiodh Ard — gives some indication that the 'dh' at the end of the first element retained its Middle Irish pronunciation rather than the one that would occur in its Modern Irish form, where Fiodh Ard would be reflected in a putative anglicised form such as Fee-ard. (There will be reason to refer to Fethard again presently.)

Before going on to look through some of the twenty-five towns whose names are treated in the IHTA, there are a couple of more general points to be made. One aspect that relates to all the names, and that must be deemed at least slightly problematical, is the way the evidence for each name is laid out. If we consult a range of scholarly works on Irish placenames, we can see the steady evolution of a number of formats that seek to display historically-attested forms of placenames. It will, I think, be readily conceded that — on the basis of experience and experimentation — the columnar form is considerably more satisfactory, being easier to read than, for example, the 'run-on' format that was commonly used up to just over a half century ago. In relation to Irish placenames, the columnar form began to be used in the journal *Dinnseanchas*, the journal of An Cumann Logainmneacha (The Placenames Society), which was established in 1964.[9] A variant of it was used in the book *Logainmneacha na hÉireann: Contae Luimnigh*, dealing with the placenames of Co. Limerick, which was issued for the Placenames Branch of the Ordnance Survey, 1990, and also in other subsequent publications of the Placenames Branch.[10] Another variant was used in the eight volumes in the series *Place-names of Northern*

Ireland, which were issued between 1992 and 2004 by the Northern Ireland Place-Name Project.[11] The thing that all these formats have in common is the practice of having one entry per line, the main point of difference being whether one puts the date before or after the entry and whether, alternatively, one numbers the entries consecutively. I would contend, however, that all of these formats are preferable to the 'run-on' one used in most of the IHTA entries. The latter may be argued to give a somewhat higgledy-piggledy impression, being often rather crowded and, yet, not achieving a particularly significant saving in space. One of the more satisfactory treatments of a name in the series seems to be that on Tuam, which conforms fairly closely (although not entirely) to the layout in the books cited above — it is not, however, arranged in columnar form, but changing to such a format would be not merely feasible but quite easy to accomplish. A format rather similar to that in the Tuam fascicle is employed by the Scottish scholar Simon Taylor in his massive five-volume series, recently completed, on *The place-names of Fife*.[12]

There is another problem that is common to most entries and that merits close consideration. It relates to citations from that most important of sources, the early and medieval Irish annals. With the exception of the *Annals of Inisfallen*, and later portions of other collections of annals, most of the annalistic material is found in manuscripts that are a good deal later than the events they record. So what date is to be given to annalistic entries — the date cited in the text or the date of the manuscript in which the annals are preserved? I would argue that, for example, in the case of, say, the *Annals of the Four Masters*, citations should be given the date under which they occur in the annals, not 'early 17th century' as has sometimes occurred in certain fascicles of the IHTA. It is of course true that the *Annals of the Four Masters* was compiled in the 1630s,[13] but it uses much earlier materials and, for the most part, does not appear to distort them too much in linguistic terms — for example, a seventeenth-century writer would not have written such a form as Dún nGaillmhe but would be more likely to have written it as Dún Gaillmhe, or perhaps even Dún Gaillimhe, or Dún na Gaillimhe. Therefore, since the form Dún nGaillmhe occurs at the date 1141,[14] that is the date that should be cited in the column of evidence.[15] To take a parallel, if one were citing a name in Thucydides's *Peloponnesian War*, one would surely refer to it as coming from the fifth century B.C., not from the tenth century A.D. (the date of the earliest surviving manuscript).

There are other aspects of the onomastic evidence as laid out in the fascicles of the atlas that will be considered critically and commented upon in the following pages, with attention being drawn to a selection of salient points that strike one on reading consecutively through the treatment of the town-names in the IHTA.[16]

INDIVIDUAL FASCICLES

No. 1   On Kildare/Cill Dara, there is not much to be said, save that the Harvard style of naming a source by the name of the editors rather than with an abbreviation can prove rather tiresome. One may recognise, for example, that 'Ó hAodha' stands for Dr Donncha Ó hAodha's edition of *Bethu Brigte*, the Old Irish life of St Brigid,[17] but it seems to me that an abbreviation such as BBr would be more satisfactory here. That, however, is a minor point. It would also be worth noting the occurrence of other instances of the placename, e.g. townlands called Kildarra, in Cos Cork and Mayo, and Kildarragh in Co. Donegal.

No. 2   On Carrickfergus/Carraig Fhearghais, it must be deemed rather astonishing that all the evidence is from English and Latin documents — *Calendar of documents relating to Ireland*; *Calendar of the justiciary rolls*, etc. — with not a single mention of the numerous annalistic references, beginning with *Miscellaneous Irish annals* for 1206.[18] Full details of the many Irish language citations of the name can be found in the Irish Texts Society's invaluable *Historical dictionary of Gaelic placenames*.[19] Another point to be noted is that the Irish form Carraig Fheargas, given as one of the two 'current spellings', has two errors in the second element.[20]

No. 3   In the entry on Bandon/Droichead na Bandan the suggested Irish version of the seventeenth-century form Drohid-Mahon, Droichead Uí Mhathún, must be deemed at the very least slightly incorrect — perhaps representing a simple, but regrettable, misprint. The correct form is either Droichead Uí Mhathúna or (perhaps) Droichead Mathúna — the former representing the well-known Co. Cork surname of Ó Mathúna/O Mahon(e)y, and the latter the Gaelic personal name formerly written Mathghamhain (in present-day standardised Irish spelling, Mathúin), from which the surname is derived.

No. 4   As for Kells/Ceanannas, the evidence for Ceanannas is set out fairly clearly, but the entry cries out for even a modicum of commentary — for example, on how the name evolved from Ceanannas to Ceanadas and, apparently, *Ceanalas (= Kenlys, Kenles) and thence to Kells and, by interesting mistranslation, to Headfort — as if the Irish name were the compound noun Ceannlios.[21] There should also be mention of the fact that the name is not unique and that Kells, Co. Kilkenny, exhibits the same development, with forms such as Kenelis and Kenles in thirteenth- and fourteenth-century sources, while the existence of Kells, Co. Antrim, should also be noted, to say the least. (It might also be desirable to include a note on what was for many years the official form of the town's name, Ceanannus Mór.)

No. 5   The entry on Mullingar/An Muileann gCearr looks strangely lopsided, given that there are only two Irish forms cited even though, as shown by that great Westmeath scholar, Fr Paul Walsh in his *Placenames of Westmeath*, the Irish form occurs on numerous occasions between the early twelfth and the early seventeenth centuries.[22] Also desirable would be even a brief note explaining that the 'g' before the 'C' in the second element of the name in its original Irish form is what gives us the anglicised form Mullingar, and why the 'g' is inserted before the 'C', thus eclipsing it.[23] A note on the genitive form of An Muileann gCearr (i.e. An Mhuilinn Chearr) would also be of assistance, since at least one signpost that I have seen in the town has an incorrect form.

No. 6   When we come to the name Athlone/Baile Átha Luain, we find two quite lengthy notes on its derivation — both taken from Paul Walsh's *Placenames of Westmeath*.[24] It would also help, however, to have a brief discussion of the respective merits of the two forms, Áth Luain and Baile Átha Luain — the latter being the form in common use while the Irish language survived in the vicinity. (Most town-names with Áth as an initial element adopted the form *Baile Átha* in the later medieval period — in or about the fifteenth century — the most noted example being Áth Cliath which regularly became Baile Átha Cliath; another instance of relevance in the present context is Trim/Baile Átha Troim.)[25]

No. 7   The entry on Maynooth/Maigh Nuad strangely lacks any reference to a somewhat puzzling alternative form, found in a number of early sources, Magh Luadhad.[26]

No. 8 The entry on Downpatrick/Dún Pádraig has what is perhaps the most comprehensive treatment of any placename in the entire atlas. This is based almost entirely on the meticulous work of that great authority on Ulster placenames, Deirdre Flanagan (1932–84).[27]

No. 9 Bray/Bré has a great number of citations listed, but there is no attempt to assess the respective merits of the two Irish forms, Bré and Brí Chualann. At the very least, mention should have been made of a pretty definitive study of the subject published over seventy years ago by the principal authority on the placenames of Co. Wicklow, Liam Price — it appeared as an article in the journal *Éigse*.[28]

No. 10 Skipping over Kilkenny/Cill Channigh,[29] we come to **No. 11** Dublin/Baile Átha Cliath which, as one might expect, has by far the longest name-entry in the atlas. Both historical forms, Áth Cliath (later Baile Átha Cliath) and Duibhlinn, are set out pretty exhaustively but there is no attempt to explain the fact that, while the latter is the basis for all forms of the name used as an exonym by speakers of English and other languages outside Ireland (even by the related Celtic language, Welsh), the former is the only one used almost exclusively by speakers of Irish. Also deserving of some discussion is the puzzling fact that Adomnán in his late seventh-century *Vita Columbae*, in latinising the Old Irish name Áth Clíath, translated the first element as *Vadum* but left the second — written as *Clied* — untranslated, despite the fact that the meaning of the latter word, *clíath* in Old Irish, would have been just as transparent as the first to the learned ninth abbot of Iona.[30] One glaring error in relation to Dublin is the inclusion of that hoary old myth that seeks to equate it with the mysterious, enigmatic name Eblana, or Ebdana, which occurs in Ptolemy's Geography compiled in the middle of the second century A.D.[31]

No. 12 The derivation of Belfast/Béal Feirste is explained in an authoritative note taken from the writings of Deirdre Flanagan,[32] but there is no explanation that the third of three 'current spellings', Bilfawst, is actually the so-called Ullans, or Ulster Scots, form.

No. 13 The most important remark to be made in relation to Fethard/ Fiodh Ard is that the second of what are termed 'current spellings' is quite simply mistaken. The form given there is Fíodh Áird, which involves no fewer than *three* errors! The correct form is Fiodh Ard (with Feadha Aird as the old genitive form).[33] (As mentioned above, it would be advisable to insert a note explaining that the current anglicised spelling reflects the Middle Irish pronunciation of the medial lenited 'd'.)

No. 15 There is not much to be said about the rather contentious name Derry-Londonderry/Doire — so-called 'Stroke City'[34] — except to note that the form Doire Coluim Chille is comparatively late, not occurring prior to the twelfth century, a point deserving of at least a brief note.

No. 16 The treatment of Dundalk/Dún Dealgan is fairly comprehensive, but there is no explanation of the significance of other variant names — cited in sources nearly a millennium old — such as Áth Leathan and Tráigh Bhaile, while another name, An Sráidbhaile, survived among local Irish speakers down to the nineteenth century as the usual designation of the town.

No. 18 On Armagh/Ard Mhacha the 'traditional' explanation, 'height of Macha, a pagan Celtic goddess', is supplemented by the alternative one, 'height of the plain', but without any acknowledgment that this was a celebrated suggestion made in the 1950s by Seán Mac Airt of Queen's University.[35]

No. 20 The coverage of Tuam/Tuaim is very full, but the explanation of the derivation is vitiated by giving credence to a purported 'explanation' from an outdated and untrustworthy source, Canon Ulick Bourke's *Life of Archbishop MacHale*, published as long ago as 1882. Bourke suggested that the form *Tuam Dá Ualann* meant 'burial mound of the two altar tombs', whereas the RIA's *Dictionary of the Irish language* indicates that *ualann* is simply an alternative form of *guala*, 'a shoulder'.[36]

No. 21 The entry on Limerick/Luimneach could do with some attempt at explaining the source of the 'r' in the anglicised form in place of 'n' in the original. The pronunciation of the combination 'mn' as 'mr' in northern dialects of Irish (e.g. *mná* pronounced as *mrá*) seems to be a comparatively modern phenomenon, thought to be scarcely earlier than the late sixteenth century,[37] so its occurrence in the case of Luimneach at least half a millennium earlier (in Old Norse sources, where it is written *Hlymrek*) is quite puzzling and has, to date, not been satisfactorily explained. Also worth mentioning are the number of other places of the name throughout Ireland, such as Limnagh, in Co. Sligo, Lumnagh, in Co. Cork, Cloonlumney, in Co. Mayo, etc., and there is also a townland called Limerick/Luimneach near Gorey, Co. Wexford.

No. 22   Treatment of Longford/An Longfort is quite comprehensive with a fairly full discussion of the name's derivation from the word *longphort*, an Irish word that seems to have been adopted at an early stage by the Vikings for their encampments.[38] Once again, there are numerous instances of the element in Irish placenames — more than a dozen consisting of that element alone, and up to ten others made up of the element with one or more words appended, as well as Ballylongford/Béal Átha Longfoirt, Co. Kerry. In at least one instance the element may not be immediately recognisable in its anglicised form: Athlunkard, in Limerick, which represents Áth an Longfoirt. (I also recall seeing an instance of Longford as a minor name somewhere on the borders of Cos Limerick and Tipperary where it appears to represent the English words 'long ford' and would therefore have as an Irish form An tÁth Fada.)

No. 23   When we come to Carlingford/Cairlinn, the section on the derivation is dismayingly cryptic. 'Logainm', listed in the general abbreviations, is cited in support of a suggested original form Cathair linn fjord, purportedly meaning 'city on the fjord'; this has no doubt been obtained by writing the first two syllables of 'Carlingford' more or less according to the rules of Irish orthography, and appending the Norse word *fjörðr*. However, the proposed form is quite simply wrong, even preposterous! The officially-sanctioned Irish form, Cairlinn, has been attested since the early sixteenth century, while earlier sources, from the thirteenth and fourteenth centuries, cite the form (an) Carrloingphort, which may be interpreted as meaning 'the port of the kerling (hag-shaped rock)' and is clearly a gaelicisation of an original Norse toponym.[39] Also meriting at least a brief discussion is the intriguing form Dún Ogalla, which occurs in the *Miscellaneous Irish annals* in 1210, where the authors explicitly equate it with Carlingford.[40]

No. 24 Next is Sligo/Sligeach, on which I published a study some years ago.[41] At the very least, a modicum of linguistic detail on the name might be in order here — if only to explain the fact that what was a feminine noun prior to the thirteenth century became a masculine one thereafter, and that there is evidence for the element *slig* in placenames elsewhere in Ireland and also in Gaelic Scotland.[42]

No. 25 In the entry on Ennis/Inis, the note on derivation contains a number of errors. The early name-form Inis Mac nInill, which occurs only in the *Annals of Inisfallen* at the year 1306, means 'the island of the sons of Ineall' (this last an otherwise unattested personal name).[43] Another early form — cited in sources dated 1370 and 1602 — should read in the nominative Inis an Laoigh.[44] Finally, the form Múr Inse — dated 1588 — is not in its totality another name for Ennis: rather than 'walled island', it means '[the] wall of Inis/Ennis', and can therefore be taken as further evidence for Inis as the Irish name of the place. (Incidentally, it should be written in the first instance as *múr Inse*, while the second occurrence appears to represent a distinct form, úr Inse.)

No. 27 In the case of Youghal/Eochaill, while the treatment of the onomastic evidence is satisfactory, it would — once again — be desirable to indicate that the same original Irish name-form is to be found elsewhere in Ireland (anglicised in various ways).[45]

No. 28 The treatment of the placename Galway/Gaillimh is probably the most satisfactory of all those in the IHTA series. The separation of 'Irish language forms' and 'Latinised/anglicised forms' into two discrete sections — the former largely transparent and the latter opaque — and with the names in each laid out in chronological order, makes for greater clarity. Note, however, that the material is not arranged in the columnar form which I suggested above as the clearest and most satisfactory format for laying out placename evidence. Finally, the note on the name's derivation is cryptic in the extreme.

CONCLUSIONS

My final observation on the subject involves reiterating something remarked upon earlier — that each of the twenty-five names occurring in the titles of the IHTA fascicles has two forms: in twenty-four cases these are, in turn, an anglicised form and the original Irish, while in the case of Carlingford/ Cairlinn, the first form derives from Norse and the second is a gaelicised version of the name's initial element. In each case, then, the first name has a meaning while the second is a meaningless cipher — using terminology employed in the preceding paragraph, they are respectively 'transparent' and 'opaque'. Some time ago, I made the suggestion, which I thought merited some consideration, that for future fascicles (or those already published that may require a reprint) it would not be too onerous to give *both* name-forms on the cover, since both now have legal recognition and equal status in law.[46] To my great satisfaction, the editorial board of IHTA agreed to the suggestion and the most recent atlas, Galway/Gaillimh, bears that double name-form in large red capitals on the front cover. It is to be hoped that this practice will be maintained in future.

Looking back over my observations on the topographical information section of each IHTA fascicle, it seems to me that what is common to most of these entries is a suggestion that explanatory notes on the names have to date been generally inadequate — and, in many cases, entirely missing. It should not be difficult to furnish a short note — usually no more than a paragraph — on each of the names, discussing its derivation, linguistic background and meaning, as well as possible alternative names for the same place, and also drawing attention to other instances of the name elsewhere in Ireland.

NOTES

[1] The Branch has since the year 2000 been part of the Department of Arts, Heritage, Gaeltacht and the Islands (later renamed, again and again: first as the Department of Community, Rural and Gaeltacht Affairs, then of Community, Equality and Gaeltacht Affairs, then of Arts, Heritage and the Gaeltacht, then of Arts, Heritage, Regional, Rural and Gaeltacht Affairs, and currently of Culture, Heritage and the Gaeltacht).

[2] The one exception is no. 23 Carlingford, while one of the forthcoming towns, Waterford, has two names, one Irish in origin and one Norse.

[3] J.C. Mac Erlean (ed.), *Duanaire Dháibhidh Uí Bhruadair, the poems of David Ó Bruadair* (3 vols, London, 1910–17), i, p. xxv.

[4] According to M.D.C. Drout (ed.), *J.R.R. Tolkien encyclopedia: scholarship and critical assessment* (New York, 2006), p. 298: 'Tolkien disliked the Irish Gaelic language, which he admits "heavily defeated him". In 1937 Tolkien stated a distaste for things Celtic'. Tolkien is also quoted as stating in 1958: 'the Irish language I find wholly unattractive' (Humphrey Carpenter (ed.), *The letters of J.R.R. Tolkien* (London, 1981), p. 298), while in a draft letter from August 1967 he declared: 'I have no liking at all for Gaelic from Old Irish downwards, as a language, but it is of course of great historical and philological interest, and I have at various times studied it. (With alas! very little success)'. To balance matters, a letter to the editor of *The Irish Times*, 17 Mar. 2012, quotes him as saying: 'Portuguese is such an unpleasant language'.

[5] We may note the comment by M.A. O'Brien, 'Irish personal names', in *Celtica*, x (1973), p. 217: 'unlike an ordinary word the meaning of which can be determined, a name has no meaning'. This provocative remark could spark a most interesting discussion — but not here!

[6] See Niall Ferguson (ed.), *Virtual history: alternatives and counterfactuals* (London, 2011; first published 1997); Robert Cowley (ed.), *What if? Military historians imagine what might have been* (London, 2001).

[7] That is: Westminster, Whitehall, Southampton, Coventry, Sheffield, Birmingham. See further examples of this process in Tadhg Ó Donnchadha's edition of a mid-seventeenth century text: 'Cín Lae Ó Mealláin', in *Analecta Hibernica*, no. 3 (1931), pp 11 (*Edurt Bon Róó* — Edward Monroe), 14 (*Muinseói* — Mountjoy), 19 (*Lord Sithsesdar, Lord Blénaidh, Lord Magumraidh* — Lords Chichester, Blaney, Montgomery).

[8] For some examples of Myles writing English according to the rules of Irish orthography, see Myles na Gopaleen (Flann O'Brien), *The best of Myles: a selection from 'Cruiskeen Lawn'*, ed. Kevin O'Nolan (London, 1977), p. 275: 'Damhn, iú réibeal cur! Aigh bhás reidhding báigh ond théard iú méic fbhait samhndad leidhc a seidisius spíts' — *Down, you rebel cur! I was riding by and heard you make what sounded like a seditious speech.* For another example of 'Haighbeirneo-Inglis' (Hiberno-English), see Breandán Ó Conaire, *Myles na Gaeilge. Lámhleabhar ar shaothar Gaeilge Bhrian Ó Nualláin* (Baile Átha Cliath, 1986), p. 264: 'Aigh nó a meán thú ios só léasaigh dat thí slíps in this clós, bhéars a bíord, and dos not smóc bíocos obh de trobal obh straighcing a meaits' — *I know a man who sleeps in his clothes, wears a beard, and does not smoke because of the trouble of striking a match.*

[9] See the feature 'As cartlann na logainmneacha' (from the Placenames' Archive) in each issue of *Dinnseanchas*, 1964–77.

[10] Art Ó Maolfabhail, *Logainmneacha na hÉireann, I: Contae Luimnigh* (Baile Átha Cliath, 1990). Pádraig Ó Cearbhaill, *Logainmneacha na hÉireann, II: Cill i logainmneacha Co. Thiobraid Árann* (Baile Átha Cliath, 2007); *Logainmneacha na hÉireann, III: Cluain i logainmneacha Co. Thiobraid Árann* (Baile Átha Cliath, 2010).

[11] I directed the Northern Ireland Place-Name Project for about a decade (1994–2004). The eight volumes in question were: Gregory Toner and M.B. Ó Mainnín, 1. *County Down I: Newry and south-west Down* (Belfast, 1992); A.J. Hughes and R.J. Hannan, 2. *County Down II: the Ards* (Belfast, 1992); M.B. Ó Mainnín, 3. *County Down III: the Mournes* (Belfast, 1993); Patrick McKay, 4. *County Antrim I: the baronies of Toome* (Belfast, 1995); Kay Muhr, 5. *County Down IV: north-west Down/Iveagh* (Belfast, 1996); Gregory Toner, 6. *County Derry I: the Moyola valley* (Belfast, 1996); Fiachra Mac Gabhann, 7. *County Antrim II: Ballycastle and north-east Antrim* (Belfast, 1997); Patrick McKay, 8. *County Fermanagh: Lisnaskea and district: the parish of Aghalurcher* (Belfast, 2004). See now the massive and magisterial ten-volume study of the placenames of Co. Mayo published in recent years by Fiachra Mac Gabhann, *Logainmneacha Mhaigh Eo* (Baile Átha Cliath, 2014).

[12] Simon Taylor, *The place-names of Fife,* I–V (Donington, 2006–14).

[13] See Bernadette Cunningham, *The Annals of the Four Masters: Irish history, kingship and society in the early seventeenth century* (Dublin, 2010).

[14] *AFM*, ii, p. 1066.

[15] Albeit with the inclusion of a 'health warning' to the effect that dates prior to the sixth century, and sometimes from a later period, may be doubtful to a greater or lesser degree, and also including a note to explain that most dates in the early portion of *AFM* (i.e. in the pre-Anglo-Norman period) may be from one to five years inaccurate. See the detailed study of this subject by D.P. McCarthy, 'The chronology of the Irish annals', in *RIA Proc.*, xcviii C (1998), pp 203–55.

[16] It has not been deemed necessary to comment in the same detail on every town or city covered by the atlas.

[17] Donncha Ó hAodha, *Bethu Brigte* (Dublin, 1978).

[18] *Miscellaneous Irish annals (A.D. 1114–1437)*, ed. Séamus Ó hInnse (Dublin, 1947), p. 84 (1206.5, Carig Feargusa), p. 88 (1210.2, Cairig Feargusa).

[19] Pádraig Ó Riain, Diarmuid Ó Murchadha and Kevin Murray (eds), *Historical dictionary of Gaelic placenames* (5 fascicles, London, 2003–13), iii, pp 91–2, s.n. *Carraig Fheargusa* (the name's Classical Irish form).

[20] See *Ainmneacha Gaeilge na mBailte Poist* (Baile Átha Cliath, 1969), p. 95; and *Gasaitéar na hÉireann* (Baile Átha Cliath, 1989), p. 47; also Logainm, www.logainm.ie (last accessed 24 Oct. 2017). The error in question may be deemed quite a minor one, but not in the context of what is intended to be an authoritative publication issued under the prestigious imprint of the RIA.

[21] Ceann = head; lios = fort.

[22] Paul Walsh, *The placenames of Westmeath*, ed. Colm Ó Lochlainn (Dublin, 1957), pp 212–14. The earliest reference is said to be in the Life of St Colmán of Lynn, which 'in its present form ... belongs to the first half of the twelfth century, but some of the materials and most of the traditions which it transmits to us are very much older' (p. 212).

[23] The reason for the nasalisation of the initial 'C' is that *muilenn* in Old and Middle Irish is a neuter noun and accordingly causes nasalisation (or eclipsis) to the initial letter of the following noun or (as in this instance) adjective. Hence the present-day Irish form An Muileann gCearr. Another celebrated example of such a development occurs in the Irish name of Lough Neagh, Loch nEchach in Old and Middle Irish, and in present-day form Loch nEathach, 'the lake of Eochu'.

[24] Walsh, *Placenames of Westmeath*, pp 107–10. See also, Ó Riain, Ó Murchadha and Murray, *Historical dictionary of Gaelic placenames*, i, pp 140–41.

[25] See *AU* (1), ii, p. 532, where the phrase 'o Baile Atha-Cliath co Baile Atha-Luain' occurs at the year 1368. Thereafter this longer form of such names gradually becomes the norm.

[26] See Edmund Hogan, *Onomasticon Goedelicum* (Dublin, 1910), p. 524, where numerous citations include one from the twelfth-century *Book of Leinster*; for this last, see *The Book of Leinster, formerly Lebar na Núachongbála*, ed. R.I. Best *et al.* (6 vols, Dublin, 1974), i, p. 202, l. 6069n., where a scribal note states explicitly the identification with Magh Nuadhat (the earlier form of Maigh Nuad): 'Mag Luadat i nH*uib* Faelain. .i. Mag Nuadat hodie'.

[27] See Deirdre Uí Fhlannagáin, 'The names of Downpatrick', in *Dinnseanchas*, iv (1971), pp 89–112.

[28] Liam Price, 'The name of Bray', in *Éigse*, iv (1943–4), pp 147–51.

[29] Perhaps it merits at least a brief note referring to the contentious theory advanced some decades ago by Pádraig Ó Riain that the name Cainneach, from which the name of the monastic foundation that later grew into a city (and a county) derived, may have represented a hypocoristic form of Colum Cille, and that therefore the saint commemorated in Cill Chainnigh is identical to the celebrated saint of Cenél Conaill who founded the great monastery of Iona. See Pádraig Ó Riain, 'Cainneach alias Colum Cille, patron of Ossory', in Pádraig de Brún, Seán Ó Coileáin and Pádraig Ó Riain (eds), *Folia Gadelica* (Cork, 1983), pp 20–35.

[30] A.O. and M.O. Anderson (eds), *Adomnan's Life of Columba* (London and Edinburgh, 1961; rev. Oxford, 1991), ii, p. 4. It is interesting to note that the same thing happens in relation to the name of Trim, Co. Meath, which is mentioned in Muirchú's Life of St Patrick (perhaps two decades earlier than Adomnán's work) as *Vadum Truim(m)*; this represents the Irish name Áth Truimm and, as with Vadum Clied, is rather puzzling since the meaning of *truimm* (genitive of *tromm*, 'alder-tree') would have been obvious to all.

[31] See some previous efforts at identification, such as T.F. O'Rahilly, *Early Irish history and mythology* (Dublin, 1946), pp 7–8; Alan Mac an Bhaird, 'Ptolemy revisited', in *Ainm*, v (1991–3), p. 13 (where it is suggested to be a badly corrupted form of the population-group name Cualainn). For much less certain views of its identity and/or location,

see Gregory Toner, 'Identifying Ptolemy's Irish places and tribes', p. 81 (nos 31 and 37) and Patrizia de Bernardo Stempel, 'Ptolemy's Celtic Italy and Ireland: a linguistic analysis', p. 102, both articles in D.N. Parsons and Patrick Sims-Williams (eds), *Ptolemy: towards a linguistic atlas of the earliest Celtic place-names of Europe* (Aberystwyth, 2000).

[32] Notably her article, 'Béal Feirste agus áitainmneacha laistigh', in B.S. Mac Aodha (ed.), *Topothesia* (Galway, 1982), pp 45–64.

[33] This older genitive form (as used in Classical Modern Irish) is now obsolete, being replaced by the standardised rendering Fiodh Ard.

[34] The late Northern Ireland broadcaster, Gerry Anderson, probably merits at least a brief footnote for his clever coinage, which reflects the politically correct attempt to skirt round the knotty problem of how to refer to the 'maiden city', where one side of the community insists on calling it Londonderry (at least in formal contexts) and the other is equally insistent on using the shorter (and older) form Derry. (Some of the former, when questioned about why they also commonly refer to Derry — at least in informal conversation — will argue that what they really mean is 'Derry, but how one should express an apostrophe in speech is not explained!)

[35] See J.B. Arthurs, 'Macha and Armagh', in *Bulletin of the Ulster Place-Name Society*, 1st ser., i (1952–3), pp 37–43 (reprinted in *Ainm*, vii (1996–7), pp 152–7). See also Nollaig Ó Muraíle, 'Seán Mac Airt, pioneering Ulster place-names scholar', in *Seanchas Ard Mhacha*, xxv, no. 2 (2015), pp 1–28.

[36] Bourke most probably confused *ualann* with a rather archaic word, *ula*, which did indeed mean something like 'altar tomb' — the meanings given in Niall Ó Dónaill's *Foclóir Gaeilge-Béarla* (Dublin, 1977) include 'Tomb, sepulchre, ... sepulchral monument'.

[37] 'This change of *n* to *r* is undoubtedly a comparatively late one. English spellings of Irish names in the late sixteenth and early seventeenth centuries show little or no trace of it' (T.F. O'Rahilly, *Irish dialects, past and present* (Dublin, 1932; reprinted 1972), pp 22–3).

[38] An earlier name for the place would appear to have been Cluain Lis Bhéice Mhic Connla, which occurs in *AFM* and *Ann. Conn.* at the year 1282.

[39] Ó Riain, Ó Murchadha and Murray, *Historical dictionary of Gaelic placenames*, iii, pp 100–01, s.n. Carrloingphort; see also Hogan, *Onomasticon Goedelicum*, p. 167 — Carrlongport.

[40] See *Miscellaneous Irish annals*, pp 86–7 (1210.2).

[41] See Nollaig Ó Muraíle, 'Sligeach – the original and correct name of Sligo', in M.A. Timoney (ed.), *Dedicated to Sligo, thirty-four essays on Sligo's past* (Ballymote, 2013), pp 97–102.

[42] For evidence of the name Sligeach in Scotland, see W.J. Watson, *The history of the Celtic place-names of Scotland* (Edinburgh, 1926), p. 412 and pp 234, 412 for instances of related forms such as Sligeachán.

[43] The basis for the proposed identification of this name as Ennis/Inis is far from clear.

[44] It should be noted that the suggested identification of this name with Ennis/Inis is dismissed quite peremptorily by Gearóid Mac Niocaill ('Duanaire Ghearóid Iarla', in *Studia Hibernica*, no. 3 (1963), p. 54).

[45] Such names include townlands named Youghal and Youghalvillage, in the parish of Youghalarra, Co. Tipperary; and more than twenty others named Oghil or Oghill, a few of which have other elements attached.

[46] See Acht na dTeangacha Oifigiúla/Official Languages Act, 2003.

4. Religion

Catherine Swift

In 2013, an important review of the literature on the monastic towns of Ireland by Howard Clarke was published, using the new data compiled and highlighted by the rolling programme of IHTA studies of individual towns. His conclusions were clearly stated:

> If the concept of proto-town can be accepted ... the early Irish (Christian) ecclesiastical sites are best regarded as a species of that essentially intellectual construct, as Anngret and Katharine Simms classified them back in 1979 ... the primary dynamic was of a religious nature, operating in some kind of ceremonial complex. The so-called Irish monastic town was not an isolated, purely insular phenomenon but an aspect of urban origins in many parts

of Europe and beyond. When we ask ourselves at what stage did the places in this sample of eight become primarily urban, the answer can be found in the relevant IHTA fascicles. A group of five located in the more forcibly colonized parts of the island were promoted as towns in the late twelfth and early thirteenth centuries. These were Downpatrick, Kells, Kildare, Kilkenny and Trim. In every case, a powerful aristocratic family of foreign origin was the agent of change … The other two examples from Ulster – Armagh and Derry – became towns only in the early seventeenth century in a programme of plantation … This leaves Tuam as something of an exception… Just as at the Anglo-Norman colonial sites, the primary dynamic towards genuine urbanisation was the castle rather than the much older monastic and episcopal centre … The lesson of Tuam is that 'monastic town' is a contradiction in terms that should henceforth be excised from all archaeological and historical discourse.[1]

Irish 'monastic towns', however, have refused to die and the formulation has continued in use although the tone of conviction, apparent in earlier IHTA fascicles,[2] is now often absent. In 2010 for example, Tomás Ó Carragáin wrote: 'Whether or not modern scholars decide to categorise these settlements as towns, it seems clear that contemporaries understood them to be representations of the great cities of Christendom'.[3] More succinctly, a recent discussion of early medieval Irish archaeology concluded: 'While some have supported the idea of the "monastic town", it has also generated heated opposition'.[4] In this short paper, my aim is to provide a broad overview of certain themes that have marked this debate and the relevance of the IHTA data to these.

As noted by many, Irish scholars have tended to use a *Kriterienbündel* approach to processes of urbanisation, using up to twelve potential indicators of town status. I shall confine this examination of the Irish monastic town model to three of the most frequently attested: evidence for manufacturing, evidence for trade and evidence for large and hierarchically defined populations not engaged in full-time agrarian pursuits. Because of constraints of space, I shall not discuss the biblical and liturgical influences on the layout of Irish ecclesiastical sites, beyond noting that interesting new material on this aspect of the monastic town debate has recently been collated and analysed by Melanie Maddox and David Jenkins.[5]

The emphasis placed by Clarke on outside influence in town formation is particularly interesting given the views of an early author on the subject, the geographer R.A. Butlin, in 1979. Previous writers such as Kathleen Hughes and Donnchadh Ó Corráin had used the term 'monastic town' loosely to refer to large monasteries but without defining these in detail. Their descriptions appear to have been influenced by Counter-Reformation writers such as the seventeenth-century antiquarian, Geoffrey Keating, who could credit even the relatively minor site of Mungret in Co. Limerick with a population of fifteen hundred monks. Butlin, however, was concerned rather with the history of Irish town formation, the implications of British scholarship that sought to examine Anglo-Saxon contributions to urbanism and the 'general theory ... of secondary urban generation resulting from primary diffusion of urban form and organisation'. He explicitly rejected what he described as the Irish 'imported urbanism only' thesis and highlighted instead the potential contribution of some of the larger monastic settlements to what he characterised as 'pre-urban nuclei or proto-urban sites' of pre-Anglo-Norman Ireland. In putting forward this hypothesis, he was predominantly concerned with population size, suggesting that such communities could have attracted 'quite substantial numbers of students and probably lay farmers and craftsmen'.[6]

EVIDENCE FOR MANUFACTURING

The existence or otherwise of craftsmen has been a constant theme in the discussion of Irish monastic towns by both proponents and dissenters. Charles Doherty, the scholar who did most to develop Butlin's original construct, concentrated on ideologies of celestial cities, but he also drew attention to documentary evidence for a tenth- or eleventh-century comb-maker who worked in antler at the side of a roadway in Kildare.[7] Excavated evidence for craft activity figures largely in the papers by the archaeologist John Bradley.[8] Contrariwise, the historian Colmán Etchingham, using exclusively documentary evidence, does not believe in the economic importance of artisanal activity in eleventh- and twelfth-century Kells and Armagh.[9] Different geographical foci have something to do with these varying perspectives, but they also reveal certain inherent characteristics of archaeological versus documentary evidence for church settlement in early medieval Ireland.

On the documentary side, as Anngret Simms pointed out, the contemporary records for individual church sites are typically made up of annals and genealogies, although these can be supplemented, to some extent, by prescriptive accounts drawn from legal texts.[10] Irish annals are, however, generally brief and many (certainly prior to the tenth century) are simply the obits of church leaders or brief notices of raids and battles, providing little detail on settlement form. This explains the reliance by commentators on the later annals (which have more detailed entries), on eleventh- and twelfth-century transaction records inserted into the Books of Kells and Durrow, and on the narrative accounts of particular foundations provided in a variety of saints' Lives. (It is widely recognised, however, that an unknown percentage of these post-date the original foundations by a considerable margin.) Given this relative paucity of textual information, it is hardly surprising that documentary commentary is often generalised and that the classic historical view of earlier forms of Irish religious settlement is still largely derived from the lengthy seventh-century *Life of Columba* by Adomnán with its many references to daily life on Iona. The relevant detail was originally summarised by William Reeves:

> The monastery proper was the space enclosed by the *vallum* and embraced the *ecclesia, refectorium, coquina* and *hospitia*, lining the *platea*; the *armarium* and probably the *officina fabri*; together with the furniture and utensils belonging to the several departments of the institution. Its extent was not great and it seems incapable of receiving many strangers; yet a visitor might be in the monastery for several days without having been seen by the abbot ... Within the enclosure was a *plateola* or *faithche* surrounding or besides which were the lodgings, *hospitia*, of the community. They appear to have been detached huts ... There was a smithy, probably inside the enclosure; and in an institution where timber was so generally used, there must have been a carpenter's workshop. All of these buildings were embraced by a rampart and fosse, called the *vallum* which, in other Irish monasteries, was of a circular figure and was intended more for the restraint than the security of the inmates. It is doubtful whether the cemetery was within the *vallum* ... Outside the *vallum*, were the various offices and appointments subsidiary to the monastery; as the *bocetum* with its cows; the *horreum* with its grain; the *canaba* with its appurtenances; the *molendium* with its pond and mill-steam; the *proelium* with its horse and cart; and the *portus* with its craft of various sizes.[11]

As Reeves remarked in a footnote to this account: 'the Four Masters at 1203 give the name *baile* "town" to this conventual establishment, in accordance with the practice which is observed in many ancient Lives, of calling a monastery *civitas*'. This is, however, somewhat deceptive as the closest analogue appears to be the agricultural unit known as a *baile feara-inn* or modern townland rather than a nucleated urban space or town. The first records of these townland units, in twelfth-century charters, contain names indicating that they were often occupied by extended families sharing a common ancestor and included associated farmlands, comprising individual holdings (which could be periodically re-allocated) as well as areas of rough grazing and other landscape features held in commonage.

In contrast to historical documents, which are often widely dispersed in time and space, archaeological research is invariably localised and, as the study of material remains, is inevitably much concerned with questions of manufacture. In recent years, craft activity has been noted on a number of ecclesiastical sites and Michael Ryan's 1988 view that evidence for fine metalwork is common on church sites still appears to hold true,[12] although the 1,300 fragments of lignite bracelets and associated manufacturing debris found in Armoy, Co. Antrim are something of a puzzle. If these indeed were produced in a monastic setting, it is hard to understand why religious authorities would have permitted production of such items within (apparently) its central religious core. (It is not, however, entirely clear that Armoy was necessarily an ecclesiastical establishment at this particular stage in its history.)[13]

A more recent excavation at Clonfad in Co. Westmeath produced 1.5 tonnes of metallurgical residue, found between two large concentric ditches and linked to them by C14 dating. Analysis suggests that this represents large-scale and highly specialised brazing and iron-working, involved in the creation of multiple iron hand-bells, used to call people to community prayer. A religious site at Clonfad is recorded sporadically in annals from the sixth to the later ninth centuries and the placename is used for a parish church in the fourteenth-century taxation lists. The excavator has concluded that this discovery represents strong evidence for specialist production on religious sites on a scale sufficient for trade and exchange.[14]

Such striking evidence has not been found on the larger, defended settlements seen as potentially having an economic impact on their hinterlands, which were originally identified as the characteristic pre-Anglo-Norman monastic town.[15] However, there has been little extensive excavation of religious sites within the urban confines of most Irish towns and it is hard to imagine that situation changing in the medium term.

Irish archaeologists generally avoid digging on functioning religious sites where Christian burials might be disturbed. As a result, research on church settlements tends to be focused either on abandoned sites or, in recent years, on previously unknown discoveries revealed by motorway or pipeline construction. Where excavation occurs in 'monastic towns' such as Downpatrick, Armagh, Kilkenny or Trim it is normally limited to relatively small areas in streets or buildings, which means that there is little information on original buildings or settlement layout.[16] At the same time, ongoing pressures on ecclesiastical income means that archaeological investigation of functioning religious buildings is often deemed a low priority. It is only when urban churches are seen primarily as tourist and heritage sites, as for example at Ennis friary,[17] that substantial and state-sponsored excavation has taken place. In such a context, it is hard to believe that Ireland will see a major programme of excavation such as has marked the investigation of the episcopal complex with associated graves at the south-western Scottish site of Whithorn.[18] It is noteworthy, indeed, that so much of the archaeological discussion on 'monastic towns' has concentrated on Clonmacnoise, where substantial work was undertaken in preparation for a state-run heritage centre and which, despite its national importance and apparent size in the early medieval period, entirely failed to become the nucleus of a later town.

Of course, all commentators acknowledge that craft activity must have taken place on larger religious sites, for monumental remains such as high crosses and graveslabs still remain visible and artefacts such as illuminated manuscripts and prestigious metalwork survive. Such items required skills to produce and their creation involved the movement of goods, often from far afield. At Armagh, for example, craftsmen produced 'reliquaries in iron and bronze along with amber, enamel and glass',[19] while vellum for the Book of Kells required the skins of some 175 calves, quite apart from the various plants, lichens and minerals to make the ink and paints.[20] The question is — what processes gave rise to the wealth necessary to create these items and what was the ultimate motivation of the manufacturers?

A valid criticism of monastic town proponents is that they treat craft on church sites purely in terms of commercial transactions. It seems equally likely, in fact, that it was understood by those involved as another way in which to glorify the God who was worshipped in communal liturgy up to nine times in every twenty-four hours (including three sessions during the hours of darkness). Their artisanship, while it clearly required resources, did not necessarily involve redistribution or even profits. When the king of the Cenél Conaill sent relics from Derry to Kells in 1090 for enshrinement, along with twenty-seven ounces of silver, was he paying the craftsmen involved or merely providing them with the metallurgical means to create a thing of beauty, matching other reliquaries produced in the same era? In twelfth-century Tuam, royalty was clearly involved in sponsoring fine metalwork, sculpture and even church buildings; we have no evidence, unfortunately, as to whether the craftsmen involved were permanent residents of the settlement or whether the royal patron and/or the local church authorities paid them for their work.

This in turn raises the question: who were the people involved in the creation of manufactured goods on ecclesiastical sites? Were they, as Butlin surmised, laymen or were they professed religious, similar to those early members of the Lindisfarne community credited in a mid-tenth-century colophon as scribes, bookbinders and metalworkers?[21] The evidence of an addendum to the *Tripartite Life* at roughly the same date agrees that at least some Irish church craftsmen may have been ecclesiastics, for that text identifies members of Patrick's household as his three smiths (*gobaind*) — including, interestingly, one who made the handbell known as Finnfáidech — his three workers in bronze and other metals (*cerda*) and his three embroideresses (*druinecha*). The description adds that similar personnel existed in the tenth-century household of the leader of Armagh.[22] Another craftsman, Tuathal the *saer* (builder in wood and stone), was honoured with a cross-marked graveslab at Clonmacnoise of the type used by ecclesiastics,[23] while the Kells transaction records refer to a *cerd* called Mac Áeda who worked in gold and silver and was involved in a deal over a *leth lainded* or half a building, apparently at Kells itself. This does not specify whether Mac Áeda was a member of the community, although his inclusion in the settlement records may imply this.

The older model of a distinctive and insular 'Celtic church' has been almost entirely discarded by modern researchers and instead the Irish church is now seen, in similar fashion to other European churches, as an eclectic mix of Christian tradition and custom, influenced to varying degrees by local culture. The same could be said of Irish monasticism, although there has been little discussion by Irish medievalists to date on the various strands in European monastic ideology that might have influenced Irish practice. Far too often, the adjective 'monastic' is simply used in the historiography of early Irish urbanism as a synonym for religious practice in general. This is a pronounced weakness in the monastic town model and, given the wealth of IHTA material now available, should be discarded. It is noteworthy, for example, that all of the 'monastic towns' in Clarke's list cited at the beginning of this article were diocesan centres during the twelfth century or earlier and this may well be an important factor in their later emergence as towns.

The involvement of monks in manual labour is something that varies considerably in different monastic communities and this, in turn, has major implications for our understanding of craft activity on church sites. Ninth-century Carolingian reforms made the Benedictine rule, with its concern that monks should work manually within self-sufficient communities, dominant in north-west Europe, although even that was not consistently applied. The popular Benedictine reform movement based in tenth-century Cluny, for example (which had its only known Irish foundation at Athlone),[24] increasingly favoured regimes in which monastic labour was limited to participation in ever longer and more elaborate liturgies. In trying to categorise the nature of monasticism in Ireland in the era of the Viking Age (when 'monastic towns' are now most commonly thought to originate), it is worth bearing in mind a description of the contemporary monasticism practised by its nearest neighbours in Anglo-Saxon England:

> In or about the year 970, at a great gathering modelled on that at Aachen, [King] Edgar and the bishops and the whole synod promulgated a set of constitutions for the English monasteries, the *Regularis concordia*, a 'monastic agreement' or agreed norm for the religious life, to be the basis for the practice in all the English monasteries. It is a nice mingling of influences from Lorraine and Burgundy with native traditions … The English church was becoming thoroughly monastic. Between the accession of Edgar and the Conquest, a high proportion of the bishops were monks: under Edgar and Ethelred II (died 1016) almost all … But the monasticising [*sic*] of the English church did not mean a separation of church and state: quite the contrary … In art and sacred literature the monastic reformation was tremendously fruitful. Close links between lay patrons and the monasteries: a powerful monastic influence at court and every kind of link between church and king; and a monastic tradition especially notable for its artistic creativity: these were the marks of the English church in the time of St Dunstan.[25]

There is no evidence that anything approaching the *Regularis concordia* was ever adopted in Ireland, although royal involvement in church affairs was certainly a contemporary reality and a quasi-permanent royal presence can be detected at Armagh, Kildare, Kilkenny, Kells, Trim and Tuam as well as at Cashel. For earlier periods, the Benedictine rule was clearly known in Ireland, for quotations from it can be found in Old Irish poetry, but so too were a number of the regulatory alternatives common in the Late Antique monasteries of the northern Mediterranean littoral. These were influenced by, amongst others, the cenobitic tradition represented by the Pachomian communities of Egypt and the *Regula Basilii,* originating in Cappadocia but translated into Latin in the later fourth century. In the Egyptian tradition, monastic communities supported themselves weaving cloth and baskets from plaited reeds as well as working in fields outside the monastery enclosure. In the *Regula Basilii,* manual work was valued as a way of providing income for the needy but also as a method for focusing the mind in prayer. (John Cassian, a writer much revered in early Irish monastic circles, wrote approvingly of the abbot Paul who burnt his baskets as soon as he had made them.) In the monastic tradition of St Augustine of Hippo, on the other hand, monks were clerics who laboured in church foundation and preaching rather than in craft.[26] It is this last model that appears to have most strongly influenced Pope Gregory the Great and, through him, the earlier English churches.

The IHTA fascicles indicate that Augustinian teaching was also highly influential in Ireland. One striking feature, almost invisible until the comparative evidence was compiled, is the consistency with which 'monastic towns' were founded on eminences within their own particular district (a possible exception is Tuam). This uniformity in chosen location suggests a very clear understanding of these settlements as foci for missionary activity and involvement with the people of the surrounding district, for it implies that their founders were actively following the exhortations of the Beatitudes:

> A city built on a hill cannot be hidden. No one after lighting a lamp puts it under the bushel basket but on the lamp-stand and it gives light to all in the house. In the same way, let your light shine before others so that they may see your good works and give glory to your Father in heaven.

Native Irish monastic rules associated with figures such as Ailbe of Emly or Mochuda of Rathin, however, indicate that Irish communities drew from the entire gamut of European monastic tradition[27] and, at this preliminary stage, it seems safest to infer that attitudes to manual labour amongst Irish monastic communities were never uniform, either chronologically or spatially. In considering the role of manufacture in 'monastic towns', therefore, future scholars must evaluate the possibility that goods were produced by churchmen who may have used, on occasion, resources donated by secular patrons. Whether such goods were intended entirely for ornamentation of their own churches or for transfer to third parties, either secular or ecclesiastical, and whether such transactions involved profit for the craftsmen involved or for the settlement authorities remain open questions.

The involvement of monks in labour has implications for our understanding of the *manaig* or agricultural workers who were attached to Irish ecclesiastical settlements. Drawing on vernacular legal texts in particular, Etchingham has attempted to differentiate between what he defines as 'para-monastic dependents' and what he sees as monks:

> Sources sometimes group these other elements together loosely as 'monastic' or sometimes portray them as two distinct sub-categories. One comprised monks, under a more-or-less conventional regime of self-mortification — including those withdrawing permanently or temporarily to the solitude of a hermitage — headed by an abbot. A second group comprised a body of 'para-monastic' dependents, who had families, farmed the church's lands, paid regular rents or dues and were subject to an ecclesiastical governor or manager. While some sources differentiate sharply between the 'para-monastic' dependents and the 'real' monks, the distinction is more commonly blurred, as illustrated by the use of Latin *monachi* and Irish *manaig* for both categories, for all were united in obedience to a superior. In keeping with this, the title 'abbot' could denote both the governor of 'para-monastic' dependents and the 'true' abbot.[28]

Elsewhere he writes:

> While *manaig* seemingly comprised several socio-economic sub-categories, they can be described as bondmen of their churches and were, essentially agrarian producers. The ecclesiastical elite appropriated the surplus product

of *manaig*, in a mix of stipulated direct labour and customary payments, the latter sometimes cast as religious dues such as tithes and first fruits of their produce and livestock.[29]

It is unclear whether this model categorises 'para-monastics' as an Irish variant of what the later Cistercian order termed lay brothers or simply as secular tenants who were practising Christians. A simpler formulation would interpret the blurred evidence provided by the sources by allowing for variability in the chosen monastic ideology on labour as outlined above. The distinction drawn here between para-monastics who have families and monks (who seemingly do not) appears somewhat forced, especially in the light of the many monastic communities in which monks took clerical orders. Until the Gregorian reforms forced a change — a process that was particularly slow in Ireland and lasted in some regions until the Reformation — clergy could and apparently frequently did marry and produce offspring. This is often seen, particularly in Ireland, in terms of a degenerative laicisation following the Viking wars. Certainly the careers of particular individuals such as the eleventh-century Amalgaidh of Armagh, *comarba Patraicc ocus abb n-Gaidhel* — heir of Patrick and abbot of the Irish — seems to stray far from modern notions of monastic celibacy. Appointed by church and laity to his office in 1020 according to the *Annals of Ulster*, Amalgaid's son Domnall was born in 1049, another son Mael Ísu (tonsured one of Jesus) took the abbacy in 1068, while his daughter Dub Esa died in 1078 as the wife of the local king of the Airthir. What may be yet another son, Findchad, died as chief of Clann Bresail in 1082. This same Amalgaid is also recorded as an abbot with a particular interest in Danish horses in a fascinating praise poem describing Armagh personnel. All of this serves to highlight the extent to which the eleventh-century Irish church (including monasteries) shared the common western European phenomenon of familial domination and secularisation of ecclesiastical office in the period before the Gregorian reforms.

On the other hand, while the universal church valued celibacy from the later fourth century, Pope Leo the Great in the mid-fifth century specifically decreed that churchmen ordained to the lower diocesan grades should simply abstain from sexual activity with their wives once they were ordained to the rank of deacon or above. Members of the lower church grades (who might therefore be legitimately married) were often involved in teaching in church schools such as existed at Derry, Armagh, Kells and Tuam. Famously, the English pope, Adrian IV, was the offspring of one such ecclesiastical family. In Ireland, an early genealogy of the first ruler of Trim specified the existence of both his secular and his ecclesiastical *progenies*, with the latter including both bishops and *principes*,[30] while at Kells the late transaction records indicate the existence of a number of high-ranking church families.[31] In short, there seems to be little historical justification for separating 'para-monastic' from 'true' monks on the basis of their sexual activity alone and it seems simplest to view the *manaig* working on church property as members of a wider monastic community that also included those teaching in the schools, manning the guesthouses and as officials running the settlement or 'obedientiaries'. This interpretation fits with Adomnán's early testimony that monks worked in the fields in Iona and Clonmacnoise. Such an approach has the effect of widening the 'several socio-economic sub-categories' of *manaig* involved on church sites and thus producing clear evidence for a hierarchically defined population whose primary role was not agrarian production. This has been seen by some as one of the criteria for identification of 'monastic towns'.[32]

It follows from the evidence for monastic marriages that, quite apart from the child oblates who are attested in the (often undated) saints' Lives and from the young students whose presence is attested in sixth-century penitentials and elsewhere, women and children may well have been present on church settlements in some numbers. It seems unnecessary to conclude, therefore, that mixed cemeteries, such as existed outside the enclosure ditch at Downpatrick, necessarily represented a lay population even if the same area also produced jewellery and gaming boards.[33] The entry of 1129 for *seoid* (treasures) stolen from the altar at Clonmacnoise, after all, included such non-religious items as a drinking horn ornamented with gold, the gift of a north Tipperary king.

EVIDENCE FOR TRADE

It is apparent that, for Etchingham, much of Irish church wealth was generated by the work of the *manaig*, particularly in producing agricultural surpluses and in transferring these to their leadership. (He sees the levy of church tithes, which all laymen are required by canon law to pay, as being in reality limited to this group.) Nevertheless, and somewhat paradoxically in works refuting the validity of the monastic town concept, he also suggests that in Viking Dublin, 'trading in agricultural and subsistence produce predominated, rather than trade in goods manufactured by specialist craftsmen'.[34] If the Irish church leadership did not simply consume the entirety of the surplus produce of their *manaig*, therefore, they must have been engaged in its redistribution and consequently in some form of trade analogous to that in operation in the coastal Viking towns. In fact, the existence of churches on ecclesiastical sites implies that they must have done so, for a basic requirement for the celebration of the Eucharist is a supply of wine. Either the early Irish churchmen (heretically) celebrated the Eucharist with blackberry or elderberry juice or they had transferable assets that could be used to pay continental producers. The fact that we have only one documentary reference to such a wine trade, in a later life of Ciarán at Clonmacnoise, probably says more about the limited nature of our sources than it does about the realities of early medieval Irish commerce.

In fact, as noted by Stephen Royle,[35] the combined evidence of the IHTA fascicles over the last thirty years makes it clear that commerce in agrarian produce has been the lifeblood of Irish towns throughout much of their existence. In more recent periods, this activity took place on urban fair greens, shambles and markets;[36] the evidence for the early medieval period is far more exiguous but a Germanic loanword, *marggad*, is found in late Viking-Age documentation and is seen by all writers as indicating trade. A pre-Anglo-Norman *marggad* existed at both Dublin and Limerick, and at Athlone the word is used to refer to a market established in 1221.[37] A *marggad* also existed on at least some ecclesiastical settlements — at Kells, for example, a *marggad* is attested between 1106 and 1153, in which cattle could apparently be kept secure,[38] and another existed at the archiepiscopal centre at Cashel in 1124, which may have influenced the subsequent plan of the market place at Fethard.[39] (Pre-Anglo-Norman crosses, later linked to markets, also exist at Tuam and Armagh as well as at Glendalough — whether these marked earlier *marggad* sites remains unproven.) A Middle Irish homily on Jesus's actions in the Temple at Jerusalem describes the people there as 'purchasing and bargaining and buying [of] their goods and their market also' — *oc creic ocus oc cúnnrad ocus oc ceannaigecht a n-indmais ocus a marcaid ár-chena.*

In an Irish context, it has been unanimously assumed that such goods were the produce of artisan craftsmen, but this is unwarranted. The famous description of *óenach Carmuin* finishes with an account of three *marggaid*, including the *marggad bíd* (market in food), the *marggad beócchraid*, the market in livestock and the *marggad mór nan Gall nGrécach i mbíd ór is ardd étach* — the great market of the Greek Foreigners in which there was gold and fine clothing.[40] Another reference in the *Book of Leinster* is to the *marggad beochruid bó ocus ech* — a market in live cattle and horses.[41] Thus, though the word *marggad* was a novel import with either Norse or English origins and could be used of later urban markets, it seems clear that many of the transactions that occurred at them in pre-Anglo-Norman contexts involved traditional Irish surpluses in agrarian goods. Whether or not there was more centralised control of these transactions, with either ecclesiastical or secular lords levying tolls or other taxes, we do not currently know. It is clear, however, that they were a feature of both the coastal towns and some ecclesiastical settlements in pre-Anglo-Norman Ireland.

EVIDENCE FOR POPULATIONS

While much of the forgoing evidence for craft and trade can be gleaned from the relevant fascicles of the IHTA, a primary focus for their authors and editors has been the respective topographical analysis of individual settlements. A number of points arise from the data when evaluating the case for 'monastic towns'. The influence of Leo Swan's 1980s aerial research into enclosures surrounding ecclesiastical sites which, in many cases, are represented by circular street patterns, is obvious. Authors of town atlases not seen as 'monastic', in contrast, have referred to circular street patterns in terms of their underlying geology, as, for example, at Dundalk, which the author identified as having secular pre-Anglo-Norman origins (Fig. 2.2).[42] Paul Gosling has recently praised the author of the Kildare fascicle for his caution in underlining the degree of interpretation required to produce clear statements from ambivalent evidence (Fig. 4.1).[43]

Fig. 4.1 *Kildare*, fig. 2, curvilinear road and fence alignments.

Opposite: Fig. 4.2 *Trim*, fig. 1, possible sites of the early ecclesiastical enclosure.

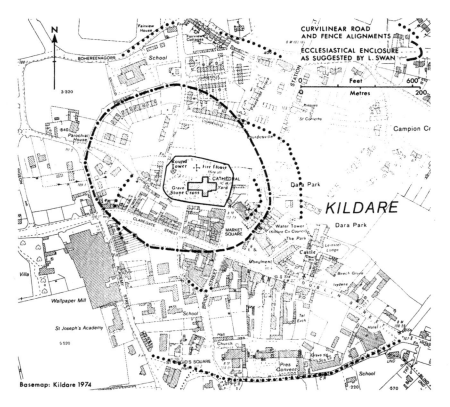

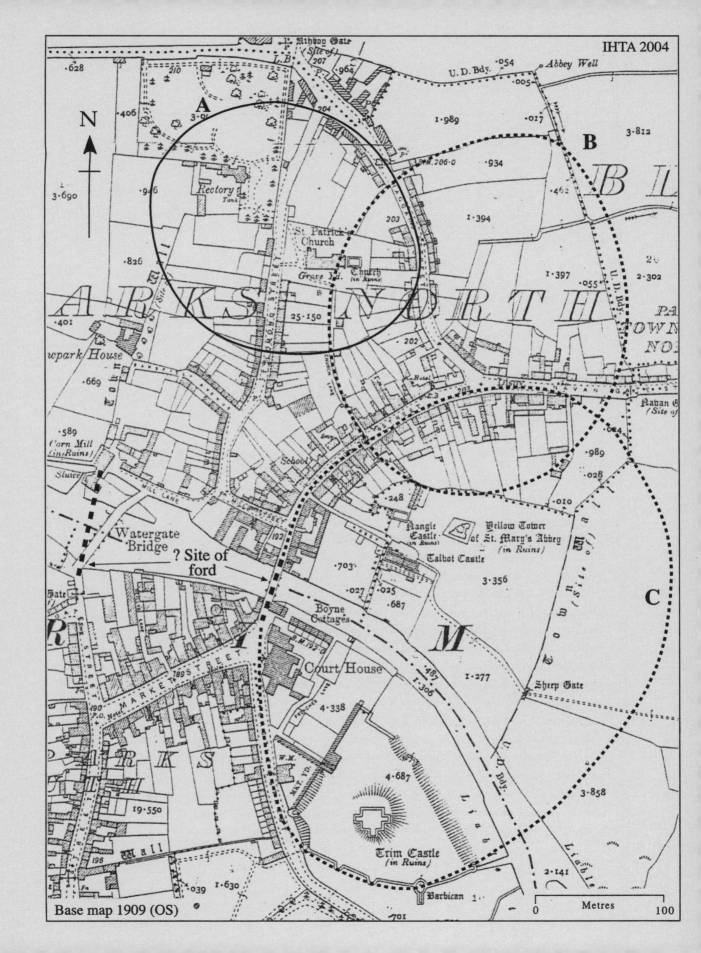

IHTA 2004

N

A

B

B IL

ARKS NORTH

Rectory
Tank

St. Patrick's
Church

Church
(in Ruins)
Grave Yd.

P A
TOWN
NO

·628

·406

3·690

·946

·825

·401

wpark House

·669

·589
Corn Mill
(in Ruins)

Sluice

Watergate
Bridge

? Site of
ford

Gate

R

MARKET STREET

190
P.O. Hotel

19·550

196

Wall

·039   1·630

Base map 1909 (OS)

School

Mill Lane

192

·703

Boyne
Cottages

Court House

4·338

Nangle
Castle
(in Ruins)

Talbot Castle

·248

·027 ·025
·687

B.M.192·0

M

4·687

Trim Castle
(in Ruins)

Barbican

·701

Yellow Tower
of St. Mary's Abbey
(in Ruins)

3·356

1·277

Sherp Gate

2·141

Raban G
(Site of)

·989

·028

·010

·044

3·858

C

U.D. Bdy.   ·054   Abbey Well

·005

·017   3·812

1·989   ·934

·462

1·394

·055

1·397   2·302

2

·202

203

Liab

0   Metres   100

25·150

204

207
964
P

Abbey Gate
(Site of)
L.B

210

3·0

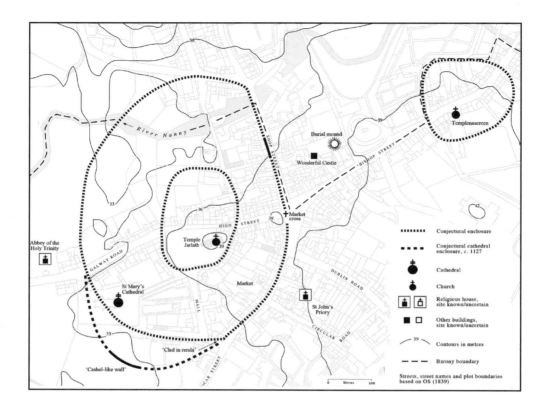

An equally strong and related early influence on individual authors has been Charles Doherty's use of material from the *Collectio canonum Hibernensis* compilation of church law and, in particular, the division of church sites into zones of graded holiness, culminating in a central sacred core.[44] This has led to struggles in a number of atlases with empirical data that indicate that, on the eve of the Anglo-Norman invasion, there were in fact a number of different ecclesiastical foci within the ground plans of the later towns at Derry, Armagh, Trim, Tuam, Kilkenny and Kells, often each with their own precinct (Figs 4.2, 4.3). Such 'sacred cores' as exist are generally represented by cathedral sites that tend to be depicted as overlapping spatially with what the authors most frequently term 'Early Christian monasteries' (drawing on terminology used in an earlier 1970 survey by Gwynn and Hadcock).[45] The strongest evidence for such a spatial overlap is the existence of round towers on later cathedral sites, although the precise function of these monuments is still debated. This is clearly an area where further research is required. Does it indicate that transfer of power and land from monastic to episcopal control during the twelfth-century reforms is key to understanding which church sites became later towns, or

Fig. 4.4 *Armagh*, map 4, 1602, by Richard Bartlett. National Library of Ireland, MS 2656 (3), extract.

does it represent more complex interactions between monastic and diocesan structures in earlier eras (Fig. 4.4)?

The situation at Kells and Tuam highlights some of the difficulties and draws attention to the under-researched links between Augustinian canons, cathedrals and earlier monasteries. Twelfth-century Augustinian foundations are often dedicated to SS Peter and Paul, as at Armagh and Trim (and indeed Ennis), indicating strong ideological affiliations with the patron saints of Rome. Augustinian houses can be found on the edge of putative enclosures as at Kells or Armagh but often, to infer from the

IHTA maps, with streets apparently linking them directly to cathedral precincts. At Kells, Maurice Sheehy pointed out that properties granted to the Columban monastery by Tigernán Ua Ruairc were later transferred to the canons and a similar transfer pattern has been identified by Tony Claffey at Tuam (Fig. 4.3).[46] Why would estates owned by a monastic community be transferred to an incoming order of what were probably priests living in community (for this is the commonest role of canons), who may or may not have acted as chapters for their local cathedral as they are known to have done at Dublin and Limerick? If they did so, did they replace the earlier monastic priests such as the Ua Breslen family from the Kells transaction records? Certainly in Limerick, we can detect some local Irish clerical families taking office as cathedral canons in the early years of the Anglo-Norman colony, while the individual prebends that provided the canons with their income appear to derive (at least in part) from older church settlements such as Mungret.[47]

The IHTA fascicles have thrown up many questions for future scholars while providing rich and complex data to help them in their searches. Rebecca Wall Forrestal has recently written that:

> At this stage, the debate stimulated by Doherty's monastic town hypothesis is at an impasse. It seems that almost everybody accepts that the largest ecclesiastical centres were more than just monasteries or churches but the vocabulary does not exist to explain their role in Irish economic networks, as Doherty set out to do.[48]

I have argued here that one potential way out of such an impasse may be a more systematic depiction of what we envisage monasticism to be, how it may have evolved, both chronologically and spatially, and whether the monks in individual settlements could also be craftsmen and farmers, family men and/or priests. Clearly their settlements were sinks absorbing local resources. Monastic communities, whose primary role was to pray, needed also to be fed and clothed, and accessories for their worship, including buildings, would have had to be manufactured. The complexity of monastic organisation was such that these communities included men labouring in fields as well as priests, teachers and overseers. At the same time, they probably functioned as hubs for the redistribution of agrarian produce and the importation of foreign substances such as wine. In the generations before and immediately after the Anglo-Norman invasion, the areas in which church sites exchanged such goods are called by the same imported term, *marggad*, as was used in Viking coastal towns. Whether all this makes such church sites towns, proto-towns, villages or cult centres depends ultimately on the viewpoint of individuals, but undoubtedly it helps to explain why some, and in particular those with multiple foci, became the nuclei around which later Irish towns coalesced.

NOTES

[1] H.B. Clarke, '*Quo vadis?* Mapping the Irish "monastic town"', in Seán Duffy (ed.), *Princes, prelates and poets in medieval Ireland: essays in honour of Katharine Simms* (Dublin, 2013), pp 277–8.

[2] Andrews, IHTA, no. 1, *Kildare*; Simms with Simms, IHTA, no. 4, *Kells*.

[3] Tomás Ó Carragáin, *Churches in early medieval Ireland* (New Haven and London, 2013), p. 219.

[4] Aidan O'Sullivan *et al.*, *Early medieval Ireland AD 400–1100: the evidence from archaeological excavations* (Dublin, 2014), p. 175.

[5] Melanie Maddox, 'Finding the city of God in the Lives of St Kevin: Glendalough and the history of the Irish celestial *civitas*', in Charles Doherty, Linda Doran and Mary Kelly (eds), *Glendalough: city of God* (Dublin, 2011), pp 1–21; David Jenkins, '*Holy, holier, holiest*': the sacred topography of the early medieval Irish church* (Turnhout, 2010).

[6] R.A. Butlin, 'Urban and proto-urban settlements in pre-Norman Ireland', in R.A. Butlin (ed.), *The development of the Irish town* (London, 1977), p. 22.

[7] Charles Doherty, 'The monastic town in early medieval Ireland', in H.B. Clarke and Anngret Simms (eds), *The comparative history of urban origins in non-Roman Europe* (2 pts, Oxford, 1985), p. 67; Andrews, *Kildare*, p. 1.

[8] John Bradley, 'The monastic town of Clonmacnoise', in H.A. King (ed.), *Clonmacnoise Studies 1* (Dublin, 1998), pp 42–56; John Bradley, 'Towards a definition of the Irish monastic town', in C.E. Karkov and Helen Damico (eds), *Aedificia nova: studies in honour of Rosemary Cramp* (Kalamazoo, 2008), pp 325–60.

[9] Colmán Etchingham, *The Irish monastic town: is this a valid concept?* (Cambridge, 2010), p. 27. Much of the same material is reproduced in Colmán Etchingham, 'The organisation and function of an early Irish church settlement: what was Glendalough?', in Doherty, Doran and Kelly, *Glendalough: city of God*, p. 38.

[10] Anngret Simms, 'Frühformen der mittelalterlichen Stadt in Irland', in *Würzburger Geographische Arbeiten*, lx (1983), p. 33; see also Brian Graham, 'Beyond fascicles: spatial form and social process', in H.B. Clarke and Sarah Gearty (eds), *Maps and texts: exploring the Irish Historic Towns Atlas* (Dublin, 2013), p. 261.

[11] William Reeves (ed.), *The Life of St Columba, founder of Hy, written by Adamnan* (Dublin, 1857), pp 257–361.

[12] Michael Ryan, 'Fine metalworking and early Irish monasteries: the archaeological evidence', in John Bradley (ed.), *Settlement and society in medieval Ireland* (Kilkenny, 1988), pp 33–48.

[13] Eiméar Nelis *et al.*, *Data structure report (no. 044 part I): St Patrick's Church, Armoy, Co. Antrim* (Belfast, 2007).

[14] Paul Stevens, 'Clonfad, Co. Westmeath: an early Irish monastic production centre', in Christiaan Corlett and Michael Potterton (eds), *The church in early medieval Ireland in the light of recent archaeological excavations* (Dublin, 2014), pp 259–72.

[15] Helmut Jäger, 'Entwicklungsphasen irischer Städte im Mittelalter', in Helmut Jäger, Franz Petri and Heinz Quirin, *Civitatum communitas: studien zum europäischen Städtewesen. Festschrift Heinz Stoob* (2 vols, Cologne and Vienna, 1984), i, pp 71–95.

[16] See comments by Avril Thomas in IHTA, no. 15, *Derry-Londonderry*, p. 2.

[17] Ó Dálaigh, IHTA, no. 25, *Ennis*.

[18] Peter Hill, *Whithorn and St Ninian: the excavation of a monastic town 1984–91* (Stroud, 1997); Christopher Lowe, *Clothing for the soul divine: burials at the tomb of St Ninian: excavations at Whithorn Priory 1957–67* (Edinburgh, 2009).

[19] McCullough and Crawford, IHTA, no. 18, *Armagh*, p. 1.

[20] Bernard Meehan, *The Book of Kells* (London, 2012), pp 219–24.

[21] Janet Backhouse, *The Lindisfarne Gospels* (Ithaca, 1981), p. 7.

[22] *Bethu Phátraic: the tripartite Life of Patrick*, ed. Kathleen Mulchrone (Dublin, 1939), p. 155.

[23] Catherine Swift, 'Sculptors and their customers: a study of Clonmacnoise grave-slabs', in H.A. King (ed.), *Clonmacnoise studies 2* (Dublin, 1998), pp 110–11.

[24] Murtagh, IHTA, no. 6, *Athlone*.

[25] Christopher Brooke, *From Alfred to Henry III 871–1272* (London, 1969), pp 67–9.

[26] T.G. Kardong, *Pillars of community: four rules of pre-Benedictine monastic life* (Collegeville, 2010), pp 57–8, 96, 107–8, 156.

[27] Uinseann Ó Maidin, *The Celtic monk: rules and writings of early Irish monks* (Kalamazoo, 1996).

[28] Etchingham, 'Organisation and function of an early Irish church settlement', pp 27–8.

[29] Etchingham, *Irish monastic town*, p. 25.

[30] Hennessy, IHTA, no. 14, *Trim*.

[31] Bairbre Nic Aonghusa, 'The monastic hierarchy in twelfth century Ireland: the case of Kells', in *Ríocht na Midhe*, viii (1990–91), pp 3–20.

[32] Brian Graham, 'Urban genesis in early medieval Ireland', in *Journal of Historical Geography*, xiii (1987), p. 10.

[33] Buchanan and Wilson, IHTA, no. 8, *Downpatrick*, p. 2.

[34] Etchingham, *Irish monastic town*, p. 29.

[35] S.A. Royle, 'Manufacturing', in Clarke and Gearty, *Maps and texts*, p. 168.

[36] Colm Lennon, 'Trades and services', in Clarke and Gearty, *Maps and texts*, pp 183–96.

[37] Clarke, IHTA, no. 11, *Dublin, part I, to 1610*; O'Flaherty, IHTA, no. 21, *Limerick*; Murtagh, *Athlone*.

[38] Simms with Simms, *Kells*; Etchingham, *Irish monastic town*, p. 24.

[39] O'Keeffe, IHTA, no. 13, *Fethard*.

[40] Edward Gwynn, 'Carmun', in *The metrical dindshenchas, part III* (Dublin, 1991), pp 24–5.

[41] See further discussion in Catherine Swift, 'Follow the money: the financial resources of Diarmait Mac Murchada', in Emer Purcell *et al.* (eds), *Clerics, kings and Vikings: essays on medieval Ireland in honour of Donnchadh Ó Corráin* (Dublin, 2015), pp 91–102.

[42] Clarke, '*Quo vadis?* Mapping the Irish "monastic town"', pp 262–3; Catherine Swift, 'Celtic monasticism — a discipline's search for romance?', in *Trowel*, v (1995), pp 21–5; O'Sullivan, IHTA, no. 16, *Dundalk*, p. 2.

[43] Paul Gosling, 'Kildare and Tuam', in Clarke and Gearty, *Maps and texts*, p. 64.

[44] Doherty, 'Monastic town', pp 58–9.

[45] Gwynn and Hadcock, pp 26–46: 'Early Irish monasteries'.

[46] M.P. Sheehy, *Pontificia Hibernica: medieval papal chancery documents concerning Ireland, 640–1261* (2 vols, Dublin, 1962–5), ii, pp 106–7, §267, n. 1; Claffey, IHTA, no. 20, *Tuam*, p. 3.

[47] *The Black Book of Limerick*, ed. James McCaffrey (Dublin, 1907), pp lxi–lxxxiv.

[48] Rebecca Wall Forrestal, 'Studying early medieval Irish urbanization: problems and possibilities', in Vicky McAlister and Terry Barry (eds), *Space and settlement in medieval Ireland* (Dublin, 2015), p. 40.

5. Derry~Londonderry

Brian Lacey

The two names used in the *Derry~Londonderry* fascicle of the IHTA,[1] and more generally for the modern city, not only reflect its historic community divisions and tragic recent past but, in effect, the separate origins of the two major historic settlements that happen to have been located there — more or less — sequentially in the same place. The anglicised form Derry — although also used contemporaneously for the short-lasting English 'city' established in 1604 by Sir Henry Dowcra — can be taken now as a shorthand way of referring to the sixth-century ecclesiastical settlement (and its earlier 'prehistoric' predecessor), which lasted for roughly a thousand years. That settlement was known initially as Daire Calgaich (and variations) and subsequently — although mainly in a poetic/cultic way rather than as a specific placename — as Doire Choluim Cille.[2] Very little of that settlement is reflected above ground now. The name 'Londonderry' on the other hand refers particularly to the planned and walled colonial city begun in 1613, which was established by the so-called Honourable the Irish Society, a collective body representing the interests of the commercial guilds of the city of London. These had been prevailed upon by King James I to finance and organise the Londonderry element of the plantations in Ulster. The change from medieval Derry to plantation Londonderry was not just another step in the evolution of the settlement but a seismic historic shift.

The historic core of the modern city is thus located on the site of a number of earlier settlements, which we either know about directly or for which there is evidence of some kind (Fig. 5.1). In chronological order these were:

i.   a late prehistoric *dún* on an isolated hillside (virtually an 'island') on the west bank of the River Foyle — earlier than the late sixth century;[3]

ii.   an early ecclesiastical (monastic?) settlement in more or less the same place — probably founded about 578;[4]

iii.   the more developed ecclesiastical settlement with some secular and even royal presence — what we might call a proto-town — for which there is strong evidence from the twelfth and thirteenth centuries, but which existed in some form earlier than that and which declined a lot afterwards;[5]

iv.   under the aegis of the powerful Uí Domhnaill family, the somewhat revived settlement based around the exploitation of a local pilgrimage in honour of St Colum Cille with a newly-built tower-house castle, dating to the first half or so of the sixteenth century;[6]

v.   an English garrison camp, which lasted from October 1566 to May 1567 laid out among, and using some of, the medieval ruins;[7]

vi.   a small English camp on the 'Iland of the Derrie' from May 1600, transformed in July 1604 until April 1608 into the tiny chartered colonial town — 'a town of war and a town of merchandize' — established by Sir Henry Dowcra, which was destroyed in 1608 by Sir Cahir O'Doherty;[8]

vii.   the larger, plantation walled city of 'Londonderry' built on the general site of the earlier settlements, which received its charter in 1613;[9]

viii.   the modern city gradually expanding in all directions beyond its walled core, on both sides of the River Foyle.[10]

Fig. 5.1 *Derry–Londonderry*, map 21, growth to 1870, extract.

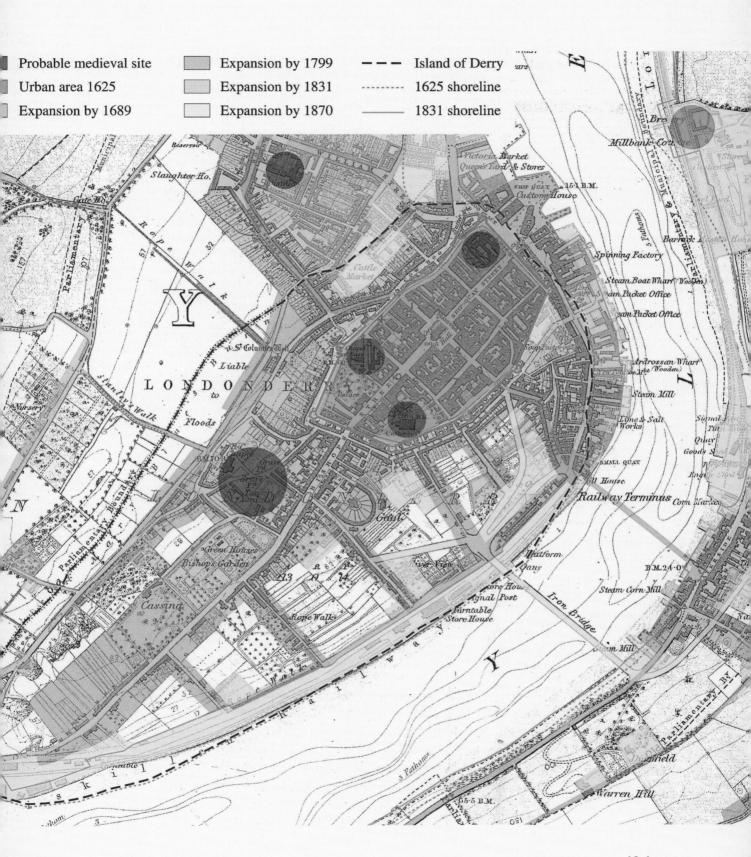

Probable medieval site

Urban area 1625

Expansion by 1689

Expansion by 1799

Expansion by 1831

Expansion by 1870

Island of Derry

1625 shoreline

1831 shoreline

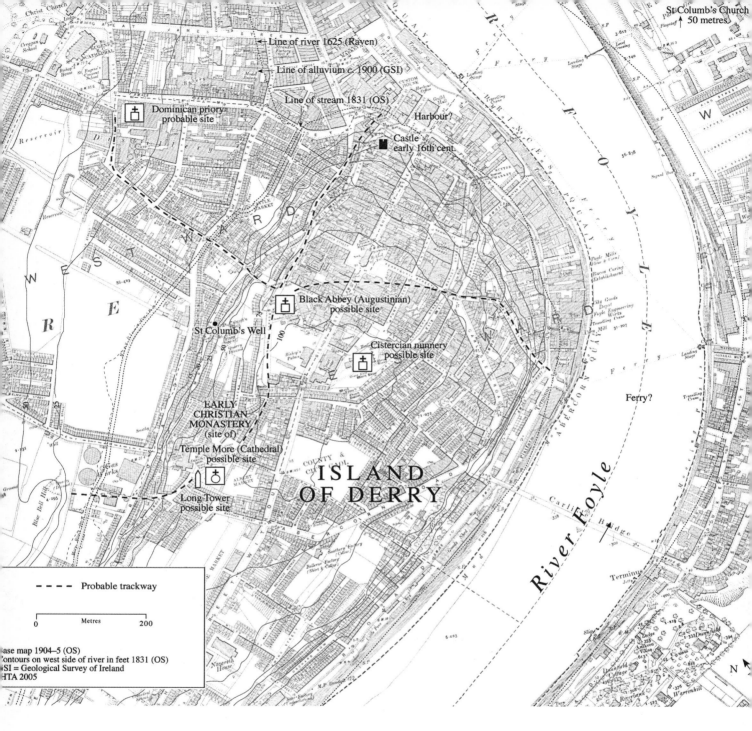

It is tempting to add to this list the apparently intended early fourteenth-century Anglo-Norman town planned by the de Burgos of *c.* 1300,
but this never seems to have got off the ground.[11] In fact the hill of Derry
may have been settled in one form or another for several thousand years.
Archaeological evidence shows that the Foyle and its tributaries had been
used as water highways since human settlers first came to Ireland in the

Fig. 5.2 *Derry~Londonderry*, fig. 2,
medieval Derry, extract.

Mesolithic — about 10,000 years ago — and that fairly permanent settlements of various prehistoric dates had been located, at very least, in the
vicinity of the later city.[12]

THE PLANTATION TOWN

The bulk of the contents of the *Derry~Londonderry* atlas concentrates on
the period after the capture of the site by the English in 1600 (vi to viii
above).[13] From then on, right through the period of the Ordnance Survey
to the present, we have an excellent series of historic maps that depict the
development of the city we know today. The author, Avril Thomas, did
not dwell to any great extent on pre-1600 Derry: there is still little in the
way of archaeological evidence for the earlier periods[14] and an attempt in
the 1980s at a reconstruction of the layout of what we knew then about
the medieval settlement was itself quite tentative.[15] Although new research
has been carried out since the atlas was published, the conclusions still
remain far from complete or certain.[16] Nevertheless, the atlas included
two specially drawn maps (Figs 5.1, 5.2) that attempted to show at least
the general whereabouts of some of the medieval buildings and features
we know about from sources such as the Irish annals and the later colonial
maps; copies of most of the latter are included in the atlas fascicle.

All the research on the city that has been carried out since 2005 — to
one extent or another — has made use of the maps and texts referred to in
fascicle no. 15.[17] It is important, however, to stress that not all these maps
should be taken at face value. The early maps particularly must be treated
like all historical sources and subjected to critical scrutiny.[18] For instance
map 7 is a copy of a drawing, which is labelled on the original as 'The platt
of the Derrie 1611' (Fig. 12.4).[19] In reality this is some kind of preliminary blueprint for a layout of the town that was not in fact constructed,
although it does bear an evident relationship to what was eventually built.
Map 10, labelled 'A plott of ye cittie and [i]land of Londonderry [wt] a
proiectment of … outworkes, and the cutting of the bogg for the better
securinge of ye cittie' and dated 1625, is obviously a combination of what
already existed at that time together with some suggestions for how the
town's defences could be strengthened in the future. But it is not immediately evident from the map itself what is already built and what is only
proposed. Map 9 provides a good example of the same problem. It is a copy
of 'The plat of the cittie of Londonderrie' by Thomas Raven, dated 1622.
This is often taken, especially when — as in the atlas — it is not accompanied by its original supporting letterpress, as a plan of what existed in the

town at the time. But as well as showing existing features it also is something of a blueprint for suggested further developments (Fig. 5.3). For instance, the building shown in the Diamond at the centre of the town is labelled on the accompanying letterpress as 'The form of a citadel fitting to have been built in the Market Place'.[20] Likewise the extensive rectangular space outside the town walls on the river bank is labelled 'A place where the new Quay were fit to be built'.[21] The 'plat' also shows an extension of Pump Street towards the south, which was certainly never built.[22] Most puzzling of all is the large church-like building shown at the junction of what are now Linenhall Street and Richmond Street. This seems to have been intended to indicate the scale and proposed location of the cathedral. But, in fact, the cathedral was built farther south up the hillside on what was almost certainly the general location of a medieval church building — most probably a Cistercian convent.[23] In what is described as an 'older manuscript volume', a copy of this drawing is accompanied by the note 'The church now building', which shows the cathedral under construction in the correct location.[24]

Fig. 5.3 *Derry-Londonderry*, map 9, 1622, by Thomas Raven. Lambeth Palace Library, Carew MS 634, ff 7v–8, extract.

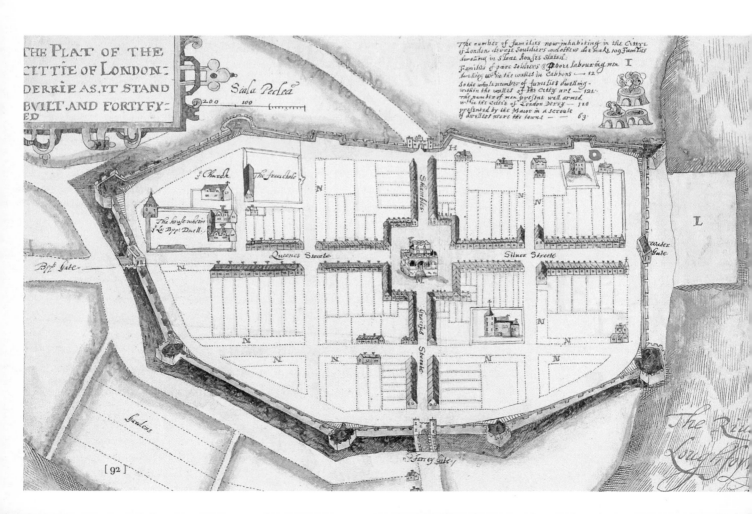

Pre-plantation Derry

The *Derry-Londonderry* atlas does not cover the pre-plantation settlement in any detail. A reviewer commenting on this pointed out that the author was 'frankly unlucky in that medieval Derry is so poorly documented'.[25] This is all the more unfortunate as Derry is arguably one of the oldest (if not *the* oldest) settlements in Ireland for which we have reasonably continuous — if admittedly limited — documentation from the late sixth century onwards. Thus, despite the challenges, the thousand years of development at the site prior to the seventeenth century cannot be ignored or dismissed just because the sources are limited or in certain cases not available at all.

Daire Calgaich first appears in history as an ecclesiastical settlement, but the earliest references and other circumstantial evidence suggest that it had a prehistoric existence as a secular, royal (and, almost certainly, border)[26] site. The admittedly late poem Estid re Conall Calma refers to Derry prior to its emergence as a church site as the *dún* of Calgach mac Aithemuin and twice elsewhere in the same poem as the *longpurt* of three kings before 'it fell to Colum of the cells'.[27] The Calgach mentioned in the poem was possibly the father of the Tipraite mac Calgaich whose death is recorded in the annals (originally compiled in Iona) in 595 and both were probably kings of Cenél nÉnnai, which almost certainly included Derry in its territory before it was later captured by Cenél Conaill.[28]

Much of the discussion about the foundation of the church at Derry — as at similar places throughout Ireland — assumes that these were founded for purely religious motives. But many churches in early medieval Ireland were effectively family businesses; we have to seek the true explanations for their origins in the secular politics of the time. The legend of the foundation of Derry as St Columba's/Colum Cille's 'first and best loved monastery' is almost a given of early Irish history. The oldest surviving text purporting to be an account of that foundation occurs in the *Liber hymnorum*, in an anthology 'apparently compiled in the tenth century' (and probably after 989).[29] The fictional 'preface' to the hymn *Noli pater indulgere* contains the alleged story.[30] It claims that the monastery was founded in the time of Áed mac Ainmerech (died *c.* 596), the Cenél Conaill king who is said to have given the land to Columba. Columba burnt the site as an act of cleansing, but the fire threatened the oak-grove that gave its name to the place, so the saint composed the hymn to protect the trees. Apart from scepticism about the supernatural aspects of the story and the fact that there is no corroborating documentation, there are inherent difficulties with the chronology. Áed mac Ainmerech was a nephew of Columba and belonged to the next generation. It is inherently improbable that Áed gave the site to the saint for the latter's first foundation.

There are three relevant references in the Irish annals to the foundation of Derry. Superficially, the earliest appears to be in the *Annals of the Four Masters* for 535. But because that text was composed in the early seventeenth century and the fact that there is no support for such a date, we can effectively ignore it as contemporary evidence. Columba, for instance, would have been at most fifteen years of age at the time. The next reference is in the *Annals of Ulster*, apparently for 545–6. It does not claim that Columba was the founder and because it contains the anachronistic title Daire Coluim Cille — not used again in those annals until 1121 — we can dismiss the entry as a contemporary record. The third earliest reference to Derry is in the *Annals of Tigernach* — a twelfth-century manuscript partially copied from earlier texts. This records the death of Fiachra mac Ciaráin in 619–20 as the *alius fundatoris* of Derry. There are good reasons — far too technical to be spelt out here — for believing that this entry records genuine contemporary information.[31] But if so, what does it mean?

The answer lies in the contemporary geopolitics of the region. Almost certainly early sixth-century Daire Calgaich — as it continued to be called for at least another four or five centuries — was a border settlement belonging to the small kingdom of Cenél nÉnnai. Before the end of the sixth century, however, Cenél nÉnnai was conquered by their neighbours, Cenél Conaill — one of the most powerful political dynasties in the Ireland of the time. Two (possibly three) of the first genuinely historical figures to be described as kings of Ireland — although that claim was greatly exaggerated — belonged to Cenél Conaill, as did Columba and Fiachra mac Ciaráin. Cenél Conaill defeated the neighbouring Cenél nEógain in a battle in 578 at a place called Druim mac Ercae, which has not been definitively identified but which was probably somewhere along the southern edge of the Inishowen peninsula.[32] As with similar church sites elsewhere, and probably in the aftermath of that battle, Cenél Conaill, having extended their territory, handed Derry (now on their northern border) over to the church — actually to Fiachra — in order to prevent any takeover of it again by the Cenél nEógain or Cenél nÉnnai. We know that Columba, although by then well-established in Iona, was in Ireland around the same time attending the convention of Drum Ceat.[33] It is possible that he played some sort of secondary role in the establishment of the church in Derry, although there is absolutely no contemporary evidence that he was its founder. The later sources, including several of the early maps reproduced in the atlas, suggest that the location of that initial church/monastery was probably in the general vicinity of the later medieval Augustinian abbey, on the site of the present St Augustine's chapel of ease (Fig. 5.4).[34] Adomnán's *Vita Columbae* written about 690–700 contains three mentions of Derry, named there as Roboretum Calgachi in Latin or Daire Calgaich in Irish.[35] The first reference is to two Columban monks who rowed to Ireland from Iona and visited Derry — the implication but not the certainty is that they had landed at Derry. The second reference is about a man who was buried in Derry in accordance with Columba's prophecy. The third reference is to a monk called Librán who boards a ship at Derry for 'Britain' from where he travels on to Iona. The three stories are set during Columba's lifetime or shortly afterwards (i.e. *c*. 520–93[36]); but all they tell us is that the saint knew about Derry, that there was a Christian burial place (and probably a church) there in his time, and that it was a place of departure for travelling to Britain and onward to Iona, and maybe also a place of arrival from Iona.

There is little contemporary evidence relating to Derry for the first couple of hundred years after its foundation. It seems that during this time it was a relatively quiet Cenél Conaill border church.[37] There is a reference in the annals to the death of Caech Scuili, the *scriba* of Derry, in 724. A *scriba* was not a lowly copyist but a senior ecclesiastical scholar such as those who compiled the broadly contemporary and highly influential *Collectio canonum Hibernensis*, which had definite Columban associations. Another possibly early reference to Derry occurs in the Latin Life of Colmán Ela. That Life belongs to the so-called O'Donohue group — dated by Pádraig Ó Riain to the thirteenth century but by Richard Sharpe to the eighth century, or 800–50 at the latest.[38] In the Life, Colmán Ela visits Iona and is given an altar cruet by Columba. The gift is left behind but later turns up miraculously beside the altar of a church in Derry. If the O'Donohue texts are as early as Sharpe believes, then this would be among the earliest references to a church in Derry.

The annals record a fire in Derry in 788. The circumstances of the fire are not recorded but it must have had a major impact — perhaps completely destroying the settlement — as, apart from a battle involving the Vikings there in 833, we hear nothing more about Derry for approximately one hundred years. For almost the whole of the eighth century Cenél Conaill, who controlled Derry, had been under severe pressure from their neighbours to the north, Cenél nEógain. The 788 fire in Derry was most likely part of that conflict. By 789 Cenél nEógain's victory over

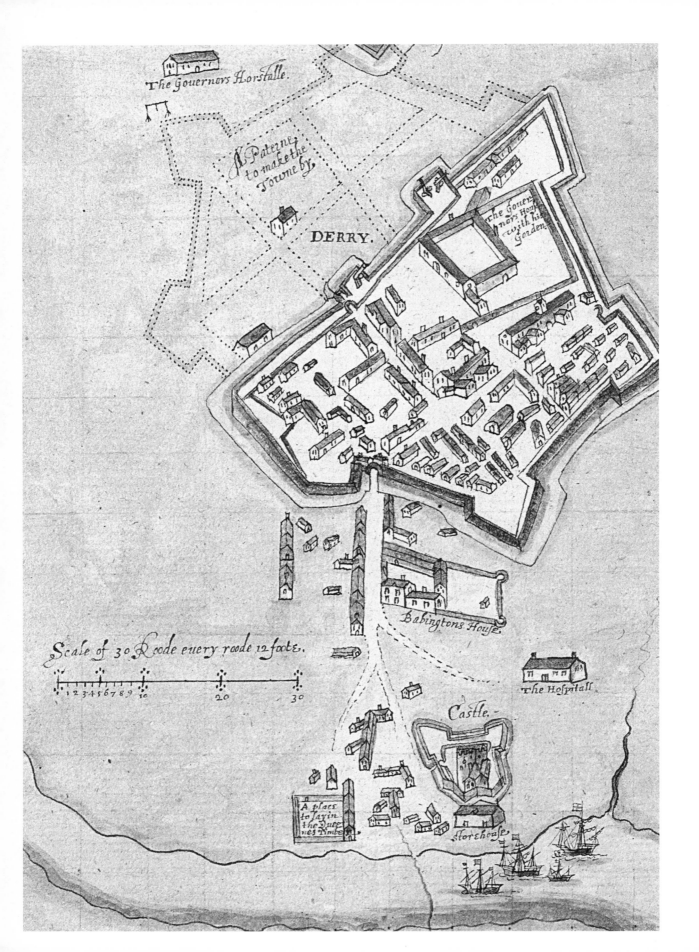

The Gouernors Horstalle.

A Paterne to make the Towne by

DERRY.

The Gouernors House with his Garden.

Babingtons House.

Scale of 30 Roode euery roode 12 foote.

1 2 3 4 5 6 7 8 9 10   20   30

The Hospitall

Castle.

A place to layin the Queenes Timber

Storehouse.

Cenél Conaill was complete and for the next five hundred years Derry remained part of Cenél nEógain territory.

There is a reference in the annals for 882 when 'Muirchertach son of Niall, abbot of Daire Calgaig and other monasteries' died. Muirchertach was almost certainly the son of the powerful king of Tara, Niall Caille, and, if so, the brother of another Tara king, Áed Findliath.[39] Although so far we have no further evidence about this, we should not underestimate the profound implications for Derry — in political, cultural and religious terms, as well as for the physical layout of the settlement — if its abbot was the son of one king of Tara and the brother of another.

DERRY IN THE HIGH MIDDLE AGES

Derry's medieval heyday was in the twelfth and early thirteenth centuries when it was under the control of the powerful Mac Lochlainn family, some of whom almost certainly lived there. By this stage Derry had developed into much more than a monastery: it was as close to being a town as anything was in Gaelic Ireland, with a vibrant secular life and its own politics.[40] Comparatively speaking we have a lot of detailed information about Derry during that period.[41]

In 1083 the powerful and ruthless Domnall Ua Lochlainn[42] became king of Ailech — a vast territory covering half of Ulster. He was soon claiming the greatly contested office of king of Ireland. It seems that he lived in Derry (or its vicinity[43]) from around 1100 if not before; he eventually died there at seventy-three years of age in 1121. By 1145 his grandson, Muirchertach Mac Lochlainn, was king of Ailech and was also bidding for the kingship of Ireland — a role he attained between 1156 and his death in 1166. Together with the important cleric Flaithbertach Ó Brolcháin, the annals tell us that Muirchertach was responsible for many 'improvements' in Derry. In 1150 Flaithbertach, presumably with the support of the king, had moved the headquarters of the *familia Columbae* to Derry from Kells (Co. Meath); Flaithbhertach simultaneously became *comarba Colum Cille* or head of that monastic federation. In 1162 Flaithbertach and Muirchertach rearranged the layout of Derry, apparently separating the secular and ecclesiastical precincts and famously demolishing eighty houses in the process. They also built some of Derry's monumental buildings such as the Tempull Mór, which would become the cathedral of the diocese of Derry in the mid-thirteenth century. Although none of the twelfth-century structures survives, to get some idea of what they may have been like we should remind ourselves that Muirchertach was patron of some of the most revolutionary new buildings in the country in his day, such as the Cistercian house at Newry and, most importantly, the Cistercian monastery at Mellifont in Co. Louth.

In the second half of the twelfth century — at least — Derry was a major centre of literature and scholarship. The names of at least six *fir leiginn* or *ard fir leiginn*[44] are listed in the annals between 1162 and 1220 — at a time when universities were beginning to emerge in various parts of Europe. A new Life of Columba was composed in Derry around this time — in effect, a new charter for its contemporary role as the leading Columban church.[45] There is a growth in the composition of poetry celebrating Derry's Columban connections and we know that the annals themselves were being compiled there around the same time.[46] One of the contemporary treasures of Derry was a book called the Soiscél Martain, which was possibly the same manuscript that we now know as the Cathach.[47]

Just at the time when Derry attained the leadership of the *familia Columbae*, however, that institution itself collapsed under the influence of various factors such as the arrival in Ireland of the new religious orders and the Anglo-Normans, and the replacement of the native church organisation by one based on dioceses. In addition Derry's chief royal patrons, the Mac Lochlainns, had fallen from national power by the middle of the thirteenth century, although they held on as erenaghs of at least the northern part of the hill of Derry through to the beginning of the seventeenth century.

Derry did not become a diocesan seat until the middle of the thirteenth century — a century or so later than most of the other centres. In this regard it was in something of an ambiguous position. The diocese of Derry, as we now know it, is effectively the territory controlled by the Mac Lochlainns in the late twelfth and early thirteenth centuries. But as a Columban centre Derry's historic connections were with the greater part of Donegal, the diocese of Raphoe. The result was ironic when viewed from a modern perspective. By the mid-fourteenth century the hill of Derry itself was partitioned: its northern half attached to the diocese of Derry; its southern half attached to the diocese of Raphoe.[48]

As we have seen, in the thirteenth and fourteenth centuries there were a number of attempts, or at least suggestions, by the Anglo-Normans to develop Derry as a town. But it was not to be. The only lasting result of those connections is, seemingly, the skeleton on the city's coat-of-arms. It is said to represent Walter de Burgo of Greencastle, who was killed in 1332. For the next 250 years or so our records for Derry are scrappy to say the least and, while there were occasional attempts to revive and reform it, the general impression is of decline and impoverishment.

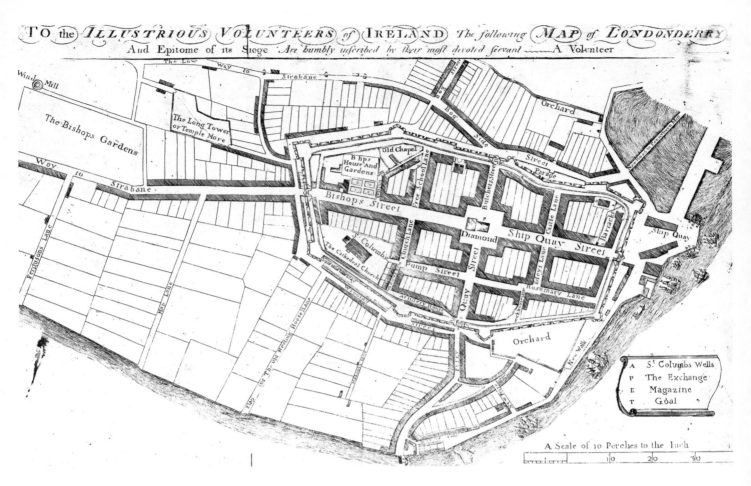

SIXTEENTH-CENTURY REVIVAL

Fig. 5.5 *Derry-Londonderry*, map 16, *c*. 1780. Trinity College Dublin, MS 1209/21, extract.

From the early sixteenth century, however, it looks as though the Uí Domhnaill were attempting to revive Derry particularly as a pilgrimage destination dedicated to St Columba. The walled city of Londonderry appears to be very close in layout to a near contemporary French town, Vitry-le-François, although there is one major — but possibly telling — difference between Londonderry and Vitry. The clear symmetrical plan behind both places breaks down in Derry on its western (Magazine Street) side, for no apparent topographical reason. This has prompted the suggestion that the line of Magazine Street and the adjacent city wall may be the survival of the medieval pilgrimage route that ran from a place called Port na Long — literally the 'ship quay' — on the River Foyle to a place called *an t-impodh deiseal*, which we know was close to what is now the Long Tower church (Fig. 5.5). Manus Ó Domhnaill's Betha Colaim Chille written in 1532 is our only documentary evidence for that pilgrimage.[49] The stories about the pilgrimage in the Betha show us that the Uí Domhnaill had a renewed interest in Derry in the early sixteenth century. Ruaidhrí Ó Domhnaill', who was bishop of Derry from 1520 to 1551, was Manus's first cousin.[50] Manus's father, Aodh Dubh, was Bishop Ruaidhrí's uncle.

The annals record that in 1512 Aodh Dubh set out from Derry on a campaign against Mac William Burke of Connacht. Derry was hardly a convenient launching pad for such an expedition. But we know that the Uí Domhnaill had a probably recently built tower-house castle in Derry, which had been erected for them by the Uí Dochartaigh in lieu of certain obligations, on land that had been bought from the Mac Lochlainn erenaghs for twenty cows.[51] The castle was located near the bottom of what is now Magazine Street, close to an old shoreline of the River Foyle (Fig. 5.2). The building survived into the plantation city and is shown on several early seventeenth-century maps.[52] We do not know exactly when it was built, but most of those castles had been constructed elsewhere in Ireland between about 1450 and 1550. Derry was only one of the Uí Domhnaill castles and was by no means the most important or most suitable in terms of a campaign against the Burkes. The reference to Aodh Dubh setting out from Derry in 1512 suggests that he may have chosen to leave deliberately from the newest of his castles, possibly in a pointed harking back to the de Burgo attempt to capture that settlement in the fourteenth century, as mentioned above.

The efforts by the Uí Domhnaill to develop Derry were not successful for a variety of reasons — not least the change in the Tudor government's policies towards Gaelic Ireland. Derry was taken by the English for the first time in 1566 and, although there are some brief references to its use after their withdrawal less than a year later, its identity as a Gaelic settlement had effectively come to an end. By May 1600 the English were back and Derry was on its way to becoming Londonderry.

The development of Derry into the modern city is recorded in great detail in the maps reproduced in the atlas and in the documents that were combed to provide the accompanying essay and itemised topographical information. No such detail is available for the thousand or so years of the site's development in medieval times. But that must not inhibit us from trying to establish as best we can how the settlement evolved over that period and what it might have looked like at any given point. One reviewer of the atlas, while praising its high quality, nevertheless lamented that because of its format 'the streets are present but the inhabitants are absent'.[53] Paradoxically it could be said that the opposite is true (in an admittedly limited way) for the medieval period. The more or less continuous references to the 'inhabitants' of Derry and the events they were involved in from the sixth century onwards imply a physical 'theatre' which, although still largely hidden from us, is becoming increasingly evident.

NOTES

[1] Thomas, IHTA, no. 15, *Derry-Londonderry*. Also in 2005, the Royal Irish Academy published *Maps and views of Derry 1600–1914: a catalogue* by W.S. Ferguson with a foreword by J.H Andrews. This extraordinarily detailed work had been a major source for those who worked on the history of the city for several decades but had been available — in almost samizdat form — only in two typescript copies: one in PRONI and the other in the library of Magee University College in Derry. Several people edited it posthumously after W.S. Ferguson's death, most particularly Mary Davies.

[2] Brian Lacey, *Medieval and monastic Derry: sixth century to 1600* (Dublin, 2012), p. 58.

[3] Ibid., pp 10–12.

[4] Ibid., pp 26–39.

[5] Ibid., pp 93–110.

[6] Ibid., pp 128–34.

[7] Ibid., pp 135–7. See also Ciarán Devlin, 'Some episcopal Lives: Eoghan O Dochartaigh (1554–68)', in Henry Jefferies and Ciarán Devlin (eds), *History of the diocese of Derry from earliest times* (Dublin, 2000), p. 119.

[8] Thomas, *Derry-Londonderry*, maps 5, 6 and 7.

[9] See, for example, ibid., maps 8–13.

[10] See, for example, ibid., maps 1–4, 15–23.

[11] Lacey, *Medieval and monastic Derry*, pp 109–10 and p. 101 for a possible earlier Anglo-Norman interest in the 'vill of Derekoneull [Doire Colm Chille?]'.

[12] See, for example, Ruairí Ó Baoill, *Island city: the archaeology of Derry-Londonderry* (Derry and Belfast, 2013), pp 5–33; Paul Logue, 'Excavations at Thornhill, Co. Londonderry', in Ian Armit *et al.* (eds), *Neolithic settlement in Ireland and western Britain* (Oxford, 2003), pp 149–55.

[13] Mainly because of the scarcity of published research on the previous periods. This lack of material has now been filled somewhat by the later published works referred to in this essay.

[14] Although see now Ó Baoill, *Island city*, especially pp 37–77.

[15] Brian Lac[e]y, 'The development of Derry, *c.* 600 to *c.* 1600', in Gearóid Mac Niocaill and P.F. Wallace (eds*)*, *Keimelia: studies in medieval archaeology and history in memory of Tom Delaney* (Galway, 1988), pp 378–96.

[16] Lacey, *Medieval and monastic Derry* and below. See also the imaginative reconstructions of the settlement at various stages in the middle ages in Ó Baoill, *Island city*. John Bryson has also produced a 'Map of Daire, *c.* 1512' (unpublished).

[17] For further commentary on some of those maps, see Annaleigh Margey, 'The emergence of Londonderry, *c.* 1600–1625: evidence from the surveys and maps', in Brian Scott (ed.), *Walls 400: studies to mark the 400th anniversary of the founding of the walls of Londonderry* (Derry, 2015), pp 57–75.

[18] These matters are not addressed to any extent in the *Derry-Londonderry* atlas but are dealt with, by and large, in Ferguson, *Maps and views*.

[19] Ferguson, *Maps and views*, p. 5, no. 10.

[20] D.A. Chart (ed.), *Londonderry and the London companies 1609–1629, being a survey and other documents submitted to King Charles I by Sir Thomas Phillips* (Belfast, 1928), p. 149.

[21] Ibid., pp 149–50.

[22] The proposed extension of Pump Street is also shown on map 8, a copy of Nicholas Pynnar's drawing of 1618–19.

[23] Lacey, *Medieval and monastic Derry*, pp 88–9.

[24] Chart, *Londonderry*, p. 167.

[25] Brian Graham, 'Review', in *IHS*, xxxv (2007), p. 390.

[26] One of the most recurring features about Derry-Londonderry throughout its long history is its continuing character as a border/frontier site.

27 W.M. Hennessy and D.H. Kelly (eds), *The Book of Fenagh* (Dublin, 1875), pp 402–5. For relevant commentary on and analysis of this poem, see Lacey, *Medieval and monastic Derry*, pp 11, 26.

28 Lacey, *Medieval and monastic Derry*, p. 11 and below.

29 Máire Herbert, 'The preface to Amra Coluim Cille', in Donnchadh Ó Corráin, Liam Breatnach and Kim McCone (eds), *Sages, saints and storytellers: Celtic studies in honour of Professor James Carney* (Maynooth, 1989), pp 69–70.

30 J.H Bernard and Robert Atkinson (eds), *The Irish Liber hymnorum* (2 vols, London, 1898), i, p. 87; ii, p. 28. The same story is repeated — more or less — in the later versions of the legend such as the Middle Irish Life of Colum Cille and Manus Ó Domhnaill's Betha Colaim Chille.

31 The issue is analysed in Lacey, *Medieval and monastic Derry*, pp 31–6.

32 Ibid., p. 13.

33 Ibid., pp 34–5.

34 Thomas, *Derry-Londonderry*, maps 5, 6; Lacey, *Medieval and monastic Derry*, pp 86–7.

35 For full references and analysis, see Lacey, *Medieval and monastic Derry*, pp 28–30.

36 Daniel Mc Carthy, 'The chronology of Saint Columba's Life', in Pádraic Moran and Immo Warntjes (eds), *Early medieval Ireland and Europe: chronology, contacts and scholarship – a festschrift for Dáibhí Ó Cróinín* (Turnhout, 2015), pp 3–32.

37 This would probably — but not certainly — mean that it was part of the Columban *familia*. A place referred to as Daire is mentioned in a marginal verse under 669 in the *Annals of Ulster*. Almost certainly Derry is not the place referred to — see Lacey, *Medieval and monastic Derry*, pp 37–8.

38 Richard Sharpe, *Medieval Irish saints' Lives: an introduction to Vitae sanctorum Hiberniae* (Oxford, 1991), p. 329.

39 Lacey, *Medieval and monastic Derry*, pp 41–3.

40 Ibid., chapters 6 and 7.

41 Using later sources relating to the system of plots and gardens allocated inside and outside the walls of plantation Londonderry, John Bryson's unpublished 'Map of Daire, *c.* 1512' attempts to locate some of the features of the medieval settlement, for example the Reilig Martain mentioned in the twelfth-century annals.

42 The names Ua Lochlainn and Mac Lochlainn are effectively interchangeable in this context.

43 Although it has been suggested that he actually lived at Enagh Lough about 5 km north-east of Derry, see Ciarán Devlin, 'The formation of the diocese', in Jefferies and Devlin, *History of the diocese of Derry*, p. 97.

44 'Professor of sacred scripture and theology in a monastic school', in *Dictionary of the Irish language: based mainly on Old and Middle Irish materials* (Dublin, 1998), p. 425.

45 Máire Herbert, *Iona, Kells and Derry: the history and hagiography of the monastic* familia *of Columba* (Oxford 1988), pp 209–86.

46 Lacey, *Medieval and monastic Derry*, p. 95.

47 Raghnall Ó Floinn, 'Sandhills, silver and shrines — fine metalwork of the medieval period from Donegal', in William Nolan, Liam Ronayne and Mairéad Dunlevy (eds), *Donegal history and society* (Dublin, 1995), p. 125.

48 Lacey, *Medieval and monastic Derry*, pp 108–9.

49 Ibid., pp 129–32.

50 Devlin, 'Some episcopal Lives: Ruairí O Domhnaill (1520–50)', in Jefferies and Devlin, *History of the diocese of Derry*, pp 115–18.

51 Lacey, *Medieval and monastic Derry*, pp 128–9.

52 See, for example, Thomas, *Derry-Londonderry*, maps 5–9.

53 Graham, 'Review', p. 289.

6. Viking Limerick

Brian Hodkinson

The Viking town of Limerick is an enigma because there are ample documentary references from the annals for its existence but surprisingly little archaeological evidence. Understanding of the development of Viking Limerick, therefore, rests upon a combination of the documentary information together with the cartographical evidence now made readily accessible with the publication of the Limerick fascicle of the IHTA.[1]

Raiding on the River Shannon commenced in the early ninth century and it is thought that the first Viking base was upstream of the present city at Athlunkard, where Eamonn Kelly and Ed O'Donovan identified what they believe to be a *longphort* (Fig. 6.1). No archaeological excavations have taken place there, but some Viking-Age material has been recovered from the site and its vicinity.[2] In the first quarter of the tenth century, settlement is believed to have moved downstream to King's Island, when

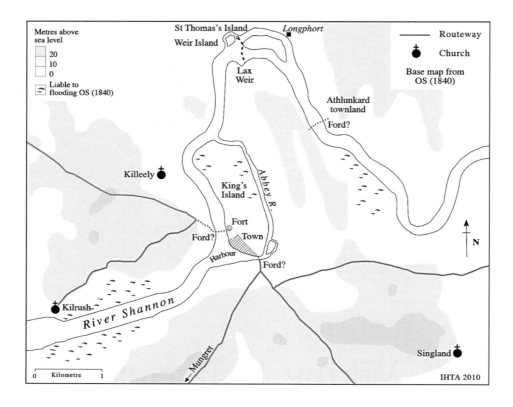

Metres above
sea level

20
10
0

Liable to
flooding OS (1840)

St Thomas's Island

Weir Island

Longphort

Lax
Weir

Athlunkard
townland

Ford?

Killeely

King's
Island

Abbey R.

Fort

Ford?

Town

Harbour

Ford?

Kilrush

River Shannon

Mungret

Routeway

Church

Base map from
OS (1840)

N

Singland

0   Kilometre   1

IHTA 2010

Fig. 6.1 *Limerick*, fig. 1, location of the Viking town.

the Vikings returned to the Shannon following a hiatus. In 968, this settlement was taken by the Dál Cais, a defeat that marked the end of an independent Viking kingdom. The King's Island site, however, continued in existence as a Norse town under Irish rule and so it still retained much of its Viking character when the Anglo-Normans arrived at the end of the twelfth century. The Ostmen were given English law and treated on an equal footing with the incomers, with the 'mere Irish' reduced to servile status. The last vestige of this separate Norse identity is found in a court case from 1295, in which the plaintiff claims to be an Ostman of Limerick and therefore due the privilege of putting forward his case, which would have been denied if he had been found to be Irish.[3]

The first entry for Limerick in the annals is in 843–4 and there are then regular references to the 'foreigners of Limerick' through to the first arrival of the Anglo-Normans in the 1170s.[4] For the most part, entries refer to the Vikings from Limerick raiding across the country but some refer to the actual town itself. There is, however, virtually no internal topographical information. Only *Chronicum Scotorum* mentions the walls of Limerick under the year 1088.[5] The *Cogadh Gaedhel re Gallaibh* mentions that the foreigners were slaughtered 'on the streets and in the houses'.[6] There is an intriguing reference in *Cathréim Cellacháin Caisil*: 'come to Limerick of the ships/ O Clan Eogan of the noble deeds/ around the gentle Cellachain/ to Limerick of the riveted stones'.[7] What exactly is meant by 'riveted stones' is not clear. Slate roofing is a possibility that springs readily to mind but is unlikely in a tenth-century context. A second reference from the same source adds further detail: 'and the soldiers were overthrown and made for Limerick to shut themselves quickly up there. And it was through the rear of the Lochlannachs that the nobles of Munster went into the town, so that the Lochlannachs were not able to close the gates, and the champions were killed in the houses and in the towers'.[8] Presumably the towers were sited on the walls, rather than free-standing within the town. One must bear in mind that *Cathréim* is a response to the *Cogadh*, both of which are much later than the era they are describing and may be imposing anachronistic detail.

Sadly there are no records relating to the town written by Norsemen, but at the very end of the period we do have the first Anglo-Norman records and one of them describes the taking of Limerick by the Anglo-Normans and gives details on the walls. So we can confirm that at least in the latter part of the Viking/Hiberno-Norse era the town had recognisable defences: 'In their efforts to repel, or rather to overpower him, the citizens met him [Meiler fitz Henry] with a hail of stones and missiles, both on the river bank and aiming from the city walls which overhung the bank'.[9] This incident follows on from a description of David the Welshman finding a ford across the river and crossing over and back to demonstrate its practicability. The ford in question is presumably in the region of the present-day Baal's Bridge, where there is a rock outcrop in the base of the river that matches the 'rough and rocky bed' (*asperum funditus et saxosum*) found by David (Fig. 6.1). If this is an accurate description of Meiler's crossing, it suggests that the walls did not then extend the full way to the ford.

The paucity of archaeological evidence from the Viking era is quite striking. There are references to the town burning in 965, 1058, 1062, 1063, 1088, 1108 and 1152.[10] While the extent of these fires is not given, one would expect that there should be recognisable fire levels within the archaeological stratigraphy, but none has been identified. In fact, to date no early Viking-Age stratigraphy has been recognised within the city. No burial is known from the vicinity and no ship remains have been found in the estuary. The major works of the Limerick main drainage in the bed of the Abbey River produced a single coin of King Cnut and a piece of decorated metalwork but little else. Nor are there chance finds from work on trenches for the various utility companies, nor reports on finds of the period garnered from old newspapers, though ones from other eras are occasionally reported on. What little we do have dates to the latter part of the Viking era, the Hiberno-Norse period, and that largely comes from the excavations at King John's Castle.[11] I worked on the first phase of the excavations and helped to excavate three sunken-featured buildings, of Scandinavian type, which were dated to the period between the first arrival of the Anglo-Normans in the 1170s and their return in the mid 1190s. Subsequent work uncovered three more similar buildings, which pre-date the Anglo-Norman ringwork castle of the 1170s, and a stone-paved roadway leading down to the Shannon.[12]

It is not possible to provide a convincing explanation for all of this, only a partial one. The main streets of the medieval town, both Englishtown and Irishtown, were once lined with late medieval and Georgian buildings, most of which had cellars or undercrofts, and the excavation of these removed earlier deposits, down to subsoil level in some cases.[13] The first phase of excavations in the late 1980s and early 1990s was carried out by Limerick City Council's informal archaeological unit and involved open-area excavations, but these were all in peripheral areas in the northern and southern suburbs and not in what is believed to be the Viking core around St Mary's Cathedral. Since the mid 1990s and the advent of privately run archaeological companies, there has been no large-scale open-area excavation within the core since pile foundations have become the method of choice, which requires small-scale keyhole excavation at best. Accordingly in Limerick there has been no large-scale excavation in the core area, unlike at Wood Quay in Dublin or Peter Street in Waterford.[14]

The hinterland of Viking Limerick seems to have stretched across the Co. Limerick side of the Shannon estuary as far as the River Deel, but there is less evidence from the Co. Clare side and it may have encompassed only the immediate environs of the town. Evidence for this settlement is drawn from a scatter of Viking-type archaeological finds and placename evidence.[15] The existence of surnames such as Siward and Harrold demonstrates Viking influence within the area, but limited DNA research has not, as yet, revealed a definitive Scandinavian gene pool.[16]

Given the lack of excavated evidence, is it possible to reconstruct Viking Limerick? It is here that the mapping in the IHTA comes into play. Returning first to the annalistic references, there is a hint that there were two separate parts to Limerick. The *Annals of Inisfallen* state, under 1108, that 'Luimnech was totally burnt save the market outside', while the *Annals of the Four Masters* state under 1171 that Cormac Mac Carthaigh 'burnt the market and half the fortress to its core'.[17] This impression of duality is further strengthened by an entry in the *Cogadh* that reads 'the fort and the

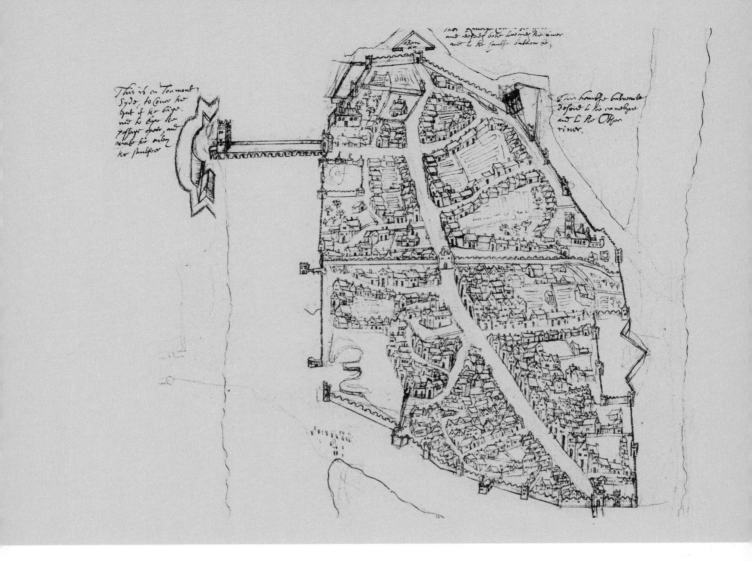

Fig. 6.2 *Limerick*, map 7, *c.* 1590.
Hunt Museum, Limerick, extract.

good town they reduced to smoke and to red fire afterwards'.[18] Jumping to the other end of the medieval period, or rather the early modern, we are fortunate to have the Civil Survey of 1654–6, which gives a property-by-property description of the town. It divides Limerick into three: 'the south suburbs or ward of the city', 'the boddy of middle ward of the city' and 'the north suburbs or warde of the citty'.[19] The southern suburb, known as Irishtown, does not concern us here because it was a later medieval development;[20] it is the other two, on King's Island and collectively known as Englishtown, that reflect the duality noted in the annals. The more detailed of the sixteenth- and seventeenth-century maps in the atlas confirm this dual nature of the town on King's Island. Map 7, an original from the Hunt Museum and dated *c.* 1590, shows the Englishtown clearly divided into two by an east–west wall with a gate astride the main street of the town (Fig. 6.2). The wall is less clear on the Hardiman map of the same date — map 6 — but the gate is very clear where it is lettered 'P' and

named as Newgate in the key (Fig. 6.3). Thomas Phillips's map of 1685 — map 12 — also shows the wall and gate, after which both disappear cartographically (Fig. 6.4).[21] The area so enclosed is the middle ward and comprises St Mary's parish, the only truly urban parish. St Nicholas's and St Munchin's in the northern suburb and St John's and St Michael's in the southern suburb all have substantial rural hinterlands. It is therefore believed that this seventeenth-century division into two parts reflects the earlier duality of the town, an interpretation that has found favour with the author of the atlas text.[22]

Fig. 6.3 *Limerick*, map 6, *c.* 1590. Trinity College Dublin, Hardiman MS 1209/57, map rotated, extract.

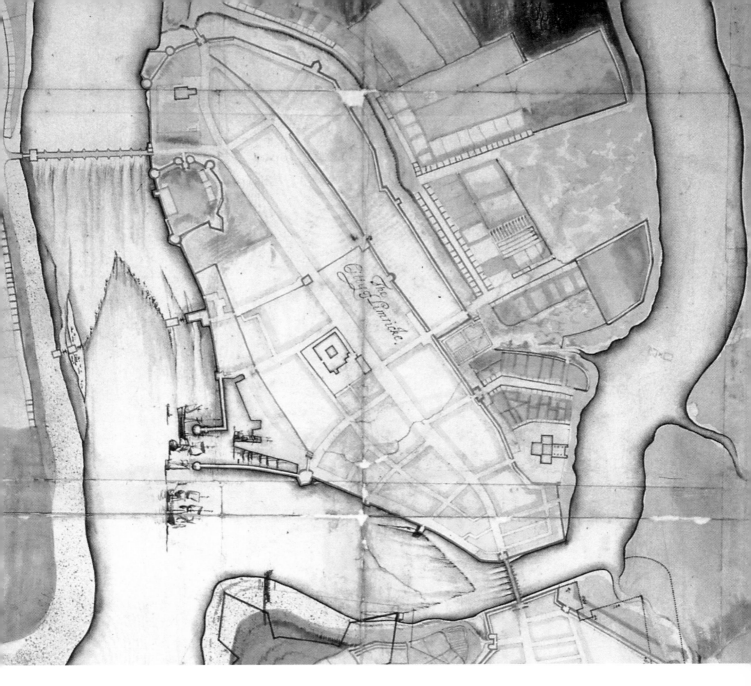

Fig. 6.4 *Limerick*, map 12, 1685, by Thomas Phillips. National Library of Ireland, MS 3137 (36), map rotated, extract.

Lacking good archaeological evidence, it is still possible from the annalistic and cartographical sources, combined with a familiarity with Viking-Age sites elsewhere, to postulate a development of Viking Limerick (Fig. 6.1).[23] Given the maritime nature of the Vikings, initial settlement was along the shoreline at the southern end of King's Island, roughly from Curragour Falls towards Baal's Bridge. The development of properties along the shoreline brought into existence a roadway on the landward side, which became the main axis of the developing town. This roadway was not the main street of the high medieval and later periods

(Fig. 6.5). That came into existence only with the construction of later infrastructure — the castle, Thomond Bridge and Baal's Bridge — by the Anglo-Normans that effectively forced a replanning of the old main route, which was blocked by the castle. The original road survives today as Crosbie Row, running along the back of City Hall, and as Courthouse Lane besides the old courthouse/school on Bridge Street. It originally ran across the front of St Mary's Cathedral, but this section seems to have become part of a cathedral close in the later medieval period. The street is very clearly marked on Phillips's map (1685, map 12) but is less clear on the Hardiman map (*c.* 1590, map 6), where a row of buildings in front of the cathedral is believed to be houses for the canons fronting the road. It is less convincing on the Hunt Museum map (*c.* 1590, map 7), but is there (Figs 6.2–5).

Farther to the north, the area of the castle and more specifically the highest point around the north-east tower served as the *þingstaðr* or assembly place for the town and its hinterland. As well as being the administrative and legal centre, the surrounding open area was probably used for casual trading around the *þing* meetings. At the time of writing the original article on the topography, I believed that when the Dál Cais took over Limerick, they established a palace in the area of the *þingstaðr*, thereby

Fig. 6.5 *Limerick*, fig. 2, conjectural layout of the Viking town (after Hodkinson, 2002).

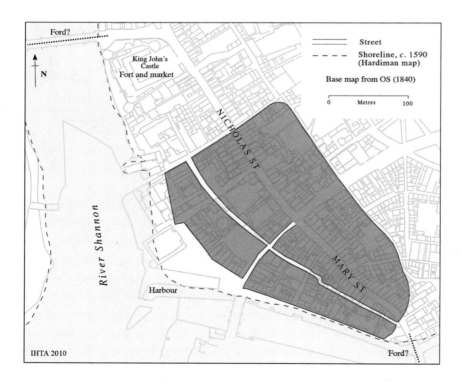

demonstrating the transfer of power. This model has been modified and I now think that there was a larger royal compound adjacent to the *þingstaðr* but farther to the north, thereby allowing the *þing* to continue in operation but under the eyes of the king. The palace probably lay in the area of the present-day St Munchin's and Villiers almshouses. The medieval bishop's palace is shown on the Hardiman map, marked 'Q', in the area later occupied by the almshouses. In a recent short article, I noted that a previously undated document in the Black Book of Limerick, seeking royal protection for church property, may possibly be dated to 1194–5.[24] When the O'Briens decided or were forced to retreat westwards from Limerick under pressure from the Anglo-Normans, they may have handed over their palace to the church as a parting gesture to prevent its use by the incomers and the church then immediately sought royal protection for its new property. St Munchin's can be seen as the family chapel of the O'Briens, which became the parish church during reorganisation under the Anglo-Normans.

In conclusion, therefore, it has to be stated that without the cartographical evidence, now easily available in the atlas, Viking Limerick would be even more of an enigma than it already is. It will be interesting to see whether the mapping for Cork, Waterford and Wexford in future fascicles plays as significant a role in the understanding of the development of those Viking towns as it does in Limerick.

NOTES

[1] O'Flaherty, IHTA, no. 21, *Limerick*.
[2] E.P. Kelly and Edmond O'Donovan, 'A Viking *longphort* near Athlunkard, Co. Clare', in *Archaeology Ireland*, xii, no. 4 (1998), pp 13–16.
[3] B.J. Hodkinson, 'The medieval city of Limerick', in Liam Irwin, Gearóid Ó Tuathaigh and Matthew Potter (eds), *Limerick history and society* (Dublin, 2009), p. 28; reprinted in B.J. Hodkinson, *Aspects of medieval North Munster; collected essays* (Limerick, 2012), p. 16.
[4] *AFM*, i, pp 466–7. This and the Irish annals and texts referred to below are available on CELT (Corpus of Electronic Texts), www.ucc.ie/celt (last accessed 6 Apr. 2016).
[5] *Chron. Scot.*, p. 255.
[6] *Cogadh Gaedhel re Gallaibh: the war of the Gaedhil with the Gaill*, ed. J.H. Todd (London, 1867), p. 79.
[7] *Cathréim Cellacháin Caisil: the victorious career of Cellachan of Cashel*, ed. Alexander Bugge (Oslo, 1905), p. 10.
[8] Ibid., p. 19.
[9] Giraldus Cambrensis, *Expugnatio Hibernica: the conquest of Ireland*, ed. A.B. Scott and F.X. Martin (Dublin, 1978), p. 151.
[10] *AFM*, ii, pp 689, 875, 883, 885, 933, 987, 1103; *Ann. Inisf.*, pp 217, 267; *ALC*, i, p. 97.
[11] Ken Wiggins, *A place of great consequence: archaeological excavations at King John's Castle, Limerick, 1990–98* (Dublin, 2016).
[12] Ken Wiggins, director of excavations, personal communication. There is the possibility of earlier deposits below the finish level of these excavations.

[13] Personal observation on sites in Broad Street and John Street, both in Irishtown. The only surviving stratigraphy was below the laneways between properties and even here there was major disturbance caused by the service trenches running down them.

[14] P.F. Wallace, *Viking Dublin: the Wood Quay excavations* (Dublin, 2015); Maurice Hurley *et al.*, *Archaeological excavations of Viking and Anglo-Norman Waterford* (Waterford, 1997).

[15] B.J. Hodkinson, 'Viking Limerick and its hinterland', in H.B. Clarke and Ruth Johnson (eds), *The Vikings in Ireland and beyond: before and after the Battle of Clontarf* (Dublin, 2015), pp 183–8.

[16] For the surnames of medieval Limerick, see B.J. Hodkinson, 'Who was who in medieval Limerick, from manuscript sources', www.limerick.ie/sites/default/files/atoms/files/who_was_who_in_medieval_limerick_2015_1.pdf (last accessed 6 Apr. 2016). Cathy Swift personally verified the statement on DNA and further suggests that the name White (Latin, Albus) in the list may reflect Norse settlement.

[17] *Ann. Inisf.*, p. 267; *AFM*, ii, p. 1185.

[18] *Cogadh Gaedhel re Gallaibh*, p. 81.

[19] *CS*, iv, pp 400, 418, 439.

[20] B.J. Hodkinson, 'The origin and dating of the name of Limerick's Irishtown', in *North Munster Antiquarian Journal*, xlix (2009), pp 1–5; reprinted in Hodkinson, *Aspects of medieval North Munster*, pp 45–51.

[21] The Civil Survey does mention the wall but it needs a really close scrutiny of the text to identify it.

[22] O'Flaherty, *Limerick*, pp 1–2.

[23] I have previously published this theory and what follows is a slightly revised version of what appears in B.J. Hodkinson, 'The topography of pre-Norman Limerick', in *North Munster Antiquarian Journal*, xlii (2002), pp 1–6; reprinted in Hodkinson, *Aspects of medieval North Munster*, pp 31–8.

[24] B.J. Hodkinson, 'St Munchin's and the bishop's palace', in *North Munster Antiquarian Journal*, liii (2013), pp 283–4.

Part III
Anglo-Norman, gaelicised and plantation towns

7. From Gaelic church settlements to Anglo-Norman towns: problems and possibilities

Cóilín Ó Drisceoil

Some twenty-three of Ireland's fifty-six Anglo-Norman towns appropriated an early medieval Gaelic ecclesiastical settlement, making this one of the chief modes by which urbanisation progressed in the decades following the conquest.[1] Charting the topography of these places as they evolved from church settlements to boroughs is therefore a key concern if we are to understand the early development of the medieval town in Ireland. But in attempting to undertake this exercise we are confronted with an array of deficiencies in the source material at our disposal: documentary records are largely silent and often unreliable about the material landscapes of these places during the critical decades of their transition; and topography and archaeology provide, at best, only vignettes and certainly not the type of macro-detail that is required. This contribution highlights some key problems with the sources that are available to us, through the lens of four Anglo-Norman towns with Gaelic church settlement antecedents that have been published as IHTA fascicles: Kildare, Kilkenny, Kells and Downpatrick.[2] The first part of the essay presents the current state of knowledge around the topographical evolution of the four towns between the late twelfth and early thirteenth centuries and includes new research and interpretations, much of it won from archaeological excavations, that has augmented or overtaken the material in the fascicles. The concluding section draws on the four townscape histories to examine key problems the sources present with regard to defining their immediate pre- and post-conquest character and topography.

TOWNSCAPE HISTORIES C. 1150 TO 1225

Cill Dara to Kildare

Before his death in 1176, Richard de Clare (Strongbow) established a borough and an earth-and-timber castle at Kildare.[3] The town was built around the royal (Uí Dúnlainge) cathedral *civitas* and pilgrimage centre of Cill Dara, which at this time comprised at least two churches (one of timber, the other stone), a round tower and high crosses, a *magnus domus*, an abbess's house, a street and domestic houses.[4] Two roughly concentric ecclesiastical enclosures (6 hectares in total) that encompassed the structures have been proposed on the basis of curving elements in the modern street pattern (Fig. 4.1). It has been argued that pre-Anglo-Norman Kildare had 'urban or "proto-urban" characteristics',[5] largely on the basis of Cogitosus's famous seventh-century description of Kildare as a 'vast metropolitan city' in the *Vita Brigitae*, in addition to tenth-century references to streets and workshops.

The exact chronology, whereabouts and topography of the initial Anglo-Norman town at Kildare are unclear, but it was probably little more than a military settlement that was located around Strongbow's castle. It was Strongbow's son-in-law, the energetic urbaniser William Marshal, earl of Pembroke and lord of Leinster (1189–1219), that was responsible for laying out the greater part of the medieval town in the early 1200s, with its main axis and market place running parallel to the cathedral. There is nothing to indicate that any substantive changes occurred at the early church site in the immediate aftermath of the conquest and it continued under the control, at least superficially, of Gaelic bishops until 1223. Its precinct boundaries were, it is argued, accommodated in the

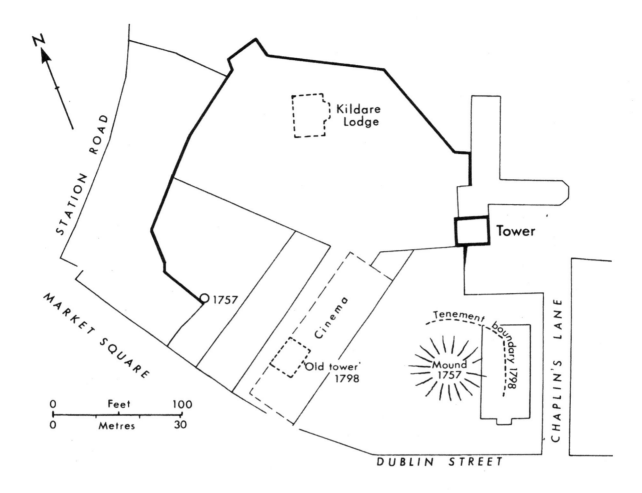

Fig. 7.1 *Kildare*, fig. 3, probable site of Kildare castle.

Anglo-Norman town plan (see below). As befitted its status as the chief administrative centre in the medieval county of Kildare, the earlier castle was re-edified by Marshal into a polygonal masonry structure that was described in 1331 as comprising four towers, a chapel and a kitchen (Fig. 7.1). The first historical references to a town wall at Kildare do not occur until the early sixteenth century but it is possible an earlier, as yet undocumented, defensive circuit of some description was constructed.[6] The tenure of the first Anglo-Norman bishop of Kildare, Ralph of Bristol (1223–32), saw the replacement of the then ruinous cathedral with the present structure — heavily 'restored' by George Edmund Street in 1875–81 — and this also acted as the parish church for the borough.[7] The mendicants did not arrive in Kildare until the Franciscan Grey Abbey was founded some time between 1254 and 1260.

Cill Chainnigh to Kilkenny

The early medieval cathedral church and political capital (Mac Gilla Pátraic) of Cill Chainnigh was one of the first ports-of-call for the contingent of Anglo-Norman adventurers led by Maurice de Prendergast in 1169 (Fig. 7.2). The settlement that greeted them was at this time the 'largest and most important inland settlement in south-east Ireland',[8] a diocesan see and centre of the once powerful, but by the twelfth century waning and divided Gaelic kingdom of Osraige.[9] The ecclesiastical settlement was occupied by a stone cathedral church decorated in Hiberno-Romanesque style (its foundations were discovered in 1845 underneath the chancel of the present Gothic cathedral), a round tower and a large stone building that may have been a residence of the kings of Ossory.[10] Other recorded structures of pre-Anglo-Norman date include fragments of a stone building beneath the foundations of the north transept of the thirteenth-century cathedral,[11] and to the south of the latter, a souterrain and a large stone-lined cesspit.[12] A densely-populated and extensive graveyard was also present: two male skeletons from directly beneath the foundations of the round tower were recently radiocarbon dated to the tenth and eleventh to mid-twelfth centuries.[13] Outlying churches dedicated to St Brigid and St Maul (a possible nunnery) and 'ostels' (presumably guesthouses) are also documented historically. Comb manufacturing was a significant industry within the church site and traces of a probable combmaker's workshop were excavated in the grounds of the former bishop's palace.[14] The modern street pattern around the cathedral was thought to preserve the circuits of two concentric ecclesiastical enclosures (6.5 hectares), but excavations have demonstrated a different circuit for the inner enclosure (see below, Fig. 7.3).[15]

About 800 m south of the church settlement, on the site of the present Kilkenny Castle, Strongbow apparently built a motte that is recorded as having been destroyed in *c.* 1173.[16] Reference around two years later to a burgage and a parish church dedicated to the Blessed Virgin Mary at Kilkenny implies that there was a resident population of some size here at this time.[17] But after the death of Strongbow in 1176 the early borough appears to have been abandoned — Kilkenny is noticeably absent from Giraldus's accounts of Ireland in the 1180s[18] — and although it was ostensibly part of Strongbow's lordship of Leinster, the Mac Gilla Pátraic kings were left in control of their heartland in central Osraige, including Cill Chainnigh, until about 1190.[19] The decades immediately following the conquest saw the continuation of Gaelic bishops of Osraige and there are no indications, in the historical or archaeological records at least, that the topography of Cill Chainnigh underwent any major changes.

Fig. 7.2 *Kilkenny*, fig. 1, principal sites *c.* 1200 to *c.* 1550.

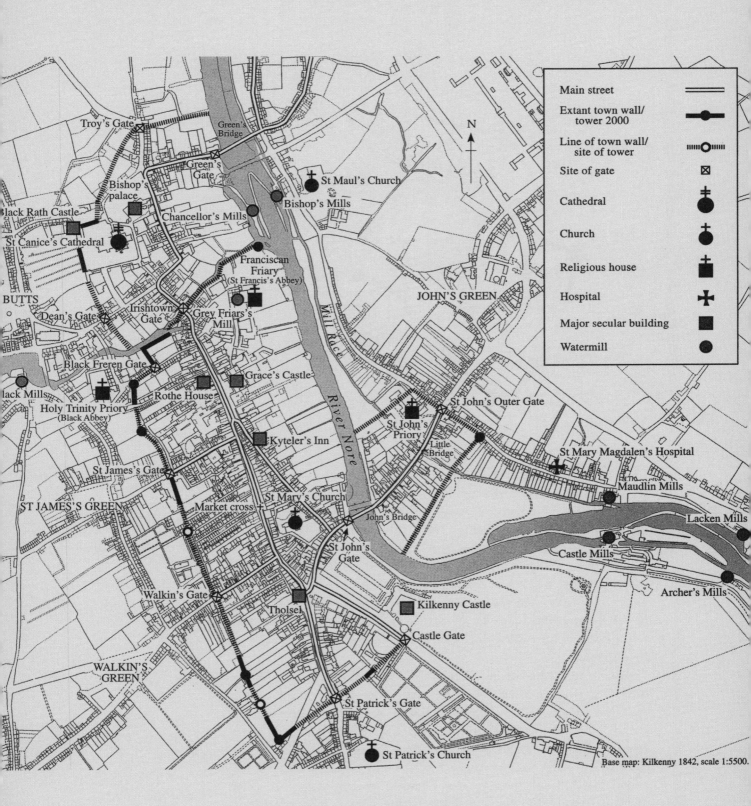

Troy's Gate

Green's
Bridge

Green's
Gate

Bishop's
palace

St Maul's Church

Black Rath Castle

Chancellor's Mills

Bishop's Mills

St Canice's Cathedral

Franciscan
Friary
(St Francis's Abbey)

JOHN'S GREEN

BUTTS

Dean's Gate

Irishtown
Gate

Grey Friars's
Mill

Black Freren Gate

Grace's Castle

Black Mills

Rothe House

St John's Outer Gate

Holy Trinity Priory
(Black Abbey)

St John's
Priory

St Mary Magdalen's Hospital

Kyteler's Inn

Little
Bridge

Maudlin Mills

St James's Gate

Lacken Mills

ST JAMES'S GREEN

Market cross

St Mary's Church

John's Bridge

Castle Mills

St John's
Gate

Archer's Mills

Walkin's Gate

Kilkenny Castle

Tholsel

Castle Gate

WALKIN'S
GREEN

St Patrick's Gate

River Nore

Mill Race

St Patrick's Church

Base map: Kilkenny 1842, scale 1:5500.

N

Main street	
Extant town wall/ tower 2000	
Line of town wall/ site of tower	
Site of gate	
Cathedral	
Church	
Religious house	
Hospital	
Major secular building	
Watermill	

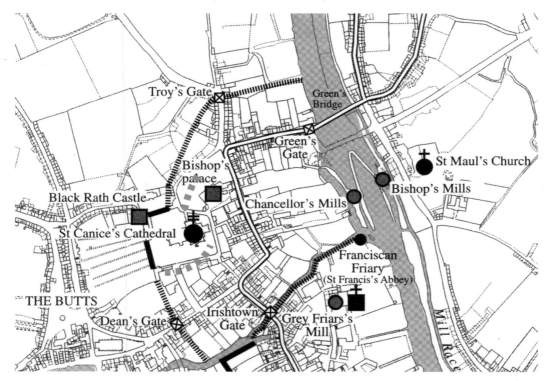

■ ■ ■ ■ ■ Excavated lines of enclosure

In recognising the strategic value of Kilkenny for the development of his vast lordship gained through his marriage to Strongbow's daughter Isabel de Clare, William Marshal selected Kilkenny for his *caput* after gaining seisin of Leinster around 1190.[20] This instituted a period of sustained development at Kilkenny. The Marshal drove out the Mac Gilla Pátraics from Kilkenny and in *c.* 1192 probably built a large ringwork castle, much of which was excavated in the 1990s beneath the present Kilkenny Castle.[21] On the occasion of his first short visit to Kilkenny in 1200, along with Isabel, he set in train the laying out of a new town to the north of the castle, which came to be known as the Hightown or Englishtown.

Shortly following the installation of the first Anglo-Norman bishop of Ossory, Hugh le Rous (1202–18), construction began on the Gothic cathedral dedicated to St Canice to replace the Hiberno-Romanesque church. Around the same time, a large English-style cathedral close and an episcopal borough — the Irishtown — were also laid out.[22] The Marshal and Isabel were in residence at Kilkenny Castle for much of the period 1207–13 and these years saw intense investment in their chief town in Ireland. The earth-and-timber stronghold at Kilkenny Castle

Fig. 7.3 *Kilkenny*, fig. 1, principal sites *c.* 1200 to *c.* 1550, extract, showing lines of enclosure excavated since publication of atlas (in red).

Opposite: Fig. 7.4 *Kilkenny*, map 6, growth to 1758, extract.

Pre-1170

13th-cent.
IRISHTOWN

Pre-1170

Pre-1170

1660-1758

1660-1758

1660-1758

13th-cent

c. 1207-c. 1231
HIGHTOWN

MARKET

c. 1207-c. 1231
ST JOHN'S

16th-cent.

13th-cent.

c. 1170-c. 1207
HIGHTOWN

1660-1758

JAMES-
GREEN

FAIR GREEN

13th-cent.

1660-1758

13th-cent.
DONAGHMORE

was replaced by an impressive stone castle, commensurate with its status as the nerve centre of Marshal's lordship. The new town doubled in size to extend, incrementally, into the former cross-lands and between whatever pre-existing settlement existed at this time around the castle and the River Breagagh, a tributary of the River Nore, which marked the division between the twin-boroughs of Irishtown and Hightown (Fig. 7.4). The town was developed along a main thoroughfare that connected the castle with the cathedral, with a market place at its centre and burgages running off it at right-angles (Fig. 7.2). The Hightown at this time appears to have been enclosed, at least partially, by a town wall that comprised a fosse and an earthen bank.[23] By c. 1205 Strongbow's parish church had been replaced by a new, much larger edifice that functioned as the chief church and burial place for the burgesses of the Hightown. Further expansion on the east side of the River Nore centred on the establishment in 1211 of the Augustinian priory of St John the Baptist, built to replace an earlier, possibly pre-Anglo-Norman, Augustinian hospital that was sited somewhere around Green's Bridge. An extensive suburb developed around the priory and further suburban expansion occurred to the south and west of the Hightown.

Marshal granted a charter to the town in 1207.[24] After his death in 1219 Kilkenny continued to prosper. Hightown was augmented by a Dominican priory (c. 1225) and Franciscan friary (c. 1231–4),[25] and a substantial masonry town wall was built around the Hightown and Irishtown in the mid-thirteenth century.[26] The suburb of St John appears to have had an earth-and-timber wall for most of the medieval period.[27] With a population by the mid-thirteenth century of at least two thousand, Kilkenny had become Ireland's largest inland town and an 'enduring strategic achievement' of William Marshal.[28]

Ceanannas to Kells

A borough, strategically sited on the edge of the lordship of Meath, was established by Hugh de Lacy (d. 1186) as the centre for the seigneurial manor of Kells. It was developed around the regionally-important, royal (Ó Ruairc) cathedral settlement and pilgrimage-centre of Ceanannas, which at this time contained a stone church and oratory (St Columb's House), a round tower, at least five high crosses and, according to the eleventh- to early twelfth-century Kells 'charters', a monastic school, guesthouse, refectory, scriptorium, metalworking workshops, granaries, a market and a street.[29] An Augustinian abbey (1140–48) dedicated to St Mary was situated west of the church site. The street-pattern around the

Fig. 7.5 *Kells*, fig. 1, medieval sites, showing lines of enclosure excavated since publication of atlas (in red).

church is regarded as retaining the concentricity of the inner and outer (9.5 hectares) ecclesiastical enclosures, but two separate excavations — at Church Street and Church Lane/Fair Green — have uncovered sections of ecclesiastical enclosure ditches that differ substantially from the layout that has been suggested (see below, Fig. 7.5).[30]

The initial Anglo-Norman settlement at Kells was probably a military stronghold centred on a motte-and-bailey castle that was sited to the east of the religious settlement. The borough of Kells was chartered by Walter de Lacy at some point between 1194 and 1211 and it was probably he who was largely responsible for the layout of the medieval town plan, with its market place and burgages occupying the area east of the church. Although the first murage grant dates to 1326 there may have been an earlier town wall, perhaps of earth-and-timber construction, in place.[31] The early medieval church site appears to have remained at least semi-independent as a Gaelic cathedral see until the death of the Irish bishop M. Ua Dobailén in 1211, at which time the see was dissolved and absorbed into the Anglo-Norman diocese of Meath. Religious provision was afforded to the new townsfolk by the re-edification of the monastic church as a parish church (1211) and on the east side of the town a hospital of the Fratres Cruciferi was founded by Walter de Lacy in 1199. Hugh de Lacy also refounded and patronised the pre-Anglo-Norman Augustinian abbey of St Mary prior to his death in 1186.

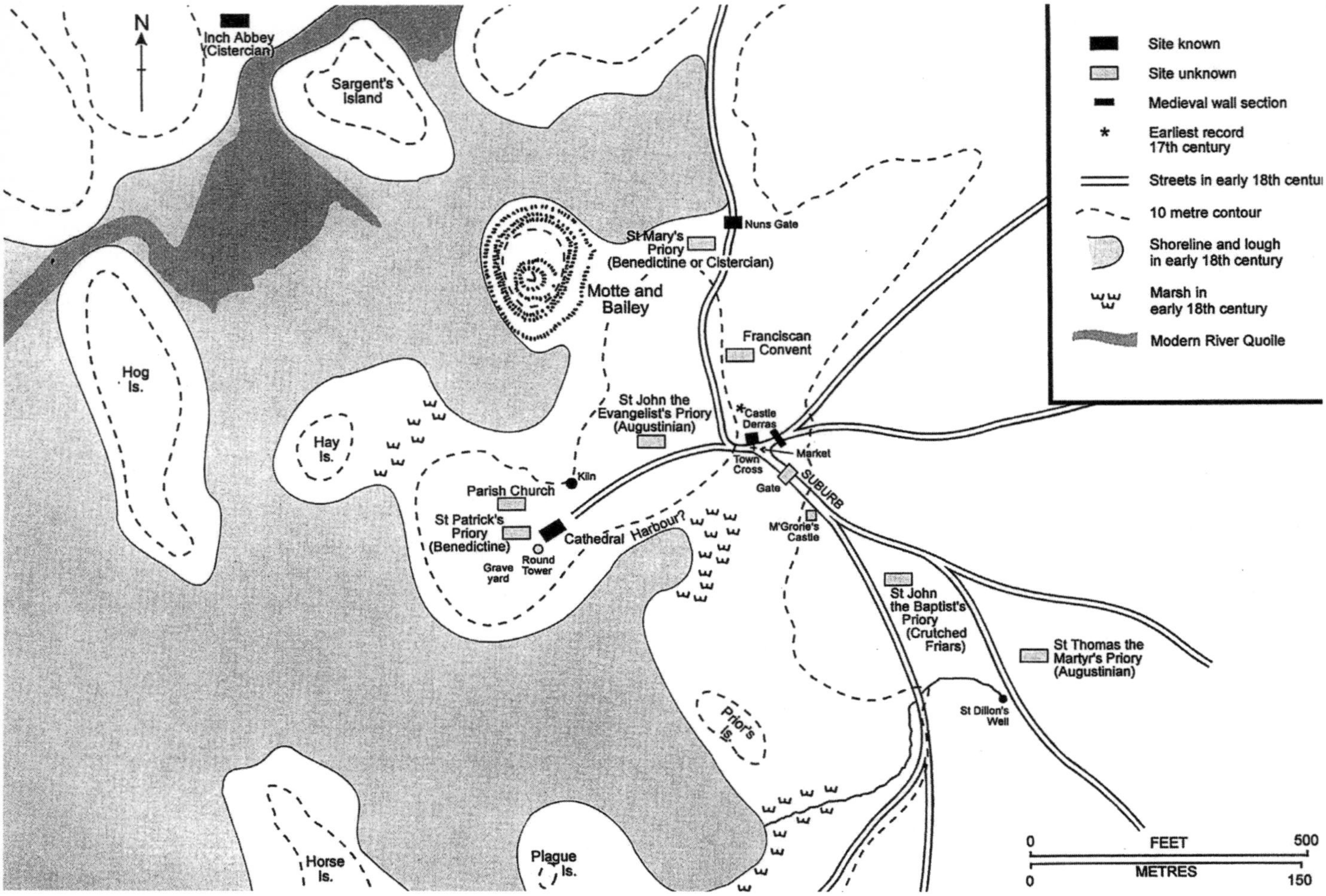
N
Inch Abbey (Cistercian)
Sargent's Island
Hog Is.
Hay Is.
Nuns Gate
St Mary's Priory (Benedictine or Cistercian)
Motte and Bailey
Franciscan Convent
St John the Evangelist's Priory (Augustinian)
Castle Derras
Market
Town Cross
Gate
SUBURB
Kiln
Parish Church
St Patrick's Priory (Benedictine)
Cathedral
Harbour?
Round Tower
Grave yard
M'Grorie's Castle
St John the Baptist's Priory (Crutched Friars)
St Thomas the Martyr's Priory (Augustinian)
St Dillon's Well
Prior's Is.
Horse Is.
Plague Is.
Site known
Site unknown
Medieval wall section
Earliest record 17th century
Streets in early 18th centu
10 metre contour
Shoreline and lough in early 18th century
Marsh in early 18th century
Modern River Quoile
0 FEET 500
0 METRES 150

Fig. 7.6 *Downpatrick*, fig. 1, medieval sites.

Dún Pádraig to Downpatrick

It was another Anglo-Norman baron, John de Courcy, who established in 1177 a military bridgehead for his colonisation of Ulster near the cathedral and centre of Gaelic power at Dún Pádraig (Cathedral Hill, Downpatrick). At this time the ecclesiastical settlement comprised a twelfth-century cathedral church, which was partially excavated beneath the present late eighteenth- to early nineteenth-century Holy Trinity Cathedral,[32] a second possible church dedicated to St Brigid, a round tower, monastic school, souterrain,[33] two high crosses and other religious buildings,[34] all set within a pair of concentric ecclesiastical enclosure ditches (*c.* 3–4 hectares) that encircled Cathedral Hill.[35] An Augustinian priory (1138) was probably located on English Street and excavations have identified extramural early medieval domestic activity on this street 100 m south-west of the cathedral.

John de Courcy's castle was almost certainly situated 450 m north of Cathedral Hill at the Mound of Down — 'Rathkeltair' (Fig. 7.6).

Excavations here in 2012 indicate that its earthworks represent an unfinished motte castle built over an earlier, perhaps eleventh-century, rath.[36] The motte was abandoned by de Courcy in favour of Carrickfergus Castle within six to eighteen months of his first arrival in Ulster in 1177 and Downpatrick was to continue throughout the middle ages without a seigneurial castle. Little is known of the topography or even the exact whereabouts of the initial Anglo-Norman settlement. It may have been focused around the abandoned motte but the discovery in excavations on Market Street, in the centre of the modern town, of a late twelfth- to early thirteenth-century ditch that may have defended the early Anglo-Norman settlement suggests it could have been sited here instead.[37] A southwards running ditch that cut through the two pre-Anglo-Norman ecclesiastical enclosure ditches on Cathedral Hill may also relate to this initial period of activity.[38] Burgage plots are referred to in 1202–5 and by 1260 the market settlement, at that stage apparently unwalled,[39] had achieved borough status and had been laid out to the east of Cathedral Hill, with English Street as its principal thoroughfare. A small harbour was sited to the west of the Town Cross and market place at the junction of English Street and Scotch Street.

Whilst it was not promoted as an administrative centre for the Ulster earldom, de Courcy positioned Downpatrick as the religious capital of his lordship by actively patronising the church. He founded a Benedictine cathedral priory on Cathedral Hill (1183), a priory of the Fratres Cruciferi (before 1189) on Mary Street and an Augustinian priory (Toberglory) (before 1183), probably somewhere between Ardglass Road and John Street. A Benedictine or Cistercian nunnery was also founded in the late twelfth century, though its assignation to de Courcy is uncertain. De Courcy famously removed to the cathedral the relics of Saints Brigid and Colum Cille to join those of Patrick, making it a major centre for medieval pilgrimage. The parish church (unusually dedicated to St Margaret) was also sited on Cathedral Hill, close to the Benedictine priory, but its exact foundation date is unknown. Around 1240 Hugh de Lacy founded a Franciscan convent on the north side of the town.

It is apparent from the town biographies presented above that reconstructing townscape history for the period in which they changed from religious centres to Anglo-Norman towns is heavily reliant on the interrogation of a very limited range of sources. In the following section three key difficulties that emerge from these sources are highlighted. Firstly, there is the question of how the historical and archaeological records can be used to address the question of precisely what were elite church settlements such as Kildare, Kilkenny, Kells and Downpatrick before the

Anglo-Normans settled their towns on them? Were they solely religious settlements? Or were they, as some have suggested, part of a horizon of indigenous pre-conquest town developments at major ecclesiastical settlements? A second, related, issue is that defining the physical extent of the church settlements in the twelfth century is beset with problems. This is largely as a result of archaeological excavations contradicting the circuits of ecclesiastical enclosures that have been reconstructed on the basis of curvilinear elements in the modern street patterns, as noted above for Kilkenny and Kells. And lastly, the topography and layout of the earliest phases of Anglo-Norman town development are very poorly understood. What did these first colonial settlements comprise and how did they engage with the pre-existing church elements? When can they be said, without reservation, to be towns? These are all questions with far-reaching implications for our understanding, not only of the origins of the town in Ireland, but also of the factors that motivated the Anglo-Normans to select these places for urban development in the first place.

ARCHAEOLOGY AND THE 'MONASTIC TOWN'

Kildare and Kells were characterised as early medieval 'proto-towns' in their respective fascicles and Kilkenny as a pre Anglo-Norman town. The authors of the Downpatrick fascicle did not explicitly define the church settlement in urban terms but did allude to the presence of a substantial 'secular settlement' outside the ecclesiastical precinct. All four were considered examples of monastic towns by John Bradley.[40] There is no need at this juncture to rehearse the 'tangled debate'[41] around pre-Anglo-Norman, non-Viking urbanism, other than to state that in the light of recent forensic deconstructions of the socio-economic and topographical indicators that have been postulated for the so-called monastic towns from documentary sources we must now turn to critiquing the arguments that originate from the physical worlds of archaeology and topography.[42] A basic problem with archaeology as a source is that, to date, excavations have not been undertaken on the scale that is required to allow for any firm conclusions. An often overlooked contribution archaeology does make to the debate, however, is the evidence it provides for the remoulding of the topography of some elite ecclesiastical sites between the tenth and the twelfth centuries.[43] Kilkenny provides a good example. Here excavations have demonstrated that the innermost enclosure ditch was backfilled in the late ninth century to accommodate the expansion into the *sanctus* of the ecclesiastical settlement of a craftworking quarter, which endured into the twelfth century.[44] The presence of craftworkers in the sacred core is a strong indication that their work was seen as a central activity in the church settlement and can be taken to entail that a cohort of the resident population here were involved in a diversity of non-agricultural and non-ecclesiastical occupations. Similar activity has been recorded on other church settlements, such as downslope of the church core at Downpatrick and at Clonmacnoise where a street of tenth- to twelfth-century craft-workers' dwellings was excavated.[45] The topographical changes, occurring as they did in parallel with substantial investment in the construction of monumental structures in the sacred cores, can therefore be seen as a material response to a new economic imperative.

Defining what exactly the aforementioned economic imperative may have been is still the key unanswered question, notwithstanding recent attempts to shift to more non-economic, anthropologically-based index for what constituted a theoretical non-Viking, pre-Anglo-Norman town.[46] Defining the socio-economic basis of the major church settlements remains a key challenge that needs to be overcome. Occupational diversity of the kind noted above is considered by some as the key 'urban touchstone' for defining a medieval town.[47] But the experiences of religious power-houses like Clonmacnoise, Glendalough and Clonfert — none of which was subjected to Anglo-Norman market-based urbanisation and none of which became a town after the conquest — would tend to suggest that over-and-above all other factors it was the degree to which the ecclesiastical centres had generated commercial settlements that made or arrested any urban trajectory they may have been on. Demonstrating, however, that commerce and trade were central functions of a church settlement in a non-monetary world where virtually everything that would have been marketed was perishable and thus generally undetectable using conventional archaeological investigation techniques, is highly problematical. While large-scale excavations at these major religious centres would of course be valuable in this regard, perhaps more direct answers will come in the future from the developing field of 'nano-archaeology', whereby molecular-scale analysis of archaeological deposits is used to recreate past land-uses.[48] Such techniques might, it is hoped, be able to identify market places, commercial structures and trade and marketing activities that have heretofore been invisible, from their residual chemical signatures.

CHURCH ENCLOSURES AND STREETS

Much of our understanding of the scale and extent of the elite church settlements, their layouts and how some were subsequently integrated into Anglo-Norman town plans is based on the premise that curvilinear alignments in the street patterns and property boundaries of town cores mirror the circuits of the former ecclesiastical enclosures.[49] In recent years, however, a note of caution around this methodology has been introduced to the effect that in some cases such correlations could be more apparent than real.[50] Adding to the air of uncertainty is the lack of any correlation between certain ecclesiastical enclosures that have been excavated and the contemporary street patterns at towns where the phenomenon has been suggested, for example at Kilkenny and Kells (previously mentioned), and Armagh.[51] Furthermore, when excavations have defined the circuits of ecclesiastical enclosures, as at Downpatrick, Dunshaughlin, Ferns, Taghmon and Trim, they have also shown no relation to the street layout.[52] Only at Lusk, Co. Dublin has there been a demonstrable association between the street pattern and an excavated *vallum*.[53] What could go some way to explaining the lack of agreement would be if the excavated enclosures had been superseded by later boundaries and it is the latter that are reflected in the street pattern. But again excavations on and near these streets suggest otherwise. For example, despite extensive excavations on the supposed line of the outer enclosure at Vicar Street, Kilkenny, no evidence for a ditch was forthcoming.[54] Likewise, excavations alongside the curving street alignments that are thought to mark the *vallum* around the ecclesiastical settlement of *Dubhlinn*, Dublin have yet to uncover any indications of a pre-Anglo-Norman ecclesiastical enclosure to correlate with the street pattern.[55] Continuity in the use of a *vallum* into the Anglo-Norman period has been established thus far at only two sites — Downpatrick and Stephen Street Upper/Longford Street Great, Dublin.[56] Elsewhere ditches were backfilled before the twelfth century and, as this was generally achieved by pushing the bank into the ditch, the enclosures must have had little or no topographical expression by the time the Anglo-Norman towns were being laid out, making it less likely that they would have been integrated into the street pattern.[57] Another factor that must also be recognised, in some instances at least, is the natural topography, for where church sites are located on hills the curving street pattern may simply reflect natural axes of movement around these heights. In sum, rather than assuming that curvilinear elements around early church cores in towns represent former enclosure circuits, a more nuanced, site-specific, methodology is required, one that takes into account the results of archaeological excavations and the local physical topography.

From church settlements to Anglo-Norman towns

The third, and final, questions to be addressed are what was the topography of the first colonial sites and how were they were knitted into the pre-existing church settlements? At the pre-Anglo-Norman ecclesiastical settlements there is little to suggest that any substantive changes occurred in the immediate aftermath of the conquest: the initial Anglo-Norman settlements seem to have been generally sited at some remove from the church cores, church buildings were retained and Gaelic bishops were left *in situ*. Nevertheless portions of the cross-lands would have had to be appropriated for the new settlements, whether by the sword or by way of accords with the Gaelic church authorities. It is also generally held that the supposed endurance of ecclesiastical precincts in the modern street plans is representative of their precincts being respected and accommodated in the Anglo-Norman town layouts, which were simply grafted onto the earlier church sites. In the light of uncertainties around defining the enclosure circuits set out above, however, this may not in fact have been the case and it is of note that at Kilkenny the *vallum* was probably cut across by the thirteenth-century town wall. A similar scenario may also have occurred at Kildare.

A direct legacy of the halting beginnings of Anglo-Norman urbanisation is that little is known about the form and layout and even the precise locations of the earliest Anglo-Norman settlements. Archaeological excavations have, thus far, presented little more than glimpses of the incipient Anglo-Norman urban landscapes and the impression they provide is that, outside the Hiberno-Norse port towns, the first foundations were little more than military strongholds centred on earth-and-timber 'colonisation' castles. On the other hand the archaeological evidence from Downpatrick indicates that they were not necessarily always based around a castle. There is also nothing to indicate that these primary settlements had any substantive economic functions and characterising them as towns before the late twelfth/early thirteenth century is, in the absence of evidence to the contrary, probably unrealistic. It is not until the first decade of the thirteenth century that we can be confident that true towns are present (outside the Hiberno-Norse ports), when a massive injection of baronial capital created the bulk of Ireland's medieval urban landscape.

Notes

[1] Based on the list of Anglo-Norman towns in John Bradley, 'Planned Anglo-Norman towns in Ireland', in H.B. Clarke and Anngret Simms (eds), *The comparative history of urban origins in non-Roman Europe* (2 pts, Oxford, 1985), pp 447–55; see Heather Swanson, *Medieval British towns* (Basingstoke, 1999), p. 15. The figure of twenty-three towns with preceding early medieval church settlements was arrived at by comparing Bradley's list with the database of early medieval church settlements compiled by the Monasticon Hibernicum project, https://monasticon.celt.dias.ie/index.php (last accessed 9 Mar. 2017), the relevant entries in the recorded monuments and places registers and a range of secondary sources. The figure excludes the five Hiberno-Norse towns. The twenty-three towns are (in alphabetical order): Athy (Ardreigh), Cashel, Castledermot, Coleraine, Downpatrick, Duleek, Dungarvan, Enniscorthy (possible), Ferns, Fethard, Gowran (possible), Kells, Kildare, Kilkenny, Kilmallock, Kinsale, Naas (possible), Nenagh (possible), New Ross, Roscommon, Thomastown, Trim and Youghal. There are also many instances of medieval boroughs that never became developed towns, for example — Dundrum, Co. Dublin and Dunshaughlin, Co. Meath — that were also founded on earlier church sites, but these lie outside the scope of this essay.

[2] Andrews, IHTA, no. 1, *Kildare*; Bradley, IHTA, no. 10, *Kilkenny*; Simms with Simms, IHTA, no. 4, *Kells*; Buchanan and Wilson, IHTA, no. 8, *Downpatrick*. Two other fascicles, Fethard and Trim, could also be included but little is known about their early medieval church settlements: O'Keeffe, *Fethard*, IHTA, no. 13; Hennessy, IHTA, no. 14, *Trim*.

[3] Adrian Empey, 'The evolution of the demesne in the lordship of Leinster: the fortunes of war or forward planning?', in John Bradley, Cóilín Ó Drisceoil and Michael Potterton (eds), *William Marshal and Ireland* (Dublin, 2017), pp 45, 54, 71.

[4] John Bradley, 'Archaeology, topography and building fabric: the cathedral and town of medieval Kildare', in *Journal of the County Kildare Archaeological Society*, xix (2000), pp 27–47.

[5] Andrews, *Kildare*, p. 1.

[6] Thomas, ii, p. 125. Archaeological excavations along the projected line of the town wall have thus far failed to identify its date of construction.

[7] Bradley, 'Archaeology, topography and building fabric', p. 38.

[8] Bradley, *Kilkenny*, p. 1.

[9] John Bradley and Ben Murtagh, 'William Marshal's charter to Kilkenny 1207: background, dating and witnesses', in Bradley, Ó Drisceoil and Potterton, *William Marshal and Ireland*, pp 206–8.

[10] Cóilín Ó Drisceoil, 'Probing the past: a geophysical survey at St Canice's Cathedral', in *Old Kilkenny Review*, no. 56 (2004), pp 86–7.

[11] Cóilín Ó Drisceoil, 'Archaeological monitoring report: Saint Canice's Cathedral Graveyard (RMP KK 19-026171), Kilkenny City (13E15)' (unpublished report, Kilkenny Archaeology, 2013), p. 73.

[12] Cóilín Ó Drisceoil, 'Archaeological assessment report: proposed carpark development at the Deanery Orchard, St Canice's Cathedral, Kilkenny City (06E0306)' (unpublished report, Kilkenny Archaeology, 2006).

[13] Cóilín Ó Drisceoil, 'Excavation and archaeological building survey at the robing room, Heritage Council headquarters (former Bishop's Palace), Church Lane, Kilkenny 2011 and 2012 (11E157)' (unpublished report, Kilkenny Archaeology, 2013), pp 36–7.

[14] Ibid., pp 51–88.

[15] Ó Drisceoil, 'Archaeological assessment report: proposed carpark development at the Deanery Orchard'; Ó Drisceoil, 'Excavation and archaeological building survey at the robing room', pp 46–7.

[16] Ben Murtagh, 'The Kilkenny Castle Archaeological Project, 1990–93, interim report', in *Old Kilkenny Review*, iv, no. 5 (1993), pp 1108–10.

[17] Empey, 'The evolution of the demesne', pp 45, 64. Bradley has also suggested that the burgage in question could have been situated in the Irishtown of Kilkenny and may have been of pre-Anglo-Norman date, see John Bradley, 'The Irish Historic Towns Atlas as a source for urban history', in H.B. Clarke, Jacinta Prunty and Mark Hennessy (eds), *Surveying Ireland's past: multidisciplinary essays in honour of Anngret Simms* (Dublin, 2004), p. 730.

[18] See Empey, 'The evolution of the demesne', p. 55.

[19] Bradley and Murtagh, 'William Marshal's charter to Kilkenny', p. 215; Bradley, 'The Irish Historic Towns Atlas as a source', p. 744.

[20] Empey, 'The evolution of the demesne', p. 65.

[21] Murtagh, 'The Kilkenny Castle Archaeological Project', pp 1108–10; Ben Murtagh, 'William Marshal's great tower at Pembroke, Wales: a view from Ireland', in Bradley, Ó Drisceoil and Potterton, *William Marshal and Ireland*, pp 172–3.

[22] It is possible that the borough was in place by the late twelfth century, to judge by excavations at No. 1 Irishtown, which uncovered a structural timber, possibly from a house, that was dated by dendrochronology to 1177–8 and a late twelfth-century house of post-and-wattle construction (I.W. Doyle, 'River Nore (Kilkenny City) drainage scheme: archaeological excavations at rear of No. 1 Irishtown, Kilkenny (02E1592)' (unpublished report, Margaret Gowen and Co. Ltd, 2004), p. 67).

[23] Cóilín Ó Drisceoil, 'Excavations at Talbot's Tower, Ormonde Road, Kilkenny City 2007–12 (E3646): final report' (unpublished report, Kilkenny Archaeology, 2017).

[24] Bradley and Murtagh, 'William Marshal's charter to Kilkenny', pp 201–48.

[25] Gerry O'Keeffe, 'St Francis Abbey 1230–1630: a history and archaeology of Kilkenny's conventual Franciscans', in *Old Kilkenny Review*, no. 68 (2016), pp 5–56.

[26] Oxford Archaeology, *Kilkenny city walls conservation plan* (Kilkenny, 2003), p. 19.

[27] Paul Stevens, 'Four excavations in Kilkenny City (1999–2001): part 1 the medieval findings', in *Old Kilkenny Review*, no. 58 (2006), pp 56–9.

[28] Empey, 'The evolution of the demesne', p. 75.

[29] Simms with Simms, *Kells*, p. 1; for an alternative interpretation of the topographical information contained in the Kells 'charters', see Colmán Etchingham, 'The organisation and function of an early Irish church settlement: what was Glendalough?', in Charles Doherty, Linda Doran and Mary Kelly (eds), *Glendalough: city of God* (Dublin, 2011), pp 50–52.

[30] Gretta Byrne, 'Kells, Townparks, Meath', in *Excavations, 1987*, no. 41; Gretta Byrne, 'Kells, Townparks, Meath', in *Excavations, 1988*, no. 57; Fintan Walsh, 'Church Street, Townparks, Kells', in *Excavations, 2010*, no. 523; Fintan Walsh, 'Interim excavation report for Church Street, Kells, Co. Meath' (unpublished report, Irish Archaeological Consultancy Ltd, 2015), pp 8–9, fig. 3. Thanks to Fintan Walsh for providing a copy of this report.

[31] Thomas, ii, p. 122; see Eoin Halpin, 'Climber Hall/Canon Street, Kells, Meath', in *Excavations, 2001*, no. 980.

[32] N.F. Brannon, 'Life and death in an early monastery: Cathedral Hill, Downpatrick, Co. Down', in Ann Hamlin and C.J. Lynn (eds), *Pieces of the past: archaeological excavations by the Department of the Environment for Northern Ireland, 1970–1986* (Belfast, 1988), p. 62; N.F. Brannon, 'Downpatrick, demesne of Down', in *Excavations, 1986*, no. 19.

[33] N.F. Brannon, 'Archaeological excavations at Cathedral Hill, Downpatrick, 1987', in *Lecale Miscellany*, vi (1988), p. 6.

[34] Brannon, 'Life and death in an early monastery', p. 62.

[35] J.F. Rankin, *Down Cathedral, the church of St Patrick of Down* (Belfast, 1997), p. 2.

[36] Philip McDonald, *Data structure report: geophysical survey and excavation at the Mound*

of Down, County Down, 2012 (Licence AE/12/29) (Belfast, 2012), pp 33–5; see T.E. McNeill, *Carrickfergus Castle* (Belfast, 1981), pp 3, 42. Thanks to Colm Donnelly (CAF, QUB) for answering queries on the report.

[37] N.F. Brannon, '"The Grove" Downpatrick, demesne of Down', in *Excavations, 1986*, no. 20.

[38] Eoin Halpin, 'Cathedral Hill, Downpatrick, Co. Down', in *Excavations, 1998*, no. 115.

[39] Thomas, ii, p. 70.

[40] Kilkenny, Kells, Downpatrick and Kildare are given as examples of monastic towns in John Bradley, 'Recent archaeological research on the Irish town', in Helmut Jäger (ed.), *Stadtkernforschung* (Cologne and Vienna, 1987), pp 330–31; and John Bradley, 'The monastic town of Clonmacnoise', in H.A. King (ed.), *Clonmacnoise studies 1* (Dublin, 1998), p. 50.

[41] Brian Graham, 'Beyond the fascicles: spatial form and social process', in H.B. Clarke and Sarah Gearty (eds), *Maps and texts: exploring the Irish Historic Towns Atlas* (Dublin, 2013), p. 261.

[42] Etchingham, 'The organisation and function of an early Irish church settlement', pp 38–53.

[43] Aidan O'Sullivan *et al.*, *Early medieval Ireland, AD 400–1100, the evidence from archaeological excavations* (Dublin, 2013), pp 148, 202.

[44] Ó Drisceoil, 'Archaeological assessment report: proposed carpark development at the Deanery Orchard'.

[45] H.A. King, 'The economy and industry of early medieval Clonmacnoise: a preliminary view', in Nancy Edwards (ed.), *The archaeology of the early medieval Celtic churches* (Leeds, 2009), pp 333–49.

[46] Edel Bhreathnach, *Ireland in the medieval world AD 400–1000: landscape, kingship and religion* (Dublin, 2014), pp 26–30.

[47] Grenville Astill, 'Medieval towns and urbanisation', in Roberta Gilchrist and Andrew Reynolds (eds), *Reflections: 50 years of medieval archaeology* (Oxford, 2009), p. 256.

[48] Martin Carver, *Making archaeology happen, design versus dogma* (California, 2011), pp 49–52.

[49] Jacinta Prunty, 'Religion', in Clarke and Gearty, *Maps and texts*, p. 123; and D.L. Swan, 'Monastic proto-towns in early medieval Ireland: the evidence of aerial photography, plan analysis and survey', in Clarke and Simms, *Comparative history of urban origins*, pp 77–102; Bradley, 'Monastic town of Clonmacnoise', p. 45. Broader studies of the organisation and function of sacred space at early medieval ecclesiastical settlements are also heavily reliant on such interpretations: for example, D.H. Jenkins, *'Holy, holier, holiest': the sacred topography of the early medieval Irish church* (Turnhout, 2010), pp 54–100; Clare Crowley, 'Sanctuary and symbolism: the origins of the curvilinear plan-form at Clondalkin, Co. Dublin', in Seán Duffy (ed.), *Medieval Dublin X* (Dublin, 2010), pp 13–48.

[50] Paul Gosling, 'Kildare and Tuam', in Clarke and Gearty, *Maps and texts*, pp 62, 64.

[51] Kilkenny: Ó Drisceoil, 'Archaeological assessment report: proposed carpark development at the Deanery Orchard'; 'Excavation and archaeological building survey at the robing room', pp 45–8; Bradley, 'Irish Historic Towns Atlas as a source', pp 729, 744. Kells: Byrne, 'Kells, Townparks, Meath', no. 41; Byrne, 'Kells, Townparks, Meath', no. 57; Walsh, 'Church Street, Townparks, Kells', no. 523; 'Interim excavation report for Church Street', pp 8–9, fig. 3. Armagh: Cynthia Gaskell Brown *et al.*, 'Excavations on Cathedral Hill, Armagh, 1968', in *UJA*, 3rd ser., xlvii (1984), p. 112; D.P. Hurl and Audrey Gahan, 'Excavations in Abbey Street, Armagh', in *UJA*, 3rd ser., lxii (2003), fig. 1, pp 107, 109.

[52] Downpatrick: Brannon, 'Life and death in an early monastery', p. 63. Trim: Matthew Seaver, 'The earliest archaeological evidence for an ecclesiastical site at Trim, Co. Meath',

in Christiaan Corlett and Michael Potterton (eds), *The church in early medieval Ireland: in the light of recent archaeological excavations* (Bray, 2014), pp 241–2. Dunshaughlin: Linzi Simpson, 'The ecclesiastical enclosure at Dunshaughlin, Co. Meath: some dating evidence', in Tom Condit and Christiaan Corlett (eds), *Above and beyond: essays in memory of Leo Swan* (Bray, 2005), pp 233–5. Taghmon: I.W. Doyle, '"Telling the dancer from the dance": the archaeology of early medieval Wexford', in I.W. Doyle and Bernard Browne (eds), *Medieval Wexford: essays in memory of Billy Colfer* (Dublin, 2016), fig. 3.4. Ferns: Doyle, 'Telling the dancer from the dance', fig. 3.8.

[53] Lusk: Aidan O'Connell, 'The early church in Fingal: evidence from Church Road, Lusk, Co. Dublin', in Corlett and Potterton, *The church in early medieval Ireland*, p. 176.

[54] Colm Flynn, 'Archaeological test trenching interim report Kilkenny central access scheme' (unpublished report, Valerie J. Keeley Ltd, 2014); Paul Stevens, 'St Canice's Place/Vicar Street', in *Excavations 1999*, no. 453.

[55] Linzi Simpson, 'Pre-Viking and early Viking Age Dublin: research questions', in Duffy, *Medieval Dublin X*, pp 56–7.

[56] Brannon, 'Life and death in an early monastery', p. 63; Tim Taylor and Mick Aston, 'Time Team dig Cathedral Hill', in *Lecale Miscellany*, xvi (1998), p. 35; Simpson, 'Pre-Viking and early Viking Age Dublin', p. 57.

[57] Kilkenny: south ditch backfilled before late ninth century (Ó Drisceoil, 'Archaeological assessment report: proposed carpark development at the Deanery Orchard'); north ditch backfilled eleventh to mid-twelfth century (Ó Drisceoil, 'Excavation and archaeological building survey at the robing room', pp 25–8). Kells: ditch contained a seventh-century brooch (Byrne, 'Kells, Townparks, Meath', no. 41; Byrne, 'Kells, Townparks, Meath', no. 57). Armagh: bank pushed into ditch after 130–600 cal. A.D. (Gaskell Brown *et al.*, 'Excavations on Cathedral Hill, Armagh', pp 109, 112–17, 156–8). Trim: ditch backfilled and paved over by Anglo-Norman road on a different alignment (Seaver, 'Earliest archaeological evidence for an ecclesiastical site at Trim', p. 241). Dunshaughlin: bank levelled into the ditch between ninth to tenth centuries and eleventh to mid-twelfth century (Simpson, 'Ecclesiastical enclosure at Dunshaughlin', pp 233–5). Pre-Anglo-Norman backfilling of enclosure ditches has also been recorded at, for example, Clonfad, Co. Westmeath (Paul Stevens and John Channing, *Settlement and community in the Fir Tulach kingdom: archaeological excavations on the M6 and N52 road schemes* (Dublin, 2012), pp 126–35); Clonmacnoise, Co. Offaly (Donald Murphy, 'Excavation of an early monastic enclosure at Clonmacnoise', in King, *Clonmacnoise studies 2*, pp 13, 26); and Lackenavorna, Co. Tipperary (Conleth Manning, 'The excavation of the Early Christian enclosure of Killederdadrum in Lackenavorna, Co. Tipperary', in *RIA Proc.*, lxxxiv C (1984), pp 242, 268).

8. Anglo-Norman towns based on castles

Margaret Murphy

The role of the castle as an instrument and symbol of domination across medieval Europe is well known. In Ireland, as in England, Scotland and Wales, the castle was, in the words of Rees Davies, the 'visible sign of a new dispensation and a foreign lordship'.[1] Domination of the landscape was almost invariably the first step in a settlement sequence that was geared towards maximum economic exploitation of local resources. Town foundation was an important element in this sequence and the Anglo-Normans were particularly committed to the dual plantation of castles and towns. Between 1066 and 1100 80% of the towns planted in England had a castle while in Wales a similar percentage of towns founded during the medieval period had a castle. In Ireland at least 70% of the urban centres founded by the Anglo-Normans developed around a castle core.[2]

The published IHTAs provide an excellent resource for the examination of Anglo-Norman towns based on castles, allowing the comparative analysis of towns such as Athlone, Carlingford, Carrickfergus, Kilkenny, Mullingar and Trim.[3] In examining the origins and development of these castle towns a number of research questions can be posed. To what extent were castles and towns 'planned' as a unit? How did the connection between the castle (a lordly or royal entity) and the town (a commercial community) evolve? What was the relationship between town defences and castle fortifications?

The variety of inter-relationships between castles and towns is reflected in the range of sources that have been used by the authors of the fascicles mentioned above. The earliest reference to a castle usually comes from an entry in the Gaelic annals or from contemporary chronicle sources such as the *Expugnatio Hibernica* of Gerald of Wales or the anonymous *The deeds of the Normans in Ireland*. This evidence can be combined with archaeological findings or analysis of architectural features, either on the surviving fabric of the castle or as shown on early drawings and maps. It is often more problematic to date the origins of the town and the precise topographical relationship between the castle and the earliest urban development. Borough charters or references to burgesses and burgage plots in early grants can assist, but a town might have been in existence some time before a formal charter was issued. Charter collections such as the *Liber primus Kilkenniensis* allow the evolving relationship between castle and town to be studied but sources of this type are rare.[4] One connection that can be studied is the relationship between town and castle fortifications where the evidence from documentary sources, such as murage charters, can be combined with pre-Ordnance Survey maps and drawings to shed light on this area.

Those working on the relationships between castles and towns continue to use the categorisation first proposed by Christopher Drage in 1987.[5] Drage distinguished between what he called 'urban castles' — those that were imposed upon existing urban centres and functioned as instruments of oppression — and what he called primary castles or castle boroughs — where a castle built in a non-urban area attracted a secondary borough or where castle and borough were planned as an integrated unit. While there are some examples in Ireland of castles imposed upon an existing urban centre, for example Dublin and Limerick, it was much more common for a castle to be built in a non-urban area on a site that subsequently attracted non-military settlement. By the time the initial earth and timber castle was replaced by a stone keep or donjon, an incipient town was already

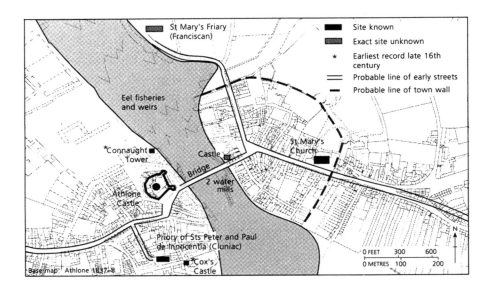

Fig. 8.1 *Athlone*, fig. 1, medieval Athlone with conjectural location of Ua Conchobair's castle.

taking shape in its shadow. Indeed in most cases, although this can be difficult to prove definitely, it seems that the lord planned castle and borough as a complementary unit.[6]

THE CASTLE SITE

The choice of castle site was first and foremost governed by strategic and military considerations. These might be primarily local, as at Carlingford where the castle was designed to defend a narrow pass at the foot of the mountains, or at Athlone, Kilkenny and Trim where the castles were tactically sited to guard important river crossings. Wider regional concerns could also come into play. The motte built by the Petits close to the ford over the River Brosna at Mullingar was one in a line of protective fortifications across the north-west of de Lacy's lordship of Meath.[7]

The strategic advantages of these sites are likely to have already attracted strongholds of some kind, but in no case can it be said definitively that the Anglo-Normans built on top of earlier fortifications. *The deeds of the Normans in Ireland* relates that Hugh de Lacy 'fortified a dwelling at Trim', leaving open the possibility that his castle was built on the site of an existing structure.[8] There is a suggestion that Kilkenny Castle was built on the site of an earlier Mac Gilla Pátraic residence, mentioned in the annals and *The deeds of the Normans in Ireland*.[9] At the time the Kilkenny atlas was published, archaeological evidence appeared to substantiate this claim but this has subsequently been questioned.[10] The presence of an Ua Conchobair 'castle' at Athlone is recorded several times in the Irish annals, but the location is unknown and it has been suggested that it was on the opposite side of the River Shannon to the Anglo-Norman castle (Fig. 8.1).[11] The features that gave strategic importance to a site — river crossings and routeways — were also likely to convey commercial benefits and these opportunities were quickly seized by the Anglo-Norman castle builders.

THE DEVELOPMENT OF THE TOWN

Thompson proposed the idea of the castle as 'midwife' to the town to describe the process whereby the castle brought a town into being.[12] The birthing process could be quick or lengthy and it is rarely possible to ascertain how many years might elapse between the foundation of a castle and the development of its dependent town. Documentary and/or archaeological evidence is rarely definitive. The earliest specific reference to a town might be the borough charter but a chance reference to a burgess in an earlier document frequently suggests that, by the time a charter was issued, the urban settlement had been in existence for some time. William Marshal's charter to Kilkenny dates to 1207 but there is a reference to a burgess living close to the castle in 1176.[13] At Carlingford and Trim there are references to burgesses and burgages very soon after the earliest castles were built.[14]

Lords might deliberately set out to attract settlers using the lure of the protection provided by the castle, but even without this the building of the castle inevitably attracted labourers and craftsmen, along with those who might supply or transport stone, timber and lead. The military community of the castle and the civilian community who clustered at the castle gate needed to be supplied with victuals, clothing and fuel. These commercial opportunities tempted others to join the embryonic settlement.

Subsequent development hampers the identification of these early 'castle-gate' settlements, but Carrickfergus might provide an example of a process that happened at a number of castle towns. John de Courcy started the first phase of building at Carrickfergus between 1178 and 1190 when a stone keep protected by two curtain walls was constructed on the southern end of Fergus's Rock, the dolerite promontory that projects into the northern shore of Belfast Lough.[15] The foundation by de Courcy of the large parish church of St Nicholas 200 m to the north-west of the castle leaves no doubt as to his intention to plan an urban settlement, but development around the church may have been slow to take off. It is likely that for the first decades following the building of the castle the remaining part of Fergus's Rock was occupied by a civilian population, who depended on

Fig. 8.2 Conjectural reconstruction of Carrickfergus Castle, *c.* 1210, by Philip Armstrong © Crown Department for Communities.

the castle for security and in turn fulfilled an important role in servicing the castle and its inhabitants. Such a settlement, including perhaps a market area, may have been protected by a timber palisade as in Philip Armstrong's reconstruction (Fig. 8.2).

Hugh de Lacy took over the castle in 1227 and between this date and 1242 the rest of the promontory was enclosed by stone walls to form an outer castle ward.[16] This doubled the area of the castle and included the construction of two polygonal towers at the west and a twin-towered gatehouse at the north. The castle now occupied the whole of Fergus's Rock and the civilian settlement was displaced, its inhabitants perhaps moving to the area outside the new gateway. Early maps of Carrickfergus, such as that by Lythe, appear to show a cluster of castle-gate dwellings surviving into the sixteenth century (Fig. 8.3).

While the gates of Carrickfergus Castle faced in towards the town, the twin bastioned entrance gate at Kilkenny was placed in the south wall of the castle, preventing direct access to the castle from the town.[17] The castle, like St Canice's Church 750 m to the north, was built on a knoll overlooking a fording place on the River Nore. A settlement that was to become known as Irishtown was already spreading southwards from the church. The Anglo-Norman town was vigorously promoted by William Marshal and his sons and started to spread from the northern wall of the castle down to the present James's Street (Fig. 7.4).

By the first decade of the thirteenth century the town was starting to expand to the east and south, but expansion to the north was halted

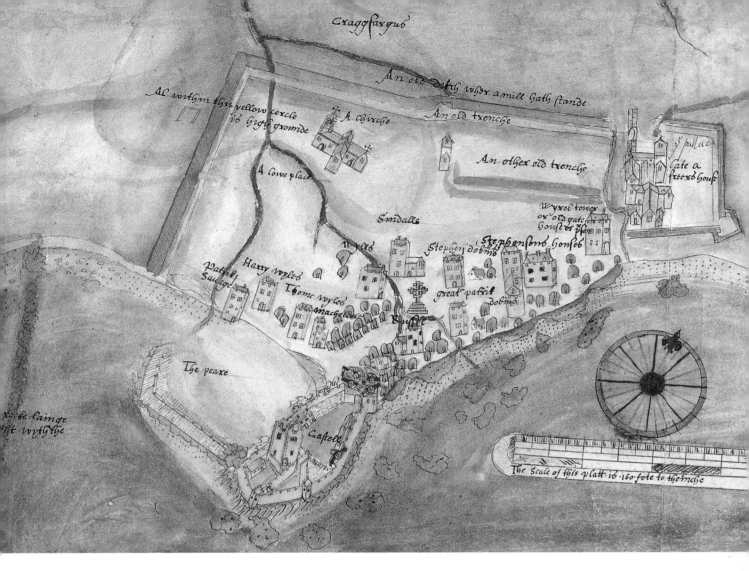

The map contains the following handwritten labels:

Craggfargus

An old Ditch wher a mill hath stande

Al within this yellow cercle is high grounde

A Chirche

An old trenche

Another old trenche

y palac

Gate a frersh house

A cove place

Smdalle

W. yrol tower or old gate house or pfon

Stephen dobins

Stephensons Houses

Wyled

great patrik dobins

Harry wyled

Patrik Sauuage

Thome wyled macgleen

Ryull

The peare

Rocke Raunge yt wyth lye

Castell

The Scale of this platt is 160 fote to the inche

Fig. 8.3 *Carrickfergus*, map 5, 1567, by Robert Lythe. Trinity College Dublin, MS 1209/26, extract.

because the land between James's Street and the River Breagagh belonged to the bishop of Ossory. What happened next might have remained a mystery were it not for the survival of a seventeenth-century transcript of a charter contained in the long-lost White Book of the bishops of Ossory.[18] This charter records that in 1207 the bishop of Ossory, in return for some other lands, agreed to give William Marshal the land that he needed to expand his town. This chance survival allows us a glimpse of the process whereby the castle builder sought actively to promote the developing urban settlement.

At Trim the town was formally established in *c.* 1194 by Walter de Lacy, son of Hugh the builder of the castle, although it is clear that an urban settlement was already in existence by this date. The town developed in a number of stages and this is reflected in the town plan, which the atlas describes as a 'composite of a number of plan units'.[19] The earliest

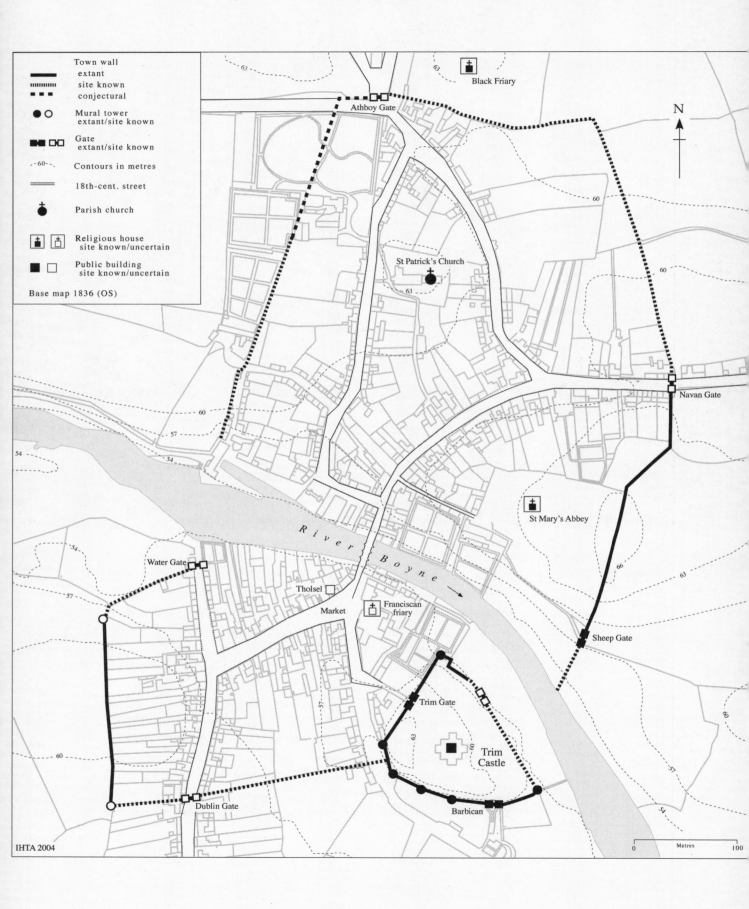

Town wall
    extant
    site known
    conjectural

● ○ Mural tower
    extant/site known

Gate
    extant/site known

−60− Contours in metres

18th-cent. street

Parish church

Religious house
site known/uncertain

Public building
site known/uncertain

Base map 1836 (OS)

N

Black Friary

St Patrick's Church

Athboy Gate

60

60

Navan Gate

St Mary's Abbey

66

River Boyne

Water Gate

Tholsel

Market

Franciscan friary

Sheep Gate

Trim Gate

Trim Castle

Dublin Gate

Barbican

IHTA 2004

Metres
0   100

Fig. 8.4 *Trim*, fig. 3, *c.* 1200 to *c.* 1600.

Anglo-Norman development was close to the castle on the south side of the river and this unit contained the market place, reflecting the desire of the de Lacys to foster a market near their power base (Fig. 8.4). Settlement also developed across the river where Hugh de Lacy had patronised St Mary's Abbey and where the parish church was also situated. Over time the settlement north of the bridge expanded to cover over twice the area as that on the south side. As a result, the castle came to occupy a peripheral position in the town. A somewhat similar development is seen at Athlone where construction of the stone castle was commenced by the Irish justiciar in 1210. The castle provided protection from the west for the town, which grew up under royal patronage initially on both sides of the River Shannon (Fig. 8.1). A later reference to the bridge lying 'between the castle and the town' suggests that over time growth on the east bank outstripped that on the west.[20]

Changes in the proprietorship of the castle could also have an impact on the way the town developed in relationship to the fortification. At Carlingford, which was initially developed by Walter de Lacy, the H-plan of the town resembled that at Trim. At Carlingford, however, this plan served to separate the market place from the castle and this may have been encouraged by the fact that the castle came under royal control in 1210, while the town remained in the hands of the landlord (Fig. 8.5).[21]

Occasionally the relationship between castle and town is not easy to discern. At Mullingar the town grew up behind the motte-and-bailey castle built by the Petits (Fig. 8.6). It is difficult to determine whether this was what the Petits envisaged or to ascertain how close the relationship was between the new settlement and the castle.[22] There is no evidence, for example, of a route or thoroughfare between the main street and the castle.

CASTLE AND TOWN DEFENCES

Town walls, gates and mural towers tend to be among the best documented features of medieval towns, as is evidenced by section **12** Defence in the topographical information included in the IHTA. In late medieval Ireland security was an issue for both municipal and central authorities and a variety of administrative sources contain petitions about town walls and grants of murage to allow taxes to be levied for the repair of existing defences or construction of new ones. Town walls are frequently depicted on early maps and plans (Figs 8.5, 8.6). Furthermore, many towns still have surviving sections of their medieval walls and in recent times a number of conservation plans have been drawn up to record and preserve these remains.[23]

In the first half of the thirteenth century Anglo-Norman towns confidently expanded from under the protective shadow of the castle that had given birth to them. Earthen defences may have been constructed to provide some security and to define the urban area from the surrounding countryside. Lords encouraged this move as tolls were more easily collected when points of entry to the urban area were limited. (At Carlingford, there is a mention of a gate as early as 1210–11, although this may have been one of the castle gates.[24]) By the second half of the thirteenth century, however, in the face of increasing attacks from the Gaelic Irish and strife between Anglo-Norman barons, the need for stronger stone defences was recognised by town and castle lords.

Many of these towns and castles had a role in the wider defence of their regions and some were key to the security of the whole Anglo-Norman enterprise in Ireland. Trim was one such town and this was acknowledged in 1290 when Geoffrey de Geneville was given a seven-year grant to impose customs on goods coming into Trim in aid of enclosing the town 'for the greater security of Ireland'.[25] The stone wall subsequently built at Trim was carefully integrated with the castle defences. The completed wall, which enclosed an area of about 23 hectares, was over 2 km long and included a 200 m section of the castle wall (Fig. 8.4).[26]

At Kilkenny the walls of Hightown enclosed an area of about 28 hectares and also linked up with the castle defences.[27] Eleven known murage grants for the construction of the walls around Hightown were made between 1250 and 1460, while references to the keeping of the gates in the fourteenth and fifteenth centuries are recorded in the *Liber primus Kilkenniensis*. The earliest grant of murage came at the request of the earl of Gloucester, who had recently come into ownership of the castle through the inheritance of his Marshal wife. He prayed the king 'to grant to his burgesses of Kilkenny a murage for seven years to enclose their vill'.[28] The southern section of the town wall ran in a straight line from the mural tower known as Talbot's Bastion across to meet and perhaps continue into the dry ditch that surrounded the castle.[29] Here Castle Gate was located and the last section of the town's defences was provided by the south side of the castle (Fig. 7.2).

Athlone, which was burnt on at least six occasions between 1218 and 1315, got a grant in 1251 to enclose the town and repair the castle.[30] It is presumed that the settlement on the east side of the river was walled at this time and that the line of the medieval walls can be reconstructed from the seventeenth-century rebuilding of defences (Fig. 8.1). In the later medieval period the castle was only nominally in the control of the Dublin

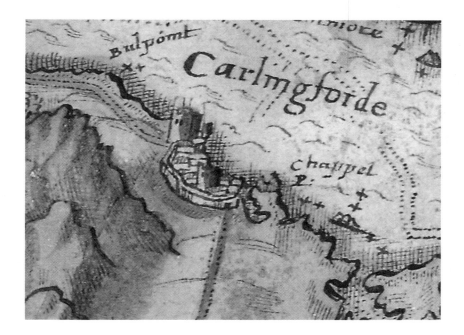

Fig. 8.5 *Carlingford*, map 6, by Richard Bartlett, *c.* 1602. National Library of Ireland, MS 2656 (1), extract.

administration and it is possible that the town all but disappeared after its burning in 1315.[31] There are signs of survival, however, not least in the fact that the settlement was capable of redevelopment when the area again came under government control in the seventeenth century.

At Carlingford the original earthen defences were replaced by stone in 1326 when a murage grant specified that a stone wall was to be built. The line of this wall can be traced from some documentary references and from surviving parts of a later wall.[32] The town wall began at the castle and there was a North Gate on Castle Hill, but the entrance to the castle was positioned outside the town wall so that it was not necessary to enter the town to visit the castle. The castle and town defences do not appear to have been conjoined as they were at Trim and Kilkenny and early maps, such as that of Richard Bartlett, show castle and walled town as separate entities (Fig. 8.5).

In late medieval Ireland the security considerations of town and castle lord or constable continued to coincide and there is later evidence of collaborative efforts to maintain, or sometimes begin, town defences. At Mullingar in 1583 the constable of the castle requested a murage grant for the town, which was described as 'lying open to all attempts'.[33] The citizens, he stressed, were willing to provide carriage and labour. It is impossible to say whether the fortifications were promptly built and to what extent the

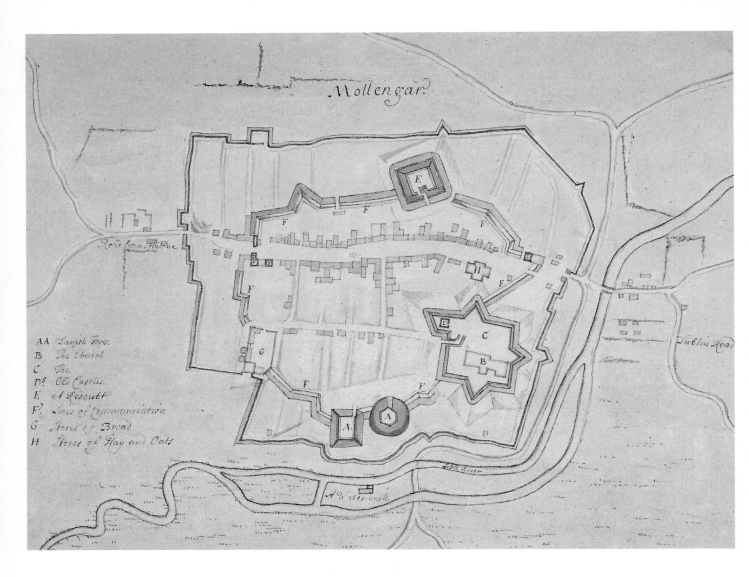

Mollengar

AA Danish Forts.
B The Church
C The
Ds Old Castles.
E A Redoubt
Fs Lines of Communication
G Store of Bread
H Stores of Hay and Oats

castle defences were integrated with them. Richards's 1691 map (Fig. 8.6) shows the motte and bailey at Mullingar (two massive structures labelled as Danish Forts) forming part of the Williamite fortifications.

Fig. 8.6 *Mullingar*, map 4, 1691, by Michael Richards. Worcester College, Oxford, MS YC 20, ccvi.

CASTLES AND TOWNS — A SYMBIOTIC RELATIONSHIP

The Anglo-Norman castle towns in Ireland shared similar origins. Lilley has described such towns as 'an expression of Norman ideology used not only to enable and enforce but to legitimize an essentially colonial settlement'.[34] Castles and towns were planted at strategically important locations where military and commercial considerations combined. Lords such as de Lacy, de Courcy and Marshal were economically ambitious and enthusiastically promoted the growth of urban centres adjacent to their castles.

The positioning of the castle and the role of the founder could significantly influence the layout and initial growth of the town, but they did not permanently determine its form or orientation. Towns developed in ways their original founder could not have envisaged. Over time, the relationships that developed between castle and town varied considerably, depending on a number of factors including the stability of lordship, the local topography and the role of the settlement in the wider region. The common need for security and the building of stone defences was one factor that frequently drew castle and town closer together again in the later thirteenth and the fourteenth centuries.

The relationship between the castle and the town it spawned was symbiotic. The castle provided protection and employment to the town from which it required labour, services and a market. When the burgesses of Kilkenny appointed municipal officers in 1231 they stressed that they were to be profitable to the lord as well as to the community.[35] In Kilkenny the protection provided by the lords of the castle, reflected in the connections between castle and town defences, allowed the town to flourish and to continue to function even when surrounded by a largely hostile hinterland. The town of Kilkenny benefited from the continuity of the Butlers of Ormond, which saw a resident lord in the castle up to the twentieth century. The fate of a town was intimately tied up with that of its castle and this could have negative as well as positive consequences. The town of Trim slipped from significance when there was no powerful lord resident in the castle.[36]

This essay has sought to examine and compare the origins and development of Anglo-Norman towns based on castles. The IHTA fascicles that facilitated this comparative study represent a significant resource for those seeking to carry out further work on aspects of this topic.

Notes

[1] R.R. Davies, *Domination and conquest: the experience of Ireland, Wales and Scotland 1100–1300* (Cambridge, 1990), p. 41.

[2] O.H. Creighton, *Castles and landscapes: power, community and fortification in medieval England* (London, 2005), p. 153; Brian Graham, 'Ireland: economy and society', in S.H. Rigby (ed.), *A companion to Britain in the later middle ages* (Oxford, 2003) p. 154.

[3] Robinson, IHTA, no. 2, *Carrickfergus*; Andrews with Davies, IHTA, no. 5, *Mullingar*; Murtagh, IHTA, no. 6, *Athlone*; Bradley, IHTA, no. 10, *Kilkenny*; Hennessy, IHTA, no. 14, *Trim*; O'Sullivan and Gillespie, IHTA, no. 23, *Carlingford*.

[4] *Kilkenny city records: Liber primus Kilkenniensis*, ed. Charles McNeill (IMC, Dublin, 1931).

[5] Christopher Drage, 'Urban castles', in John Schofield and Roger Leech (eds), *Urban archaeology in Britain* (London, 1987), pp 117–32.

[6] For a Europe-wide consideration, see Anngret Simms and H.B. Clarke (eds), *Lords and towns in medieval Europe: the European historic towns atlas project* (Farnham and Burlington, VT, 2015).

[7] Andrews with Davies, *Mullingar*, p. 1.

8 Evelyn Mulally (ed.), *The deeds of the Normans in Ireland: a new edition of the chronicle formerly known as the song of Dermot and the earl* (Dublin, 2002), p. 135; Hennessy, *Trim*, p. 2.

[9] Bradley, *Kilkenny*, pp 1, 8.

[10] Cóilín Ó Drisceoil *et al.*, 'The Kilkenny Archaeological Project (KKAP). Report for the Irish National Strategic Archaeological Research (INSTAR) Programme' (unpublished report, Kilkenny Archaeological Project, 2008), p. 81.

[11] Murtagh, *Athlone*, p. 1.

[12] M.W. Thompson, *The rise of the castle* (Cambridge, 1991), p. 145.

[13] Bradley, *Kilkenny*, p. 1.

[14] O'Sullivan and Gillespie, *Carlingford*, p. 1; Hennessy, *Trim*, p. 2.

[15] Robinson, *Carrickfergus*, p. 2.

[16] Ibid.

[17] Bradley, *Kilkenny*, p. 2.

[18] H.F. Berry, 'Ancient charters in the *Liber albus Ossoriensis*', in *RIA Proc.*, xxvii C (1907–9), p. 124.

[19] Hennessy, *Trim*, p. 2.

[20] Murtagh, *Athlone*, p. 2.

[21] O'Sullivan and Gillespie, *Carlingford*, p. 2.

[22] Andrews with Davies, *Mullingar*, p. 2.

[23] Oxford Archaeology, *Kilkenny city walls conservation plan* (Kilkenny, 2005); 'Trim town walls conservation plan' (unpublished report, Meath County Council and the Heritage Council, 2008).

[24] Ibid.

[25] *Cal. doc. Ire., 1285–92*, pp 277–8.

[26] Michael Potterton, *Medieval Trim* (Dublin, 2005), p. 182.

[27] Bradley, *Kilkenny*, p. 2.

[28] *Cal. doc. Ire., 1171–1251*, p. 112.

[29] *Kilkenny city walls conservation plan*, p. 128.

[30] *Cal. doc. Ire., 1171–1251*, p. 469.

[31] Murtagh, *Athlone*, p. 2.

[32] O'Sullivan and Gillespie, *Carlingford*, p. 2.

[33] Andrews with Davies, *Mullingar*, pp 2–3.

[34] K.D. Lilley, '*Non urbe, non vico, non castris*: territorial control and the colonization and urbanization of medieval Wales and Ireland under Anglo-Norman lordship', in *Journal of Historical Geography*, xxvi (2000), pp 517–31.

[35] *Liber primus*, p. 1.

[36] Potterton, *Medieval Trim*, p. 156.

9. Anglo-Norman towns based on coastal and riverine trading activity

Andy Halpin

This essay focuses on four Anglo-Norman towns — Dublin,[1] Dundalk,[2] Limerick[3] and Carlingford,[4] although Dublin and Limerick were, of course, urban settlements long before the Anglo-Norman conquest. As Anglo-Norman settlements these four towns share in a relatively rich (by Irish standards) heritage of surviving documentary sources for the period 1170–1600. The late John Bradley demonstrated almost forty years ago the relative wealth of documentary sources available for Drogheda, a near neighbour of Dundalk and Carlingford.[5] These include official records produced by the government of the English colony (mainly of a financial or judicial character but often containing important incidental topographical information), ecclesiastical records of both monastic houses and secular diocesan government, and documents produced by some of the great landowning families. Limerick is an outlier in this respect, but is reasonably well represented in the records of central government and in addition has some local records, such as the fourteenth/fifteenth-century *Black Book* and the Arthur manuscript. Its seventeenth-century vicissitudes have meant that Limerick is well endowed with cartographical sources that preserve a wealth of information on the physical fabric of the late medieval town. Dublin, needless to say, has all of this and more. As the seat of central government and the location of some of the most important religious houses in medieval Ireland, it figures prominently in such records but in addition has good local records, particularly those of the corporation of Dublin. It is also well served by cartographical sources.

Besides documents and maps, the major source of information for reconstructing the topography and development of medieval towns such as these is archaeology. The quality and quantity of data vary greatly, however, mainly because of the nature of archaeological activity in Ireland. Excavation tends to be a by-product of commercial development, rather than being planned on the basis of research strategies. Hence it concentrates in the areas of greatest developmental activity — notably, in this case, Dublin to a far greater degree than the other towns. Commercial considerations impact not only on the quantity of archaeological excavation but also on its nature. Large-scale excavation tends to be extremely — often prohibitively — expensive and thus tends to be confined to areas where commercial buoyancy is sufficient to support the costs involved, which again are mainly in Dublin. Most archaeological excavation is very small-scale and exploratory ('test excavation' or 'trial trenching'), designed to establish the presence, quantity and nature of archaeological deposits rather than actually to investigate these deposits to any significant degree. Test excavation can, on occasion, produce useful archaeological information on urban topography and layout, but this is essentially a happy accident rather than its primary purpose. In Carlingford and Dundalk, practically all excavation to date has been of this small-scale, exploratory nature and even in Limerick large-scale excavation has mainly been confined to King John's Castle. In effect, large-scale 'full' excavation — the process best designed to deliver high-quality information about the topography and development of urban areas — has been common only in Dublin. Even in Dublin, it has long been clear that for various reasons (perhaps only partially understood) both the quality and the quantity of archaeological deposits for the Anglo-Norman and later medieval periods are substantially poorer than for the preceding Hiberno-Norse period.

Apart from excavation, archaeological information can also be obtained from the study of upstanding medieval buildings, including churches and monastic buildings, houses, castles and town defences. The spread of this source material between the four towns is more even with Dublin having, perhaps, less than might be expected given its importance and with Carlingford having more; Dundalk is probably the least well-served in this respect. These surviving medieval structures have been surveyed and analysed, generally, by the Archaeological Survey of Ireland and more specifically by the Urban Archaeology Survey. Dundalk and Carlingford benefit from inclusion in the only full county survey published to date by the Archaeological Survey of Ireland.[6] The Urban Archaeology Survey, regrettably, remains unpublished and difficulty of access to its reports may account for the low rate of usage of this important source in most fascicles.

COMPARISONS AND CONTRASTS

These four towns present a range of comparisons and contrasts which, between them, cover many of the major themes in the study of Irish medieval urbanism. Some are obvious, like the contrast in scale — today — between the city of Dublin and the small town of Carlingford. This leads, however, to a consideration of a more significant theme — the question of success and failure — always a prominent question in any study of Ireland's (and, indeed, Europe's) medieval towns. By definition, all places featured in the IHTA were relatively successful in the sense that they still exist as towns today but they have had, of course, varying degrees of success. The reasons for success or failure can also be complex. Carlingford was never really in competition with Dublin, but it was in many respects in earnest competition, for much of the middle ages, with its near neighbour Dundalk. Despite having a better natural harbour, Carlingford ultimately lost out to Dundalk — probably mainly because its location was more remote from the centres of economic and political power, especially in the late middle ages when English control in Ireland was greatly reduced. Conjectural evidence for a reduction in the size of the town behind a new line of defences[7] reveals the difficulties faced by Carlingford, at least in the fourteenth century. Nevertheless the evidence of surviving buildings points to some degree of economic recovery in the fifteenth and sixteenth centuries. Even Dundalk along with Limerick could, like Carlingford, be characterised as an increasingly isolated frontier town in the late middle ages. Like many other Irish towns, these were profoundly affected by the changing political balance of power and other factors over which they had no control. Limerick, in many respects, was even more remote than Carlingford was from Dublin and the Pale, and this clearly had an impact on the lives and culture of its inhabitants. Despite this, its strategic importance was such that there was never any likelihood of it failing, albeit that it endured some difficult days in the late middle ages. Here too, however, the surviving medieval fabric of the town is evidence of enduring prosperity, which must be set alongside the evidence for isolation and vulnerability. The success of Dublin was effectively guaranteed, given its political status as the seat of English government in Ireland, but it could be argued that, in view of the apparent advantages it was afforded, Dublin was actually not a particularly successful town in the late medieval period, economically and otherwise. This in turn, however, is at least as much a reflection on the success of the English colony generally as it is on Dublin in particular.

An obvious point of comparison between all four towns is that they are located on the coast. Equally obviously, this 'pattern' is largely determined by the criteria used to select this particular group of towns for study. Nevertheless, it is noteworthy that Dublin, Limerick and Dundalk are all located where a river meets the sea and, more specifically, at the last practical crossing point before the river met the sea. This concern with proximity to both river and sea tells us that water-borne transport — and hence potential for trade — were significant considerations in the original selection of these sites. More broadly it reminds us of how Anglo-Norman urbanisation continued and intensified the shift in settlement emphasis towards the coast, particularly the east and south-east coasts, which began in the Hiberno-Norse period. This is probably one of the most profound and lasting changes in the history of settlement in Ireland.

Origins provide another clear point of comparison between these towns. Although dealt with here as Anglo-Norman towns, all (with the possible exception of Carlingford) have clear evidence for pre-Anglo-Norman settlement — which, indeed, is a feature of most Anglo-Norman towns. Very few of them were entirely new settlements on virgin ground — most were established at or near existing ecclesiastical or secular sites. Carlingford is apparently the exception that proves the rule, a rare example of an Anglo-Norman settlement established on virgin ground in the late twelfth century. This, however, may not be the case. The name Carlingford is derived, rather speculatively, from the Scandinavian *kerling fjörðr* or from the even more implausible Irish-Scandinavian hybrid *cathair linn fjörðr*. But the atlas gives the first recorded Irish version of the name, in early thirteenth-century annalistic sources, as Carlongphort.[8] This could be a clumsy phonetic spelling by Irish-speaking annalists but it raises the possibility — not specifically addressed in the fascicle — that there was a Viking *longphort* on the site. While there is no definite supporting evidence for this, there is historical evidence strongly suggesting the existence of a Viking base somewhere on Carlingford Lough in the ninth century.[9] Dublin and Limerick, of course, were Viking settlements and in this context the coastal and riverine location was critical to their original selection by their Viking founders. Dublin may also have had both a church site and a secular Gaelic settlement predating even the Viking *longphort*. The location and, indeed, the name of Dundalk are derived from an Irish royal site, the stronghold of Dún Delca with an associated *aonach* (ceremonial assembly) site. This was taken over, probably in the 1180s, by Bertram de Verdon and a borough developed, but at some point in the thirteenth century a new town was established almost a kilometre to the east, at the lowest fording point on the Castletown River, specifically to take advantage of better access to the sea. Over time the new town eclipsed the original settlement, to the extent that even the name Dundalk became associated with it, whereas the original Dún Delca is now known as Castletown.

Proprietorial status divides these towns in the late middle ages into two groups: royal towns (Dublin and Limerick) and private baronial towns (Dundalk and Carlingford). The latter were both probably founded by Bertram de Verdon and subsequently belonged to a succession of different English or Anglo-Irish noble families. Royal proprietorship of Dublin and Limerick highlights the fact that these were major towns (by Irish standards) and of critical strategic importance to English rule in Ireland. They are thus in quite a different category from Dundalk or Carlingford. Nevertheless Carlingford shares with Dublin and Limerick the presence of a major royal castle (albeit one that was originally built by Hugh de Lacy and only subsequently confiscated by the crown). Dundalk, by contrast, is unusual in the apparent absence of any seigneurial castle. This, no doubt, is because the original de Verdon motte-and-bailey castle was on the site of Dún Delca at Castletown. This castle does not appear to have continued in use beyond the thirteenth century, but the extinction of the de Verdon line in 1316 and the subsequent subdivision of the estate between four female heiresses removed any impetus for erecting a seigneurial castle in the town. This experience — of the lordship being subdivided between multiple female heirs on the extinction of the male line — was a surprisingly common one in Ireland and contributed significantly to the difficulties experienced by many Irish towns in the late middle ages.

A final and interesting point of comparison is the presence of churches dedicated to St Nicholas in Dublin, Limerick and Dundalk from at least the early thirteenth century. This, presumably, is explained by the fact that St Nicholas, among his other attributes, is the patron saint of merchants and sailors. Unfortunately, little evidence survives of any specific links between these churches and guilds or associations of merchants or sailors, or of any specific functions, that the churches performed for such groups. Nevertheless, the fact that the main parish church of Dundalk was dedicated to St Nicholas can surely be seen as further evidence that maritime trade was the primary consideration in the founding or relocation of this new town.

THE TOWNS AS PORTS AND TRADING CENTRES

What information do the fascicles provide on these towns as ports and trading centres? The atlas is not an economic history, so one should not expect to find detailed discussion or statistics on trading volumes, customs receipts and so on. But we do learn, for instance, that fishing was the mainstay of Carlingford's economy throughout the middle ages and beyond,[10] that Dundalk was trading with east Ulster, Dublin, England and even France by the fourteenth century,[11] that Dundalk merchants were trading significantly into Ulster (presumably overland) during the sixteenth century[12] and that by 1635 Dundalk was second only to Drogheda in the export of linen yarn to England.[13] Interestingly, surviving customs receipts for the years 1277–1333 appear to show Limerick as a relatively unimportant port, contributing far less than 1% of national receipts and nothing at all after the Bruce wars. But O'Flaherty wisely questions the reality behind these statistics, pointing out that the prosperity that is clearly evident in the physical remains of late medieval Limerick must be based on significant economic activity and especially trade.[14]

Surviving evidence for the physical form of these medieval ports is very limited, with practically no evidence in Dundalk or Carlingford. This, as noted above, is mainly due to the lack of large-scale archaeological excavation (assuming any archaeological remains survive to be excavated). In Dublin, Clarke refers to the well-known evidence for a succession of timber and later stone docks constructed at Wood Quay in the late twelfth and thirteenth centuries.[15] He is able to integrate this with documentary and cartographical evidence, such as descriptions of the fifteenth-century crane and crane-house at the bottom of Winetavern Street, as evidence that the port at Wood Quay continued to function in the late medieval period, despite the well-known problems with silting in the River Liffey and the need to offload large ships at Dalkey.[16] The Wood Quay area continued to function as Dublin's port until the early seventeenth century, when a new

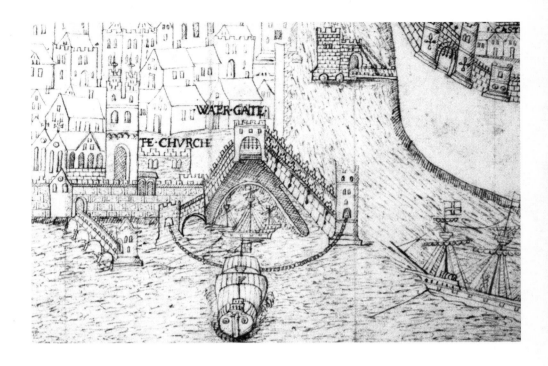

Fig. 9.1 *Limerick*, map 5, 1587. The National Archives: Public Record Office, MPF 1/96, extract.

customhouse was built on reclaimed ground just to the east, now Essex Street East, in 1621, along with a new crane and wharf. Unfortunately, there is little evidence, whether documentary, cartographical or (as yet) archaeological, for the form or layout of the late medieval port at Wood Quay. The most impressive evidence for late medieval port structures comes from Limerick. The earliest known map of Limerick, dating to 1587 (Fig. 9.1), shows an elaborately defended harbour, with an enclosed dock, at the south-western corner of King's Island where the Abbey River re-enters the Shannon. Two towers project from fortified walls at either end of the harbour and between them a large chain is hung, presumably to prevent unwelcome access to the harbour. That this is not simply a cartographical flight of fancy is confirmed by a detailed description written in 1618 and also by a perspective view drawn in 1685 by the English military engineer Thomas Phillips — a man not much given to flights of fancy and a very accurate recorder of what he saw (Fig. 9.2). These elaborate structures, probably of fifteenth-century date, are testimony both to the importance of maritime trade to Limerick and to the wealth that it created. Sadly, no traces survive above ground today, although archaeology may reveal sub-surface remains at some point in the future. It is, perhaps, curious that there is no evidence for such elaborate defensive structures at the port of Dublin, but presumably this reflects the fact that they were not considered necessary, whereas in Limerick they clearly were.

A very interesting contribution to the Limerick fascicle is the mapping and analysis of the distribution of building types (stone-built versus

timber-framed houses, and so on) in the town, based on the 1654–6 Civil Survey (Fig. 9.3). From this a clear division within the Englishtown emerges, with stone-built houses predominant in the southern half, while most timber-framed houses were to be found in the northern half.[17] Although recorded in 1654, this division within the Englishtown presumably reflects much older patterns, ultimately linked to the earliest development of the Hiberno-Norse town. It is also interesting to note that even in 1654 there is still little evidence for development — or even habitation — on the very substantial lands of the dissolved monastic houses along the eastern edge of the Englishtown. Apart from work on the outer defences in the 1640s, there is little evidence of significant change to the physical fabric of the town until after the Restoration. This pattern is also noted in Dublin, where again the physical impact of the Reformation is not really seen until the seventeenth century. Apart from demolition of monastic buildings, new developments on former monastic lands did not get under way for some time, the earliest being that of Trinity College on the grounds of All Hallows Priory in the 1590s.[18] The early seventeenth century also witnessed a new initiative in Dublin — the resumption of land reclamation along the Liffey banks for the first time in centuries. Initially focused on the area of the Poddle–Liffey confluence, this relatively small-scale development began a trend of reclamation along the south bank of the river, east of the medieval city, that gathered momentum as the century progressed. The revival of Dublin as a port, along with the gradual eastward shift of that port, was under way.

Fig. 9.2 *Limerick*, plate 2, view, 1685, by Thomas Phillips. National Library of Ireland, MS 3137 (25), extract.

Opposite: Fig. 9.3 *Limerick*, fig. 5, House types and land use in Englishtown, 1654, from the Civil Survey.

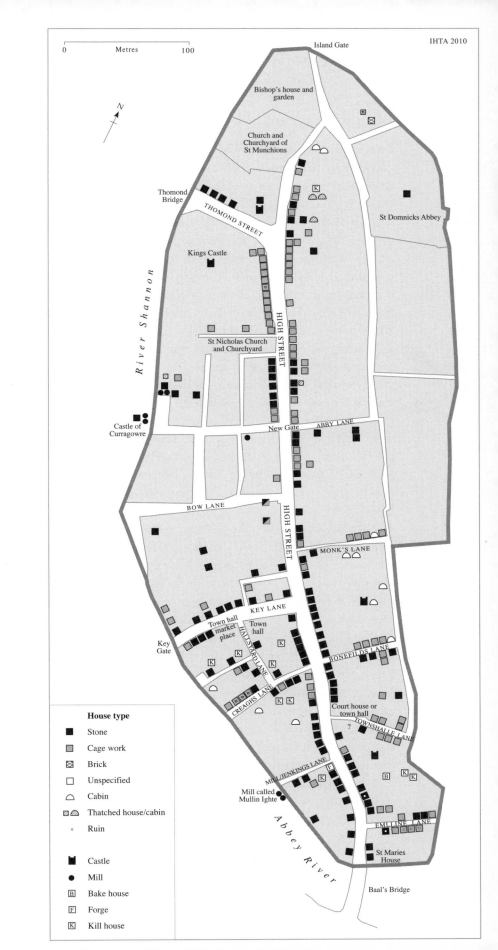

IHTA 2010

0   Metres   100

Island Gate

Bishop's house and
garden

Church and
Churchyard of
St Munchions

Thomond
Bridge

THOMOND STREET

K

St Domnicks Abbey

Kings Castle

HIGH STREET

St Nicholas Church
and Churchyard

New Gate   ABBY LANE

Castle of
Curragowre

BOW LANE

HIGH STREET

MONK'S LANE

KEY LANE

Town hall
market
place

Town
hall

K

HALLYARD LANE

Key
Gate

K   K

K

K

BONEFILDS LANE

K   K

CREAGHS LANE

K

Court house or
town hall

?

TOWNSHALLE LANE

MILL/JENKINGS LANE

F

B   K

K

Mill called
Mullin Ighte

EMILINE LANE

St Maries
House

Abbey River

Baal's Bridge

House type

■	Stone
▨	Cage work
⊠	Brick
☐	Unspecified
⌂	Cabin
▨ ◠	Thatched house/cabin
∘	Ruin
■	Castle
●	Mill
B	Bake house
F	Forge
K	Kill house

River Shannon

Use of archaeological evidence

Some comments on the IHTA, from the specific perspective of an archae-ologist, may be offered in conclusion. The first thing that must be said is that, given the broad scope of the project, it would be difficult for any one person to master all of the various fields encompassed, especially for larger towns and cities such as Limerick and, of course, Dublin. Archaeological evidence is a vital source for the early development of these towns and, indeed, continues to be crucial even into the sixteenth and seventeenth centuries in cases such as Carlingford, where historical documentation is scarce. As it happens, all four fascicles in this group were written by historians and, for the most part, relatively modern historians at that, with the exception of Howard Clarke. On the whole, the authors handle archaeological evidence quite well, probably better, indeed, than most archaeologists would handle modern history. One of the big difficulties with archaeological evidence in Ireland is that so much archaeological work still exists only as 'grey literature' and it is understandable that his-torians may not be well versed in how to access unpublished reports and other material. The major disappointment in the atlas, for this writer, is the fact that the Urban Archaeology Survey was hardly used in any of these fascicles.[19] The Dublin fascicle can be excused, as no full Urban Archaeology Survey report has been completed for Dublin, but there are reports for Carlingford, Dundalk and Limerick that would have signifi-cantly added to the atlas. The problem, of course, is that the Urban Survey still has not been published, but it is relatively easy to consult a copy if one knows where to find it, as most archaeologists would be aware. There may, perhaps, be an argument for making some professional archaeolog-ical advice available to future authors of fascicles, specifically to assist in sourcing and interpreting material such as this.

The other major source of archaeological information, relevant to the atlas project, is excavation reports. While many of these remain unpub-lished, there are published summaries available through the annual *Excavations* volume or online at www.excavations.ie. It must be borne in mind that these are not only summaries but early summaries at that, often compiled before post-excavation research and analysis have been completed. Thus they have to be handled carefully but can often be infor-mative. In general, this resource is reasonably well used by the authors of these fascicles. The one exception is the Dundalk fascicle, where there is little or no direct reference to excavated evidence — perhaps because the author felt that including Paul Gosling's work[20] covered him, as it were, in terms of archaeology. But as good as Gosling's work is, it cannot substitute for the evidence of excavations — especially those that took place after Gosling's paper appeared in 1991. The Dundalk fascicle was published in 2006 and www.excavations.ie lists at least 130 excavations carried out in Dundalk between 1991 and 2006, for which information might have been included in the atlas. The great majority of these were of the test-trenching variety, rather than large-scale excavation, and it must be admitted that the results, in most cases, were not particularly useful for the purposes of the atlas. However, there is evidence for significant medieval archaeological deposits along Bridge Street, at the northern end of the town, including traces of a pottery kiln on the western side of Bridge Street, operational in the period 1250–1350.[21] Other work in 1995 and 1997 provided evidence for the town's defensive fosses on the western and southern sides of the town; perhaps most significantly a test excavation in 1995 on a site at the corner of Clanbrassil Street and Jocelyn Street (more correctly Crowe Street/Market Square at this point) revealed the town's defensive fosse running east–west across the southern end of Clanbrassil Street and apparently dating not later than the late thirteenth or early fourteenth centuries.[22] This is considerably farther south than where O'Sullivan places the southern line of the original defensive circuit[23] and this information really ought to have been included in the Dundalk fascicle. In fairness to the author, the late Harold O'Sullivan, by the time he came to prepare the Carlingford fascicle, published in 2011, a different approach was adopted and good use was made of the limited excavation evidence that was available. Indeed, because documentary source information for the development of the medieval town was so limited, the Carlingford fascicle relies quite heavily on archaeological evidence.

The Limerick fascicle does the same for the reconstruction of the earliest phases of the town's topographical development and gives much weight to Hodkinson's thesis of the extent and development of the Hiberno-Norse town. Much of this is, inevitably, speculative because of the lack of early documentary source material and the relatively poor record, to date, of excavated archaeological evidence. The overall picture of the early town, centred around the port and the site of the later cathedral, is probably broadly correct and some discussion of analogies with Dublin and Waterford might have been helpful in this respect. One wonders whether the Irishtown on the southern bank of the Abbey River might be a possible alternative location for the *villa Oustmannorum* (town of the Ostmen), recorded in the aftermath of the Anglo-Norman seizure of the town at the end of the twelfth century.[24] The proposed location, in the northern part of what became the Englishtown, is perhaps problematic, given the presence of the castle (and the strategically important crossing-point on the Shannon) from the early thirteenth century. Within the Irishtown, excavated evidence exists for thirteenth/fourteenth-century occupation deposits off the eastern side of Broad Street, at the rear of plots presumably fronting onto Broad Street itself. The street frontages, where the most substantial evidence (including traces of buildings) might be expected, had unfortunately been cleared of archaeological deposits by later cellars. Excavation in the angle between Broad Street and Charlotte's Quay also produced evidence of features associated with pottery of late twelfth- to fourteenth-century date.[25] Such evidence for relatively early occupation in the Irishtown may be relevant in the context of the *villa Oustmannorum* and might, perhaps, have been discussed by O'Flaherty.

The Dublin fascicle was written by a specialist medieval historian who is also familiar with using and discussing archaeological evidence. The discussion of pre-Norman Dublin is based almost entirely on archaeological evidence and archaeology remains very much to the fore up to the end of the twelfth century. This section of the fascicle effectively provides a very good and thorough summary of the state of archaeological knowledge as it existed prior to 2002. Research, of course, never stands still and it is only to be expected — and, indeed, hoped for — that the various fascicles of the atlas will to some extent be overtaken by ongoing research, almost from their first appearance in print. Indeed, the ink was scarcely dry on the Carlingford fascicle when a paper appeared querying its identification of the church of the Holy Trinity and the chapel of St Michael mentioned in a will of 1485.[26] Inevitably, for reasons outlined earlier, recent research — especially archaeological — has concentrated overwhelmingly on Dublin rather than any of the other three towns. This, combined with the fact that the Dublin fascicle is the oldest of the four, means that new research has added to the Dublin atlas to a far greater extent than to the others in this group.

More recent research

Perhaps the most significant development in the period since the Dublin fascicle appeared is the arrival of the *Medieval Dublin* publications as an established, regularly-appearing series, thanks largely to the work of the indefatigable Seán Duffy. Although the first volumes appeared before 2002 — and indeed are referenced in the Dublin fascicle — the majority of the current fifteen volumes have appeared more recently. The strength of the series is its multi-disciplinary focus, exploring medieval

Dublin from historical, archaeological, literary, geographical and other viewpoints. Almost inevitably, however, it is the regular appearance of relatively detailed accounts of archaeological excavations that makes the most important contribution for our present purposes. Since 2002 significant papers have appeared dealing with the priory of All Hallows and the early Trinity College;[27] the site of the Hospitaller priory of St John of Kilmainham;[28] human remains from the cemeteries of the leper hospital of St Stephen; the church of St Peter and the abbey of St Thomas;[29] riverside reclamation, timber docks, stone quay walls and late medieval watermills on both the south bank of the Liffey at St Augustine Street and on the north bank at Arran Quay and at Strand Street Great; on the topography of the area known as the Pill;[30] and, of course, the town defences.[31] In addition there are valuable papers on Dublin Castle;[32] the early development of Dublin's western suburb and the influence of St Thomas's Abbey;[33] the northern suburb of Oxmantown;[34] the largely hidden archiepiscopal palace of St Sepulchre in Kevin Street;[35] the architecture — and roof timbers — of Christ Church and St Patrick's Cathedrals;[36] the layout and surrounding topography of Christ Church Cathedral and of St Mary's Abbey;[37] the foundation of the Dominican priory;[38] the progress and processes of the dissolution of Dublin's monastic houses;[39] and medieval Dublin's chronicles, annals and other archives.[40] It must be admitted that none of these contributions fundamentally changes the general picture of the Anglo-Norman town as presented in the atlas — in contrast to the pre-Anglo-Norman period, where the results of recent excavations have radically altered our ideas, especially regarding the earliest phases of Dublin's development. Other important contributions have appeared in the National Museum of Ireland's Medieval Dublin Excavations series, including McCutcheon's study of the pottery from Wood Quay, which sheds light on many of the trading connections of the ships that would have berthed at the quay there.[41] Reports on the excavation of the parish church of St Audoen and the Augustinian friary have also appeared.[42] While it does not deal in any detail with the physical form or development of the town, Murphy and Potterton's *Dublin region in the middle ages* is an essential guide to the hinterland and agricultural economy on which the medieval development of Dublin was largely based.[43]

Little of note has appeared in relation to Carlingford or Dundalk since their respective fascicles were published. In the case of Limerick a useful paper on the development of the castle — and its place in the early development of the Anglo-Norman town — appeared in 2013 and the final publication of excavations within the castle in the 1990s is imminently expected.[44] A number of papers on various details — archaeological,

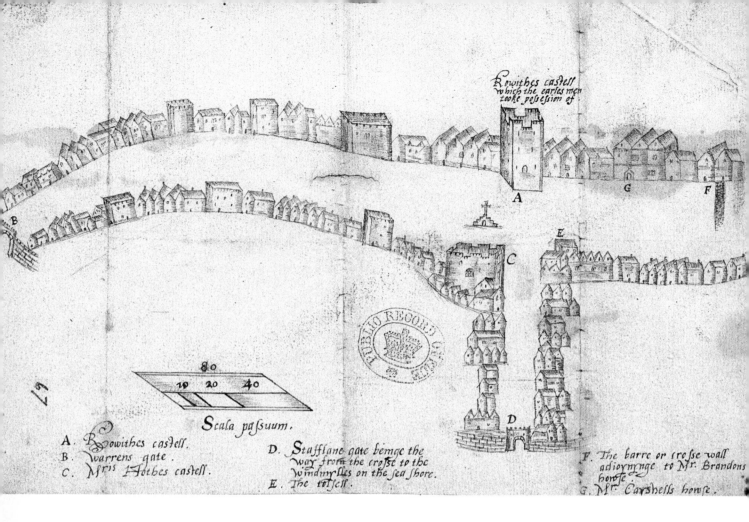

A. Bowithes castell.
B. Warrens gate.
C. Mris Hothes castell.

D. Stafflane gate beinge the
   way from the crosse to the
   windmylles on the sea shore.
E. The tolsell.

F. The barre or crosse wall
   adioyninge to Mr Brandons
   howse.
G. Mr Carshells howse.

architectural and historical — of some of Limerick's important late medieval stone houses have also appeared.[45]

CONCLUSIONS

Being overtaken by subsequent research is simply one of the occupational hazards that all researchers must accept (and, for the most part, do so happily). With all due respect to the learned authors, in many ways it is the illustrations that are the real stars of the IHTA. Each fascicle includes both reproductions of historic maps, paintings and prints and many fine interpretative maps drafted by the authors specifically for their fascicle, including reconstructed maps of the medieval layout and features, and maps illustrating the stages of growth of each town. Maps such as the latter are invaluable to historians and archaeologists and can effectively function as research agendas for future work — especially archaeological work — in a town. As with the authors' essays, however, all interpretative maps will eventually become obsolete as new research modifies what we

Fig. 9.4 *Dundalk*, map 4, 1594, by Henry Duke. The National Archives: Public Record Office, SP 63/175, no. 5, xxiii.

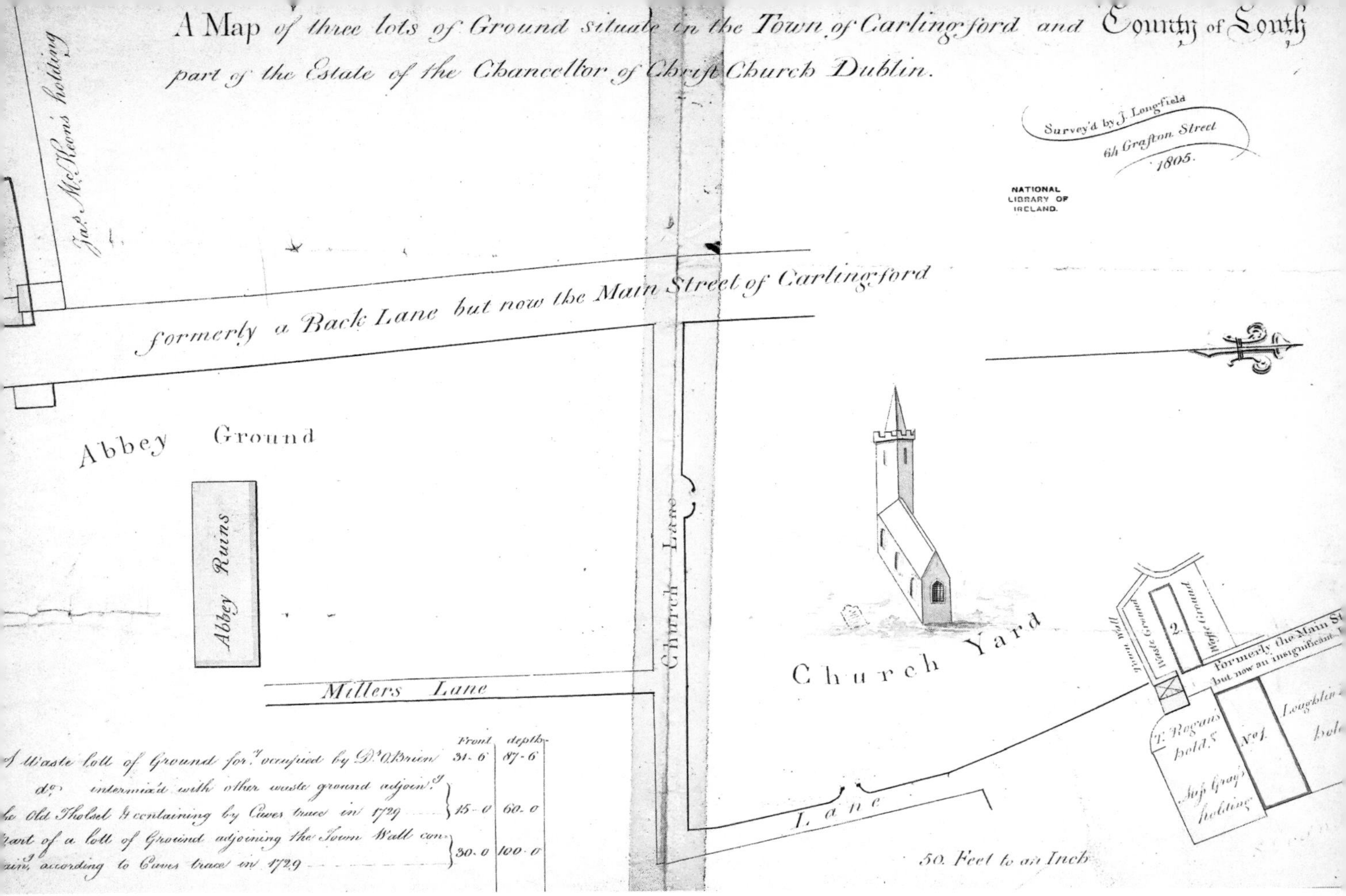
A Map of three lots of Ground situate in the Town of Carlingford and County of Louth
part of the Estate of the Chancellor of Christ Church Dublin.
Survey'd by J. Longfield
6½ Grafton Street
1805.
NATIONAL
LIBRARY OF
IRELAND.
Jas. McKeon's holding
formerly a Back Lane but now the Main Street of Carlingford
Abbey Ground
Abbey Ruins
Church Lane
Millers Lane
Church Yard
Town Wall
Waste Ground
Waste Ground
2.
Formerly the Main St
but now an insignificant
T. Rogan's hold.g
No 1.
Loughlin
Jas. Gray's holding
Lane
50 Feet to an Inch
Front
depth
A Waste lott of Ground for.y occupied by D. O'Brien
31 - 6
87 - 6
do intermix'd with other waste ground adjoin.g
The Old Tholsel & containing by Caves trace in 1729
15 - 0
60 - 0
Part of a lott of Ground adjoining the Town Wall con-
tain.g according to Caves trace in 1729
30 - 0
100 - 0

Fig. 9.5 *Carlingford*, map 12, 1805, by John Longfield. National Library of Ireland, MS 21/F/40 (34).

thought we knew. What will never go out of date are the historic maps and views of the period and the inclusion of high-quality reproductions of many of these is one of the most valuable features of the entire atlas project. These include the earliest known maps of the towns — and some of the earliest surviving Irish maps of any kind — such as the wonderful map of Dundalk dating from 1594 (Fig. 9.4) and humbler, relatively modern maps and surveys preserving details of older features, such as a lease map of part of Carlingford in 1805, showing a section of the town wall (now destroyed) on the western side of the gatehouse known as the Tholsel (Fig. 9.5). Contrasting the enduring value of such maps with the inevitably provisional nature of the authors' interpretations is in no way intended to belittle the value of the latter. These fascicles will undoubtedly stand for many years to come as the definitive statements of current knowledge of the towns concerned and as an important contribution to the wider themes of urbanism and of English and Anglo-Irish settlement in medieval Ireland generally.

Notes

[1] Clarke, IHTA, no. 11, *Dublin, part I, to 1610*.

[2] O'Sullivan, IHTA, no. 16, *Dundalk*.

[3] O'Flaherty, IHTA, no. 21, *Limerick*.

[4] O'Sullivan and Gillespie, IHTA, no. 23, *Carlingford*.

[5] John Bradley, 'The topography and layout of medieval Drogheda', in *Journal of the County Louth Archaeological and Historical Society*, xix, no. 2 (1978), pp 98–127.

[6] Victor Buckley and P.D. Sweetman, *Archaeological survey of County Louth* (Dublin, 1991).

[7] O'Sullivan and Gillespie, *Carlingford*, pp 2–3, fig. 1.

[8] Ibid., p. 7.

[9] Ibid.

[10] Ibid., pp 3–4.

[11] O'Sullivan, *Dundalk*, p. 2.

[12] Ibid., p. 3.

[13] Ibid., p. 4.

[14] O'Flaherty, *Limerick*, p. 4.

[15] Clarke, *Dublin, part I, to 1610*, pp 6–7. For the most recent discussion of the excavated evidence, see P.F. Wallace, *Viking Dublin: the Wood Quay excavations* (Sallins, 2016), pp 154–81.

[16] Ibid. For a discussion of the range of harbours available to medieval Dublin in the wider area, see Niall Brady, 'Dublin's maritime setting and the archaeology of its medieval harbours', in John Bradley, Anngret Simms and A.J. Fletcher (eds), *Dublin in the medieval world: studies in honour of Howard B. Clarke* (Dublin, 2009), pp 295–315.

[17] O'Flaherty, *Limerick*, pp 5–6; figs 5–6.

[18] Clarke, *Dublin, part I, to 1610*, p. 10.

[19] The Urban Archaeology Survey is listed as a source (Urb. Arch. Survey) in the general abbreviations of the Limerick fascicle (O'Flaherty, *Limerick*, p. 60), but this writer could find no evidence of it actually being used in the text.

[20] Paul Gosling, 'From Dún Delca to Dundalk: the topography and archaeology of a medieval frontier town A.D. *c.* 1187–1700', in *Journal of the County Louth Archaeological and Historical Society*, xxii, no. 3 (1991), pp 221–353.

[21] Rob Lynch, 'Townparks, Dundalk', in *Excavations 2000*, p. 229; Kieran Campbell, '78 Bridge Street, Dundalk', in *Excavations 1997*, pp 130–31.

[22] Deirdre Murphy, 'Carrolls Village, Church Street, Dundalk', in *Excavations 1997*, p. 131; Cia McConway, 'Clanbrassil Street, Dundalk', in *Excavations 1995*, pp 62–3.

[23] O'Sullivan, *Dundalk*, p. 2, fig. 2.

[24] O'Flaherty, *Limerick*, p. 2.

[25] Christine Tarbett, 'Broad Street, Custom House', in *Excavations 1987*, pp 19–20; Kenneth Wiggins, 'Broad Street/Curry Lane, Abbey C Ward', in *Excavations 1989*, pp 34–5; Edmond O'Donovan, 'Broad Street/George's Quay/Abbey River, Limerick', in *Excavations 1999*, pp 169–71; Ken Hanley, 'Broad Street/Charlotte's Quay (rear of), Limerick', in *Excavations 2001*, pp 235–6. See also B.J. Hodkinson, 'The medieval city of Limerick', in Liam Irwin, Gearóid Ó Tuathaigh and Matthew Potter (eds), *Limerick history and society* (Dublin, 2009), pp 20–22.

[26] Noel Ross, 'Carlingford churches in 1485', in *Journal of the County Louth Archaeological and Historical Society*, xxvii, no. 3 (2011), pp 448–9; see also the response by Raymond Gillespie, 'More on Carlingford churches in 1485', in *Journal of the County Louth Archaeological and Historical Society*, xxvii, no. 4 (2012), pp 593–9.

[27] Linzi Simpson, 'The priory of All Hallows and Trinity College, Dublin: recent archaeological discoveries', in Seán Duffy (ed.), *Medieval Dublin III* (Dublin, 2002), pp 195–236;

Linzi Simpson, 'The priory of All Hallows and the Old College: archaeological investigations in Front Square, Trinity College Dublin', in Seán Duffy (ed.), *Medieval Dublin XIII* (Dublin, 2013), pp 246–316.

28 Linzi Simpson, 'Dublin's famous "Bully's Acre": site of the monastery of Kilmainham?', in Seán Duffy (ed.), *Medieval Dublin IX* (Dublin, 2009), pp 38–83.

29 Laureen Buckley and Alan Hayden, 'Excavations at St Stephen's leper hospital, Dublin: a summary account and an analysis of burials', in Duffy, *Medieval Dublin III*, pp 151–94; Tim Coughlan, 'Excavations at the medieval cemetery of St Peter's Church, Dublin', in Seán Duffy (ed.), *Medieval Dublin IV* (Dublin, 2003), pp 11–39; Laureen Buckley, 'Health status in medieval Dublin: analysis of the skeletal remains from the abbey of St Thomas the Martyr', in Duffy, *Medieval Dublin IV*, pp 98–126.

30 Alan Hayden, 'Excavation of the medieval river frontage at Arran Quay, Dublin', in Seán Duffy (ed.), *Medieval Dublin V* (Dublin, 2004), pp 149–242; Claire Walsh, 'Archaeological excavation of the Anglo-Norman waterfront at Strand Street Great, Dublin', in Seán Duffy (ed.), *Medieval Dublin VI* (Dublin, 2005), pp 160–87; Alan Hayden, 'Archaeological excavations at the west side of Augustine Street, Dublin: a summary', in Seán Duffy (ed.), *Medieval Dublin X* (Dublin, 2010), pp 241–66; Teresa Bolger, 'Defining the "Pill": the contribution of excavations at Ormond Quay Upper to the interpretation of the original topography of the Liffey foreshore', in Seán Duffy (ed.), *Medieval Dublin XI* (Dublin, 2011), pp 161–9.

31 Linzi Simpson, 'The medieval city wall and the southern line of Dublin's defences: excavations at 14–16 Werburgh Street', in Seán Duffy (ed.), *Medieval Dublin VIII* (Dublin, 2008), pp 150–77.

32 James Lydon, 'Dublin Castle in the middle ages', in Duffy, *Medieval Dublin III*, pp 115–27.

33 Cathal Duddy, 'The role of St Thomas' Abbey in the early development of Dublin's western suburb', in Duffy, *Medieval Dublin IV*, pp 79–97. See also Edmond O'Donovan, 'The growth and decline of a medieval suburb? Evidence from excavations at Thomas Street, Dublin', in Duffy, *Medieval Dublin IV*, pp 127–71 and Judith Carroll, 'Excavations at 58–59 Thomas Street/Vicar Street and 63–64 Thomas Street, Dublin 8', in Seán Duffy (ed.), *Medieval Dublin XII* (Dublin, 2012), pp 161–88.

34 Emer Purcell, 'Land use in medieval Oxmantown', in Duffy, *Medieval Dublin IV*, pp 193–228; Emer Purcell, 'The city and the suburb: medieval Dublin and Oxmantown', in Duffy, *Medieval Dublin VI*, pp 188–223.

35 Danielle O'Donovan, 'English patron, English building? The importance of St Sepulchre's archiepiscopal palace, Dublin', in Duffy, *Medieval Dublin IV*, pp 253–78.

36 Rachel Moss, 'Tales from the crypt: the medieval stonework of Christ Church Cathedral, Dublin', in Duffy, *Medieval Dublin III*, pp 95–114; Michael O'Neill, 'St Patrick's Cathedral, Dublin and its prebendal churches: Gothic architectural relationships', in Duffy, *Medieval Dublin V*, pp 243–76; Charles Lyons, 'Dublin's oldest roof? The choir of St Patrick's Cathedral', in Seán Duffy (ed.), *Medieval Dublin VII* (Dublin, 2006), pp 177–213; Máire Geaney, 'Christ Church Cathedral, Dublin: a survey of the nave and south transept roofs', in Duffy, *Medieval Dublin VII*, pp 233–49. See also Michael O'Neill, 'Design sources for St Patrick's Cathedral, Dublin, and its relationship to Christ Church Cathedral', in *RIA Proc.*, c C (2000), pp 207–56.

37 Michael O'Neill, 'Christ Church Cathedral and its environs: medieval and beyond', in Duffy, *Medieval Dublin XI*, pp 298–319; Geraldine Stout, 'The topography of St Mary's Cistercian Abbey and precinct, Dublin', in Duffy, *Medieval Dublin XII*, pp 138–60. See also Stuart Kinsella, 'Mapping Christ Church Cathedral, Dublin, *c.* 1028–1608: an examination of the western cloister', in Bradley, Simms and Fletcher, *Dublin in the medieval world*, pp 143–67.

[38] Bernadette Williams, 'The arrival of the Dominicans in Ireland in 1224 and the question of Dublin and Drogheda: the sources re-examined', in Duffy, *Medieval Dublin XIII*, pp 150–82.

[39] Brendan Scott, 'The religious houses of Tudor Dublin: their communities and resistance to the dissolution, 1537–41', in Duffy, *Medieval Dublin VII*, pp 214–32.

[40] Mary Clark, 'People, place and parchment: the medieval archives of Dublin city', in Duffy, *Medieval Dublin III*, pp 140–50; Bernadette Cunningham, 'Dublin in the late medieval Gaelic annals', in Duffy, *Medieval Dublin VIII*, pp 178–93; A.J. Fletcher, 'The annals and chronicles of medieval Dublin: an overview', in Duffy, *Medieval Dublin VIII*, pp 194–212; Raymond Gillespie, 'Dubliners view themselves: the Dublin City chronicles', in Duffy, *Medieval Dublin VIII*, pp 213–37; Ellen O'Flaherty, 'Manuscript sources for the history of medieval Dublin in Trinity College Library, Dublin', in Duffy, *Medieval Dublin XII*, pp 289–306. See also A.J. Fletcher, 'The earliest extant recension of the Dublin Chronicle: an edition, with commentary', in Bradley, Simms and Fletcher, *Dublin in the medieval world*, pp 390–409.

[41] Clare McCutcheon, *Medieval pottery from Wood Quay, Dublin: the 1974–6 waterfront excavations*. Medieval Dublin Excavations, 1962–81, series B, vii (Dublin, 2006).

[42] Mary McMahon, *St Audoen's Church, Cornmarket, Dublin: archaeology and architecture* (Dublin, 2006); Seán Duffy and Linzi Simpson, 'The hermits of St Augustine in medieval Dublin: their history and archaeology', in Bradley, Simms and Fletcher, *Dublin in the medieval world*, pp 202–48.

[43] Margaret Murphy and Michael Potterton, *The Dublin region in the middle ages: settlement, land-use and economy* (Dublin, 2010).

[44] Daniel Tietzsch-Tyler, 'King John's Castle: staged development, imperfect realization', in *North Munster Antiquarian Journal*, liii (2013), pp 135–71; Ken Wiggins, *A place of great consequence: archaeological excavations at King John's Castle, Limerick, 1990–8* (Bray, 2016).

[45] Brian Hodkinson, '"Indeed a town of castles": the castles of Limerick city', in *North Munster Antiquarian Journal*, li (2011), pp 53–60; Jim Higgins, 'Some late medieval sculptured chimney-pieces from Limerick', in *North Munster Antiquarian Journal*, liv (2014), pp 81–94. See also Tracey Collins, 'Stone undercrofts at Mary Street, Limerick', in *North Munster Antiquarian Journal*, xliv (2004), pp 67–74.

10. Gaelic towns? Tuam, Longford, Sligo and Ennis

Sarah Gearty

The 'Gaelic town' is not a familiar term within the study of medieval Ireland or its urban history. Just two places are designated with 'Gaelic market town' status on the urban origins map in the *Atlas of Ireland*, making it the lowest-ranking category symbolised.[1] Secondary literature continues to classify the significant periods of town formation in medieval Ireland under headings that reflect the dominant influence — 'monastic', Viking or Hiberno-Norse and Anglo-Norman or English.[2] The Gaelic, Irish or native element is more implied than obvious. Pre-colonial ecclesiastical settlements such as Armagh, Kells, Kildare and Tuam were essentially Gaelic but classification of these sites as 'genuine' towns is a topic of much debate with the term proto-town being introduced as a compromise.[3] Urbanisation in its fullest sense is associated with the coming of the Anglo-Normans in the twelfth century to new and established settlements, where the defining factors of commerce, legal independence, communal organisation, social hierarchy and specialist activity can be identified from documentary and archaeological sources.[4] Of the twenty-five towns covered by the IHTA to date, seventeen can be classed as Anglo-Norman and nine of the first ten publications in the series had firm origins in this category. Consequently, the first comprehensive comparative overview on the IHTA, carried out by John Bradley in 2004, has an Anglo-Norman emphasis but fully recognises the degree to which the landscape had been settled prior to arrival of the colonists and the effects of the Gaelic revival in the fourteenth and fifteenth centuries.[5] In recent years, four midland and western towns within the Gaelic sphere of influence have been published in the IHTA series — *Tuam* (2009) by J.A. Claffey, *Longford* (2010) by Sarah Gearty, Martin Morris and Fergus O'Ferrall, *Sligo* (2012) by Fióna Gallagher and Marie-Louise Legg and *Ennis* (2012) by Brian Ó Dálaigh. Thus, the opportunity has opened to assess and compare the topographies of towns in Gaelic regions during the medieval period.

GAELIC IRELAND AND IRISH TOWNS

The native Gaelic world within Ireland has been acknowledged as a neglected subject across the relevant disciplines up to relatively recently, particularly for the period after the arrival of the Anglo-Normans, when many towns originated. Without a straightforward timeline or boundary, 'Gaelic Ireland' itself is hard to define. Katharine Simms in her book on sources for the subject has described the term as 'a convenient label to describe communities and territories in Ireland which were still ruled by Gaelic chieftains between the Norman invasion of 1169 and the sixteenth-century Tudor re-conquest'.[6] Two societal arrangements were in operation, each with its own language, laws and administrative procedures. Part of this contrast involved the indifference of the Gaelic lords to keeping official records. This has produced an emphasis in the record on native literary texts and official gleanings from medieval English and Anglo-Norman sources. Historians have had to contend with this lack of documentation and difficulties of interpretation. Meanwhile, research archaeologists have focused mainly on the earlier Christian period where their expertise may be considered to have most impact and, with little evidence from the documents or on the ground, historical geographers have tended towards reconstructing earlier landscapes from later topographical sources.[7] Exploring more complex issues, Tadhg O'Keeffe has noted 'a tendency in narrative histories of mediaeval Britain and Ireland to present Gaelic culture as a marginal issue in marginal space, deserving of attention only at its interface with an "English" polity'.[8]

The number of scholars considering the subject of Gaelic Ireland has increased in recent years, via interdisciplinary scholarly publication and national research programmes such as the Discovery Programme's Medieval Rural Settlement project.[9] In discussing the medieval population, where people lived and how they operated, the general pattern that consistently emerges is a divided one — Gaelic (or Irish) and Anglo-Norman. It has been convincingly argued that demarcating medieval Ireland 'on the basis of the national origin of the ruling lineages is one which cannot survive an investigation of the actual facts'.[10] There is acknowledgment of an interdependency of the two worlds and that they were not 'closed cultural systems'.[11] Part of the issue is that assessing their interaction on the ground is difficult. Here, too, there is a demarcation that could be described in modern terms as a rural/urban divide, with the Gaelic peoples almost exclusively associated with the former and with towns — as John Andrews has put it — 'intruding belatedly as an alien force'.[12] Urbanism itself has been on the fringe of broader historical study within Ireland. Anngret Simms suggested that 'the past reluctance to accept towns as part of the Irish heritage' may be linked to questions of cultural identity, colonial history and its expression through the urban network.[13] The question of the Gaelic Irish town emerges as a peripheral one, both thematically and spatially.

Gaelic influence is recogisable topographically in all of the published IHTAs to varying degrees. The Irishtowns adopted at different times at Kilkenny and Limerick are obvious examples, while the persistence of Áth Cliath in the naming record is perhaps the starkest evidence for ongoing Gaelic influence in Dublin.[14] Many published towns firmly categorised as Anglo-Norman in relation to origin illustrate tantalisingly various degrees of settlement (castle or church) pre-dating the arrival of the colonists.[15] Authors engaged in comparative studies using the atlases have been making similar observations. Bradley pointed out the tendency of the Anglo-Normans to locate near existing nodal and individual church sites.[16] Patrick Duffy has noted the diverse nature of the morphological development of Armagh and Kells despite their common origins as Early Christian monastic sites — 'both settlements in many ways present a microcosm of the separate historical experiences of Gaelic and Anglo-Norman Ireland'[17] — while Paul Gosling has observed similar 'cultural divergences' with regard to the evidence in Kildare and Tuam.[18] Howard Clarke has compared eight published Gaelic ecclesiastical sites in the

IHTA series from the perspective of their urban origins.[19] This paper attempts to make a further contribution by teasing out the Gaelic elements in the atlases of Tuam, Sligo, Longford and Ennis and questioning how they interacted with other influences in the townscape.

The stories of the four towns are quite different. Sligo stands apart in a locational sense as an Atlantic coastal settlement, dramatically overlooked by Ben Bulben (527 m). Its river, the Garvoge connecting Lough Gill in the east to the bay in the west, is broad and fast-flowing. The other towns have a degree of inland remoteness — low-lying, characterised by nearby marshlands and bog. The weaving course of the River Fergus, though a dominant feature in Ennis, is secondary to the expansive Shannon estuary about 15 km to the south, while the Rivers Nanny (Tuam) and Camlin (Longford) are tributaries of nearby larger water systems (River Clare/ Lough Corrib and River Shannon).

Culturally too, at least within the definition of a medieval Irish town, Sligo is in its own class as an Anglo-Norman foundation of the thirteenth century. A less straightforward story is quickly revealed, however, with the dominating forces of the local Gaelic lords making their mark on the Anglo-Norman borough and port.[20] Tuam, Ennis and Longford are harder to pin down. Tuam's role as an early monastic site brings the date of that settlement back to the Early Christian period. Its long history as primarily a monastic and an episcopal centre blurs the evidence for when it changed into a fully-functioning town and for who was responsible for this development, though it does seem likely that the agency was native despite Anglo-Norman incursions.[21] Appearing later in the period (fourteenth–fifteenth centuries), Ennis and Longford have been defined as Gaelic townships but their form as 'fledgling urban centres' is difficult to establish. Both places were markets in territories of Gaelic lords within reach of nearby Anglo-Norman strongholds and there is evidence of vibrant trade with English merchants.[22] As in Sligo and Tuam, the Gaelic emphasis in Ennis and Longford is strong but it is one that is interacting with other authoritative influences — colonial and ecclesiastical — to varying degrees and with different chronologies.

Gaelic evidence

Placename evidence for Tuam and Sligo reveals settlements that have their roots in prehistory. References to Tuaim dá Ualann or Tuaim dá Gualann (burial mound of the two altar tombs or two shoulders) appear from A.D. 781 and preserve the memory of the earliest feature of prominence at Tuam. The Bronze Age burial occupied a ridge in the north-east quadrant of what was a crossroads site just south of the River Nanny. Sligigh or Sligeach (the shelly place) is referred to in the annals from A.D. 543 and may also be linked to early prehistoric activity at Sligo, where archaeology has revealed shell middens. In contrast, Ennis (*Inis*, island) and Longford (*longphort*, stronghold) are more recent names, in use from the fourteenth and fifteenth centuries respectively. Where the early settlement histories do converge, however, is in their primary consideration as nucleated sites — on routeways at crossing points on rivers. The crossroad location at Tuam was just south of a ford on the River Nanny. The first indication of settlement at Sligo is a reference to a bridge in 1188, over fifty years before the Anglo-Norman castle was established. Meanwhile the fording points of the Rivers Camlin and Fergus were the determining factors for Gaelic lords when positioning their strongholds at Longford and Clonroad, Ennis.

Tuam is the only one of the towns under discussion whose morphology was considerably influenced by events prior to *c.* 1200. With the coming of Christianity, it developed significance through its association with St Jarlath and its origin as a monastic site was apparently established at Toberjarlath, about 1 km south-east of the crossroads/burial mound location of earlier times. By the eleventh century, focus returned to the site just south of the River Nanny where Temple Jarlath church was established, probably under Áed Ua Conchobair (Áed of the gapped spear), chieftain of Uí Briúin Aí. In 1119, Toirrdelbach Mór Ua Conchobair became high-king of Ireland. Political contact with Hiberno-Norse Dublin and ecclesiastical competition with Munster increased Toirrdelbach's ambition for Tuam as 'a royal and an episcopal showpiece'. The monastic complex at Temple Jarlath was extended to include St Mary's Cathedral, a number of high crosses were erected and St John's Priory of Augustinian canons was established (*c.* 1140), all under Toirrdelbach's patronage. By 1166, Toirrdelbach's son Ruaidrí was high-king and had built a castle at Tuam on a site adjacent to the old burial mound. Within a decade Ruaidrí had built a new parish church, Templenascreen, east of the castle, indicating that Tuam, 'an entirely Gaelic settlement, had acquired an urban dimension by the late twelfth century'.[23]

Some of the elements of this developing Gaelic settlement are reconstructed from documentary, archaeological and morphological evidence in the atlas (Fig. 4.3). The annals are the source of evidence for the monastery of Temple Jarlath (abbot, 1032), its monastic school (lector, 1097), church (1127), and guest house (*teach n-aighed*, 1127). The church is represented in the present townscape by the ruins of a later medieval structure, while the D-shaped curve of the associated graveyard along with the curvilinear nature of Church Street and Sawpit Lane preserve the inner enclosure of the site. Shop Street and Vicar Street mark the eastern line of the outer enclosure of the monastery, which the annals tell us extended from *clad in renda* (corner dyke or trench) in 1127 to enclose St Mary's Cathedral. Excavations have revealed a 'thick cashel-like wall' and this has been interpreted as part of the cathedral boundary.[24] A further enclosure associated with Templenascreen church has been conjectured, partially following the curved alignment of Back Lane north of Bishop Street. The church itself represented a separate parish and, although there are no longer any remains, its name and site are remembered on the Ordnance Survey maps from the nineteenth century to the present day.

The ecclesiastical and secular elements of Gaelic twelfth-century Tuam are defined topographically. The market place and cross (*c.* 1127) have been located at the eastern entrance to Temple Jarlath, just south-west of Ruaidrí's 'wonderful castle'. The castle itself was contained in an area bounded by the enclosures of Temple Jarlath to the west, Templenacreen to the east, the connective route of Bishop Street to the south and the natural boundary of the river to the north. The barony boundary takes an unusual route to unite the enclosed monastic, church, cathedral and priory sites to the east, west and south, while separating the castle complex to the north, giving functional coherence to this patchwork of separate settlement components.

The period post *c.* 1170 is when many of Ireland's towns have their origins, but for the four towns in question it is a mixed story. The coming of the Anglo-Normans did have an impact on Gaelic Tuam. The town was located on a main route into Connacht and Ruaidrí gave allegiance to the king of England in 1175. The battle for Connacht continued and Tuam suffered as a consequence. By *c.* 1200 with the death of Ruaidrí and the archbishop, Cadla Ua Dubthaig, crown control of Tuam increased. The town, however, was left in control of the archbishop, who continued to be Irish as did the majority of tenants. The Anglo-Norman lord William de Burgh founded the Premonstratensian abbey of the Holy Trinity on the western outskirts in *c.* 1204 and there is evidence for an archbishop's residence in the thirteenth century. Archbishop William de Bermingham was responsible for rebuilding the choir of the cathedral but it was still incomplete by 1312. Tuam was developing urban functionality yet its elevated 'metropolitan status' declined from the late twelfth century (Fig. 4.3).

Farther west, Sligo was just establishing itself as one of the few 'peripheral outposts' in an estimate of some fifty 'genuine' Anglo-Norman towns

(Fig. 10.1).[25] Maurice Fitzgerald built his castle at the Sligo crossing point in 1245, where he had already established a hospital and soon would found a Dominican priory (1252). By 1289 Sligo is referred to as a manor. The political history of the late thirteenth-century town is reflected in 'the repeated destruction and reconstruction of Sligo Castle', which is described as 'symptomatic of the fact that its possession was contested between various Gaelic and Anglo-Norman families'. By the early fourteenth century, the castle and town were firmly under the control of Gaelic lords (the O'Connors), though the bridgehead site remained contested by the O'Donnells throughout the medieval period.[26]

The fording points at Ennis and Longford may not have been chosen locations for the Anglo-Normans, but the arrival of the foreigners provided the motivation for the Irish to defend their territories at these well-appointed sites that would mature in the early modern period, like Sligo, to county towns (Figs 10.2, 10.3). The O'Briens, formerly kings of Munster, in retreat to Thomond in the aftermath of their surrender of Limerick, built their stronghold in *c.* 1210 at Clonroad (Inis an Laoigh) rather than at the more obviously strategic site of Clare (where the Anglo-Normans would build in the mid-thirteenth century) or at the established ecclesiastical centre of Drumcliff 4 km away. O'Brien commitment to Clonroad was reinforced in *c.* 1240 when the Franciscans, by invitation, established a friary 1 km to the west at the modern site of Ennis (Inis Mac nInill). O'Brien dominance in the district continued and the settlement at Ennis expanded in the fifteenth century, the friary was improved and urban life developed.[27] The evidence for the stronghold at Longford is more uncertain: it is likely that it was built by the O'Ferralls, lords of Annaly, in the thirteenth century in response to encroaching Anglo-Norman influence, indicated most notably by the de Lacy castle and manor at Lissardowlan, 6 km south-east of Longford and on the western fringe of the lordship of Meath. Continued settlement at the site is implied by the foundation of a Dominican priory near the stronghold in *c.* 1400 and by the end of the fifteenth century Longford had developed at least some of the defining elements of a market town.[28]

TOPOGRAPHICAL COMPARISONS

How did this Gaelic, Anglo-Norman and Anglo-Irish control and influence play out topographically in the four towns and what comparisons can de drawn? It is 1613 before any of the four towns received official legal independence through a charter of incorporation, though references to Sligo having 180 burgesses illustrate that it was functioning in an urban way from the thirteenth century. Descriptions of the bridge (1236), hospital (1242), castle (1245) and 'street town' (*sráid bhaile*, 1257) from the *Annals of Loch Cé* provide the initial documentary evidence for the reconstruction of the early medieval borough.[29] The castle at Longford was located in a position overlooking the bridge crossing, the two 'intimately connected'.[30] This pattern of paired river crossing/stronghold locations is replicated at Tuam, Clonroad and Longford but there are variations in the form and evolution of these defensive sites (Table 10.1). As for Sligo, the first documentary references to the castle site come from the annals and Irish-language sources where there are issues of interpretation. It has been

Fig. 10.1 *Sligo*, fig. 1, medieval Sligo.

Opposite: Fig. 10.2 *Ennis*, fig. 1, medieval Ennis.

Fig. 10.3 *Longford*, fig. 2, seventeenth-century Longford.

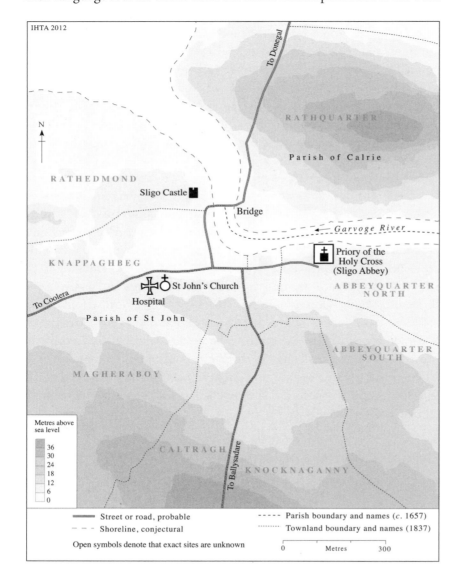

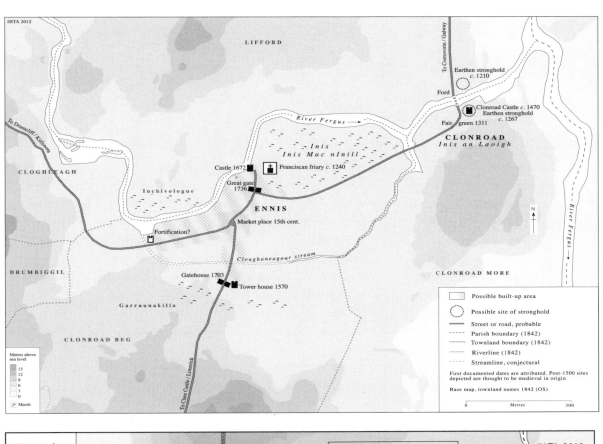

LIFFORD

To Corrovoin / Galway

Earthen stronghold
c. 1210

Ford

Clonroad Castle c. 1470
Earthen stronghold
c. 1267

River Fergus

Fair green 1311

CLONROAD
Inis an Laoigh

To Drumcliff / Kilfenora

*Inis
Inis Mac nInill*

CLOGHLEAGH

Castle 1672

Franciscan friary c. 1240

Inchivologue

Great gate
1736

ENNIS

Market place 15th cent.

N

River Fergus

Fortification?

CLONROAD MORE

DRUMBIGGIL

Cloughaneagour stream

Gatehouse 1703

Tower house 1570

Garraunakilla

CLONROAD BEG

Metres above
sea level

15
12
9
6
3
0

Marsh

	Possible built-up area
	Possible site of stronghold
	Street or road, probable
	Parish boundary (1842)
	Townland boundary (1842)
	Riverline (1842)
	Streamline, conjectural

First documented dates are attributed. Post-1500 sites
depicted are thought to be medieval in origin.

Base map, townland names 1842 (OS)

0   Metres   300

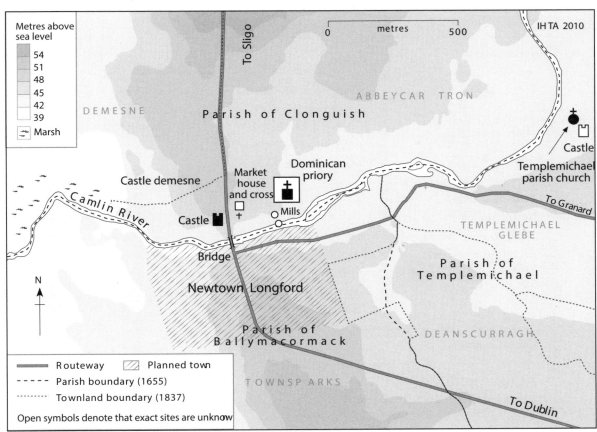

Metres above
sea level

54
51
48
45
42
39

Marsh

To Sligo

0   metres   500

IHTA 2010

ABBEYCAR TRON

DEMESNE

Parish of Clonguish

Castle

Templemichael
parish church

Castle demesne

Dominican
priory

Market
house
and cross

To Granard

Camlin River

Castle

Mills

TEMPLEMICHAEL
GLEBE

Bridge

Parish of
Templemichael

N

Newtown Longford

DEANSCURRAGH

Parish of
Ballymacormack

TOWNSPARKS

Routeway   Planned town

Parish boundary (1655)

Townland boundary (1837)

Open symbols denote that exact sites are unknown

To Dublin

TABLE 10.1: CHRONOLOGY AND DESCRIPTION OF CASTLE SITES AT TUAM, ENNIS, SLIGO AND LONGFORD

TUAM	ENNIS	SLIGO	LONGFORD
Location			
Riverside, near crossing, main routeway, market 50 m, churches/priory 300 m	Riverside, bridgehead, main routeway (Clonroad), market/friary (Ennis) 600 m	Riverside, bridgehead, main routeway, market 300 m, priory 500 m	Riverside, bridgehead, main routeway, market 50 m, priory 200 m
Overlordship			
1164, Gaelic, O'Connor 1574, Gaelic, archbishop	1210, Gaelic, O'Brien	1245, Anglo-Norman, Fitzgerald 1395, Gaelic, O'Connor	1430, Gaelic, O'Ferrall
Description			
Stone castle	Stronghold, moved to new site across river *c.* 1267, replaced by tower house *c.* 1470, 'white castle' *c.* 1551	Stone and lime castle, rebuilt 1269, 1293, 1310; in ruins 1602	Stronghold, replaced by castle or gaol 1571
Post-medieval buildings			
Archbishop's palace c. 1720, shopping centre 2018	Manor house 1713, distillery 1809/ Clonroad House 1837–2018	Stone fort 1659, part stores 1800, Town Hall 1865–2018	Rebuilt *c.* 1671, demolished 1971, derelict shopping centre 2018
Extant remains			
No standing remains, turret excavated 1995	No standing remains	No standing remains, excavated 2002	No standing remains

suggested that Cluain Lis Becc (meadow of the enclosure of Bec), which is referenced from 1282 and had significant associations with the O'Ferralls, is the former name for Longford. This would explain the seemingly late date of the first stronghold at *sean longphort*.[31]

The castles at Tuam, Sligo and Longford were located centrally within the developing town. Strikingly, there are no remains of the early fortifications at any of the sites, each having been adapted to defensive, administrative, residential or commercial priorities during the modern period. Excavations have revealed walls that confirm the siting of the thirteenth-century castle at Sligo, illustrating the importance of archaeology in understanding these fortified sites, which seem to have been critical to these emerging towns.[32] In survival and locational terms, Sligo is more akin to its Gaelic counterparts whose physical memory has faded within the urban space over time, as compared to the resilient, more removed Anglo-Norman strongholds. Of the IHTAs published, twelfth- or thirteenth-century castles/fortifications have survived at Athlone, Carlingford, Carrickfergus, Downpatrick, Dublin, Dundalk (Castletown), Kilkenny, Limerick, Maynooth and Trim and many of these are located at an 'extremity of the town', a common feature noted by Bradley in his study of Anglo-Norman towns.[33] It is worth noting in this context that a stronghold associated with Ruaidrí Ua Conchobhair, probably in the east town, preceded the familiar Anglo-Norman castle at Athlone, strengthening the argument for an earlier twelfth-century Gaelic strategic settlement there.[34] Meanwhile, the ambiguous 'wonderful castle' at Tuam has parallels at the monastic/Anglo-Norman settlements at Kildare and Kells where castles were part of the twelfth-century settlements but no longer survive above ground.[35] Town walls, or lack of, are another common link in the defensive story of the four towns, perhaps reflecting the looser boundary between town and country in Gaelic Ireland and the urge of the natives to escape rather than retreat inwards in times of trouble.[36] References to 'town walls' in Tuam from 1499 most likely refer to the monastic and cathedral enclosures rather than to a defensive circuit of the type found in many Anglo-Norman boroughs.[37]

Religious life is expressed topographically in each of the four towns in various ways. In 1244 there are no fewer than four churches recorded at Tuam (not including St Mary's Cathedral), an indication of the complexity involved in reconstructing ecclesiastical sites in towns with long monastic connections. At Sligo, Ennis and Longford there are challenges too. There are no references to a parish church until the early seventeenth century except at Sligo, as one would expect, but even here the evidence is presented in the atlas as speculative.

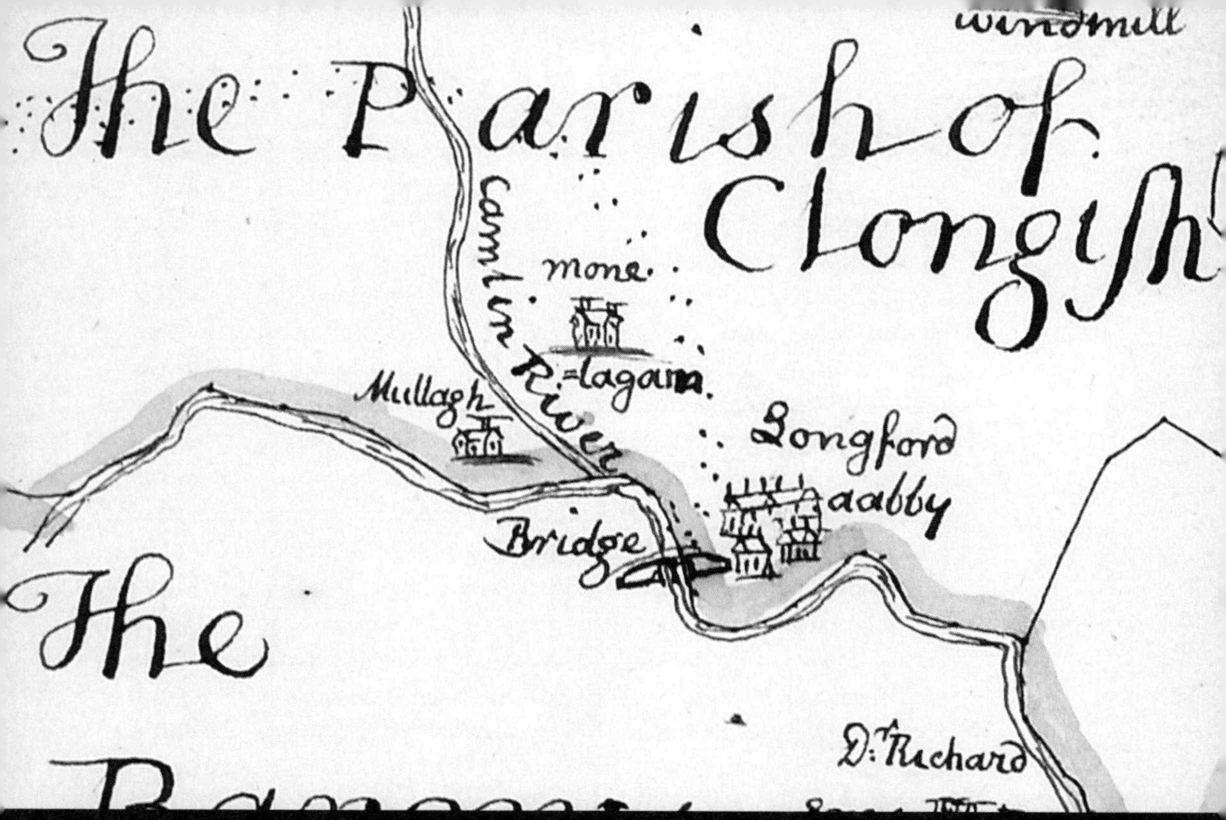

The Parish of Clongish

windmill

Camlin River

mone

=lagara

Mullagh

Longford aabby

Bridge

D: Richard

The

Ba...

Parrish

Slygoe

Castle

Abie

Fort

The common link is the presence of religious houses, their location
on the fringe of the settlements and their key role in urban development. At Tuam, the coupled Gaelic/Anglo-Norman influence is
detected in St John's Priory (canons regular of St Augustine) founded
by Toirrdelbach Ua Conchobair in *c.* 1140 and the abbey of the Holy
Trinity (Premonstratensian) founded by William de Burgh in *c.* 1204.
Both houses occupy spaces in the 'suburbs', outside the outer enclosure
of St Mary's Cathedral. The Augustinians are located more centrally just
south of the market and west of the parish church, Templenascreen.[38]
Otherwise, it is the mendicant or begging orders of friars that establish themselves at Sligo, Ennis and Longford. The priory of the Holy
Cross (Sligo Abbey) was built by Maurice Fitzgerald in *c.* 1252 and St
Brigid's Priory was established by the O'Ferralls at Longford in *c.* 1400.
Both were Dominican foundations on lands at an easterly remove from,
but connected on the same side of the river via street and market to the
founding lord's castle or stronghold. The mid-seventeenth-century Down
Survey and other early regional maps depict schematically the 'abbeys' of
Longford and Sligo as consistent, enduring features from the medieval
past (Figs 10.4, 10.5).[39] At Ennis, a Franciscan establishment was founded
by Connchad Cairprech Ó Briain in *c.* 1240 at a site about 1 km upriver
from Clonroad. The friary is the first identifiable feature of the site of
the modern town and the relationship of the two settlements is recorded
in a topographically descriptive fourteenth-century Gaelic poem where
Inis an Laoigh is distinguished from the bell of Inis to the west.[40] The
O'Briens invested in the Ennis friary and there are references to improvements through the subsequent centuries, as there are at Sligo's priory. St
Brigid's at Longford appears to have been slower and less ambitious in its
improvements. Despite the process of the dissolution of the monasteries
from *c.* 1540, the Ennis and Sligo friaries remained in use until the 1570s
and were adapted afterwards as the location of law courts and parish
churches. Both sites were handed over to the Office of Public Works
in 1893 and are the most significant tourist attractions in Ennis and
Sligo today. The Longford priory was granted to Richard Nugent, baron
of Delvin, in 1556–7 and over the next two centuries slowly disappears
from the records; its former site was partly replaced by St John's Church
and the gaol in the eighteenth century. A similar pattern of transformation occurs at Tuam where St John's Priory and the abbey of the Holy
Trinity are recorded as being in ruins by 1672 and remain only as 'sites
of' on the Ordnance Survey maps of the nineteenth century, gradually
having been replaced by modern housing and roads.

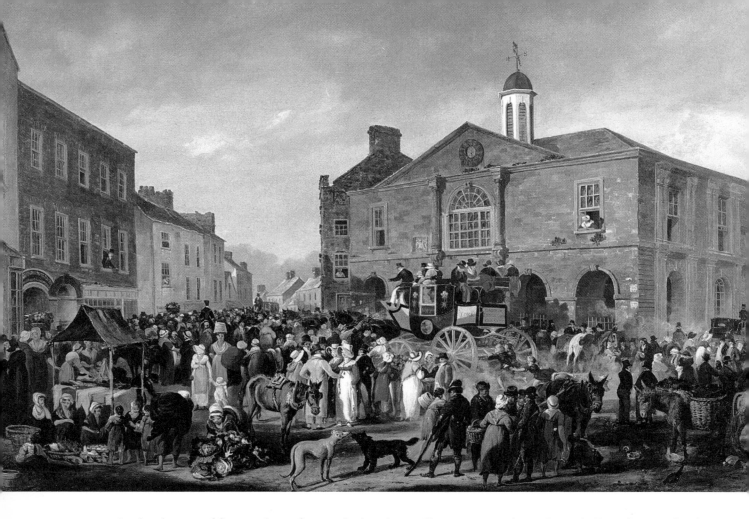

In the absence of firm evidence for parish churches at Sligo, Ennis and Longford, the possibility emerges that religious activity in these towns revolved around the local priory or friary, which would also have provided an impetus for craft and trade. Sligo was in operation as a port from at least 1392 and there is some evidence that the early market place was situated at the eastern end of Castle Street, near Sligo Abbey. Trade increased during the fifteenth century and several Irish merchant families, such as the O'Creans, are associated with Sligo during this period. Sir Henry Sidney, lord deputy of Ireland, mentions the castle, friary and merchants' houses, many of which were in ruins, when he visited Sligo in 1566, his observations reinforcing the main elements and urban nature of the nucleated settlement. By *c.* 1570, Bishop Andrew O'Crean had erected a market cross at the western end of Castle Street, where it meets with Grattan Street and Market Street to form the classic triangular-shaped space for such purposes. There is a comparable triangular market place arrangement at Ennis and Tuam where the main routeways meet and the market cross was located. These historical market places have remained the commercial core of each of the three towns (Figs 10.6, 10.7). Longford's

Fig. 10.6 *Ennis*, plate 2, market place at Ennis, 1820, by William Turner de Lond. The Merrion Collection.

Fig. 10.7 *Tuam*, cover illustration, Market Square, 1953, by T.G. Canny.

position as a midland, frontier trading place between the Pale and the Irish led to its development as a market centre in the fifteenth century, but it is difficult to establish exactly where this trade was taking place. The most likely location was between the castle and friary sites, on present-day Church Street and close to where a market house was built probably in the early seventeenth century. Another suggestion is that the market was south of the river, where the Aungier 'new town' would develop in the seventeenth century. It is possible that, as at Sligo, the siting of the market place changed over time. At Tuam, fairs are recorded from 1260 and it is thought that a cobbled surface uncovered in excavations on the west side of Vicar Street may represent an early market site, the precursor to the modern Market Square location.

In conclusion, the above observations are made with regard to the themes of religion, defence and trade in Tuam, Sligo, Ennis and Longford. Galway was published in the IHTA series in 2016 and Cavan is due in the future. Both will contribute to the history of Irish towns in Gaelic regions. The interconnection of the Gaelic and Anglo-Norman populations is expressed topographically and there is certainly scope for further comparisons encompassing a broader sample from the IHTA. The recent seminal publication *Lords and towns* includes comparative studies from the wider European atlas scheme and in its opening chapter asks whether we can define the identity of the European town?[41] A similar question can be posed with regard to the Irish town and its personality. The Gaelic medieval experience, though elusive, is part of this story.

NOTES

[1] Anngret Simms and Katharine Simms, 'Origins of principal towns', in *Atlas of Ireland*, ed. J.P. Haughton (Dublin, 1979), no. 43; reproduced more recently in Jacinta Prunty and H.B. Clarke, *Reading the maps: a guide to the Irish Historic Towns Atlas* (Dublin, 2011), p. 160.

[2] See, for example, the sub-headings used in *AAI*, i, pp 365–8; and Prunty and Clarke, *Reading the maps*, pp 162–89.

[3] For an overview, see H.B. Clarke, '*Quo vadis?* Mapping the Irish "monastic town"', in Seán Duffy (ed.), *Princes, prelates and poets in medieval Ireland: essays in honour of Katharine Simms* (Dublin, 2013), pp 262–5. See also Anngret Simms, 'The origin of towns in medieval Ireland, the European context', in Jean-Marie Duvosquel and Erik Thoen (eds), *Peasants and townsmen in medieval Europe: studia in honorem Adriaan Verhulst* (Ghent, 1995), pp 99–116.

[4] List of defining factors from John Bradley, 'Planned Anglo-Norman towns in Ireland', in H.B. Clarke and Anngret Simms (eds), *The comparative history of urban origins in non-Roman Europe* (2 pts, Oxford, 1985), pp 418–19.

[5] John Bradley, 'The Irish historic towns atlas as a source for urban history', in H.B. Clarke, Jacinta Prunty and Mark Hennessy (eds), *Surveying Ireland's past: multidisciplinary essays in honour of Anngret Simms* (Dublin, 2004), pp 729–30, 735.

[6] Katharine Simms, *Medieval Gaelic sources* (Dublin, 2009), p. 9.

[7] P.J. Duffy, David Edwards and Elizabeth Fitzpatrick, 'Introduction: recovering Gaelic Ireland, *c.* 1250–*c.* 1650', in P.J. Duffy, David Edwards and Elizabeth Fitzpatrick (eds), *Gaelic Ireland c. 1250–c. 1650: land, lordship and settlement* (Dublin, 2001), pp 22–35.

[8] Tadhg O'Keeffe, *The Gaelic peoples and their archaeological identities, A.D. 1000–1650* (Cambridge, 2004), p. 2.

[9] See Duffy, Edwards and Fitzpatrick, 'Introduction: recovering Gaelic Ireland', pp 21–33.

[10] K.W. Nicholls, *Gaelic and gaelicised Ireland in the middle ages* (Dublin, 2003), p. 4.

[11] O'Keeffe, *The Gaelic peoples and their archaeological identities*, p. 4.

[12] J.H. Andrews, 'The study of Irish country towns', in Anngret Simms and J.H. Andrews (eds), *More Irish country towns* (Dublin, 1995), p. 10.

[13] Anngret Simms, 'The origin of Irish towns', in Anngret Simms and J.H. Andrews (eds), *Irish country towns* (Dublin, 1994), p. 12.

[14] Jennifer Moore, 'Kilkenny and Limerick', in H.B. Clarke and Sarah Gearty (eds), *Maps and texts: exploring the Irish Historic Towns Atlas* (Dublin, 2013), p. 48; Clarke, IHTA, no. 11, *Dublin, part I*, pp 1, 11.

[15] Murtagh, IHTA, no. 6, *Athlone*, p. 1; Horner, IHTA, no. 7, *Maynooth*, p. 1; Hennessy, IHTA, no. 14, *Trim*, pp 1–2.

[16] Bradley, 'The Irish historic towns atlas as a source', p. 729.

[17] P.J. Duffy, 'Armagh and Kells', in Clarke and Gearty, *Maps and texts*, pp 28–9.

[18] Paul Gosling, 'Kildare and Tuam', in Clarke and Gearty, *Maps and texts*, p. 64.

[19] Clarke, '*Quo vadis?* Mapping the Irish "monastic town"', pp 261–78.

[20] Mary O'Dowd, 'Sligo', in Simms and Andrews, *Irish country towns*, p. 142; Nicholls, *Gaelic and gaelicised Ireland in the middle ages*, p. 140.

[21] See Brian Graham, 'Urbanisation in Ireland during the high middle ages, *c.* 1100 to *c.* 1350', in Terry Barry (ed.), *A history of settlement in Ireland* (London, 2000), p. 5; Bradley, 'Planned Anglo-Norman towns in Ireland', p. 420; H.B. Clarke, 'Planning and regulation in the formation of new towns and new quarters in Ireland, 1170–1641', in Anngret Simms and H.B. Clarke (eds), *Lords and towns in medieval Europe: the European historic towns atlas project* (Farnham and Burlington, VT, 2015), p. 278.

[22] Brian Ó Dálaigh, 'Ennis and Longford', in Clarke and Gearty, *Maps and texts*, pp 70–71.

[23] Claffey, IHTA, no. 20, *Tuam*, pp 2–3.

[24] Ibid., p. 3.

[25] Prunty and Clarke, *Reading the maps*, pp 180, 187.

[26] Gallagher and Legg, IHTA, no. 24, *Sligo*, pp 1–2.

[27] Ó Dálaigh, IHTA, no. 25, *Ennis*, pp 1–2.

[28] Gearty, Morris and O'Ferrall, IHTA, no. 22, *Longford*, pp 1–2.

[29] *ALC*, i, pp 335, 359, 369, 423; Gallagher and Legg, *Sligo*, pp 8, 14, 21–2.

[30] Gallagher and Legg, *Sligo*, p. 1.

[31] Gearty, Morris and O'Ferrall, *Longford*, p. 1.

[32] Archaeology has also revealed plots on the eastern side of O'Connell Street running westwards to the river (Eoin Halpin, 'Archaeological site assessments, 1993–1994, Rockwood Parade, Sligo', in M.A. Timoney (ed.), *A celebration of Sligo: first essays for the Sligo Field Club* (Sligo, 2002), pp 119–201; Gallagher and Legg, *Sligo*, p. 2).

[33] Bradley, 'Planned Anglo-Norman towns in Ireland', p. 444.

[34] Murtagh, *Athlone*, pp 1, 10.

[35] Andrews, IHTA, no. 1, *Kildare*, pp 2–3, 9; Simms with Simms, IHTA, no. 4, *Kells*, pp 2, 9.

[36] See, for example, Claffey, *Tuam*, p. 3 for a description of the Irish retreating to local fastnesses when under attack by the Anglo-Normans in 1177.

[37] Claffey, *Tuam*, pp 3, 12.

[38] Ibid., p. 3.

[39] Gearty, Morris and O'Ferrall, *Longford*, maps 4, 6; Gallagher and Legg, *Sligo*, maps, 4, 6a–c.

[40] Ó Dálaigh, *Ennis*, p. 1.

[41] Anngret Simms, 'The European historic towns atlas project: origin and potential', in Simms and Clarke, *Lords and towns in medieval Europe*, p. 32.

11. Colonial towns, 1500–1700: Carrickfergus, Downpatrick and Belfast

Raymond Gillespie

Between 1500 and 1700 one of the most striking features of settlement in Ireland was the growth of towns. In part this was the result of the influx of settlers and the consequent changes in political, economic and social structures. Towns were needed as places to trade for the increasingly commercialised economy as well as the location of local administrations and centres of cultural exchange. The older medieval towns to the south and east of the country developed considerably and some evolved new roles as regional centres in the polity that expanded its control after 1603. To the north and west of Ireland there was almost no urban tradition on which to build and here government and settlers had to create an urban network by fiat rather than allowing it to emerge organically as it had done in other parts of the country. Thus in the Ulster plantation, at the beginning of the seventeenth century, government guidelines laid down clear rules for the creation of towns and created chartered boroughs with their own system of local government.[1] These 'plantation' towns created by government as part of a process of social shaping were rather different entities from the older 'colonial' towns in east Ulster that had emerged more slowly as a result of medieval Anglo-Norman settlement and had benefited from the population influx of the early modern period. This essay will focus on the experience of the 'colonial' towns of east Ulster in the seventeenth century, as the 'plantation' towns of the west of the province are dealt with elsewhere in this volume. Three of these towns have been published as part of the IHTA project — Carrickfergus, Downpatrick and Belfast. The last of these was a new creation of the seventeenth century on the site of an older settlement while the other two were medieval centres that were reinvigorated by the colonisation of the seventeenth century.

PROBLEMS OF SOURCES

However we classify the towns of seventeenth-century Ulster, they all have one common feature: they are poorly documented. The corporation records of Carrickfergus, while existing from 1569, survive only in a fragmentary eighteenth-century transcript made by Dean Dobbs who seems to have copied most of the sixteenth-century entries from the original book but became more selective in his extracts for the seventeenth century.[2] The surviving Belfast corporation book begins in the late 1630s, although a few earlier entries have been copied into it.[3] For Downpatrick no early modern corporation records are extant. Since all three towns were controlled by their landlords, an alternative approach to reconstructing urban life might be through the papers of those landowners. Unfortunately, like the corporation records, the papers of the owners of the towns have not survived well. For Downpatrick almost nothing survives of the papers of the landlords before 1703, the Cromwell family. The situation is rather better for Carrickfergus and Belfast, which were both under the control of the Chichester family, but even here the gleanings on urban life are thin with almost no correspondence from landlords about their town and few leases that might say something about how it was to be structured. It is in this context that the topography of these towns has a particular significance as a source for reconstructing urban life and structures among the 'colonial' towns of east Ulster.

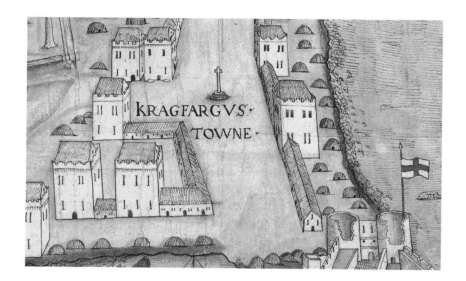

Fig. 11.1 Market cross. *Carrickfergus*, map 4, *c.* 1560. British Library, Cotton MS Augustus I.ii.42, extract.

CARRICKFERGUS

The importance of topographical evidence is that it provides a way of looking at more than morphology. Urban topography is not simply dictated by physical form, although that is clearly a variable in the way in which a town is laid out. Urban form is determined at least as much by the social, economic and cultural priorities of those who lived in individual towns and had considerable agency in how their town developed, making topography an important source for understanding the priorities of town dwellers. This is clearest in a comparative context. The topography of Carrickfergus by the seventeenth century, for instance, was the result of the slow evolution of an urban community with a distinct social and political structure. The town had acquired a mayor and burgesses in the thirteenth century, although the first surviving charter is late, dating from 1568. The public buildings and spaces that articulated the community's assumptions about government are relatively easy to identify by the late sixteenth and early seventeenth centuries. Central to this was the public space of the market place. Here a wide range of activities, typical of streets in an early modern town, happened. For instance in 1576 it was ordered by the corporation that some soldiers of the town's garrison who had insulted the mayor in the street were to be openly whipped through the town and banished to stand 'publicly in the day time on the pillory three or four hours ... and afterwards to be disarmed in the market place as a note of infamy and so banished the town forever'.[4] This use of the market place highlighted the public nature of the punishment, which used shame as much as physical punishment as a weapon. The main business of the market place, however, was buying and selling. Carrickfergus had had a twice weekly market since at least the middle of the sixteenth century and probably much earlier. Crucially for the evolution of the town the right to hold the market, and hence to collect tolls, was vested in the corporation rather than in the landlord and was confirmed in the 1613 charter. The market place was thus closely integrated into the street pattern, although it was not a planned public space but rather had evolved from the emerging street pattern of the town. The late sixteenth-century maps of the town show it as a point where West Street and High Street met, marked on some of the maps by a plain cross on a stepped stone plinth (Figs 11.1, 13.1).

If one aspect of the town was the complex of streets that marked it out on the landscape over a prolonged period, the second feature was the density of population that also serves to mark the settlement. For most contemporaries it was the sheer density of the Carrickfergus population that made the town distinct from the surrounding countryside rather than its economic or social functions. That distinction was given topographical expression by the town walls. These did not mark the edge to the town's authority since that extended out into the surrounding 'county' of Carrickfergus and had been refined in 1601 and again in 1609. What the walls did was to mark out the edge of the physical urban settlement rather than defining legal space. There had been some form of ditch enclosing the town from the thirteenth century and an earthen rampart surrounded it in the early sixteenth century. This was replaced by a stone wall in the mid-sixteenth century (Fig. 8.3). In the early seventeenth century a new stone defensive line was constructed around the town, enlarging its physical area although settlement in this newly enclosed part was limited.[5] The function of this stone wall is rather unclear since such walls were rapidly going out of fashion in an age of canon where complex earthen fortifications offered more effective protection. It seems that the main concern of the builders of the stone wall was display — to highlight the importance of the concentration of population and to reveal the status of the landlord. The parallel clearly was Derry-Londonderry, and possibly less consciously Bandon, where the roughly contemporaneous construction of stone walls was at least partly for display of the wealth and power of the landlord. Neither Belfast, owned by the same landlord, nor Downpatrick had any form of defensive line before the 1640s, presumably because they were less prominent in the landscape than was Carrickfergus as centres of population density and of landlord status.

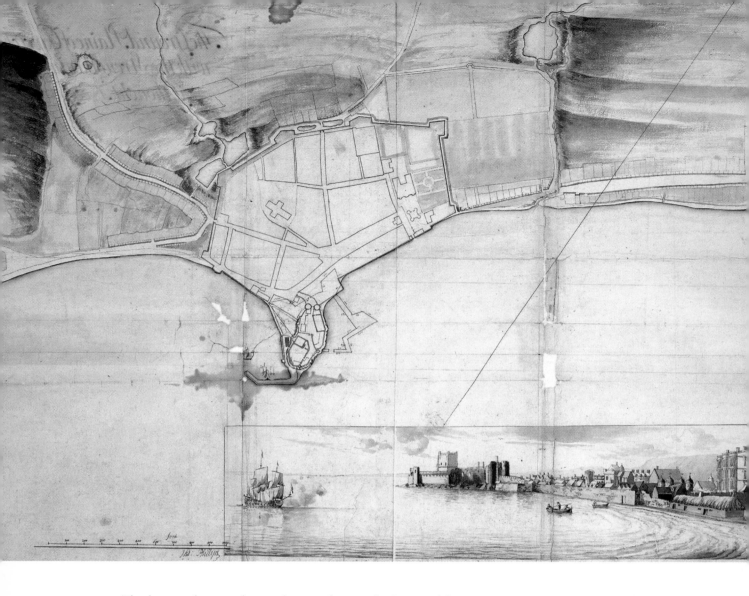

Fig. 11.2 *Carrickfergus*, map 7, 1685, by Thomas Phillips. National Library of Ireland, MS 3137 (42).

The key to the population density that marked Carrickfergus out in the landscape was the presence of a garrison in the town. In 1660 the number of poll tax payers recorded for the town was 664, of whom 349 were soldiers. This clearly affected the character of the settlement in which those classified as 'English' outnumbered the 'Irish' by a factor of more than 3 to 1.[6] Exactly how the tax assessors judged who was native and who newcomer is not known, but one rather crude method may have been religious affiliation. This garrison was quartered there because of the castle at Carrickfergus, built in the late twelfth century but much enlarged and altered through the middle ages.[7] The castle was not the property of the landlord but rather was a royal castle, although for most of the seventeenth century the governor of the castle was also the landlord of the town. In practice it was the importance of the army as a source of economic activity and royal authority that mattered, despite the fact that relations between the garrison and the urban population could be fraught. Thus Carrickfergus was the principal port in the expanding economy of east Ulster before 1660 largely because the garrison of the castle had to be supplied and it is no accident that the harbour is dominated by the castle in the sixteenth-century maps of the town. With the rise of Belfast in the late seventeenth century and the reduction in military presence in the eighteenth century Carrickfergus lost out. In the early seventeenth century neither Belfast nor Downpatrick had the economic pulling power generated by the army or the administrative status of the medieval seat of royal authority of Carrickfergus and these variables certainly shaped the development of the early modern town.

The final topographical feature that provides evidence of a particular type of community comprised the public buildings in Carrickfergus. Most distinctive was the parish church. It was probably built in the late twelfth century to judge from the surviving architectural features but was extensively rebuilt and extended by the Chichesters in the early seventeenth century.[8] It seems that this building served as a topographical symbol of the community of the town. In the late 1560s and early 1570s, for example, the corporation book records that meetings of the corporation were held in the parish church partly because it was the largest, most suitable building in the town. How old this practice was is not clear but by the early 1590s the gatehouse known as Castle Worraigh at the east end of the town had been fitted up as the mayor's courthouse or the 'town house'. Its position, at the edge of the town, is unusual and sixteenth-century town halls or tholsels in the Pale were usually located more centrally. Nevertheless, its marginal position seems to be attributable to its late arrival as part of the urban fabric (Fig. 11.2).[9] Taken with the late date of the first known charter and the late start date of the surviving corporation records it may point to the slow evolution, culminating only in the late sixteenth century, of the corporate sense of the town as a distinctive community with public infrastructure. That sense of a clear corporate identity was present by the late sixteenth century, as reflected in the building of the town hall and the language of the surviving corporation records that is corporatist, referring to the 'common weal' of the town in 1576 and more usually to decisions being made by all the categories of urban residents. Again in 1576 the dates of meetings of the town assembly were standardised for 'more certainty', pointing to a regularisation and routinisation of civic authority that may also be connected with the walling of the town at that time. Finally in 1600 the townscape of the town was more ordered by the creation of wards for the management of street cleaning and repair and defence.[10]

The topographical evidence, together with such fragmented documentary evidence as exists, suggests that Carrickfergus developed a distinct sense of itself in the late sixteenth century. That such a sense carried into the seventeenth century was probably reinforced by other developments such as the building of the new walls by Chichester. The increase in trade, and probably growth of population, that accompanied the settlement of Ulster in the wake of the Nine Years War undoubtedly contributed to this sense of distinctiveness of the town from the surrounding area as suggested by the enclosure within a stone wall. In that sense Carrickfergus was a colonial town of the seventeenth century that was firmly rooted in its medieval past and drew from that topographical legacy to articulate its position in a new world.

DOWNPATRICK

In some respects the evolution of Downpatrick has similarities to that of Carrickfergus. Both were medieval settlements built around a substantial complex of buildings that had an institutional character. In the case of Carrickfergus this was the royal castle but in the case of Downpatrick it was the Benedictine cathedral priory, founded on the site of an older monastic community *c.* 1180. In the case of Downpatrick, however, the settlement that developed around the cathedral was a great deal looser than the compact and legally defined one at Carrickfergus. The position of the cathedral priory on a hill separated it from the other medieval religious houses and the known secular buildings that lay at the foot of the hill on what seem to have been the main communication routes along which the town grew up. The dissolution of the cathedral priory by 1540 and the apparent decay of the building throughout the sixteenth century, a state in which it remained until the late eighteenth century, removed much of the focus, economic as well as religious, for the town.[11] When the settlement revived in the early seventeenth century it was as a result of the colonial spread of English and Scottish settlers throughout the Lecale. The poll tax for 1660 recorded 308 taxable persons in Downpatrick split roughly between 146 settlers and 162 native Irish.[12] The sort of settlement that emerged was rather different from its medieval predecessor. In comparison with Carrickfergus it was similar in size. Disallowing the 349 soldiers in the garrison, Carrickfergus comprised 315 tax payers as opposed to 308 in Downpatrick. The population in Downpatrick, however, was a much less coherent one. By comparison with Downpatrick's roughly equal balance between natives and newcomers, Carrickfergus was dominated by 218 taxpayers of settler origin in contrast to only ninety-seven natives.[13]

Downpatrick was clearly a much more ethnically, and presumably religiously, diverse community than Carrickfergus.

This rather diffuse settlement that grew up at Downpatrick as a result of colonial spread in the early seventeenth century contains a number of topographical complexities that reflect the rather haphazard nature of the town. These can be highlighted by a comparison with Carrickfergus. There the evolution of the town over time had created a core of a market place, a town hall and a centrally located church within a walled context. Downpatrick by contrast had no market place. This is a striking omission in the topography of the town and marks it off as distinctive from the planned plantation towns of Ulster on virtually green-field sites such as Derry-Londonderry and Coleraine that each had a market place at their centre. Even Armagh, less formally planned, had a market place by 1618.[14] The contrast with the eighteenth-century planned towns of Co. Down is even more marked. Nearby Rathfriland, for instance, is built around its market square, which was both the focus and the rationale of the settlement. This does not mean that Downpatrick was not a market centre. There is at least one reference to a port at medieval Downpatrick on the River Quoile and in the early seventeenth century the port books for the Lecale contain references to small Scottish ships trading with Downpatrick.[15] While this quay reappears in the early eighteenth century, no infrastructure was provided there and it never developed despite the fact that the hinterland of Downpatrick, the Lecale, was one of the agriculturally richest areas in east Ulster. A Saturday market and two fairs each year were granted in 1617, but crucially the grant here was made not to the corporation but to the landlord, Edward Baron Cromwell, who was an absentee for most of the early seventeenth century. In 1641, when the town was attacked, there was clearly a merchant community since five of those living there were described as merchants, all of whom had Irish names.[16] Nevertheless there is little evidence for trading infrastructure. A market house was not built until 1660 and a focal point for the market with a market cross was provided only as late as 1729 when one of the Early Christian crosses from the cathedral was re-erected in the town (Fig. 11.3).[17] As late as the 1830s the municipal corporations report noted that 'the markets are held in narrow streets of the town; no accommodation of any kind is furnished to the public by the owners of the market and every exaction is enforced with rigour'. Such stalls as were provided were said to be 'placed in the most inconvenient positions'.[18] Clearly such 'inconveniences' served to limit the scope for economic and social development and most of the attempts at providing it came late.

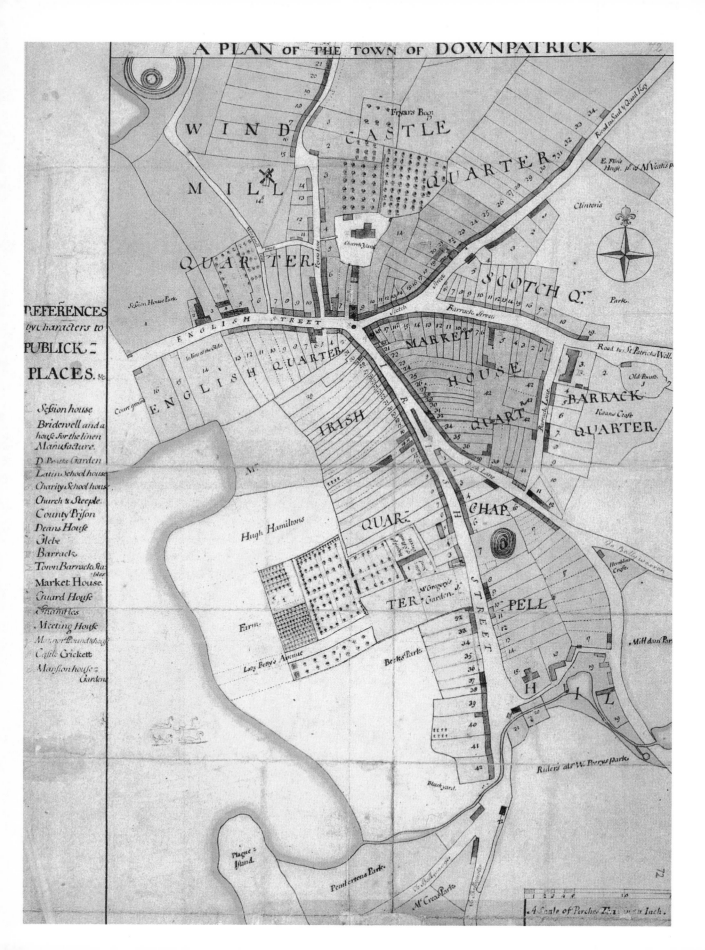

A PLAN OF THE TOWN OF DOWNPATRICK

WIND

MILL

QUARTER

CASTLE QUARTER

Fryars Bog:

Church Yard

Session House Park.

SCOTCH Q.

Park.

Clintons

E. Flins Hoge. pt of M.Veahs p.

Road to Saul & Quol. Key

REFERENCES
by characters to
PUBLICK
PLACES. &c.

Session house
Bridewell and a
house for the linen
Manufacture.
D. Deans Garden
Latin School house
Charity School house
Church & Steeple.
County Prison
Deans House
Glebe
Barrack
Town Barrack Sta-
bles
Market House.
Guard House
Shambles
Meeting House
Marger Roundshead
Castle Crickett
Mansion house &
Garden

ENGLISH STREET

ENGLISH QUARTER

IRISH QUARTER

Court green

In lieu of the Globe

MARKET HOUSE QUARTER

Barrack Street

BARRACK QUARTER

Road to St Patricks Well.

Keans Croft

Old Bouts

Barrack Lane

Back Lane

CHAP

STREET

PELL

HILL

Hugh Hamiltons

Farm

Lady Bettys Avenue

Berles Park.

Mr Gregorys Garden.

To Bally weaver

Hewlins Croft.

Mill dam Par

Riders als W. Berrys Park.

Black yard.

Plague Island.

Pembertons Park.

M.Creash Parks

A Scale of Perches Ten in an Inch.

The second topographically problematic element in Downpatrick was the parish church. Unlike Carrickfergus this was not placed prominently at the core of the town but was located away from the centre where the main streets meet. Moreover, it was set back from the main body of the town, being at the end of Church Lane. The history of the parish church is rather enigmatic. It is unclear where the medieval parish church had been located. The earliest reference to the present building comes from the visitations of the early seventeenth century and a piece of communion silver of 1630. It has been suggested that part of the present building is of sixteenth-century date, but there is no evidence to support this. It is clear that the building has two phases. The main body of the church was reconstructed in 1733–5, but the tower is clearly older and there is evidence from the vestry books that the tower may have been built in 1710–15.[19] It seems likely that the early seventeenth-century structure was on a different site and was relocated, possibly in the late seventeenth century. This might partly explain the marginal position of the parish church at Downpatrick as opposed to the central position of the medieval church at Carrickfergus. Whereas at Carrickfergus the medieval church sat beside the market place and served as a focal point for the community, the confessional balance of Downpatrick when the church was built, possibly after 1660, made it less emblematic of the community as a whole and as a result it was located in a position some distance away from the town. Differential patterns of migration in a colonial world could produce differing topographical results and this may be an example of such a development.

The final problem with Downpatrick is the absence, in contrast to Carrickfergus, of any topographical expression of a sense of urban identity such as a town hall or other corporate building. Taken together with the lack of a market place as a public space, this raises the question as to whether any indications of urban distinctiveness, such as a charter, ever existed. There are certainly medieval references to a mayor and later to the 'commonality' of Downpatrick, which implies some form of corporate government, but the municipal corporations report in the nineteenth century could find no trace of a charter, although the borough had had two MPs 'by prescription' since at least 1585.[20] Most towns in this situation had their position regularised in the early seventeenth century as part of the preparations for the parliament of 1613–15 when a large number of Ulster towns were given charters to allow them to return MPs. Downpatrick, however, did not receive a charter. Some attempt was made to regularise this position in 1635 with the issuing of a king's letter for the incorporation of the town with its rights. While part of the context of this grant may have been the new parliament, it is also clear that there was a major dispute, whose origins and details are murky, about the government of the town in circumstances that may have necessitated the grant of a charter.[21] Whatever the reason for the granting of a king's letter for a charter, it is clear that no grant was made and that Downpatrick operated through the seventeenth and eighteenth centuries with no charter or body corporate to act as a framework for local life. This is reflected in the absence of any town hall or corporation house where local government might be conducted and give topographical expression to the corporate existence of the town.

Much of the local administration of Downpatrick was carried on through the manorial courts rather than by a corporation. The framework for the town was the manor erected in 1617, when the property was granted to the Cromwell family, and confirmed by royal grant in 1638. For most of the early seventeenth century the Cromwell family were absentees and it was not until the late 1630s that they built a residence in Downpatrick. This house was, by the standards of Chichester's houses at Belfast and Carrickfergus, very modest and located well outside the core of the town. All of this suggests a rather limited engagement by the landlord with the town and certainly no investment in the shape of the town as Chichester provided by walling Carrickfergus. This may partly be explained by the heavy debts that Cromwell incurred in the early seventeenth century, but since Chichester had similar financial difficulties it cannot fully explain the divergence between the two places.[22]

The topographical differences between Carrickfergus and Downpatrick in the early modern period were striking. Both had similar inheritances, both centres of trade and administration in the middle ages. Both developed their administrative roles in the seventeenth century as the assize towns for their own areas and the main centres where inquisitions were taken. Both had similar possibilities in the seventeenth century with the expansion of economic activity in east Ulster and the dramatic population growth that took place as a result of informal colonisation. Nevertheless Downpatrick failed to congeal as a town in the seventeenth century while Carrickfergus had succeeded by the late sixteenth century. The former failed to develop sites and institutions, such as the town hall, market place or the parish church, where an urban sense could be created and community coherence generated. At least some of this was the result of an absentee landlord who, though he held the rights and income from the markets, failed to provide any infrastructure to develop trade or the physical fabric of the town itself. While the Cromwell family did reside in Downpatrick in the late 1630s after the Restoration, they were absentee for two decades.

BELFAST

The third example of a town that grew as a result of seventeenth-century colonial spread in east Ulster was Belfast. Like Carrickfergus and Downpatrick, Belfast had a medieval history, albeit a more insubstantial one. The town grew up around the lowest fordable point on the River Lagan, where the River Farset entered the Lagan, and a Chapel of the Ford established itself there in the middle ages. By the fifteenth century this chapel had been joined by a castle, probably a tower house, that controlled the ford. The way in which this settlement evolved was unlike either Carrickfergus with it medieval corporate tradition, or Downpatrick with its rather less coherent expression of corporate identity. Rather, Belfast chose to turn its back on its medieval past. The seventeenth-century town was built on a green-field site not near the castle and chapel but on the other side of the River Farset. Belfast was to all intents and purposes a newly founded town.[23] For that reason the parish church, the reconstructed Chapel of the Ford, was somewhat removed from the main centre of the town in the seventeenth century. Applying the criterion of background, ethnic or religious, suggests that the town in the 1660s was a diverse mix of people with a predominance of settlers over Irish, 366 as against 223. Extending the area to include some of the townlands adjacent to the immediate urban area would not affect that balance significantly.[24]

Unlike both Downpatrick and Carrickfergus, Belfast was a town that had not evolved slowly but rather was the product of landlord planning. Thus, when the plantation commissioners visited the town in 1611 they noted 'the town of Belfast is plotted out in good form', suggesting that it was surveyed and formally laid out.[25] Control on urban development was through the lease and in particular the building leases granted by the Chichesters early in the settlement process. In this way much of the long-term responsibility for the development of the town was devolved on its tenants, so that the landlord had little involvement in shaping its fabric and there was little infrastructural investment in areas such as defence. Belfast, like Downpatrick, had no line of defences before the construction of a rampart in the 1640s to protect the town during the wars of that decade, this being paid for by levies imposed by the corporation rather than by the landlord.[26] Unlike Downpatrick, however, this absence of defences does not seem to have arisen through landlord parsimony but was instead part of a strategy. Belfast's function was intended to be that of a port, acting as an entrepôt for the large Donegall estates in south Antrim. As such it did not require much in the way of defence. Carrickfergus, by contrast, was intended to be the status and administrative centre for the Chichester

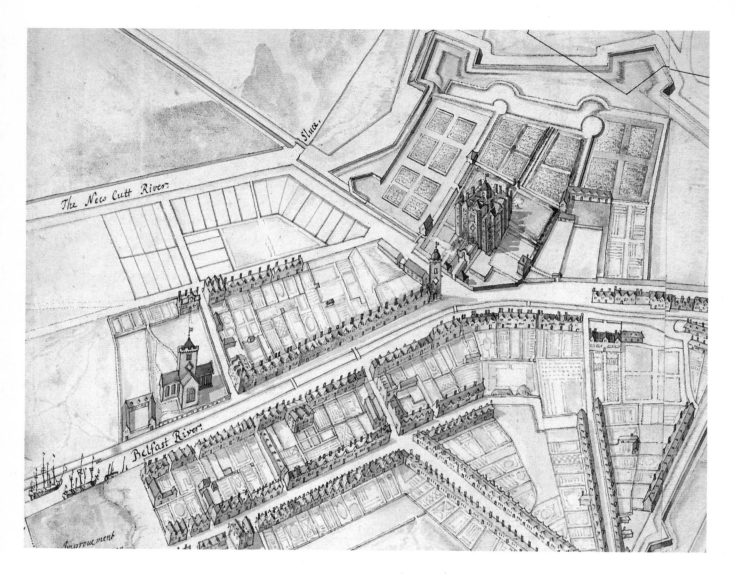

The New Cutt River.

Sluce.

Belfast River.

estate and hence display of apparent wealth and power was more appropriate in that case. This made walls a necessity, even though their military function may have been limited.

This concentration on trade in Belfast, booming in the colonial context of the seventeenth century, had a number of effects. Paradoxically it was this concentration that allowed Belfast to flourish, outstripping Carrickfergus in the middle of the seventeenth century and leading to the Chichesters moving their main residence from Joymount in Carrickfergus to a rebuilt Belfast Castle. This was located on the site of the sixteenth-century tower house and thus provided a link between the older settlement and the newly developed part of the town that in the eighteenth century allowed the two parts to be integrated. The rise in importance of the castle as a real landlord residence in the later seventeenth century saw the relocation of the town hall away from the older market place to a new site opposite the

Fig. 11.4 *Belfast, part I*, map 4, by Thomas Phillips. British Library, Maps, K Top 51 38, extract.

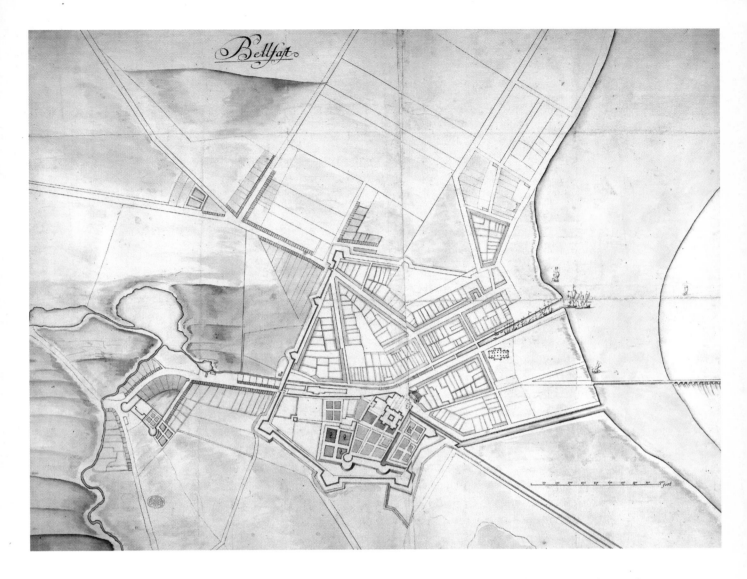

Fig. 11.5 *Belfast, part I*, map 5, by Thomas Phillips. British Library, Maps, K Top 51 37.

castle gate, a process that did not occur in Carrickfergus since the castle was a royal one and not a landlord residence. Since trade was central to urban life, the market place, as the physical manifestation of trade, was central to the town. In contrast to Downpatrick where no market place emerged, that at Belfast was at the core of the new landlord planned town and was located at the junction of an older route marked by North Street and Broad (or Waring) Street, which was the spine of the new town and the main residence of its new elite (Fig. 11.4).[27] Something of the significance of this trade is clear from a comparison with Carrickfergus. There trade was concentrated in a central market place, although a separate fish shambles was built on the 'hill against the castle' in 1576.[28] The sixteenth-century maps suggest that this was an uncluttered area and stalls were presumably erected temporally for the market. In Belfast, however, the market was more clearly organised and managed. By 1639 there were rules for the operation of the market and the reference to 'standings to be made about the walls of the market place' suggests that permanent structures were being developed, indicating more intensive trading activity than simply weekly markets.[29] In the late seventeenth and eighteenth centuries, as the Carrickfergus market remained centralised, Belfast markets broke up into more specialised spaces reflecting the greater complexity and sophistication of trading activity in the town. The corn market emerged by 1670, a market near the barracks is shown on the map of 1696 and it may be that the large open area beside the parish church with a chimneyless building adjacent to the new quay on the Phillips view of 1685 was intended to be developed as a market. As in Carrickfergus the market place in Belfast was also an important public space. Its seems likely that this was the location of the town hall when that was built, or adapted from existing buildings, in the 1630s. It was also the place for significant events and dramatic public statements, such as the tearing in pieces of the colours of the royalist forces by the parliamentary commander Major General Munroe after he had seized the town in 1644.[30]

Unlike Downpatrick, Belfast was one of the Ulster towns that obtained a charter in 1613. This can certainly not be seen as evidence of a sense of corporate identity so early in the settlement's history. Indeed most of those named as burgesses do not seem to have been resident in the town at this date. Unlike Carrickfergus, which also received a charter in 1613, the Belfast charter was imposed from central government whereas that for Carrickfergus emerged as part of a long tradition of obtaining charters from the mid-sixteenth century. The Belfast charter, however, is important since it provided a framework for an emerging sense of urban identity. Here topographical evidence is important in elucidating the formation of this sense of corporate belonging. The building of a town hall is one such indication. Belfast's first town hall was built in the late 1630s, whereas Carrickfergus had a town hall from the 1590s. A chamber for the Belfast sovereign's court was fitted out and silver maces acquired for the town. Other aspects of the town were reorganised, reflecting a greater articulation of the sense of an urban community. From the late 1630s town records were independently kept and some older material was written into the new corporation book by the same clerk who made the entries in the late 1630s. Markets were increasingly regulated by the corporation and standard weights and measures were held in the town hall. The location of the town hall is unclear, but in all probability it was directly beside the market place, which would have placed it at the centre of the newly emerging town. This conjunction of the manuscript evidence with topography and material culture all suggests that Belfast in the late 1630s was beginning to demonstrate evidence for the coherence of an urban community.

Central to this process was the corporation, yet little is known about its internal workings and problems. Here topography can shed some light on the question. A case in point is the micro-topography of the quays in seventeenth-century Belfast (Fig. 11.5). The evolution of the quays, and in particular the slow rate of change in the infrastructure at a time of rapid trade and more general economic expansion, present something of a paradox in the history of the town. Part of the explanation is the shortage of finance. While the charter of 1613 had assigned the 'common key' to the corporation, it had not provided for any income to fund that and the corporation had little by way of alternative sources of income. Unlike Carrickfergus, where the corporation had control of a substantial land bank around the town, all the lands of Belfast and the income from markets and fairs were vested in the Chichester family. While in 1674 Chichester was prepared to grant the profits of the office of water bailiff to the corporation for the maintenance of the quays, that relationship did not last and broke down in the disputes between the Donegalls and the town at the end of the seventeenth century.[31] The problem with the quays was only one facet of a much larger problem of the government of a town over which the governors had no real financial control. It was not an issue that either Carrickfergus or Downpatrick was to encounter.

CONCLUSION

These three case studies of the formation of east Ulster towns in a colonial context, unencumbered by the regulation characteristic of the plantation process, demonstrate that even with sparse evidence from traditional sources it is possible to reconstruct something of early modern Irish urban experiences. In that process topography can usefully be analysed alongside the surviving manuscript material. Since topography is not a given but the result of a set of social and economic processes, evidence of contrasting topographical development points to significantly differing social experiences of colonial town formation.

NOTES

[1] R.J. Hunter, 'Towns in the Ulster plantation', in *Studia Hibernica*, no. 11 (1971), pp 40–79.
[2] PRONI, T707/1.
[3] R.M. Young (ed.), *Town book of the corporation of Belfast* (Belfast, 1892).
[4] PRONI, T707/1, p. 13.

[5] Ruairí Ó Baoill, *Carrickfergus: the story of the castle and walled town* (Belfast, 2008), pp 35–7, 59–60, 71–5.

[6] *Census 1659*, p. 20.

[7] Ó Baoill, *Carrickfergus,* pp 16–27.

[8] Ibid., pp 42–57.

[9] For the position of town halls see Anngret Simms, 'Interlocking spaces: the relative location of medieval parish churches, churchyards, market places and town halls', in H.B. Clarke and J.R.S. Phillips (eds) *Ireland, England and the continent in the middle ages and beyond* (Dublin, 2006), pp 222–34.

[10] PRONI, T707/1, pp 13, 26–7.

[11] Fred Rankin, *Down Cathedral: the church of St Patrick of Down* (Belfast, 1997), pp 81–102.

[12] *Census 1659*, p. 69.

[13] Ibid., pp 20–21.

[14] McCullough and Crawford, IHTA, no. 18, *Armagh*, p. 3.

[15] For instance, R.J. Hunter (ed.), *The Ulster port books, 1612–15* (Belfast, 2012), p. 102.

[16] TCD, MS 837, ff 31–31v; MS 810, f. 128.

[17] There may have been an earlier market cross since in 1617, at a Catholic funeral in Downpatrick, the beir was said to have been carried 'about the cross' (Brian Mac Cuarta, 'A Catholic funeral in County Down, 1617', in *Archivium Hibernicum*, lx (2006–7), p. 324). Given the liturgical role of the cross, however, this is more likely to have been a wayside cross or a cross in the cathedral graveyard.

[18] *Mun. corp. Ire. rept,* p. 799.

[19] For a description of the building, see E.M. Jope (ed.), *An archaeological survey of County Down* (Belfast, 1966), pp 324–5 and for the communion silver of 1630 see Anthony Wilson, *Saint Patrick's town* (Belfast, 1995), p. 87.

[20] *Mun. corp. Ire. rept,* p. 797.

[21] *Cal. S.P. Ire., 1633–47,* p. 108; Sheffield Archives, Wentworth Wodehouse MS, Strafford letters books 15, no. 303.

[22] For Cromwell's debts see Raymond Gillespie, *Colonial Ulster: the settlement of east Ulster, 1600–1641* (Cork, 1985), pp 138.

[23] Raymond Gillespie, *Early Belfast: the origins and growth of an Ulster town to 1750* (Belfast, 2007), pp 24–64.

[24] *Census 1659*, p. 8.

[25] Gillespie, *Early Belfast*, p. 58.

[26] Ibid., pp 75–7.

[27] Ibid., pp 63–5, 69.

[28] PRONI, T707/1, p. 13.

[29] Young, *Town book*, pp 14–15.

[30] Gillespie, *Early Belfast*, p. 69.

[31] Raymond Gillespie, 'Reconstructing the quays of seventeenth-century Belfast', in *Áitreabh*, no. 20 (2015–16), pp 6–9.

12. Plantation towns: Bandon, Derry~Londonderry and Armagh

Annaleigh Margey

The sixteenth and seventeenth centuries witnessed a distinct watershed in the evolution of Irish towns. At this juncture, new towns emerged under the auspices of Tudor and Stuart policies of plantation. At first, these plantations gave rise to urban settlements that grew around fortifications in the Irish midland counties of Laois (Queen's County) and Offaly (King's County) in the 1550s and 1560s. Yet, by the early seventeenth century, urban development had shifted apace, as plantation in Munster witnessed formal town development by enterprising landlords, such as the future earl of Cork, Richard Boyle. Furthermore, under the auspices of the Ulster plantation, the use of towns to aid in social regulation and anglicisation came to the fore, when twenty-five corporate towns were planned across the six plantation counties.

For the urban historian, this programme of building has left behind numerous sources to help us understand the evolution of towns during the decades of plantation. In recent years, these sources have been deployed by the IHTA project to study three plantation towns: Bandon, Derry-Londonderry and Armagh. These atlases have enabled analysis of the development of these towns during the plantations within the wider context of their long-term growth, from their origins to the present day, across themes including topography, morphology, settlement, governance and the economic and social world. This essay aims to explore the source-driven nature of these studies by offering a comparative analysis of the three plantation towns completed by the IHTA. Beginning with an overview of the range of sources available, the essay will move to focus specifically on the content of the three fascicles to explore the similarities and contrasts in the plantation histories of these towns, with a particular emphasis on how the sources have been deployed.

THE SOURCES

While all of the towns in question — Bandon, Derry and Armagh — fall under the umbrella of 'plantation towns', each had very distinctive origins in its own right. Bandon emerged as the centrepiece of the Boyle estates in Munster and was entirely a private enterprise. Armagh developed from an existing medieval settlement, dominated by ecclesiastical foundations and under the control of the archbishop of Armagh. 'Londonderry', on the other hand, became a condition of the grant of lands to the city of London at the beginning of the Ulster plantation. The diverse origins of many plantation towns have given rise to a wide range of sources, which are spread between public repositories and private collections. In the main, the documents roughly follow a prescribed chronology from pre-plantation descriptions of the region, materials relating to the planning of, and preparation for, settlement, and reports on the early growth and development of the town. These sources cover the formative years of the Irish plantations from *c.* 1550 to the 1620s, as well as tracing their continuing success in the seventeenth century. In the case of Derry, the records of the Irish Society run to the present day.

One of the most distinctive features of these towns is the physical evidence of their existence. Raymond Gillespie has argued that perhaps our main source for plantation towns is their streetscape.[1] While basic town plans are represented on contemporary maps, the grid-iron street pattern is, for example, still intact within the walls of Derry, while street names in towns such as Coleraine and Bandon reflect their plantation past. This tangible evidence of plantation from the streets also helps us to understand something of the complexities in their modern usage. In recent times planners have grappled with how to integrate the early modern heritage into the present townscape. At Derry, for example, evidence of changes to the plantation walls bears witness to this. The continuing evolution of the city ensured that in previous centuries the local authorities broke down sections of the original walls to accommodate new gates and entry points as the urban area expanded. More recently, the Derry walls have been adapted to provide a walkway around the historic core.[2]

This physical evidence has also been elucidated by archaeological excavation. While we have definite evidence of plantation from the walls in Derry, other plantation towns have been less fortunate in the survival of their defences. Only sections of the Bandon wall, for example, are still to be found. These have seen continual archaeological digs since the early 2000s, as part of a period of construction and development in the town.[3] What has been more informative, however, is the archaeological evidence that emerged previously, from the seventeenth century onwards. In the 1970s, a programme of rescue archaeology was carried out in Derry at the height of the Troubles. These digs found a range of evidence including wells, potsherds, clay tobacco pipes and two seventeenth-century houses in Linenhall Street.[4] As a source for plantation towns, archaeological remains can be both enlightening and frustrating in equal measure. The remains of waste pits, household objects and even houses themselves enable us to piece together something of the social and economic world of plantation towns. Yet, the piecemeal nature of the remains due to soil disturbance and rebuilding over the intervening centuries often inhibits our attempts to reconstruct fully the physical fabric of these worlds.

Plantation towns are ably recorded cartographically and maps usually survive for the many stages in their development. In their earliest guise, maps often acted as blueprints for the town. As the town matured, plans recorded its growth, quite often monitoring the overall development of the urban environment for plantation officials. Taking our three plantation towns from the IHTA, the usefulness of maps as a source comes to the fore. Richard Bartlett depicted pre-plantation Armagh in 1602 (Fig. 4.4).[5] This map shows the destruction that had rained down on medieval Armagh during the Nine Years War of the late sixteenth and early seventeenth century. As such, it offers the historian a view of the site on the eve of plantation, allowing analysis of how new settlement both integrated into, and adapted within, the existing landscape. For Bandon, three maps have survived. The first dates from 1613, while the other two seem to depict intentions for the earl of Cork's developments at Bandonbridge in *c.* 1620 (Figs 12.1, 12.2).[6] A gatehouse plan has also survived for Bandon, showing the scale of the fortified gates embedded in the town wall.[7]

The most extensively mapped plantation town, however, is Derry. Maps provided the outline plan for the town and thereafter became monitoring tools as the twelve great livery companies of London and the Irish Society sought to examine development. The earliest plan of the town can be compared to the later maps showing, for example, walls on three sides of the circuit only, with the river acting as a natural barrier to the north.[8] In reality, as plans continued to evolve, the entire circumference of the town was walled. Further cartographical evidence for many plantation towns has recently been made publicly available by the online publication of the Down Survey maps of Ireland.[9] The walled town of Bandonbridge, straddling both sides of the Bandon River, features prominently on the map of Co. Cork, for example.[10] The value of maps as a source for plantation towns cannot be disputed. They offer an insight into both planning and construction and give an indication of the dates for the development of key morphological and architectural features. They do, however, need to be used in conjunction with other sources. Recent archaeological work suggests that we need to be aware that some maps embellished reality, often including planned features that had not been built by the time the map was made and that, thereafter, were never constructed. This is true of Thomas Raven's 1622 map of Derry, which included a small fortification at the centre of the modern Diamond that was supposed to act as a store for weaponry (Fig. 5.3).[11] The fortification, however, never came to fruition.

Unsurprisingly, much evidence for town development can be found in the official records of government, such as the *Calendar of the state papers relating to Ireland*. These, for example, record the formal incorporation of each town on receipt of its charter. Often, correspondence between town officials and the London government can be found here. They are, however, not so fruitful for research on towns as other elements of plantation history, owing to the diversity of many towns' origins. Among the most important official sources for towns during the period are the reports of the government-issued commissions that surveyed the progress of plantations in Ireland. These reports survive for Ulster from 1611, 1614 and 1619, and include vivid descriptions of towns and their inhabitants. Moreover, a commission in 1622 included reports for the whole of Ireland, giving an introduction to the extent of urban development across the country in the seventeenth century. As sources, these reports are invaluable, offering some of the most extensive descriptions of the towns, their buildings, their fledgling economies and the extent of habitation. Their chronological sequence allows for judgements to be made on the growth

Fig. 12.1 *Bandon*, map 4, 1613, by Christopher Jefford. Trinity College Dublin, MS 1209/39.

Following pages:
Fig. 12.2 *Bandon*, map 5, *c.* 1620. Trinity College Dublin, MS 1209/41.

S.r Richard Boyle

A New Way

Dithe

S.r Richard Boyle

way into Mußcre

Beachers

towne Nuces part

S.r R.B.   S.r R.B.   S.r R.B.   S.r R.B.

northe stret

S.r R.B.   S.r R.B.   S.r R.B.   S.r R.B.

stret to corke

out the towne for the lord
president of mounster

S.r R.B.   S.r R.B.   S.r R.B.   S.r R.B.

chirch

A hye way to leg-o-northe

west stret

market place

S.r R.B.

Cop: Nuce   Cop: Nuce

Carnes
of the fort:
Cop: Nuce

Cop: Nuce   Cop: Nuce

S.r R.B.

S.r Richard Boyle

S.r R.B.   S.r R.B.

The great reuer with the myles on it

A mylle of browne Nuces

a Richard Boyle

Shepards   Part.

N.

The braw

A Way to

The brid

The great reuer with the myles on it

a saile with an inch deuided
into 16 parts

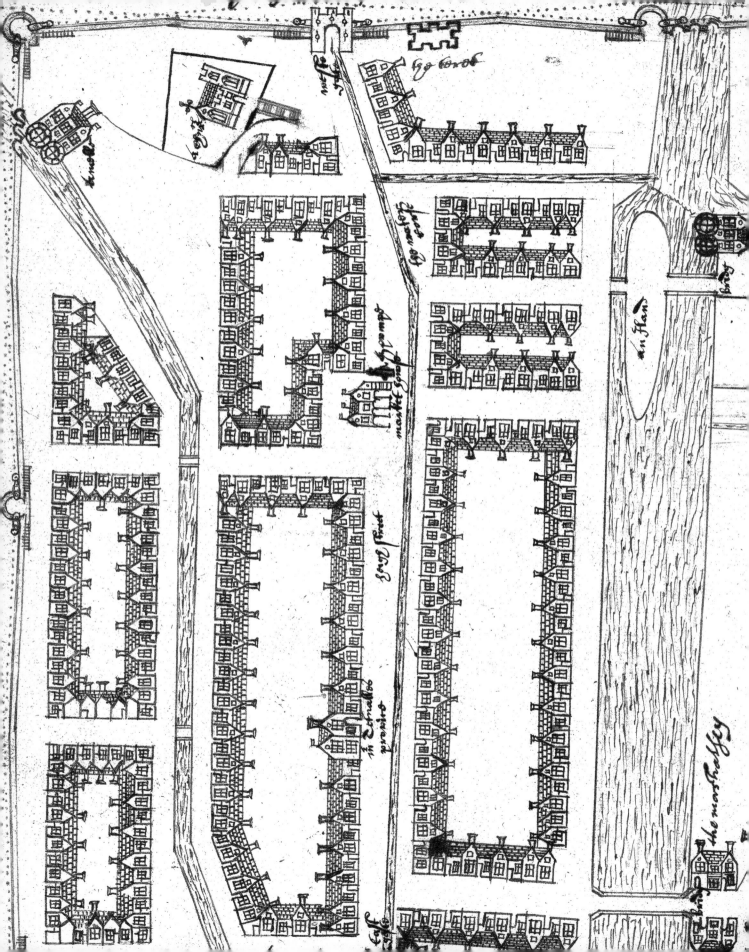

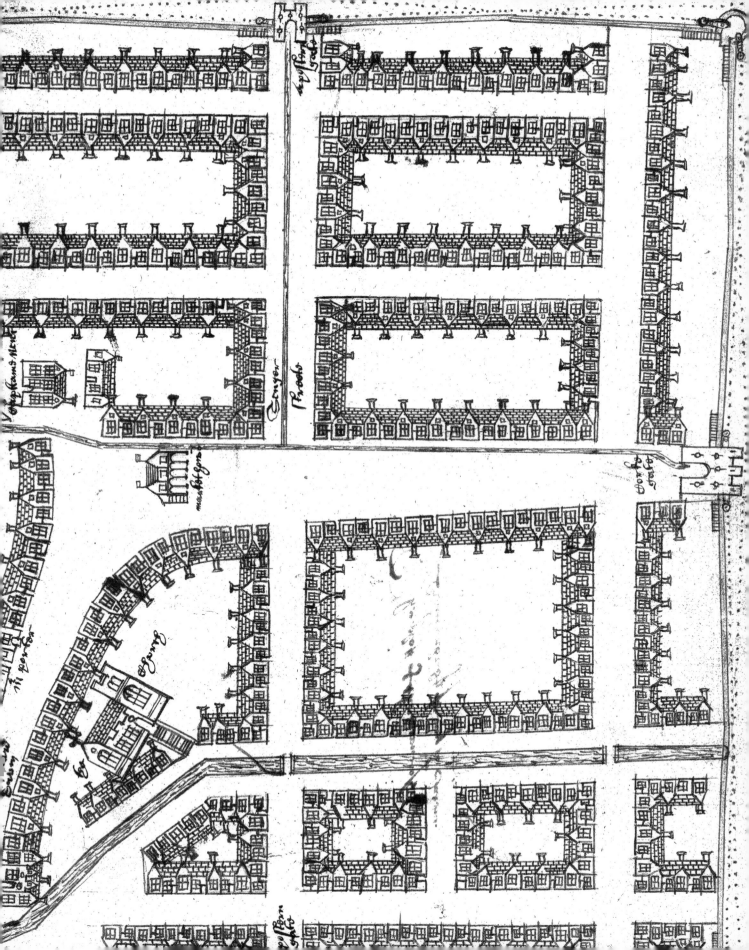

of the towns and how, in fact, they developed across the decades. They are, however, geographically limited, offering a more extensive insight into the development of Ulster's planation towns than those elsewhere. What makes these reports stand out is how relatively easily they can be accessed by researchers. Recent transcriptions by the historian, Victor Treadwell, have given rise to the publication of the 1622 commission report. Others, such as Bodley's 1614 survey, were published at earlier dates in the Historical Manuscripts Commission reports. Pynnar's 1619 survey was first made available by George Hill in the nineteenth century and more recently by the Ulster Historical Foundation, which digitised his book and made the 1622 maps by Thomas Raven available in a CD-ROM pack.[12]

While the physical development of the towns during the plantation period was at the forefront of many sources, others record the economic and social growth of urban areas across Ireland. Port books, for example, recorded the import and export of a range of goods to Derry and Coleraine in the 1610s.[13] Muster rolls also survive in full and, in part, for many towns in Ireland, offering a distinct look at the numbers of urban settlers and how well many of these were armed. The Ulster Historical Foundation recently posthumously published the 1630 muster roll for Derry, transcribed by R.J. Hunter.[14] These muster rolls are most effective when taken in tandem with other sources that offer an insight into the population of towns in Ireland in the seventeenth century. The Civil Survey of 1654, for example, provides the names of proprietors in Ireland prior to the 1641 rebellion and locates them geographically in the landscape by barony, parish and townland.[15] While useful, the results do not survive for the whole country, although records do remain for Derry. The 1659 census of Ireland provides further evidence for settlement detailing the parishes, the townlands, the names of the principal settlers and denoting the numbers of English, Scottish and Irish settlers.[16] Further evidence for the principal landowners exists in the Books of Survey and Distribution that continue to record the changing pattern of landownership in Ireland in the 1670s.[17] Moreover, a lot can be gleaned about the social and economic character of plantation towns from the 1641 depositions, which have recently been made available online.[18]

While much of what has been discussed thus far relates to the 'official' records of plantation, given that many of the relevant towns emerged as private enterprises, pertinent sources can also be found in private collections such as estate papers. The estate papers of the archbishop of Armagh, for example, are of paramount importance for studies of the evolution of both the pre- and post-plantation town. They include original records such as rentals for the town from 1628, 1660 and 1661, as well as several transcripts of documents such as survey material and inquisitions.[19] Similarly, early records of the town of Bandonbridge have survived in the Lismore Papers, now at Chatsworth House, Derbyshire, Cork University Library and the National Library of Ireland. The papers include rentals of the estate from the late seventeenth century and property deeds. Furthermore, extracts of many elements of the collections have been published in journals, including the *Journal of the Royal Society of Antiquaries of Ireland* and the *Journal of the Cork Historical and Archaeological Society*. While the estate collections are a fine source for studying the plantation towns in question, the evidence is quite fragmentary and offers information of substantive value only when supplemented with other sources from the period.[20]

One of the most special collections of papers that record the early history of plantation towns is perhaps that of the Irish Society, which had the responsibility for spearheading the development of two corporate towns at Derry and Coleraine. Despite its foundation in 1613, however, its papers are rather fragmentary until after 1660, from when corporation minute books survive. The material, now at the London Metropolitan Archives, provides a strong sense of what a collection of papers for a plantation town possibly should look like had we been fortunate enough for all of them to survive. The papers include the original founding charter from King James I, as well as the renewed charter from Charles II. Moreover, they contain material relating to the Irish Society's control of fisheries; its interaction with the livery companies; its receipt books and ledgers from the period after 1660; rent rolls for Derry and Coleraine for the end of the seventeenth and into the eighteenth centuries; and maps. The collection, however, is not comprehensive, having been victim of a fire in the Guildhall in London in the eighteenth century.[21] This fire managed almost to destroy a key source for the city — the Great Parchment Book of 1639 — a survey commissioned under Charles I to examine the estates of the Irish Society and the livery companies.[22] Most astoundingly, however, the London Metropolitan Archive, University College, London and Derry City Archives and Museum Service worked together to conserve, digitally restore, transcribe and publish the Great Parchment Book online. It now enables a key bridge to be made across the history of the city, as historians can trace a picture of the estates on the eve of the 1641 rebellion.[23]

THE SOURCES AND THE ATLAS

Given the plethora of sources available for plantation towns, it is not surprising that the IHTA has employed them extensively to understand the development of Bandon, Derry and Armagh. Using the full range of sources, the atlas gives an extensive synthesis of many of the core themes of the plantation town: origins, topography, morphology, settlement, governance, economy and society. While the fascicles emphasise the comparative aspects across these elements, they also distinguish each town's own distinctive peculiarities. This is particularly obvious in the essay discussions on town origins. While all three towns had distinct plantation development and redevelopment, each, as noted earlier, had radically different beginnings. Evidence of settlement at Armagh and Derry, for example, stemmed from pre-Christian and Early Christian times, while Bandon originated in the medieval period. At Bandon, O'Flanagan noted how the Anglo-Normans had not settled in the Bandon valley, west of Inishannon, with the only notable settlement in the area being that of the Fleming family at Cloghmacsimon.[24] Armagh had much deeper origins, with evidence of land occupancy in the area going right back to the Iron Age, the nearby Emhain Mhacha stronghold giving the impetus for development on the current site of Armagh. The settlement itself emerged as a strong site of pre-Christian worship with two enclosures, one at the core of Armagh that encompassed a 'principal church, subsidiary churches and the round tower'. This site had, in turn, sparked a larger religious settlement and a cluster of houses in the surrounding landscape by the sixteenth century.[25] Derry's origins date to A.D. *c.* 546 or 590, as two probable dates for the monastic foundation are given.[26] Despite their diverse origins, however, each of these three towns underwent its plantation metamorphosis across the same decades, roughly between 1610 and 1630.

TOPOGRAPHICAL AND MORPHOLOGICAL COMPARISONS

Given their differing origins, it is not surprising that each fascicle under discussion contains evidence of topographical and morphological differences in the development of a plantation town. They were not greenfield sites and the sources point to a distinct grappling with the earlier history as planners sought to develop plantation settlements. At Armagh, for example, Richard Bartlett had exposed the complex physical topography of undulating hills to planners in his maps of the Nine Years War campaign (Fig. 4.4). This, combined with the existing morphology of a strong network of ecclesiastical foundations across the hills, shaped the plantation settlement that emerged. As McCullough and Crawford noted in their discussion of Armagh, much of the land north of the cathedral was engulfed in a pre-existing abbey site, while pre-plantation settlements were clustered on the eastern slope of the hill around further ecclesiastical buildings.[27]

The designation of Armagh as a corporate town under the plantation scheme should have dictated its growth in a regulated and controlled manner, akin to an English country town or village. The existing settlement, however, made this impossible, since much of the land still belonged to the Church of Ireland archbishop of Armagh. McCullough and Crawford elucidated how the plantation records show this proprietorial complexity at Armagh, which was exacerbated by the grant, in error, of the Nun's Church at Tempul na Ferta to Sir Francis Annesley in 1619. This, in turn, captured a large part of the lands for the corporate town in the adjoining manor of Mountnorris. In addition, the former abbey of SS Peter and Paul was granted to Sir Toby Caulfield, who drew these lands into his manor of Charlemont.[28] The ensuing proprietorial geography saw responsibility for the town's development in the hands of three individuals.

Despite this, however, contemporary sources show that much of Armagh's development thereafter was spearheaded by the archbishop, particularly Archbishop Hampton who sketched a reconstruction plan for the town in 1615. He also attempted to spark regrowth by leasing out areas of the town to interested parties, including Edward Dodington of Dungiven in Derry. The archbishop's plan remained cognisant of the existing morphology. The second thematic map in the fascicle succinctly captures the plantation geography of the town, depicting the dominant hilltop medieval cathedral and churchyard at the centre of the settlement with new roads in the hinterland forming a radial pattern (Fig. 12.3). A market place had emerged at the base of the hill, while the plantation settlement had appeared confined to the east of the existing site.[29] The centrality of the church continued to be a strong urban feature, with other corporate towns in Ulster, such as Virginia, placing the Church of Ireland in a prominent location overlooking the town.

The atlas allows for some distinct comparisons to be made between the morphological growth of this atypical plantation settlement with a more typical example at Derry. Topographically, the site of Derry offers some comparisons to that of Armagh. The plantation town emerged on the Island of Derry, a remarkably hilly site on the banks of the River Foyle, still notable in the steepness of many of the city's present-day streets. Morphologically, however, what developed at Derry was the ideal plantation settlement: a walled town. Unlike Armagh, Derry had free rein to develop at its chosen location, owing to the destruction of the existing fort by Sir Cahir O'Doherty in 1608. The development of the site was also granted to one landowner — the Irish Society. This ensured that only one

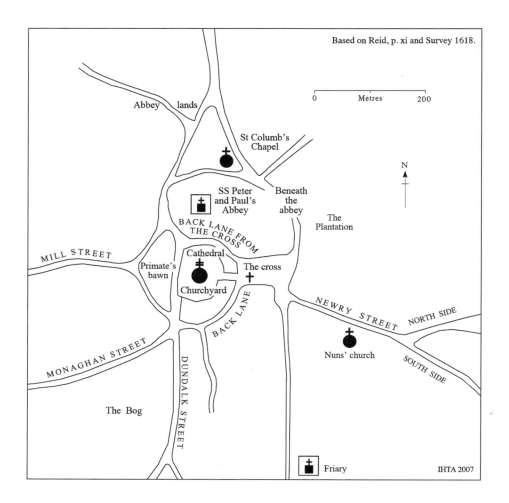

Based on Reid, p. xi and Survey 1618.

0   Metres   200

N

Abbey   lands

St Columb's
Chapel

SS Peter
and Paul's
Abbey

Beneath
the
abbey

The
Plantation

BACK LANE FROM
THE CROSS

MILL STREET

Primate's
bawn

Cathedral

The cross

Churchyard

BACK LANE

NEWRY STREET   NORTH SIDE

Nuns' church

SOUTH SIDE

MONAGHAN STREET

DUNDALK STREET

The Bog

Friary   IHTA 2007

master was in place, giving the city of London the opportunity to focus on developing a strong, plantation settlement that embodied order and civility.

The town's development is recorded in a series of contemporary maps, reproductions of which accompany the fascicle, enabling both the emergence of Derry to be visibly traced in its most formative years and to be compared to other towns. The first cartographical representation dates from 1611 and seems to be the blueprint for the town. In its earliest guise, the authorities proposed a town that would be walled on three sides, with the river offering a natural defence on the fourth side (Fig. 12.4).[30] By 1618, however, the next map shows that a fully, enclosed walled circuit had been developed (Fig. 12.5).[31] Unlike what emerged at Armagh, Derry formed around an ordered and planned series of grid-iron streets, which were bounded by houses and gardens as per the conditions of the grant to

Fig. 12.3 *Armagh*, fig. 2, street layout, 1618.

Opposite: Fig. 12.4
Derry-Londonderry, map 7, 1611.
Trinity College Dublin, MS 1209/24*.

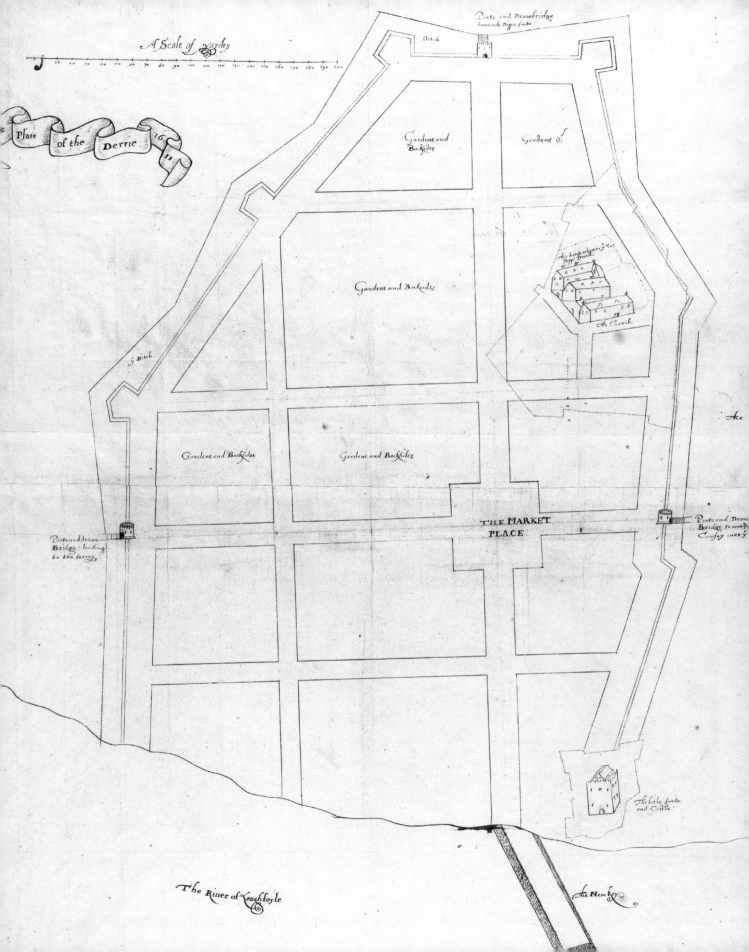

A Scale of yardes

Platt of the Derrie 1611

Porte and Drawbridge
towardy Bigoe forte

Ditch

Gardens and
Backsides

Gardens &

ye Ditch

Gardens and Backsides

The house wherein ye Lo:
Byss: Dwell

The Church

Gardens and Backsides

Gardens and Backsides

THE MARKET
PLACE

Porte and Draw
Bridge towardy
Cawsey quee ye

Porte and drawe
Bridge: leading
to the ferry

The litle forte
and Castle

The Riuer of Loughfoyle

The New key

the Irish Society. By 1622, the Raven map gives an insight into the growth of the town. Avril Thomas noted how the plan shows the asymmetry of the town, with the Diamond located slightly farther west than it possibly should have been (Fig. 5.3).[32] Furthermore, the map showed the differing tenement plot sizes that had developed along the streets. By 1625, Raven was recording the extent of spill-over settlement in the town, as houses began to develop along the roads leading into the walled area.[33]

In comparison, the history of Bandon exudes some of the characteristics of both Derry and Armagh. Like Derry, it emerged at the heart of a private venture of plantation in Munster, yet, similarly to Armagh, its development fell to several individuals. Its site, however, had little pre-existing settlement history, which meant that the earliest proprietors, Capt. William Newce and John Shipward, could develop the town according to

Fig. 12.5 *Derry-Londonderry*, map 8, 1618–19, by Nicholas Pynnar. Trinity College Dublin, MS 1209/22*.

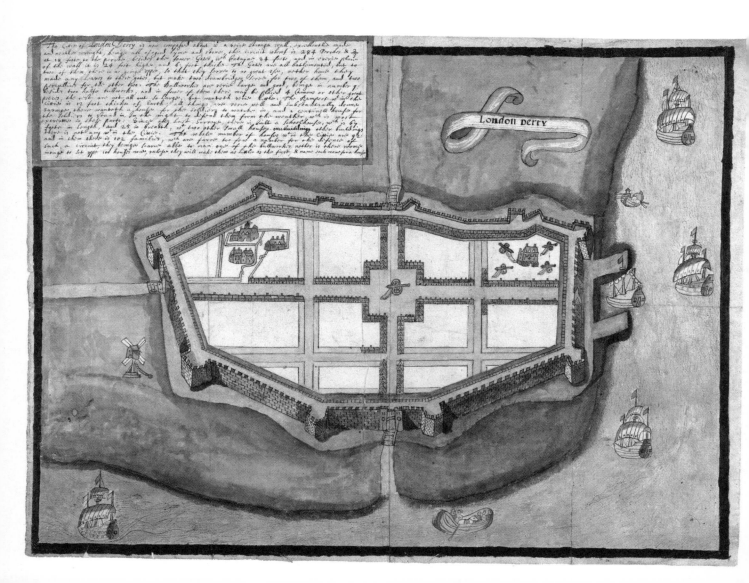

their own plans. The growth of Bandon reflected the control of both men, with each man's holdings straddling separate sides of the river. As a result, early Bandonbridge had two market houses and differing street patterns. The town plan, however, owes most to Richard Boyle, who had bought Newce's share by 1612, followed by Shipward's in 1618.[34]

The plantation morphology of Bandon has been ably discussed in the fascicle by Patrick O'Flanagan, who concentrated on the surviving maps of the town. The first dates from 1613 and appears to be a blueprint for Newce's, showing 'a compact rectangular grid-iron settlement of some 360 houses with a market cross, a sessions house and a church' (Fig. 12.1).[35] It also depicted a wall, which seems to have been proposed by Newce. The influence of Boyle, however, is reflected in two maps from *c.* 1620, which are the first to show both original settlements enclosed in one large town (Fig. 12.2). These maps offer comparisons with Derry, as the two walled towns developed almost contemporaneously.[36] Of all the authors, O'Flanagan has teased out these comparatives most, contrasting the style of fortification at both Derry and Bandon. Moreover, he traced the development of Bandon's walls through to the Down Survey, which gave the first depiction of the completed walled circuit of the town.[37]

Settlement

The atlas and its use of a wide spectrum of sources also enables comparisons to be made between the patterns of settlement that emerged in each of the three plantation towns, much of which is gleaned from the reports of the contemporary plantation surveys alongside available rentals. These surveys provided descriptions of settlement patterns, completed buildings and settler numbers for each town. At Armagh, for example, McCullough and Crawford recognised the distinct pattern of 'coalescence between native and newcomer' despite the strict social regulations laid down in the plantation conditions. In their discussion, they employed the archbishop's 1615 rental, which revealed that of the residents noted in the ninety-six houses in the town only fourteen names were English, with eighty-two being Irish. By 1618, the Pynnar report recorded the continuance of this pattern, as the number of houses had grown to 123, but only twenty-seven were non-Irish. Again, much of the settlement form was dictated by the unusual patterns of land ownership within the town's boundaries. By 1622, the commissioners reported that Toby Caulfield had emerged as a relatively diligent landowner, having built his own premises as a 'strong and convenient dwelling house of lime and stone with a stable' and having brought fifteen English families to his holdings at Armagh.[38] By 1641, the depositions revealed a town that had carved out a distinct role for itself as the county town with a cathedral, jail, sessions house and market.[39]

In contrast to Armagh, the Derry fascicle acknowledges how many of the contemporary reports focused on the extent of house building in the confines of the walled town. The original articles of agreement with the city of London from 1610 dictated that 200 houses should be built, leaving room for 300 more. The fascicle, however, reflects on the fact that Pynnar's report estimated that only ninety-two of these houses had been built by 1618, despite the Irish Society reporting that 215 were available in 1616. This, as Thomas notes, might have had more to do with differing definitions of what a house was in each of these reports. If, however, Pynnar's figures are somewhat accurate, this would mean that Derry, the flagship plantation town in Ulster, had a potentially smaller number of comparable houses and population than Armagh at the same date. Unlike for Armagh, the Derry fascicle has the good fortune to be able to relate this house-building and population programme to a contemporary map from the work of the 1622 commission. This gives a distinct view of the extent of house building in the town and, in doing so, shows the extent of non-developed areas by this date. Despite this slow pattern of settlement growth in its initial years, Derry did grow significantly. The fascicle highlights this growth using the 1628 rent roll, which gave a figure of 265 houses in the town. The 1660 census recorded over a thousand poll tax payers, half of whom lived inside the walls.[40]

Settlement at Bandon is more difficult to judge in its formative years, as the Munster plantation remained outside the reporting bounds of many of the surveys of the early seventeenth century. O'Flanagan, however, has offered something of a comparable analysis to Armagh and Derry using a range of other fragmentary sources. He acknowledges how using surviving leases — for example, an estimate of Bandon's 1611 population at around 135 — with the 1622 commission reporting that 250 houses had been built in the town at this date would make Bandon roughly comparable in size to Derry by 1622.[41]

GOVERNANCE

The atlas also explores the area of governance in each of the towns, using relevant sources such as their charters. While the comparisons are most easily drawn out by using the topographical information, the governance of each town is also dealt with in the essays in each fascicle. All three towns were formally incorporated by royal charter in 1613.[42] Under the terms of plantation schemes in Ireland, incorporation entitled the towns to hold fairs and markets, appoint municipal governments and return burgesses to parliament. In reality, however, how this system operated in each town was radically different. At Armagh, for example, the normal rights of incorporation were complicated by the fact that ownership of the town remained in the hands of the archbishop. Under the terms of its charter, the corporation of Armagh received 'no land to fund its operation', remaining solely beholden to the income generated from fines that the corporation could impose at the weekly court of record. Moreover, the rights granted by charter to the corporation were further distilled, as the archbishop reserved the rights to hold fairs and markets.[43]

At Derry, the picture is similarly complex. The original articles of agreement between the king and the city of London regulated much of the early direction of the town. With formal incorporation, the town became a parliamentary borough electing two members of parliament right down to 1800. Yet Derry remained susceptible to upheaval in governance owing to the control of the Irish Society. The early corporations were composed of representatives from this body and the London companies. Their efforts were regularly scrutinised by government-appointed observers, who reported back to London and the king on their progress. The early governors remained particularly vulnerable, as they traversed the complexities of establishing a walled town. Such was the dissatisfaction of the king that Charles I suspended the charter to the town, as a result of the trial of the Irish Society in the Star Chamber for its apparent mismanagement of the plantation. In effect, Derry entered a period of limbo in its governance, a complication that no other plantation town felt. New charters were, however, granted in the interregnum and, after the restoration of Charles II, they enabled the Irish Society to regain control of the town.[44]

Similarly, Bandon's incorporation made possible a full flourishing of early modern town governance. As O'Flanagan noted, 'as a chartered borough Bandon had a provost, a portreeve and burgesses. Members were returned to the Irish parliament and there was also a clerk of the market and a merchant guild'. Town control, however, remained in the hands of the men who had directed its growth. The incorporation, coming in 1613, placed it at the juncture of Boyle's purchase of the estate. This was reflected in the names of the first town burgesses, identified by O'Flanagan as including Newce, Shipward and Nicholas Blacknell, Boyle's agent. Thereafter, the town gained many significant roles, including a juridical one that saw the emergence of 'a market court, a court of record, a manor court, a court of d'oyer hundred, a prison and a marshalsea'. Furthermore, the corporation gained responsibility for the military defence of the town and its surroundings, placing an emphasis on the supply of weaponry and horsemen.[45]

SOCIAL AND ECONOMIC LANDSCAPE

At the core of seventeenth-century plantation in Ireland was the objective of anglicisation. While the morphological structures of the planned towns acknowledged this objective, the societies and economies that developed within their bounds often became a microcosm of the equivalent in their English counterparts. This is perhaps the thematic area that the atlas tends to emphasise least. In fact, only the Bandon fascicle gives a full description of the economic and social diversity that marked the new town. Using the 1622 commission report and surviving estate papers from the Chatsworth House collections, O'Flanagan points to a real economic flourishing in the town. He notes, for example, the range of artisans within the town as including 'bakers, blacksmiths, butchers, carpenters, chandlers, clothworkers, comb-makers, coopers, curriers, cutlers, dyers, feltmakers, glaziers, glovers, masons, metalmen, pewtermen, shoemakers, stainers, tailors, tanners, turners and weavers'. He also acknowledges the presence of merchants and yeomen, attesting further to a diverse economy and indeed society. This was combined with a note on the number of shops and alehouses and evidence of an export trade from the town, which highlighted its prominence in the economic landscape of Munster as a whole.[46]

No real attempt has been made to conduct a similar analysis for Armagh and Derry. The authors, or indeed the fascicles, are not at fault in this regard. The reason for the disparity is the diversity and lack of sources. As historians, we can report only what the evidence suggests. The estate records for Bandon are more complete for the early years of the plantation, making this wider analysis more possible. For Derry and Armagh such a comparative analysis can be completed from the late seventeenth and early eighteenth centuries onwards, as more documents become available. Some further knowledge might be gleaned by a more complete exploration of previously damaged and inaccessible sources such as the Great Parchment Book for Derry and the 1641 depositions.

CONCLUSION

The decades of plantation witnessed a fundamental reshaping of Ireland. This reshaping is often discussed by historians, historical geographers, sociologists, archaeologists and political scientists, who seek answers to the reasons for our current complex cultural and political landscapes. Yet these decades also had a far-reaching impact on the urban topographical landscape. In the main, plantation gave rise to a widespread programme of town building, which offered distinct centres for regulation and control over the newly emerging plantations across the country. These urban centres ranged from the flagship plantation towns of Bandon and Derry, as discussed here, to small villages that emerged on plantation estates across Ireland. Moreover, much of this town building also engulfed existing settlements, such as Armagh, fundamentally restructuring their urban morphology.

As scholars of urban settlements in Ireland, we are fortunate that this urban growth has left its mark in the sources. These sources offer a unique snapshot of the evolution of these towns across a range of themes, including their growth, settlement patterns, governance, society and economy. The survival rate of many of these documents means that the IHTA can offer a clear overview of the salient histories of towns and their growth during the plantations. Their focus on what the sources can tell us offers a strong opportunity for comparative analysis across core themes. This thematic approach is also embedded in the topographical information that condenses the major elements of the topographical, social, economic and political evolution of these towns across the centuries. Yet this approach also ensures that the analysis cannot be standardised for all plantation towns. Like every area of history, our understanding can be shaped only by what survives and, while we have solid evidence for the three towns discussed here, such an analysis might not be possible for all plantation towns. As is obvious in the atlas to date, there cannot be complete uniformity of discussion where sources do survive, particularly when these sources are so diverse.

Notes

[1] Raymond Gillespie, 'Plantation towns', in William Nolan and Anngret Simms (eds), *Irish towns: a guide to the sources* (Dublin, 1998), p. 79.

[2] 'The fabric of the city walls', http://appsc.doeni.gov.uk/ambit/docs/LDY/LDY_014/LDY_014_033/Public/SM7-LDY-014-033-04.pdf (last accessed 6 May 2017).

[3] Tober Archaeological Services and Carraig Conservation, 'Bandon town walls: conservation, management and interpretation plan', http://www.corkcoco.ie/co/pdf/46386829.pdf (last accessed 9 Dec. 2016).

[4] Brian Lacey, 'Archaeology and war in an Irish town', in *History Ireland,* xvii, no. 6 (2009), pp 60–61.

[5] McCullough and Crawford, IHTA, no. 18, *Armagh,* pp 1–2 and map 4.

[6] O'Flanagan, IHTA, no. 3, *Bandon*, maps 4–6.

[7] 'The plott of the gate alreddy neer fynished at Bandon Bridge and of the 2 gates or castles', [*c.* 1620] (TCD, MS 1209/40).

[8] Thomas, IHTA, no. 15, *Derry~Londonderry*, map 7.

[9] 'The Down Survey of Ireland', http://downsurvey.tcd.ie/index.html (last accessed 9 Dec. 2016).

[10] William Petty, 'The barony of Kinealmeaky in the County of Corke', *c.* 1655 http://downsurvey.tcd.ie/down-survey-maps.php#bm=Kinealmeky&c=Cork&indexOfObject-Value=-1&indexOfObjectValueSubstring=-1 (last accessed 9 Dec. 2016).

[11] 'The platt of the cittie of Londonderrie as it stand bvilt and fortyfyed' (Thomas, *Derry~Londonderry*, map 9).

[12] Victor Treadwell (ed.), *The Irish Commission of 1622: an investigation of the Irish administration, 1615–1622 and its consequences, 1623–1624* (Dublin, 2006); Francis Bickley, *Report on the manuscripts of the late Reginald Rawdon Hastings Esq. of the Manor House, Ashby de la Zouche* (4 vols, London, 1928–47), iv; George Hill, *An historical account of the plantation of Ulster at the commencement of the seventeenth century, 1608–1620* (Belfast, 1877); *The dawn of the Ulster-Scots: the plantation in Ulster*, CD-ROM (Belfast, 2009).

[13] R.J. Hunter and Brendan Scott, *The Ulster port books, 1612–15* (Belfast, 2012).

[14] R.J. Hunter (ed.), *'Men and arms': the Ulster settlers, c. 1630* (Belfast, 2012).

[15] *CS*.

[16] *Census, 1659*.

[17] R.C. Simington, *Books of survey and distribution* (4 vols, Dublin, 1949–67).

[18] 'The 1641 depositions online', www.1641.tcd.ie (last accessed 9 Dec. 2016).

[19] 'Introduction: Armagh Diocesan Registry Archive', https://www.nidirect.gov.uk/sites/default/files/publications/armagh-diocesan-registry-archive.pdf (last accessed 6 May 2017).

[20] O'Flanagan, *Bandon*, pp 8, 15–16.

[21] 'The London Metropolitan Archives', https://www.cityoflondon.gov.uk/things-to-do/london-metropolitan-archives/Pages/search.aspx (last accessed 9 Dec. 2016).

[22] 'The Great Parchment Book of the Honourable The Irish Society', http://www.great-parchmentbook.org/ (last accessed 9 Dec. 2016).

[23] New works on many of the towns discussed in the atlas are constantly being produced. Some of the more recent materials include: B.G. Scott (ed.), *Walls 400: studies to mark the 400th anniversary of the founding of the walls of Londonderry* (Derry, 2015); R.J. Hunter, *The Ulster plantation in the counties of Armagh and Cavan, 1608–1641* (Belfast, 2012); Annaleigh Margey, '1641 and the Ulster plantation towns', in Eamon Darcy, Annaleigh Margey and Elaine Murphy (eds), *The 1641 depositions and the Irish rebellion* (London, 2012), pp 79–96, 217–21; Annaleigh Margey, 'Making the documents of conquest speak: plantation society in Armagh and the 1641 depositions', in P.J. Duffy and William Nolan (eds), *At the anvil: essays in honour of William J. Smyth* (Dublin, 2012), pp 187–213; A.J. Horning (ed.), *Post-medieval archaeology of Ireland, 1550–1850* (Bray, 2007).

[24] O'Flanagan, *Bandon*, p. 1.

[25] McCullough and Crawford, *Armagh*, p. 1.

[26] Thomas, *Derry~Londonderry*, p. 1.

[27] McCullough and Crawford, *Armagh*, pp 2–3.

[28] Ibid., p. 2.

[29] Ibid., p. 3.

[30] Thomas, *Derry~Londonderry*, map 7.

[31] Ibid., map 8.

[32] Ibid., map 9.

[33] Ibid., map 10.

[34] O'Flanagan, *Bandon*, pp 1–2.

[35] Ibid., p. 1 and map 4.

[36] Ibid., p. 2 and maps 5, 6.

[37] O'Flanagan, *Bandon*, p. 2.

[38] McCullough and Crawford, *Armagh*, pp 2–3.

[39] 'Depositions from County Armagh', TCD, MS 836, www.1641.tcd.ie (last accessed 5 Jan. 2017); McCullough and Crawford, *Armagh*, p. 3.

[40] Thomas, *Derry-Londonderry*, pp 2–4.

[41] O'Flanagan, *Bandon*, p. 4.

[42] R.J. Hunter, 'Towns in the Ulster plantation', in *Studia Hibernica*, no. 11 (1971), p. 79.

[43] McCullough and Crawford, *Armagh*, p. 2.

[44] Thomas, *Derry-Londonderry*, p. 9.

[45] O'Flanagan, *Bandon*, p. 3.

[46] Ibid.

13. An art-historical perspective on the Irish Historic Towns Atlas

Rachel Moss

With the publication of each fascicle of the IHTA comes greater clarification of the morphological development of Irish towns in the high and late middle ages and the manner in which distinctive street and plot patterns have evolved over time. The actual experience of a town though is not of its plan, but rather of its elevations — the spaces and the vistas created by particular configurations of structures and the manner in which certain symmetries, use of materials and application of decorative features convey different messages about the status and function of buildings and their patrons. This is the field of the art and architectural historian.

The earliest commentators on Irish urban topography only rarely commented on the nature of street patterns and plot sizes, but rather focused their attention on the key buildings in the streetscape and on regional characteristics. Travelling through Ireland in 1620, Luke Gernon, for example, singled out the dominant structures of the typical Irish medieval town, albeit by then in decay: 'Here lieth an old ruyned castle ... there, a broken forte ... and in another place, an old abbey with some turrets standing'.[1] His contemporary Fynes Moryson, on the other hand, was most struck by the diverse character of housing across the country: 'the houses of Cork, Galway and Limerick (the fairest of them for building), are built of unwrought freestone or flint, or unpolished stones, built some two stories high and covered with tile. The houses of Dublin and Waterford are for the most part built of timber, clay and plaster'.[2]

Early pictorial maps are typically untrustworthy in their representation of individual buildings, but what they do portray are these dual aspects of architectural hierarchy and materiality.[3] The c. 1560 view of Carrickfergus, for example, gives primacy to the castle in the foreground and distorts the topography of the town so that the castle, parish church and Franciscan friary form the three points of a triangle that enclose it, with a prominently located market cross at the centre (Fig. 13.1). A clear differentiation is also made between the sturdy, semi-fortified, stone tower houses of the merchant classes and the disproportionately small, but obviously thatched creats that occupy the spaces set back from the main thoroughfares. Building design not only responded to function and availability of material, but was also a means of imposing social order, status and, increasingly as the medieval period progressed, a sense of civic pride.

In the late twelfth and early thirteenth centuries high-status or public building projects were typically initiated by episcopal or seigneurial potentates but, as time progressed, upwardly mobile mercantile populations had both the desire and the financial wherewithal to sponsor prestigious building programmes.[4] The manner in which they did this, given their exposure to architectural trends abroad through trade, meant that towns became the main conduits of architectural innovation. In spite of this, urban architectural design is a much neglected branch of Irish architectural history, with the range and evolution of building types present in the medieval town only now gradually becoming exposed through the immensely valuable topographical sections of the IHTA series.[5] Though typically information relating to individual buildings can be quite scant, taken collectively, dated references to particular building types reveal both general patterns of building and patronage and more specific details

The freres

KRAGFARGVS
TOWNE

KRAGFARGVS
CASTELL

concerning the form and development of now-lost building types. Placed in a broader historical context, they can also demonstrate how building activities often hold up a mirror to history and reflect more subtle influences, such as political concerns and collective memory.

TOWERS IN THE URBAN ENVIRONMENT

Writing in 1323–4 the Clonmel friar, Symonis Semeonis, described the architecture of Paris: 'its walls are admirably built of cut stone and strongly fortified with lofty towers … it is provided in wonderful manner … with lofty steeples and bell-towers and other beauties of church architecture'.[6] To the traveller approaching a town, it was the skyline that created the first impression, with the number and height of towers creating a particularly significant impact. This was not just a reflection of the piety of the population, as might be inferred by a proliferation of church towers, but was also an assertion of prestige and authority.[7] It is no coincidence that when municipal authorities commissioned images of their towns, as for example on the late fourteenth-century Waterford charter roll, inevitably the result was a strongly fortified townscape enclosing a coppice-like cluster of towered buildings.[8] Similarly, on seal matrices it was not unusual for a corporation to represent itself by means of a well-fortified, towered gatehouse, even when such buildings did not exist — this was the ultimate image of collective identity, rights and privileges.[9]

Towers were both technically challenging and expensive to build, to the extent that the early rules of religious orders such as the Dominicans and Franciscans imposed detailed restrictions on the height of buildings and deemed towers superfluous extravagances.[10] The relatively numerous accounts of the collapse of such structures, and the damage that this wrought, highlights the costly and, some might argue, unnecessary gamble undertaken by their very construction. In light of this, tracing the vertical growth of towns has the potential to reveal much in relation to the social, political and religious imperatives in Irish towns.

The IHTA for Kilkenny provides a useful example, with sections **11** Religion and **12** Defence revealing a fairly radical change in the town's skyline during the first half of the fourteenth century. At the opening of the century the northern hill of the town was capped by the ancient ecclesiastical round tower, deliberately preserved when the other pre-Anglo-Norman church buildings had been swept away to accommodate construction of the new thirteenth-century cathedral. On the southern hill stood the (by then) de Clare castle, delineated by four corner towers so that Hightown and Irishtown were bookended by the two largest, tallest stone structures of the settlement. By 1305, construction of the wall around Hightown, with its towers and fortified gatehouses, was well under way with at least six of the towered gatehouses completed during the course of the century.[11]

In 1328 the tower of St John's Priory on the eastern bank of the Nore collapsed, an event echoed just four years later when the collapse of the 'recently erected' tower of St Canice's caused considerable damage to the choir and chapels of the cathedral.[12] One might expect that this would have acted as a deterrent to building upwards. In 1343, however, as the tower of St Canice's was being rebuilt, a new tower was commissioned for the parish church of St Mary, and just four years later a confraternity was founded to construct a tower at the Franciscan friary.[13] The tower of St Mary's was built at the west end of the church, so aside from the probable destruction of some graves it would not have interfered too much with activities in the church. The tower at the Franciscan friary, however, was inserted at the junction of nave and choir, necessitating removal of part of the roof and inevitably disrupting worship for both laity and friars, similar to the disruption presumably also being experienced in the nearby cathedral.

Tower building was not just limited to Kilkenny at this time. In Dublin, the authorities at Christ Church Cathedral were granted a licence for a crenelated bell-tower in 1330, to replace the belfry that had been destroyed in a storm of 1316.[14] This storm had also damaged the tower of St Patrick's, which was evidently rebuilt before 1362 when it was once more damaged, this time by fire.[15] Meanwhile, the Dominican friary of St Saviour received a bell-tower, sponsored by the mayor, Kenewrek Scherman (d. 1349).[16] An Athenry burgess, William Wallace (d. 1344), initiated building the tower at the Dominican friary there — its construction completed after his death by another burgess, James Lynch — the earliest recorded act of patronage by burgesses at the friary, which had previously been patronised solely by the Anglo-Norman and Gaelic nobility.[17] In other towns, such as Drogheda, Dundalk and Waterford, records of construction do not survive, but the style of remaining friary towers also suggests a fourteenth-century date.[18]

What was it that prompted this flourishing of towers, even in the face of the obvious risk and disruption involved? The majority of towers were integrated with the fabric of churches, so there has been a tendency to focus on their liturgical function. The bells hung in towers were rung to call the populace to prayer, to commemorate anniversaries of the dead, and had a talismanic function, for example, to encourage prayer during storms.[19]

Fig. 13.2 *Kilkenny*, plate 2, view, *c.* 1760, by Thomas Mitchell. National Gallery of Ireland, 4467.

But urban towers fulfilled other functions too. The 1592 map of Trinity College, occupying the former site of All Hallows, Dublin, labels the sole surviving remnant of the priory, the belfry, as a 'seamarke'.[20] Concern with the maintenance of the tower, and its weathervane, is reflected in leases of the 1570s, confirming the role of towers in navigation and medieval meteorology, of particular significance to port towns.[21] Hints towards other functions appear in other sixteenth- and seventeenth-century cartographical contexts. For example, statistical information compiled as part of the Down Survey in 1656–8 noted that the bell-tower of St Mary's Abbey, Trim was the only watchtower in the barony.[22] It also described the round tower at Kells as a watch tower, a common designation for this type of monument during the period.[23] 'Watch' towers would certainly have been useful at times of conflict, but also in peacetime, for exerting social control or even fire-spotting, with churches frequently used to store the parish's fire buckets and ladders.[24]

Although no longer standing, Thomas Mitchell's eighteenth-century view of the tower of St Mary's, Kilkenny, and archaeological excavation of its foundations confirm a substantial structure (Fig. 13.2).[25] From shortly after its completion, the tower accommodated meetings of the town councillors, thus extending their relationship with the church fabric, which they already maintained through collection of an annual payment of 4*d*. from each stall (shop).[26] This overlap of the secular and the sacred space suggests that in all probability the construction of the tower was funded by the town council, providing a safe place to meet and perhaps to store items of particular value.

Motivation for the construction of the nearby Franciscan tower is harder to explain, contradicting as it did the Franciscan ethos of poverty and simplicity.[27] It may simply represent an act of piety, building towards the heavens, but its construction by a confraternity so close in time to the council's tower of St Mary's and the bishop's tower of St Canice's hints at a firmer statement. Friaries, like parish churches, were used for a number of secular functions, not least as a meeting place for guilds and fraternities.[28] Carved corbels (structural supports) on the interior of the tower depict merchants supporting the very fabric of the building, a clear and enduring statement of its patronage. The proportions of the tower, a particular characteristic of Irish friary towers, are unnecessarily tall simply to carry the sound of the bell and are perhaps most reminiscent of the tall, slender urban towers that once proliferated in many Italian cities. While many of these continental examples were built by wealthy families, others were built by confraternities as a means of expressing status and delineating shared interests within the urban environment.[29]

While the earliest examples of towers in Irish towns are associated with episcopal or seigneurial patronage, by the fourteenth century most were apparently built at the behest of the merchant classes, reflecting a trend common throughout Europe at the time. In the Low Countries, for example, numerous examples of the sponsorship of church towers by municipal authorities and confraternities are documented, and in certain cases the towers remained their property long after the rest of the church had fallen out of use.[30] Although dated records of the construction and patronage of Irish towers are relatively rare, comparison of standing remains of some towns with dated records of patronage in others can be informative. Thus, secular patronage and use of the medieval tower of Holy Trinity in Carlingford may explain its retention when the church was rebuilt in *c.* 1665 and may also account for the preservation of the Franciscan tower in Dundalk, now standing alone and known by the distinctly secular appellation of Seatown Castle.[31]

THOLSELS

Whatever their uses, church towers ultimately became a common sight in both urban and rural settlements. But other types of building were more specific to the urban environment, in particular those relating to local administration and trade. Owing to the changing nature of administrative structures and commerce, many of these purpose-built structures no longer exist, so that the topographical sections of the IHTA provide a unique record of their development, form and ultimate demise.

By the twelfth century Dublin had a *domus grandis* or 'large house' that provided the venue for commercial negotiations.[32] The building was located in modern-day Winetavern Street and what was probably the same building was referred to in 1210 as a guildhall and in 1254 as a tholsel. A new, purpose-built tholsel was constructed in 1305, in Christchurch Place, also known as the king's market, and seems to represent a strengthening of the link between municipal authority and the hub of commercial activities in the town.[33] The timing of this may be coincidental, but it is noteworthy that it coincides with efforts during the first decade of the fourteenth century to move the holding of fairs and markets away from their traditional location in churchyards and to establish new, more secular settings for commercial activity.[34]

The first mention of the stallage house in Kilkenny comes just two years later, in 1307.[35] This building, subsequently referred to as the tholsel, was prominently located at the intersection of High Street, Patrick Street, Castle Street (now the Parade) and Rose Inn Street. This was a short distance away from the principal market place, which was mid-way down High Street, close to St Mary's Church, and it remained at this location until *c.* 1579 when a 'new' tholsel was built closer to the market. This physical separation of tholsel and market place may have been due to a lack of suitable building space in the fourteenth century and possibly explains the maintenance of the town council's particularly strong links with the more adjacent church, an arrangement that was later echoed in Carrickfergus.[36]

At Dublin, the leasing of six 'warehouses' under the new guildhall/ tholsel in Dublin in 1311 implies a vaulted structure of six bays, with a hall above that was 'reserved to the commonalty'.[37] Subsequent records confirm that it was used variously as a court, council chamber and prison, and possibly treasury, and that by 1466 it was the location of the town clock.[38] During the sixteenth century it underwent a number of improvements including the stabilisation of fabric, the insertion of new windows and the addition of stucco fretwork in the 'netherloft'.[39]

In Kilkenny, the tholsel was used for the legal and public proceedings of the council and assemblies, probably as a prison, and from the mid-fifteenth century accommodated the town clock.[40] A lease of four shops under the 'old tholsel' in 1628 suggests that it may have been smaller than the Dublin building, with the meeting chamber located over a four-bayed opening and cellars beneath. Use of the tower of St Mary's for council meetings and, down to 1517, of the chapter house in the Dominican priory for the election of the town sovereign suggests that the original hall may not have been very large. In 1517, extensive renovations included the addition of a 'great solar' (literally a well-lit, 'sunny' room) and the small room below, together with a new stone entrance on the east side that was closed with a war trophy — an iron grate taken by force from the MacGilla Patrick castle at Cullahill. Notice of these renovations refers to the tholsel as a timber building.[41]

By the end of the sixteenth century the guildhalls of many European towns were lavishly decorated expressions of civic pride. Late sixteenth- and early seventeenth-century pictorial maps of Irish towns do not, however, give the impression that Irish medieval examples were designed to dominate the townscape in the same way as churches or castles. The tholsel in Dublin is marked by a number on Speed's map, but it is impossible to distinguish it from the surrounding buildings. Similarly, the drawing of the 'tolsell' on Henry Duke's 1594 plot of Dundalk shows a relatively modest structure projecting into the market place in Church Street East, but it is dwarfed by adjacent merchants' castles (Fig. 9.4).[42] A pictorial map of Galway of the mid-seventeenth century shows perhaps the most detail — depicting the tholsel as a long hall, its first floor accessed by external steps and with its loft level lit by gable windows (Fig. 13.3).[43] In scale and design, however, it is remarkably similar to the stone merchants' houses

Fig. 13.3 *Galway*, map 12, mid-17th cent. Trinity College Dublin, MS 1209/73, extract.

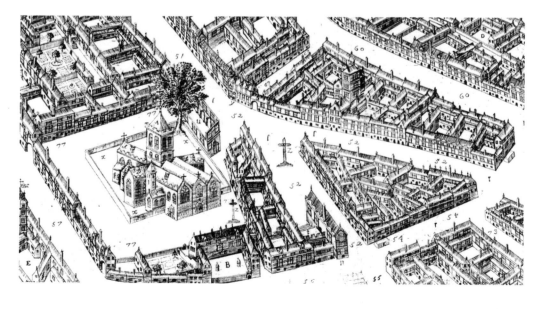

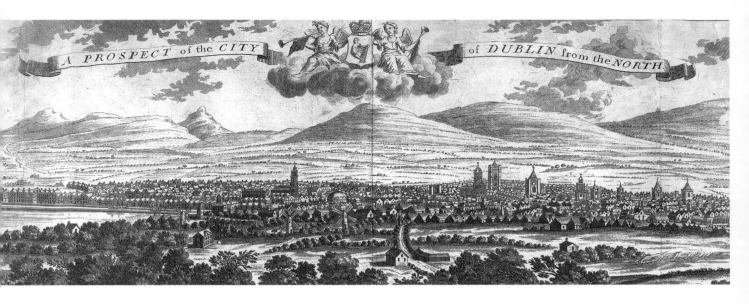

Fig. 13.4 *Dublin, part II*, 1728, view. From Charles Brooking, *A map of the city and suburbs of Dublin*. Royal Irish Academy © RIA.

and shops around it. While the Galway building was constructed from stone, it seems likely that, like Kilkenny, the Dublin tholsel was a timber-framed building and timber was also the specified material used for the new market house built at Athlone in 1586.[44] In this, medieval Irish tholsels appear to fit into the typology of English provincial public halls — first-floor halls with external stairs and strong undercrofts, as found at Ipswich and Great Yarmouth, constructed in the prevalent material of local domestic architecture.[45]

This design was the precursor of the sixteenth- to eighteenth-century market house carried on an arcade with an open market space beneath, which ultimately replaced the Galway, Dublin and Kilkenny tholsels, incorporating details that were among the earliest examples of provincial classical design embodying the idea of civic order. By the early eighteenth century the topographical views continued to be dominated by church spires, but replacing the 'castle' and the 'fort' of Gernon's experience were the tall cupolas of tholsels and market houses — an architectural expression of the shift of power in early modern towns (Fig. 13.4).

MARKET CROSSES

Just over twenty years after the construction of the new tholsel at Dublin comes the first reference to the 'new cross of the city tholsel'.[46] Market crosses demarcated the location of fairs and markets, a function clearly illustrated in relation to the establishment of a new market place in Ardfert, where the bishop and the prior of Kilmainham jointly 'erected a certain wooden cross in sign of a market there to be held'.[47] Although inherently religious in their form, ultimately market crosses also became the backdrop for trade, public dramas, the reading of proclamations and meting out of punishments on the town stocks or gallows, hence their inclusion in the IHTA across sections **11** Religion and **16** Trades and services.

As with larger buildings, images of medieval market crosses on sixteenth- and seventeenth-century maps are not particularly trustworthy, but some, as J.H. Andrews has pointed out, carry 'an aura of antiquity', even though that which features, for example, on a seventeenth-century map of Omagh must have been newly erected.[48] Andrews's comment is of particular interest when one comes to survey the form and age of surviving market crosses. Those at Armagh, Clones, Downpatrick, Kells and Tuam are of early medieval date, and have been used in the past as evidence of the markets associated with Early Christian settlements. However, this pattern of survival is deceptive; not all market crosses necessarily stand in the place for which they were first made and only the minority were of this early form.

At Kilkenny, an elaborate canopied cross, adorned with religious statues, was erected in the market place in 1335 (Fig. 13.5).[49] The cross erected by Bishop O'Crean at Sligo in *c.* 1570 appears to have been of similar form, comprising a stepped base and canopy supported by four pillars.[50] The Sligo cross incorporated heraldry of the O'Crean and Hart families and remnants of other market crosses also preserve heraldic devices, most likely commemorating the merchants responsible for their erection.[51] Certainly there are a number of examples that were paid for by individuals, such as the cross at Drogheda erected by the merchant John Ballard in 1501, even though ultimate responsibility for their maintenance lay with the municipal authorities.[52] Religious imagery was also common, as for example on the pillar cross at Dublin and the lantern cross at Athenry, which bore images of Christ and the Pietà.[53]

The overtly Christian form of the cross and devotional imagery found on some of the monuments is of particular interest when it comes to the fate of these monuments following attempts at church reform in the mid-sixteenth century. For roughly a century following the ban imposed on the public display of devotional imagery, the long-established tradition of marking the nexus of a town with a cross prevailed over any concerns there may have been about the prominent display of religious imagery. Indeed crosses continued to be seen as the most appropriate way to demarcate the market space, demonstrated, for example, on the 1613 'plot of the towne of Bandon Bridge'.[54] As the events of the 1641 rebellion unfolded, however, market crosses increasingly became the stage for the performance of religious difference. The market cross at Belturbet, Co. Cavan, was the backdrop of a provocative act of iconoclasm, when the Roman Catholic community of the town and surrounding area assembled there and burnt

Fig. 13.5 *Kilkenny*, cover illustration, market cross, *c.* 1760. From *RSAI Jn.*, ii (1852–3), frontispiece.

Protestant books and bibles 'in great heapes' at its foot.[55] The sole record of the market cross at Longford is in relation to the display of a proclamation relating to murders in the town, again in 1641.[56]

As the Confederate wars of subsequent years rumbled on, public high crosses became deliberate targets for iconoclastic destruction by Protestant forces. In 1647 the cross at Kilkenny fell prey to troops, who smashed the statues of the Irish saints that adorned its canopy, while a near-contemporary account of the Wexford barony of Forth recounted the complete obliteration of all public crosses, whether of timber, metal or stone.[57] In the following decades of uneasy peace, gradually those crosses that had not succumbed to the iconoclasts' hammers were simply taken down: that in Carrickfergus known as Great Patrick in the middle of the century; in Tuam, Co. Galway, in 1653; and in Drogheda, Co. Louth, in 1666, this last to be replaced by a new market house.[58]

A brief reversal of this activity occurred between 1685 and 1688, coinciding with the reign of the Roman Catholic monarch, James II, and a temporary respite in restrictions on Roman Catholic land ownership and membership of municipal governing bodies. An inscription on the market cross at Kells reveals that it was erected, or perhaps re-erected, by the town's sovereign Robert Balfe in 1688.[59] At the same time, the great granite cross at Ballymore Eustace was either re-erected or repaired — an act commemorated through inscription — and, although not dated, it was probably at this time too that the ancient cross at Clones, Co. Monaghan, was restored and given a new capstone.[60] Although the market cross had been removed just twenty-two years earlier in Drogheda, in 1688 an order was passed that 'a decent and substantiall market cross be erected, and built in ye ancient and former ground where a cross stood'.[61] Such repairs may also have been carried out on other ancient monuments: the medieval tower of St Mary's in Tuam bears a plaque recording its repair in 1688.[62] For a brief period of time this insecure section of society sought to strengthen its standing through the restoration of ancient monuments that reflected the long-established connection between their faith and urban power.[63] This was not, however, to last and, as the maps and topographical sections of the IHTA demonstrate, by the early eighteenth century the creation of new focal points of commercial activity and the broadening out of streets and squares led to the almost total demise of all but a handful of these monuments.[64]

At Kells in 1694 the local assembly ordered that sergeants give notice to Roman Catholics 'that if they wish to preserve the cross, that they remove it into another place for that the judgement of the said assembly is that the said cross now blocks the way, where it stands in the market street and that it should be removed from thence'.[65] For whatever reason, the cross was not removed and survived in Market Street until the 1990s. But at Ennis the fate of the cross was not so felicitous: its stones were removed from O'Connell Street in 1711 and used in the construction of the quay.[66] At Downpatrick, the early medieval cross was moved from the centre of English Street in 1729 and re-erected at the east end of the cathedral.[67] As the market place that it demarcated was some distance from the early ecclesiastical site, it seems likely that this was not the first time it had been moved and it may well have been returning to the vicinity of its original ecclesiastical location after several hundred years of more commercial function.

Although by definition two-dimensional, the maps and texts of the IHTA provide an invaluable source for reconstructing the third dimension of Irish towns. Provision of closely dated references to structures helps to elucidate the manner in which the architecture of towns developed, with a distinct shift towards mercantile patronage from the beginning of the fourteenth century. Traditionally, art historians have drawn clear distinctions between the sacred and the secular in the study of medieval architecture, but one of the many useful insights that the IHTA provides is the blurring of that division and the many factors that must be considered in assessing the form, function and ultimate preservation of the urban built environment.

Notes

[1] Caesar Litton Falkiner, *Illustrations of Irish history and topography mainly of the seventeenth century* (London, 1904), pp 355–6.

[2] Fynes Moryson, *An itinerary, containing his ten yeeres travell through the twelve dominions of Germany, Bohmerland, Sweitzerland, Netherland, Denmarke, Poland, Italy, Turky, France, England, Scotland & Ireland* (4 vols, Glasgow, 1907–8), iii, p. 498.

[3] Caoimhín Ó Danachair, 'Representations of houses in some Irish maps of *c.* 1600', in R.M. Dorson and J.G. Jenkins (eds), *Studies in folk life: essays in honour of Iorwerth C. Peate* (London, 1969), pp 91–104.

[4] H.B. Clarke, 'Planning and regulation in the formation of new towns and new quarters in Ireland, 1170–1641', in Anngret Simms and H.B. Clarke (eds), *Lords and towns in medieval Europe: the European historic towns atlas project* (Farnham and Burlington, VT, 2015), pp 321–53; John Bradley, 'The purpose of the Pale: a view from Kilkenny', in Michael Potterton and Thomas Herron (eds), *Dublin and the Pale in the Renaissance c. 1540–1660* (Dublin, 2011), pp 54–67.

[5] For the architecture of medieval towns see, for example, the section entitled 'Neither churches nor castles', in Tadhg O'Keeffe, *Medieval Irish buildings, 1100–1600* (Dublin, 2015), pp 55–9.

[6] *Itinerarium Symonis Semeonis ab Hybernia ad Terram Sanctam*, ed. and trans. Mario Esposito (Dublin, 1960), pp 29–31.

[7] Derek Keene, 'Tall buildings in medieval London: precipitation, aspiration and thrills', in *The London Journal*, xxxiii, no. 3 (2008), pp 201–15.

[8] Eamonn McEneaney and Rosemary Ryan, *Waterford treasures: a guide to the archaeological treasures of Waterford city* (Waterford, 2004), p. 58.

[9] See, for example, the medieval seals of Athenry, Callan, Carrickfergus, Clonmines, Kilkenny Hightown, Kilmallock and Knocktopher.

[10] R.A. Sundt, '*Mediocres domos et humiles habeant fratres nostri*: Dominican legislation on architecture and architectural decoration in the thirteenth century', in *Journal*

of the Society of Architectural Historians, xlvi (1987), pp 394–407; Wolfgang Braunfels, *Monasteries of western Europe: the architecture of the orders* (Princeton, 1980), appendix 14, p. 246.

[11] Bradley, IHTA, no. 10, *Kilkenny*, p. 14.

[12] Ibid., p. 13; *Kilkenny city records: Liber primus Kilkenniensis*, ed. Charles McNeill (Dublin, 1931), p. 64; *The Annals of Ireland by Friar John Clyn*, ed. Bernadette Williams (Dublin, 2007), p. 207.

[13] Bradley, *Kilkenny*, p. 13; William Carrigan, *The history and antiquities of the diocese of Ossory* (4 vols, Dublin, 1905), iii, p. 90; *Annals of Friar Clyn*, p. 242.

[14] Clarke, IHTA, no. 11, *Dublin, part I, to 1610*, p. 17.

[15] Ibid., p. 18; William Monck Mason, *History and antiquities of the collegiate church and cathedral of St Patrick* (Dublin, 1820), p. 118.

[16] Clarke, *Dublin, part 1*, p. 18; *Chartularies of St Mary's Abbey, Dublin … and annals of Ireland, 1162–1370*, ed. J.T. Gilbert (2 vols, 1884–6), ii, p. 391.

[17] 'Regestum monasterii fratrum praedicatorum de Athenry', ed. Ambrose Coleman, *Archivium Hibernicum*, i (1912), p. 206.

[18] H.G. Leask, *Irish churches and monastic buildings* (3 vols, Dundalk, 1955–61), iii, pp 41–58; Canice Mooney, 'Franciscan architecture in pre-Reformation Ireland (part III)', in *RSAI Jn.*, lxxxvii (1957), pp 1–12.

[19] Colmán Ó Clabaigh, *The friars in Ireland, 1224–1540* (Dublin, 2012), pp 236–40; *Calendar of ancient records of Dublin in the possession of the municipal corporation*, ed. J.T. Gilbert and R.M. Gilbert (19 vols, Dublin, 1889–1944), ii, pp 114–15.

[20] Clarke, *Dublin, part 1*, pp 19, 29.

[21] *Calendar of ancient records of Dublin*, ii, pp 64–5.

[22] Charles McNeill, 'Copies of some Down Survey maps in private keeping', in *Analecta Hibernica*, no. 8 (1938), p. 424.

[23] Ibid., pp 425–6. Round towers at Cork and Clones are both given this designation on sixteenth-century maps. See F.H. Tuckey, *City and county of Cork remembrancer* (Cork, 1837), p. ix; Anon., 'Notices of the round towers of Ulster', in *UJA*, 1st ser., iii (1855), p. 28.

[24] *Calendar of ancient records of Dublin*, ii, p. 253.

[25] Bradley, *Kilkenny*, plate 2.

[26] Ibid., pp 3, 13; *Liber primus Kilkenniensis*, pp 18, 14, 13, 48, 57.

[27] Discomfort with Irish friary tower building is implied in a 1482 permission for the construction of two Irish friaries by Pope Sixtus IV, which specifies low belfry towers (*cum … campanilibus humilibus*) (Mooney, 'Franciscan architecture', p. 2).

[28] Jens Röhrkasten, 'Secular uses of the mendicant priories of medieval London', in Paul Trio and Marjan de Smet (eds), *The use and abuse of sacred places in late medieval towns* (Leuven, 2006), pp 135–52.

[29] Carol Lansing, *The Florentine magnates: lineage and faction in a medieval commune* (Princeton, 2015), pp 84–106.

[30] Marjan de Smet, 'Heavenly quiet and the din of war: use and abuse of religious buildings for purposes of safety, defence and strategy', in *Use and abuse of sacred places*, p. 6.

[31] O'Sullivan and Gillespie, IHTA, no. 23, *Carlingford*, p. 9; Christine Casey and Alistair Rowan, *North Leinster: the counties of Longford, Louth, Meath and Westmeath* (London, 1993), p. 178; O'Sullivan, IHTA, no. 16, *Dundalk*, p. 13.

[32] J.T. Gilbert, *History of the city of Dublin* (3 vols, Dublin, 1854–9), i, p. 153.

[33] Clarke, *Dublin, part I*, p. 23.

[34] For the 1308 prohibition see *Statutes and ordinances and acts of parliament of Ireland: King John to Henry V*, ed. H.F. Berry (Dublin, 1907), p. 257; Karina Holton, 'From charters to carters: aspects of fairs and markets in medieval Leinster', in D.A. Cronin, Jim

Gilligan and Karina Holton (eds), *Irish fairs and markets: studies in local history* (Dublin, 2001), pp 20–24.

[35] Bradley, *Kilkenny*, p. 15.

[36] Robinson, IHTA, no. 2, *Carrickfergus*, p. 11.

[37] Clarke, *Dublin, part I*, p. 23; *Calendar of ancient records of Dublin*, i, p. 110.

[38] Clarke, *Dublin, part I*, p. 23.

[39] *Calendar of ancient records of Dublin*, ii, p. 274.

[40] John Hogan, 'The three tholsels of Kilkenny', in *Journal of the Royal Historical and Archaeological Association of Ireland*, 4th ser., v, no. 41 (1880), pp 236–52.

[41] Hogan, 'The three tholsels of Kilkenny', p. 236; *Liber primus Kilkenniensis*, pp 138–9.

[42] O'Sullivan, *Dundalk*, map 4.

[43] James Hardiman, *History of the town and county of Galway* (Dublin, 1820), p. 29.

[44] Murtagh, IHTA, no. 6, *Athlone*, p. 12.

[45] S.E. Rigold, 'Two types of court hall', in *Archaeologia Cantiana*, lxxxiii (1968), pp 1–22.

[46] Clarke, *Dublin, part I*, p. 27.

[47] Miss Hickson, 'Notes of Kerry topography', in *Journal of the Royal Historical and Archaeological Association*, 4th ser., vi, no. 58 (1884), pp 301–2.

[48] J.H. Andrews, 'Mapping the past in the past: the cartographer as antiquarian in pre-Ordnance Survey Ireland', in Colin Thomas (ed.), *Rural landscapes and communities: essays presented to Desmond McCourt* (Dublin, 1986), p. 47.

[49] Bradley, *Kilkenny*, p. 19; J.G.A. Prim, 'The market cross of Kilkenny', in *RSAI Jn.*, ii (1852–3), pp 219–30.

[50] Gallagher and Legg, IHTA, no. 24, *Sligo*, p. 19; NAI, M 2533, p. 364.

[51] Heather King, 'Late medieval crosses in County Meath, *c.* 1470–1635', in *RIA Proc.*, lxxxiv C (1984), pp 79–115.

[52] Heather King, 'A possible market cross fragment from Drogheda', in *Journal of the County Louth Archaeological Society*, xx, no. 4 (1984), pp 334–9.

[53] Peter Harbison, 'A long-lost stone "cross" from late fifteenth-century Dublin: its illustrators, iconography and echoes of a medieval play', in John Bradley, A.J. Fletcher and Anngret Simms (eds), *Dublin in the medieval world: studies in honour of Howard B. Clarke* (Dublin, 2009), pp 345–68; Rachel Moss, 'Athenry market cross', in *AAI*, i, p. 384.

[54] O'Flanagan, IHTA, no. 3, *Bandon*, map 4.

[55] W.J. Smyth, *Mapmaking, landscapes and monuments: a geography of colonial and early modern Ireland c. 1530–1750* (Cork, 2006), p. 130.

[56] Gearty, Morris and O'Ferrall, IHTA, no. 22, *Longford*, p. 13; TCD, MS 817, 235v, depositions.

[57] Prim, 'The market cross of Kilkenny', pp 219–30; John Synott, 'An account of the barony of Forth in the county of Wexford, written at the close of the seventeenth century', in *RSAI Jn.*, iv (1856), pp 444–60.

[58] Robinson, *Carrickfergus*, p. 11; Claffey, IHTA, no. 20, *Tuam*, p. 12; *Council book of the corporation of Drogheda*, ed. Thomas Gogarty (Drogheda, 1915), p. 136.

[59] Simms with Simms, IHTA, no. 4, *Kells*, p. 8. The survey of Kells in 1659 refers to only two standing crosses, both of them in the churchyard (McNeill, 'Copies of some Down Survey maps', pp 425–6).

[60] Peter Harbison, *The high crosses of Ireland* (3 vols, Bonn, 1992), i, pp 45, 103; Heather King, 'Late medieval Irish crosses and their European background', in Colum Hourihane (ed.), *From Ireland coming* (Princeton, 2001), pp 333–50.

[61] *Council book of the corporation of Drogheda*, p. 228.

[62] Claffey, *Tuam*, p. 11.

[63] For further examples of this, see Rachel Moss, 'Appropriating the past: seventeenth-century preservation of the Romanesque in Ireland', in *Architectural History*, li (2008), pp 63–86.

[64] For early modern attitudes to the past, see Colm Lennon 'The medieval town in the early modern city: attitudes to Dublin's immediate past in the seventeenth and eighteenth centuries', in Bradley, Fletcher and Simms, *Dublin in the medieval world*, pp 436–47; and Rachel Moss, 'Collective memory and municipal identity in the early modern Irish town *c.* 1550–1750', in Dany Sandron (ed.), *Le passé dans la ville* (Paris, 2016), pp 193–210.

[65] Headfort Estate Papers, NLI, MS 25446, Records of the corporation of Kells, 1685–1787, 26 Mar. 1694, quoted in Anngret Simms, 'Change and continuity in an Irish country town: Kells 1600–1820', in Peter Borsay and Lindsay Proudfoot (eds), *Provincial towns in early modern England and Ireland: change, convergence and divergence* (Oxford, 2002), p. 137.

[66] Ó Dálaigh, IHTA, no. 25, Ennis, p. 19; *Corporation book of Ennis, 1660–1810*, ed. Brian Ó Dálaigh (Dublin, 1990), pp 56, 75, 91.

[67] Buchanan and Wilson, IHTA, no. 8, *Downpatrick*, p. 9.

Part IV
Georgian and
Victorian Towns

14. The Big House and town improvement

Toby Barnard

Big Houses are to be found in IHTA, but seldom bulk large. The IHTA is not an inventory of individual buildings, although it tries to list those falling into particular types. It is unusual to find more than one Big House in any single fascicle. Modest towns could not support more. A single one is prominent in the plans and maps of Dundalk, Fethard and Maynooth. Also, under section **22** Residence of the topographical information, can be found a few sizeable and venerable dwellings, such as Myrtle Grove and The College at Youghal (Fig. 14.1). The scarcity warns that — at least in the mainly middling-sized towns mapped so far — Big Houses are not conspicuous. Nor indeed is the IHTA concerned with aesthetic judgements but with settlement, morphology and subsequent development.

Fig. 14.1 *Youghal*, Myrtle Grove, *c.* 1900. National Library of Ireland, L_CAB_00797.

Freer with opinions, especially recent developments and replacements, is the Buildings of Ireland volume *South Ulster*.[1] For several places, not yet covered by IHTA (and perhaps unlikely to be), the interested can turn to the stimulating discussions by Brian Graham and Lindsay Proudfoot of the ingenuity with which proprietors' houses were juxtaposed alongside humbler dwellings.[2]

There are two obvious but rather different ways in which the uncertain relationship between 'Big' Houses and the IHTA may be approached. 'Big House' may be no more than short-hand for a landowner living nearby (seldom in the town itself) and who possessed a substantial part, if not all, of the ground on which the town stood. Indeed, remembering how much land in sixteenth- and seventeenth-century Ireland (and earlier) was confiscated, an individual might have been granted the place, with requirements to build and promote something akin to urbanisation. Among the authorities and proprietors of the soil there seems to have been near-universal agreement that towns were desirable, both ideologically and in practice. Accordingly, they were watched over benignly, with support from parliament and government. At the same time, and darkening this bright picture, towns — and their promoters — competed against one another. They intrigued for benefits, including turnpike roads, canals, bridges, and subsidies for corn, linen and flour. The location of the regular meetings of the assizes and sessions or the building of a barracks could be the making of a town. Popularising the markets and fairs with new buildings and lower tolls, the aim was to steal business from neighbours. Social, cultural and recreational activities were also favoured: race meetings, hunts, balls, assemblies, musical concerts, lectures on electricity and astronomy, spectacles. In these ways some of the thinking and values of the Big House may have been incorporated into the programme of urban improvements. Proprietors who initiated and underwrote physical improvements were praised for public spirit; their reputations were enhanced; also their properties increased in value. Too often the impression was conveyed that they had acted on their own, but in practice physical improvements were favoured by shopkeepers, professionals and civic worthies.

Some of the Irish manifestations, notably in the seventeenth and eighteenth centuries, were linked with the formulation in England of a conscious urban renaissance, to revive declining towns.[3] They parallel, too, actions in eighteenth-century Scotland that have been studied recently.[4] In the Irish context, the distinctive role of towns has gained yet more prominence thanks to investigations of associational cultures, both in Dublin and the provinces, and the commercialisation of sport.[5] Another activity important to the custom and ambience of a town was education.[6] These developments are recorded in the topographical information of the IHTA. Excellent use has been made of newspapers to spot teaching. However, the poor survival of copies before the nineteenth century and the sheer volume thereafter probably mean that many references have been overlooked. Also, it is easier to note advertisements for teachers in named premises at set hours than to track the peripatetic who moved hourly from private house to house. The humblest did not need to advertise in the press: word of mouth sufficed.

A second possibility for acknowledging the Big House is as part of an urban spatial ensemble, either central to it as the architectural focus, or as a crucial accent. In Ireland outside Dublin this second phenomenon is rare, particularly in the towns so far, or prospectively to be, covered by the atlas. An owner's stronghold that determines much of the look and character of Alnwick, Arundel and Petworth (ducal enclaves in England), the duke of Argyll's Inverary, or, further afield, the Villa d'Este at Tivoli, Frascati (Villa Aldobrandini) and on Sicily at the Lampedusas' Santa Margherita de Belice, in Ireland arguably occurs at Kilkenny, Lismore or Hillsborough.

Living cheek by jowl was not always relished either by the landlords or by the tenants. If substantial houses in provincial Irish towns owned and used regularly by grandees were rare, it did not mean that the latter were abstaining from local and cultural affairs. How these preferences were expressed, and the likelihood of their being adopted, depended most obviously on how much urban ground they owned. There were, too, enduring habits of deference. These sometimes masked a more independent attitude on the part of a corporation, traders and town dwellers, who welcomed the utilitarian. The ostentatious, unless it carried no additional premium, might be rejected.[7]

There was a powerful doctrine of urban improvement across Europe, which filtered into early modern Ireland. Much in this was pragmatic and self-interested but for those very reasons might be endorsed enthusiastically. The state and its agencies, those charged with the governance and security of towns, as well as those who had been granted substantial tracts within them, agreed on the desirable measures and together forwarded them.[8] Regularity, even symmetry were valued; buildings with public and communal functions — court rooms, market halls, customhouses, guard rooms, barracks and places of worship — ideally should be differentiated in look and materials, as well as in size. This axiom was readily accepted and hardly had to be promoted by a proprietor from a Big House. Travel and reading familiarised the rudiments. The supervisory boards employed their own architects and engineers, thereby achieving some uniformity in the public buildings that were erected. Characteristic building types have been classified.[9] By the nineteenth century, banks had their own architects.[10]

Increasingly grandees valued privacy, health, recreation and domesticity. Even when secluded behind a demesne wall, owners wished their mansions to have creditable approaches. Rather than a huddle of insalubrious cabins at the lodge gates, regular and decent houses would be admired. These ancillary settlements were often modest — for example, at the Flowers' residence at Castle Durrow or the Veseys' at Abbey Leix — and hardly merit the term 'town'. They lie outside the remit of the atlas. However, one conspicuous example is within its bounds and that is Maynooth. Here, it was possible for the Leinsters to continue the long avenue to Carton into the reordered and extended town and to create an axis that terminated with the agent, Stoyte's House, now the central and oldest feature of Maynooth University. The ambitious scale and its completion (at least in part) attest to the exceptional status of the Leinsters. In social terms, as Ireland's only resident dukes, they were pre-eminent. They had an income commensurate with their status, if never altogether adequate for their ambitions, including those of urban improvement.

So the Big House as a feature in the purely urban landscape is rare. For a variety of understandable reasons, most proprietors preferred to locate themselves away from the towns that they might own. An exception which attracted attention in the eighteenth century was the Catholic Lord Kenmare's Killarney. Few towns in eighteenth-century Ireland were prosperous and populous enough to need many private residences of scale and pretension. No provincial magnate maintained a grand town house to which he repaired for set months of the year and expected to lure others into doing the same in order to share a calendar of recreations and diversions. There were administrative and judicial routines but they did not match the courts — legal and princely — provincial governorships, diets and assemblies that functioned throughout western and central Europe. To participate in the Irish events — the assizes, race meetings and balls — it was practicable for participants to ride over daily from their country houses and, if necessary, to overnight uncomfortably with neighbours and acquaintances or to hire lodgings. A consequence was the absence of quarters adjacent to the landowners' *hôtels* where professionals and dependants lived in a manner that reflected their status and aspirations. Taking, rather randomly, cities in continental Europe, Modena, a grand duchy with its own resident ruling family, retained early in the twentieth century palazzi that require three volumes to describe and illustrate.[11] Similarly, the wealth and importance of the maritime state of Genoa can be judged by the architectural survivals of Strada Nuova.[12] Even moving beyond the more modest towns to be covered by the IHTA, Cork, Kinsale, Limerick and Waterford lack anything comparable. Perhaps lighter tenurial, legal, economic and social systems left townspeople in Ireland freer to follow their own inclinations in the design of housing.

Faced with only modest evidence, there is a second aspect of the issue: landlords influencing the physical development of towns. Their ability to do so varied, most obviously, depending on how much of the ground and urban property they owned and how much money they had to deploy in improving schemes. Hughes, half a century ago, argued that an income of £10,000 per annum was needed for a proprietor to sustain a model or remodelled village.[13] In the eighteenth century, only a handful of landowners in Ireland commanded revenues of that size.

Other factors that might come into play and determine success or failure included the relationship between the proprietor and the corporation and leading citizens of the place. Sometimes, of course, the corporation was entirely in the pocket of the proprietor, its members nominated by and dependent on him. But this was not universal and corporations or individuals sometimes resented landlord influence and resisted it. In some cases this brought obstruction of and opposition to planned regeneration. Occasionally, where rival landowners from the neighbourhood vied with one another for dominance, they might try to outdo each other with generous subsidy to town improvements.

The temperament of a landlord could come into play. A few became passionately, even irrationally, committed to their projects and were prepared to spend lavishly in order to accomplish them. The earl of Donegall in mid-eighteenth-century Belfast illustrates this.[14] The skilful prepared their campaigns by cultivating local interests, bringing in outside expertise with architects and engineers and, above all, through offering inducements.

By the eighteenth century there were two primary calculations that recommended urban development to owners. The first was financial; the second, aesthetic and reputational. Their thinking often converged with that of leading town dwellers: for example, a wish to improve the health of a town and to compete successfully for trade and traffic against rivals. In some cases, since interests coincided, it was possible for proprietors and the corporation to co-operate in improving projects, notably in constructing new market houses, assembly rooms, fair grounds, promenades (malls) and recreational centres such as bowling greens and race courses. They could also join together to lobby for the construction or replacement of bridges, the route of a turnpike road, the grant of patents for fairs and markets, and, by the eighteenth century, a canal (and later the railway). Proprietors, especially when members of one or other house of the Irish parliament, were well placed to direct government funds towards infrastructural improvements.[15] Moreover, with relations and acquaintances or themselves on the board for inland navigation, the linen and barrack boards, they exerted themselves to secure benefits both for themselves and for the town. Because of the way in which the information is set out in IHTA, the extent of these improvements, and whether or not they belonged to synchronised campaigns, can be hard to gauge. Elements that might have been conceived as a programme are separated under different headings: trades and services, defence, transport, housing, entertainment, education, even religion. In such projects, intended to please the eye and sometimes organised as a spatial sequence to be apprehended when walking or riding a specific route through the town, the intention and original effect are lost in the presentation of the information.

Investing in the enlargement and modernisation of an estate town could make good sense financially. By attracting more trade to markets, fairs and shops, by developing within the population specialised skills, notably in the manufacture of textiles but even such attributes as fishing, by securing a barracks, county courts, a school, demand for goods and services was increased. In time, this quickening of economic activity was felt by the landlord. Most obviously demand for holdings grew and with it the ability to charge higher rents. Even so, as with agricultural and rural leases, the freedom to exploit the situation was limited by the length and terms of the leases: three lives or ninety-nine years deferred the extra profiteering. In the shorter term, the surrender to the urge to build to enhance the attractiveness of a town, like other indulgences, involved spending that might ruin. This may be the case of the Everards who impressed Fethard with their physical stamp in the later seventeenth century (Fig. 14.2). Within a few decades, they were heavily indebted and soon withdrew from the place, to be replaced in the mid-eighteenth century by the absent Bartons.

A contrast with this rather sorry story is the record of landlord involvement in Dundalk. It was a town with natural advantages: on a main route between Dublin and the north, and close to the sea. Landlord interventionism becomes apparent after 1695 when the Hamiltons from Tollymore in Co. Down acquired a substantial stake. First Anne, the widow of the original Hamilton, and then her son, later ennobled as Viscount Limerick and earl of Clanbrassil, concerned themselves with the town. Anne Hamilton, to whom for example the foundation of a school can be traced, reminds us appropriately that proprietorial intervention was never exclusively and sometimes not primarily male. She had been described by a contemporary as a 'clever sensible managing person'.[16] Notable to sustaining the economic base of the physical improvements were the establishment of a textile factory, manufacturing cambrics, and a new harbour.

The elder James Hamilton is recorded travelling in Europe and married into a Dutch family that had accompanied William III to England. From

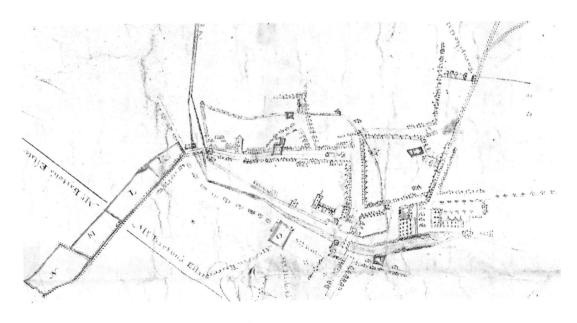

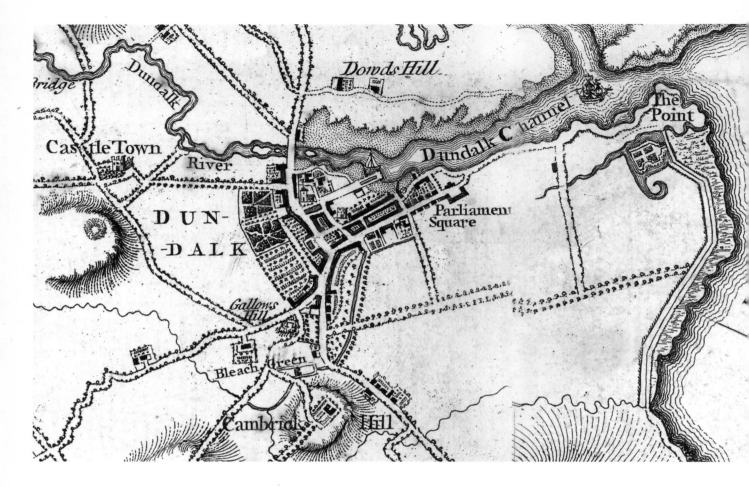

Fig. 14.3 *Dundalk*, map 9, 1766.
From Matthew Wren, *A topographical
map of the county of Louth*. Royal Irish
Academy © RIA.

Holland, Limerick (as he had become) enticed Peter Johann Shravendyke
to oversee the cambric works at Dundalk. This initiative was one of several
intended to invigorate the town that marched with his demesne. It paralleled the interventions of the Abercorns at Strabane and the Fitzgeralds
at Maynooth.[17] On the larger public stage, Limerick promoted a preco-
cious if unsuccessful measure of Catholic relief; on his lands at Dundalk
and Tollymore, Co. Down, he allowed free rein to a polymath from Co.
Durham whose proclivities were towards the Gothic. Limerick's heir,
second earl of Clanbrassil, devoted himself to the beautification of the
demesnes and may himself have written a tract about pine trees. One
visitor surprised Clanbrassil, hatchet in hand, tending his improvements,
which included the introduction of 'American sheep'. The peer, enjoying
£3,000 per annum from a sinecure and £7,000 from his Louth and Down
estates, a member of both the Westminster parliament and the Society of
Dilettanti, was judged 'a most domestic man'.[18] Not so active as his father
in parliament, Clanbrassil was portrayed by Liotard and had Stubbs paint
himself and his hunter 'Mowbray'.[19] In addition, he owned a good collection of antique (or supposedly antique) gems that he allowed James Tassie
to copy.[20] Disjointed as the outline is, through these Hamiltons, a series

Fig. 14.4 *Dundalk*, map 11, 1777, Dundalk demesne, by Bernard Scalé. Private collection.

Following pages:
Fig. 14.5 *Armagh*, map 6, 1766, by Robert Livingston (redrawn by J.T. Noble in 1835). Armagh County Museum, Trustees of National Museums Northern Ireland.

of potentially useful and innovative activities can be detected: ones that, unusually, suggested a benign influence of the Big House over its district (and beyond). The Hamiltons projected back onto Cos Louth and Down, and farther into Ireland, ideas from Britain and continental Europe.

Hamilton's public activism, in parliament, in semi-state boards such as the linen trustees and inland navigation, assisted greatly in securing subsidies and contracts. He was active, too, in trade with the Americas. In addition, the more ornamental and visible features associated with improvement appeared in the town: an inn, court and market houses (Fig. 14.3). Unusually, the Hamiltons had a house in the town as well as creating an extensive and much admired demesne and residence bordering on the town (Fig. 14.4). Nor did they jettison their interests in Co. Down at Tollymore. Towards the end of the eighteenth century when the male line of the Hamiltons failed, their holdings were inherited by the earls of Roden, who continued the Hamiltons' constructive engagement.

Giving a secure economic base to a town, or strengthening it, as the Hamiltons did at Dundalk, was the best method to underpin the more cosmetic or superficial improvements. Other than through employment in the house, gardens and demesne, what most proprietors could offer was

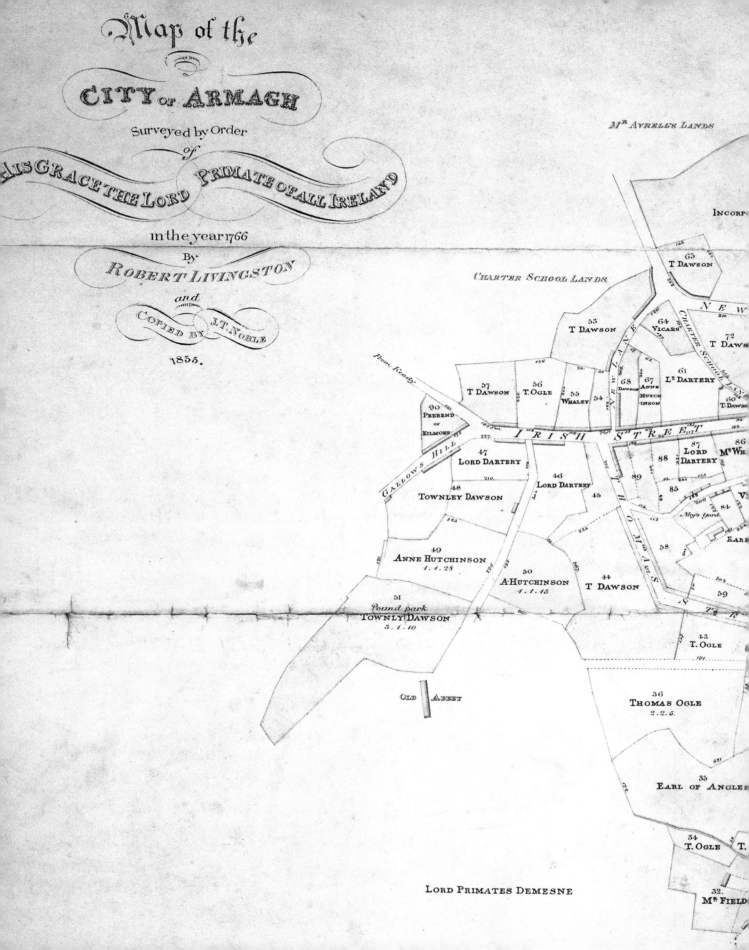

Map of the
CITY of ARMAGH

Surveyed by Order

of

His Grace the Lord Primate of all Ireland

in the year 1766

By

Robert Livingston

and

Copied by J. T. Noble

1835.

Mr Avrell's Lands

Incorp

Charter School Lands

New

From Keedy

Gallows Hill

Irish Street

Thomas St

53 T Dawson

64 Vicars

65 T Dawson

72 T Daws

57 T Dawson

56 T. Ogle

55 Whaley

54

68 Dawson

67 Anne Hutchinson

61 Lᵈ Dartery

60 T. Daws

90 Prebend of Kilmore

47 Lord Dartery

48 Townley Dawson

46 Lord Dartery

45

88

89

85

87 Lord Dartery

86 Mr Wh

Mess yard

49 Anne Hutchinson 4.4.28

50 A. Hutchinson 4.4.43

44 T. Dawson

58

59

Earl

V

51 Pound park. Townly Dawson 3.4.10

43 T. Ogle

Old Abbey

36 Thomas Ogle 2.2.5

35 Earl of Angles

34 T. Ogle

T.

Lord Primates Demesne

32. Mr Field

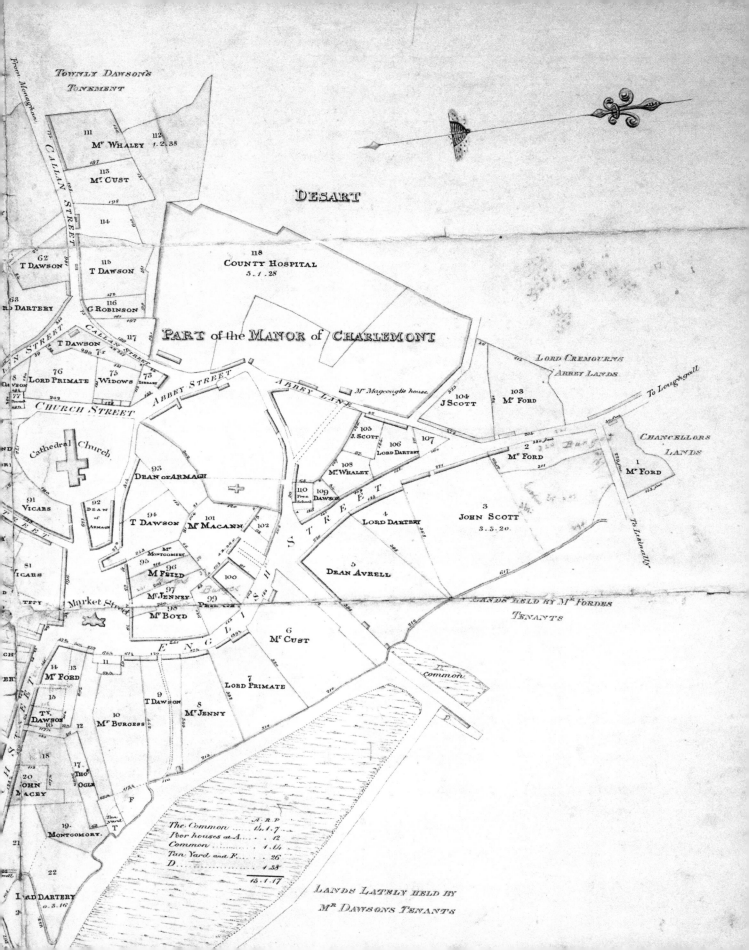

TOWNLY DAWSON'S
TONEMENT

111
Mr WHALEY

112
1.2.38

113
Mr CUST

DESART

114

62
T DAWSON

115
T DAWSON

118
COUNTY HOSPITAL
5.1.28

63
RD DARTERY

116
G ROBINSON

PART of the MANOR of CHARLEMONT

117
T DAWSON

LORD CREMOURNS
ABBEY LANDS

76
LORD PRIMATE

75
WIDOWS

73
ABBEY STREET

ABBEY LANE

Mr Magcough's house

104
Mr FORD

103
Mr FORD

To Loughgall

CHURCH STREET

8

77

Cathedral Church.

DEAN of ARMAGH

Mr WHALEY

105
J. SCOTT

106
LORD DARTERY

107

108
Mr WHALEY

J SCOTT

2

CHANCELLORS
LANDS

Mr FORD

1
Mr FORD

91
VICARS

92
DEAN
of
ARMAGH

93

94
T DAWSON

101

Mr MACANN

102

110
Free
School

109
DAWSON

4
LORD DARTERY

3
JOHN SCOTT
3.5.20

81
VICARS

95

96
Mr FEILD

Mr
MONTGOMERY

100

99

5
DEAN AVRELL

Market Street

97
Mr JENNEY

98
Mr BOYD

6
Mr CUST

LANDS HELD BY Mr FORDES
TENANTS

14 13
Mr FORD

11

ENGLISH STREET

7
LORD PRIMATE

The
Common

15

9
T DAWSON

8
Mr JENNY

Ty
DAWSON 16

12

10
Mr BURGESS

18

17
THo OGLE

20
JOHN
MACEY

F

19
MONTGOMORY.

T

A. R. P
The Common 45.1.7
Poor houses at A 12
Common 1.14
Tan Yard and F 26
D. 1.38
                    15.1.17

21

22

LORD DARTERY
0.3.16

LANDS LATELY HELD BY
Mr DAWSONS TENANTS

small. No landed estate, no matter how well endowed and well run, could achieve self-sufficiency. Traders, shopkeepers and professionals, such as attorneys, surveyors, physicians, apothecaries, tutors and clergy, could be used, but for the most prestigious and lucrative commissions the grandees customarily turned to a provincial centre, such as Cork, Limerick or Belfast, or more typically Dublin, London and continental Europe.

An owner might donate the ground on which a market or sessions house or assembly room was to be built, might head the published list of subscribers for additions and improvements to the Protestant church and, by the later 1760s, a county infirmary. Indeed, it could be within the church — of the conforming minority — that the Big House was most assertive. Even when enlarged, the space was intimate. It was likely to be dominated by a pew in a prominent position for the family from the Big House and another for the servants obliged to attend public worship. Monuments to members of the family might adorn the walls, as of Sir Thomas Taylor and his wife in Kells parish church, or a grandiose mausoleum might occupy disproportionate space in the graveyard.

Later in the eighteenth century, proprietors like Sir James Caldwell gave land and some money on which Protestant dissenters or Catholics could erect a place of worship. The design of any buildings with architectural pretensions — a church or courthouse or an integrated terrace or mall of houses — required plans. Some of the otherwise obscure figures, such as William Elgee employed on works in Dundalk, had been trained on the estate, acquiring familiarity with the modish classicism of the eighteenth century not just on the job but also from the instructions of their well-travelled employers. Possibly the latter lent the artificers pattern-books and other manuals and drawings from which the rudiments of Palladianism could be gleaned. Even so, it accords too much privilege as architectural and cultural innovators to dim squires and dizzy aristocrats if we ignore the presence within the towns of professionals, traders, their children and even skilled craftworkers who had themselves travelled and who were conversant with the styles of building and decoration prevalent in Britain and western Europe. Furthermore, the Taylors' altruism did not then lead them to encourage Adam to couple designs for the interiors at Headfort with other commissions in the neighbourhood.[21]

Interventions by local grandees in urban planning only occasionally had a transformative impact, as in Armagh city through Archbishop Robinson (Fig. 14.5). It was not only a town's appearance, but also its atmosphere that concerned active proprietors. The presence of reputable teachers, a salubrious inn, assembly room, stationer, bookshop and printer, agreeable promenades, communal gatherings catering to self and collective improvement and curiosity about wider worlds all helped. A discerning proprietor could create a congenial atmosphere for such developments: notably by providing premises and recommending operators. However, for such initiatives to survive, let alone thrive, support from the townspeople and hinterland was vital. The landed and their families set powerful examples in underwriting and attending such events, but with numerous other calls on their time and money, and frequently away in Dublin, England or on military and government service, they were unlikely ever to be constant patrons. Possibly diaries, engagement books and minutes, if exhaustively analysed, might show how assiduous were supporters. Even with the role of Archbishop Robinson, his importance in implanting civility, sociability and refinement in Armagh is not universally agreed. Robinson chose to erect his palace away from the principal public buildings of the town and indeed returned with increasing frequency to his own mansion in the north of England.[22]

The IHTA has exploited surviving and excavated structures. Thanks to the archives of, for example, the Taylors, formerly at Headfort, the Hamiltons and Rodens and the Boyles (Bandon and Youghal), much detail about leases, rents, building materials, regulation and oversight can be found and applied to the urban history. In some cases, more thorough research, the discovery and availability of more such material and the emergence of unsuspected sources may illumine presently dark phases. Detailed surveys of estates, handsomely conceived and executed, often sumptuously bound, have sometimes escaped from the bulk of a collection and resurface in unexpected places.[23] A noteworthy example is the album of Hugh Douglas Hamilton's *Cries of Dublin*. Everyday life and the characters of Dublin at the accession of King George III are vividly portrayed. Its migration to Australia and the uncertainties of its provenance (bearing the bookplate of Gaussen) must stir hopes that materials that will illumine a smaller Irish town will one day be unearthed.[24] Meanwhile, the lengthening line of fascicles offers a surfeit of information to compare and ponder.

Notes

[1] K.V. Mulligan, *South Ulster: Armagh, Cavan and Monaghan* (New Haven and London, 2014).

[2] B.J. Graham and L.J. Proudfoot, *Urban improvement in provincial Ireland, 1700–1840* (Dublin, 1994), pp 3–12.

[3] Peter Borsay, *The English urban renaissance: culture and society in the provincial town, 1660–1770* (Oxford, 1989).

[4] Bob Harris and Charles McKean, *The Scottish town in the age of enlightenment* (Edinburgh, 2014).

[5] James Kelly, *Sport in Ireland, 1600–1840* (Dublin, 2014); James Kelly and M.J. Powell (eds), *Clubs and societies in eighteenth-century Ireland* (Dublin, 2010).

[6] T.C. Barnard, 'Educating eighteenth-century Ulster', in D.W. Hayton and A.R. Holmes (eds), *Ourselves alone? Religion, society and politics in eighteenth- and nineteenth-century Ireland* (Dublin, 2016), pp 104–25; Anngret Simms, 'Education', in H.B. Clarke and Sarah Gearty (eds), *Maps and texts: exploring the Irish Historic Towns Atlas* (Dublin, 2013), pp 226–35.

[7] J.H. Gebbie, *An introduction to the Abercorn letters (as relating to Ireland, 1736–1816)* (Omagh, 1972), pp 129, 152–3; W.J. Roulston, *Abercorn: the Hamiltons of Barons Court* (Belfast, 2014), p. 73.

[8] For reflections, see Toby Barnard, 'An Irish urban renaissance?', in Catherine Armstrong and John Hinks (eds), *The English urban renaissance revisited* (Newcastle, 2018, forthcoming).

[9] Edward McParland, *Public architecture in Ireland, 1680–1760* (New Haven and London, 2001).

[10] Mulligan, *South Ulster*, pp 62–3.

[11] Giordano Bertuzzi, *Palazzi a Modena: note storiche su alcune dimore gentilizie cittadine* (3 vols, Modena, 1999–2002).

[12] Raffaella Besta (ed.), *Musei di Strada Nuova a Genova* (Milan, 2010).

[13] T.J. Hughes, 'Historical geography in Ireland from *circa* 1700', in G.L. Herries Davies (ed.), *Irish Geography: the Geographical Society of Ireland golden jubilee 1934–1984* (Dublin, 1984), pp 156–60.

[14] Raymond Gillespie, 'Belfast and Derry-Londonderry', in Clarke and Gearty, *Maps and texts*, pp 86–99.

[15] Eoin Magennis, 'Coal, corn and canals: parliament and the dispersal of public moneys, 1693–1772', in D.W. Hayton (ed.), *The Irish parliament in the eighteenth century: the long apprenticeship* (Edinburgh, 2001), pp 71–86.

[16] O'Sullivan, IHTA, no. 16, *Dundalk*, p. 4.

[17] John Ellis to Lord Limerick, 12 Sept. 1749; Arthur Newburgh to same [May 1746]; Stephen Poyntz to Edward Weston, 25 Apr. 1757; Thomas Waite to same, 10 Dec. 1748 (PRONI, MIC 147/9; T 3019/863; T 3019/1214); *Proposals for carrying on the cambric-manufacture* (Dublin, 1739) (TNA: PRO, 30/26/46); Robert Stephenson, *An inquiry into the state and progress of the linen manufacture of Ireland* (Dublin, 1757), p. 160; Robert Stephenson, *Observations on the present state of the linen trade of Ireland* (Dublin, 1784), p. 7.

[18] Sir James Caldwell to Lady Caldwell, 4 Oct. 1772 (John Rylands Library, Manchester, B 3/29/30).

[19] Brian de Breffny, 'Liotard's Irish patrons', in *Irish Arts Review*, iv, no. 2 (1987), p. 38; Eileen Harris, 'Thomas Wright and Viscount Limerick at Tollymore Park, County Down', in *Irish Architectural and Decorative Studies*, xvi (2013), pp 132–43; Robert Jocelyn, *Tollymore: the story of an Irish demesne* (Belfast, 2005); Peter Rankin, *Tollymore Park, the Gothick revival of Thomas Wright and Lord Limerick* (Belfast, 2011); *Some hints on planting. By a planter* (Newry, 1773 and 1783).

[20] *A catalogue of impressions in sulphur of antique and modern gems from which pastes are made and sold by J. Tassie* (London, 1775).

[21] John Harris, *Headfort House and Robert Adam: drawings from the collection of Mr and Mrs Paul Mellon* (London, 1973).

[22] T.C. Barnard, 'Delusions of grandeur? "Big" Houses in eighteenth-century Ireland', in *Eighteenth-Century Ireland*, xxx (2015), pp 143, 148.

[23] William Laffan and Christopher Monkhouse (eds), *Ireland: crossroads of art and design, 1690–1840* (Chicago, 2015), p. 233.

[24] Anne Crookshank and Desmond FitzGerald, 'Preface', in William Laffan (ed.), *The cries of Dublin, drawn from the life by Hugh Douglas Hamilton, 1760* (Dublin, 2003), p. 9.

15. Exploring the impact of the canals: Limerick, Maynooth, Mullingar and Longford

Arnold Horner

Before introducing the experience of the four towns under review in this discussion, it may be useful to offer some perspective on the general development of inland waterways in Ireland. Schemes for improving the navigability of rivers and for the building of canals were being proposed from the seventeenth century. In the following century, these ideas found expression in a series of construction projects. [1] As well as developments affecting several of the principal rivers such as the Shannon in the midlands, the Barrow, Nore and Suir in the south-east, and the Boyne and some other rivers on the east and north coasts, several major purpose-built canal schemes were initiated. The most significant of the eighteenth-century canals were, in the north the 30 km Newry to Lough Neagh canal and, running west from Dublin to link with the Shannon, the 130 km Grand Canal and the 148 km Royal Canal. Completed in 1742, the Newry canal has the distinction of being one of the earliest purpose-built canals in either Britain or Ireland. Operating commercially for almost two hundred years, it has been recognised as being one of the preconditions that facilitated the economic transformation of the Newry to Lough Neagh corridor during the eighteenth century.[2] In some contrast, the two canals starting from Dublin were built later and experienced rather more mixed fortunes. The Grand Canal was commenced in 1756 and was undoubtedly the greatest engineering project in eighteenth-century Ireland. With a long branch to Athy and the Barrow, and later short offshoots to Edenderry, Mountmellick and Kilbeggan, its progess was slow. It took until 1804 to reach Shannon Harbour and 1827 to continue beyond the Shannon as far as Ballinasloe. Passing through some areas of solid agriculture and also near extensive bogland, the Grand Canal was able to carry a significant traffic in agricultural and fuel products. In addition, during its early decades it offered a passenger service that was enhanced by such initiatives as canal hotels and onward coach connections.[3]

Whereas the Grand Canal was able to operate profitably for long periods, the Royal Canal was much less soundly based. Started in 1789, possibly as a result of some sort of row within the Grand Canal hierarchy and perhaps further stimulated by the canal mania that took hold in 1790s Britain, it headed west and north-west from Dublin and took a route that demanded some very significant investment.[4] A major aqueduct had to be built at Leixlip and later high costs were incurred to stabilise the canal in bogland. Reaching Maynooth about 1795 and Mullingar in 1806, financial issues forced the canal to be paused for several years. Not unlike some major companies in recent years, a new round of investment was required to complete the project. At least if the canal could reach the Shannon, there was the possibility that some sense could be made of the scheme, especially if it were in some way possible to link the canal into the development of the 'Connaught coalfield' in Leitrim. Even though this was a highly speculative prospect, a re-capitalisation was undertaken in 1812, with a new company — the New Royal Canal Company — being created in an attempt to put the whole venture on some sort of rational footing. It was under the aegis of this body that the canal reached the Shannon about 1817, with the short 8 km branch to Longford being built around ten years later.

In Britain, where an extensive network was developed during the second half of the eighteenth century, canals played an important role during the early decades of the industrial revolution.[5] Canals facilitated the movement of coal away from the coalfields and on a broader level they promoted the growth of inter-, as well as intra-, regional trade. Their success was such that, as already noted, they became a speculative prospect that reached an investment frenzy during the early 1790s.[6] In Ireland, however, their development was much more selective, as might be expected given their more limited resource base and the smaller volumes of longer-distance trade. The establishment in 1800 of the Directors-General of Inland Navigation, with a capital grant of £500,000, offered some prospect of enhanced government support for canal and river navigation projects, with the result that, particularly over the following decade, some schemes were completed.[7] About the same time, the prospects of linking the Grand Canal to the collieries of Kilkenny and south Laois (Queen's County) inspired a variety of proposals for new canals. Many lines were drawn on maps and some survey work was undertaken, yet little of this planning ever became expressed in actual infrastructure.[8] Part of a rural scene, and with modest levels of traffic, the Irish canals that were actually built may have had a relatively limited impact across the broader economy, at least when compared to some of their counterparts in Britain.

Specific data on traffic volumes on Irish canals indicate that the Grand Canal consistently carried much greater quantities than the Royal Canal. In 1810 the Grand carried over 200,000 tons, about four times the volume recorded for the Royal. Fifty years later the Grand was averaging 300,000 tons whereas the Royal was carrying just under 100,000. From the mid-1870s traffic on the Royal began to decline sharply, to less than 25,000 tons in the early twentieth century, at which time the Grand was still carrying some ten times that volume.[9] A traffic map, made for the railway commissioners in 1838, gives some indication of the broader pattern of freight movements across Ireland.[10] This map shows light traffic over much of the country, with much of it focused on the nearest port. Nevertheless, a significant flow volume is represented from Limerick along the Shannon and thence via the Grand Canal to Dublin. Smaller, but noticeable, flows are also evident from the south-east and along the Royal Canal. Grand Canal data for the 1840s (by which time the canal was carrying nearly 300,000 tons annually) indicate that bricks and other building materials, turf, flour and grain were being moved in substantial quantities towards Dublin, whereas manure, coal and culm, and various 'sundries' were going in the opposite direction into the country. Places handling at least 20,000 tons annually included (in descending order) Tullamore, Sallins, Hazelhatch, Athy and the section of the Barrow between St Mullin's and Athy, with at least 10,000 tons being moved annually at Robertstown,

Mountmellick, Ticknevin, Shannon Harbour, Ballinasloe and Limerick.[11] Spread over most of its routeway, the Grand Canal had evidently become embedded in the economy of the south midlands.

Attention can now be given to the towns under review. Of the four, Limerick, part of the Shannon navigation, was by far the largest. Its population was already close to 50,000 about 1800. In comparison, Maynooth, Mullingar and Longford, each on the Royal Canal, then had populations of under 5,000. The last two listed were county and market towns. The first, Maynooth, was essentially a substantially remodelled landlord village, with a population of around 1,000 and only just beginning to absorb the new Roman Catholic college that had been founded there in 1795. It is proposed to consider the impact of the canal on each of these towns in turn, with particular reference being given to any relevant information in the IHTA.

LIMERICK

In its long and distinguished history, Limerick, as the IHTA makes clear, has developed to be both morphologically and functionally complex, fulfilling a variety of roles as a regional and manufacturing centre, as a port, as a garrison town, and as the centre of many administrative and institutional activities. Between 1700 and 1830 its population increased from around 10,000 to over 65,000, a peak that it did not again reach until the late twentieth century. During that eighteenth-century surge, the elegant 'new town' of Newtown Pery, together with extensive stretches of new quays, docks and associated stores, were laid out. Limerick enhanced its role as an entrepôt, being the point of import and also of export for a substantial hinterland in south-west Ireland. The River Shannon played a crucial role in the prosperity of the city during this period, as Limerick acted as both a gateway to the outside world and a link to inland Ireland, a role that acquired some significance once the river above Limerick was made more navigable as a result of various initiatives from the 1760s on.[12] The precise level of significance that should be accorded to the inland waterway link remains unclear, however, as an effective development of the Shannon navigation was really achieved only during the 1830s. Even then it would appear that traffic was limited by narrow locks on the Limerick–Killaloe section, together with difficulties in negotiating the short section from the canal to the harbour at Limerick. During the early 1830s around 30,000 tons and some 14,000 passengers were being carried on the Limerick–Killaloe section in particular years. An 1845 statistic that over 5,000 tons of goods were being moved in each direction between

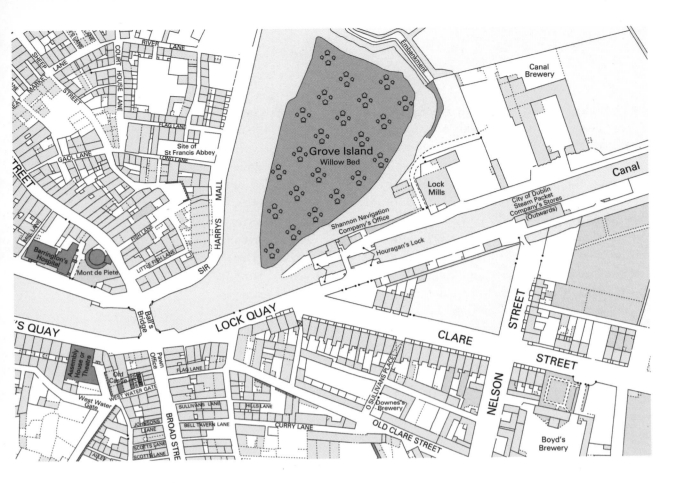

Fig. 15.1 *Limerick*, map 2, canal area, 1840, extract. A lock complex linked the canal to the river.

Limerick and Dublin may initially seem impressive, yet this averages at only 15 tons, perhaps a boatload, per day.[13]

The essay for the IHTA on Limerick gives the inland navigation link very limited attention. It is also difficult to develop any profile on how canal development related to the general surge in the growth of the city during the later eighteenth century from the dauntingly large number (over 4,000) of topographical information entries. Nor is it possible to establish much about the landholding or property ownership context from either the topographical information or the accompanying maps. In some contrast, however, the large number of maps included with the fascicle makes it possible for readers to undertake their own interpretation of the morphological impact of the canal. Map 1, Limerick and its surroundings at a scale of 1:50,000, shows that the canal that enters the city from the east runs only for a short distance and is in fact a short straight stretch that had been built to avoid two weirs and a major meander of the Shannon (between Groody and the city). More local detail is then found on map 2, the 1:2500 coloured plan of Limerick about 1840 (Fig. 15.1). This clearly shows the canal approaching the city at Lock Quay, with Houragan's lock regulating a junction with the Abbey River which, after passing under

Baal's Bridge, is then flanked by George's Quay and Charlotte's Quay before joining the Shannon beside New Quay and Custom House Quay. Several canal-related buildings flanking the canal east of the lock are named. These are Canal Brewery and Lock Mills, both occupying quite large sites, the Shannon Navigation Company's Office and the City of Dublin Steam Packet Company's Stores (Outwards). Two more breweries, Boyd's and Downes's, and a cotton factory are located in nearby streets. Perhaps significantly, these buildings and the canal itself are very much on the edge of the city. The older city lies to the west and north, with Irishtown and the newer developments of the late eighteenth century lying to the south. It is only when the older maps are consulted that a reason for this pattern emerges. The Englishtown of the older city is an island between the Abbey and Shannon rivers. The canal, as Christopher Colles's map of 1769 (map 18) indicates, runs through 'low boggy ground', an area that had been for long avoided for intensive settlement. As well as confirming that the Lock Mills were already in place by 1769, the Colles map has the additional interest that its marginal information includes a written description of the development of Limerick. Here the recent surge of growth is noted in the following comments:

> Since the Year 1760 these famous Walls and Fortifications have been levelled in many places, to make way for new Streets and Buildings which are of late very numerous and stately from the Trade and Spirit of the Inhabitants. A new additional Town on an extensive and elegant Plan, now building by the Encouragement of Edmond Sexton Pery Esqr ... and the Canal now cutting from here to Killaloe, so as to lay open a Navigation to the Grand Canal from Dublin, promises in a few years so to extend its Limits and Trade, that it will very much exceed both this Plan and Description.

The contrasts between the Colles map and those of the Limerick area made by William Eyres around 1752 (maps 15 and 16) are striking. On these earlier plans there is no sign of either the new town or the canal. Nevertheless, map 17, a plan of the new quay (New Kay) about 1764, shows that the lock was apparently by then in place and that the main focus at that stage was to make new walls for the link between the new quay and the Abbey River under Baal's Bridge.

In summary, even though the IHTA is largely silent on landowner-ship and tells us relatively little directly about the trade of the canal from

Fig. 15.2 *Maynooth*, map 8, *c.* 1821, by Sherrard, Brassington and Greene. National Library of Ireland, MS 22,004 (12), extract. Land was reserved for the Royal Canal Company along Canal Place (later Leinster Street), which linked the canal harbour to the main street.

Limerick, comparisons between maps in the IHTA collection allow some deductions to be made as to the scale and phasing of the canal development. It is also easy to make a visual appraisal of how the canal relates to and fits in with the general morphology of the city.

MAYNOOTH

Because of its proximity to the starting point at Dublin, Maynooth was an early connection on the Royal Canal. It was a small place, however, and very much incidental to the main goal of developing a link with the Shannon. More than any local pulling power, its inclusion on the selected route may have been because its landlord, the duke of Leinster, was a member of the the board of directors of the canal. His influence has been cited for the expensive routing of the canal across the aqueduct at Leixlip.[14] He was also no doubt instrumental in ensuring that a short quayside was constructed close to Wharton Bridge, opposite the main entrance to his demesne and residence at Carton. At Maynooth, 3 km farther west, the canal was routed south of the main built-up area. A large harbour was

constructed, with a link to the main street being provided via Canal Place, a newly laid-out street. As the IHTA essay records and as IHTA map 8 showing the town in 1821 depicts, building ground flanking the harbour was assigned to the canal company, with its holding being gated off from that part of Canal Place nearer the main street (Fig. 15.2). Even so, as the IHTA map 2 showing the town about 1837 also indicates, the canal appears to have made little further impact, with not even a single store being located near the harbour. The main role of the canal was then said to be to supply coal to the town.[15]

Yet even if its functional significance was minor, in terms of urban morphology the canal was of some importance. As well as defining the location of the railway line, which arrived in 1846, the canal has significantly influenced the pattern of twentieth-century urban growth, with traffic from the south being channelled via two bridges over the canal, and — as is clearly shown on plate 1, the aerial photograph of Maynooth in 1994 — with building activity leap-frogging to Greenfield and Railpark to the south of the canal line.

MULLINGAR

At the larger centre of Mullingar, 60 km to the west and reached ten years after Maynooth, the canal also took a peripheral route. A manuscript map, which is not included in the IHTA and which was drawn by William Larkin as part of his survey of the Dublin to Sligo mail coach road in 1810,[16] is among the earliest fairly detailed depictions of the canal in relation to the town (Fig. 15.3). Approaching the town from the south-east, the canal is shown following an extended semi-circle to the north and on to the west — what the IHTA essay describes as a 'great northern horseshoe'. Avoiding the developed town area, and featuring an embankment to cross the River Brosna and elsewhere a cutting through a ridge, this route also allowed the canal to be easily connected with a water supply channel from Lough Owel. Near the northern apex and either side of a bridge carrying the Longford road, the canal widened to make a town harbour, beside which at least one dry dock (the IHTA topographical information suggests that two docks existed, but the maps do not confirm this) was built. On map 2, depicting Mullingar in 1837, two small clusters of buildings, incorporating canal stores, are shown beside the harbour area. A canal-side corn store, which may later have been used as an auxiliary workhouse during the 1840s famine, is also marked on this map. An aerial photograph taken in the 1970s gives some impression of the harbour complex as it was once and map 3, depicting Mullingar in 1953 at a scale of 1:5000, records a

Fig. 15.3 The first Mullingar by-pass. The recently-built Royal Canal, from mail coach road map, 1810, by William Larkin. National Library of Ireland, 15/A/4, extract.

Fig. 15.4 *Mullingar*, plate 1, aerial photograph, 1987. Ordnance Survey Ireland. The impact of the canal and the later railway on the urban morphology is striking.

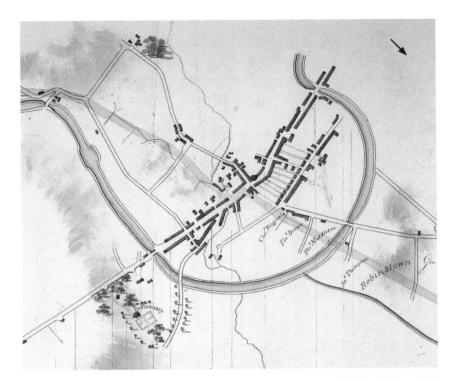

dry dock, the harbour quay and canal stores. In general, however, it is the limited extent of the canal-side buildings that is striking. The Royal Canal Company plot on Harbour Street appears to have still been vacant in 1858 (map 5b). A daily passenger boat service operated to Dublin for a few years and the canal was used to export small amounts of oats and butter, and to import fuel, timber and building materials, but — notwithstanding an 1837 comment that the town derived 'a great increase in trade' from the canal[17] — the functional impact was evidently very limited. As plate 1, the aerial photograph of the town in 1987, makes plain, the canal had, as in Maynooth, a much more enduring and continuing impact on the urban morphology, significantly regulating the road pattern and influencing the broader progress of urban expansion (Fig. 15.4).

LONGFORD

Following from the construction of a short spur section from the main line to Cloondara, the canal reached Longford in the late 1820s. IHTA map 12, part of an estate map by John Hill showing the manor of Longford in 1830, depicts the canal approaching the town from the south and terminating in a rectangular basin beside the market square and market house that had been recently developed at the southern end of the town. Comparison with map 13, featuring the town as it appears on the 1813 map of Co. Longford by William Edgeworth, indicates that the area where the canal basin and market square were to develop had then been part of the Longford town parks. The 1830 map shows much of the development area as being leased by the representatives of John Stafford and John Young. From the IHTA alone it is not possible to determine whether these men, or their representatives, were significant in the development process. Nonetheless, Lewis in 1837 records the key role of the town proprietor, the earl of Longford. As well as being responsible for the construction of the canal basin, he had built the market house and corn stores, and had 'erected a butter market and shambles at his own expense'.[18]

Comparison with the later map 16, showing Longford in 1884 by Thomas Gill, indicates that the Fair Green had by then a location close to the market square and canal basin, a position that was of course also near to the railway station (Fig. 15.5a). No buildings appear to be directly beside the canal basin. The IHTA topographical information, however, identifies the canal harbour as being the location for stores including corn stores, a slate yard and at least one timber yard. These facilities operated at various times during the nineteenth century. No doubt drawing from the contemporary comments in Lewis, the IHTA essay states that the arrival of the canal 'contributed hugely to the growth of the southern part of the town and confirmed its dominance over the old town in commercial terms'. It would be useful to have further information on the volume

Fig. 15.5 Canal harbour area. (a) *Longford*, map 16, 1884, by Thomas Gill. Longford County Library and Archive, M/T/2, extract; (b) *Longford*, map 3, 2009. Ordnance Survey Ireland, extract.

of Longford traffic on the canal and in particular to assess how it was affected by the arrival of the railway in 1855. Almost certainly the hey-day of the canal was short-lived and before that date. In the twentieth century, according to the IHTA topographical information, the canal probably declined rapidly, with the harbour being sold to Longford County Council in 1951. Following its infill, part of the harbour site came to be used for a town swimming pool. On map 3, the 1:5000 plan of Longford in 2009 (Fig. 15.5b), and on plate 5, the aerial photograph of the town in 2007, the market square and market building are still evident. The line of the disused canal is also apparent as it approaches the town. Even so, there is nothing in the present layout of the area to suggest the past existence of the canal harbour itself. Only a couple of buildings and the names of a street, Harbour Row, and an apartment block, Harbour Point, remain as enigmatic reminders of an otherwise erased past.

CONCLUSION

Overall, it cannot really be claimed that the coming of the canal made a significant long-term economic impact on any of the four towns under review. In the case of the Royal Canal traffic volumes were always quite modest and, in the case of the much larger city of Limerick, the volume of inland traffic using the Shannon navigation, although appreciable, was also modest relative to the size of the city and to the overall level of trade. Morphologically, however, the canals were more significant, with their routes coming to define lines, patterns and rates of urban development. The IHTA records the morphological impact of the canal, showing it to be especially significant at Maynooth and Mullingar. At Longford, however, the place where the canal penetrated closest to an urban core, the main later 'impact' of the harbour was to provide a development site. Comparisons between various IHTA maps and plates show how the canal has been instrumental in a variety of ways by creating a form that has been relevant for future growth. The accompanying topographical information identifies many of the relatively limited number of ancillary buildings that related to canal development. Less satisfactorily, perhaps, the IHTA is usually silent on the property holders and land transactions that must have been part of the canal development process. More property information will almost certainly be found embedded among the vast accumulation of records in the Registry of Deeds. Essentially, the IHTA may best be seen as a valuable resource for focusing on urban development issues, perhaps stimulating enquirers to later probes into the processes that underlie the various features and changes involved in urban growth. These characteristics will become yet further apparent as the atlas expands to cover the small number of other Irish towns with significant canal connections, for example Newry, on the borders of Cos Down and Armagh, and Tullamore, Co. Offaly.

NOTES

[1] W.A. McCutcheon, *The canals of the north of Ireland* (Dawlish, 1965); V.T.H. Delany and D.R. Delany, *The canals of the south of Ireland* (Newton Abbot, 1966).

[2] B.M.S. Campbell, 'Economic progress in the canal age: a case study from Counties Armagh and Down', in David Dickson and Cormac Ó Gráda (eds), *Refiguring Ireland: essays in honour of L.M. Cullen* (Dublin, 2003), pp 63–93.

[3] Ruth Delany, *The Grand Canal of Ireland* (Newton Abbot, 1973).

4 Ruth Delany and Ian Bath, *Ireland's Royal Canal 1789–2009* (Dublin, 2010); see also, Delany and Delany, *Canals of the south of Ireland*, pp 77–91.

[5] Charles Hadfield, *British canals: an illustrated history* (Newton Abbot, 1974).

[6] Ibid., pp 107–31.

[7] Many of the records of the Directors-General of Inland Navigation (1800–31) are preserved in the National Archives of Ireland, Dublin. For an introduction to these and other navigation records, see the chapter on inland navigation in Rena Lohan, *Guide to the archives of the Office of Public Works* (Dublin, 1994), pp 189–218.

[8] See the list of 'canals authorised or projected but not begun' in Delany and Delany, *Canals of the south of Ireland*, pp 236–7. Many of the routes proposed during the early nineteenth century are included on maps in NAI, OPW 5HC and in NLI, 16/E/17.

[9] Delany and Delany, *Canals of the south of Ireland*, pp 85, 140–47.

[10] Redrawn in T.W. Freeman, *Pre-famine Ireland: a study in historical geography* (Manchester, 1957), p. 117.

[11] Delany and Delany, *Canals of the south of Ireland*, pp 65, 67.

[12] Ruth Delany, *The Shannon Navigation* (Dublin, 2008); Delany and Delany, *Canals of the south of Ireland*, pp 98–123.

[13] Delany and Delany, *Canals of the south of Ireland*, pp 67, 214–15, 246.

[14] Ibid., p. 83.

[15] Lewis, ii, p. 349.

[16] NLI, 15/A/4.

[17] Lewis, ii, p. 411.

[18] Ibid., p. 311.

16. Military barracks in an age of revolt and war

David A. Fleming

Buildings designed for the accommodation of large numbers of soldiers are a relatively recent phenomenon in European history. The development and ever increasing demands of a standing or permanent military establishment, especially from the seventeenth century, obliged governments to assess how best to house, feed and provide for soldiers, horses and equipment. Up to the seventeenth century soldiers had been accommodated in the existing garrisons or castles and fortifications belonging to the state, while additional accommodation was met by billeting officers and men on the populace at large. Increasingly citizens bemoaned this imposition, especially as numbers multiplied. Others, such as taverners and innkeepers may have been reluctant to see any change in the arrangements, but change there was. An increasingly professional army required discipline and training, which might be more easily provided for in dedicated accommodation. France and Spain were among the first to build barracks for their soldiers, while in Britain the first barracks were erected in the 1670s.[1] Yet, Britain did not witness any large-scale barrack building programme, mostly owing to the British parliamentarian's reluctance and ambivalence towards a large standing army, which was based on fears that soldiers could be used by an overbearing monarch to subdue parliament, as had happened in the 1640s. As a result legislation prevented the king from stationing more than 7,000 soldiers in Britain during peacetime.[2] Similar legislation, in 1699, had limited the number of soldiers in Ireland to 12,000.[3] Thus Ireland became an important link in the emerging imperial nexus, where soldiers constantly moved between the home islands, parts of Europe, the American plantations and later India. As the empire expanded in the eighteenth century the government argued that there was need for more soldiers than the 1699 legislation allowed for. Thus in 1769 the army, paid for by the Irish establishment, grew to 15,325 after a heated parliamentary and public debate.[4] How many men and animals were actually stationed in Ireland at any one time is difficult to answer, yet it is safe to say that the numbers involved were substantial and had a significant influence on the political, economic and social worlds of both the capital and the provinces.

While nineteenth-century barracks and their occupants have been well treated, studies for the eighteenth century are relatively sparse.[5] Understanding the development of military defence and architecture is a necessary precursor for establishing why certain barracks were built where they were. Harman Murtagh's study of defensive fortifications serves as a starting point.[6] Contributions by Ivar McGrath, Alan Guy and Sean Connolly provide the financial, imperial and political context in which these buildings emerged.[7] Several useful studies concentrate on specific examples and local areas.[8] Recently attention has turned to the factors that prompted their location, the impact soldiers had on the locality where they were stationed, and the emergence of a distinctive style of military architecture.[9] Ivar McGrath's project to create a database, which will identify and map over two hundred barracks known to have been built in eighteenth-century Ireland, should advance our knowledge of major as well as minor buildings and may prompt further studies.[10]

Identifying eighteenth-century barrack locations and the evolution of barrack building in a locality can be challenging. The availability of contemporary maps is often a useful starting point. Maps surveying the island often provide indicative locations, sometimes differentiating between barracks for infantry and those for cavalry.[11] Detailed city and town plans typically identify the exact locations of official buildings including barracks. Quite often these maps provide the outline of buildings and any enclosing walls or defences. What is more difficult to determine is the location of less important and more rural buildings called 'redoubts' that were used in the earlier part of the century to accommodate smaller army units, typically in areas where bandits or raparees were active.[12] Some may not classify these buildings as barracks *per se*, given their temporary use and their relatively simple construction, yet they formed part of the emerging network of places where soldiers were accommodated. We know of their existence chiefly from official documents, such as the *Journals of the house of commons of Ireland* and war office papers in the British Library and The National Archives, London.[13] Some redoubts may have developed into permanent barracks, while most, located in isolated places, were abandoned. Archaeology may in the future provide us with a better insight into the location and development of these structures. Other, mostly manuscript sources, such as lists of the 'quarters of the army in Ireland', which identify regiments and the number of units to be accommodated in specific barracks, are very useful where they exist.[14]

Identifying when a barracks was built can be even more challenging. For the larger towns and cities, a barrack's foundation as well as the number of companies it could accommodate was often recorded in directories, almanacs, newspapers or contemporary histories. In smaller and more isolated places the historian must rely on official and estate papers where property was either leased or sold to the government for building barracks.[15] In all likelihood such sources may not offer a precise date, but a best estimate based on comparisons of official barracks lists or a first mention in correspondence or other official papers. Again for larger barracks in prominent locations, an architect may have been identified and can be found on an online database compiled by the Irish Architectural Archive.[16]

The IHTA series of fascicles provides a very useful means of assessing the development of barracks from the 1690s. Of the 125 locations[17] where barracks were built in the period 1690 to 1809, eighteen have been covered by fascicles.[18] This amounts to 12% of barracks locations, which therefore should caution us from making concrete conclusions on the general nature of barrack building when using the fascicles. Nevertheless a general picture of the development of these buildings can be gleaned from evidence in the series. Using these eighteen fascicles, this essay examines three key elements for researching barracks within towns and cities: (i) determining the dates when barracks were built; (ii) the reasons for their location within or near towns and; (iii) the impact these buildings had on the urban landscape.

Dating barrack construction

Two intense periods of barrack building at the beginning and end of the eighteenth century are noticeable from data provided in the fascicles, which generally correspond with other documentary evidence for barrack construction in Ireland. Twelve barracks have been identified as being built in the first two decades after 1691. The same number has been recorded in the period 1790–1809. This is explained by two periods of warfare that book-end the century. The wars between Britain and France and their respective allies, which lasted from the 1690s to 1715, with a couple of gaps, provided the backdrop to the initial drive to acquire land and built a network of barracks, as well as the improvement of existing garrisons and fortifications. Likewise, the wars with revolutionary France beginning in 1793 and continuing to 1815 provide the second. In the intervening period a number of factors prompted the establishment of barracks. The decision to close smaller barracks and to concentrate larger numbers in some places prompted rebuilding or extensions to existing barracks, or alternatively a move to a new site in the same town. Longford provides a useful example. It had a cavalry barracks by 1708, which was substantially enlarged with the addition of a new building to its rear in 1774 (Fig. 16.1). Later, between 1806 and 1810, an artillery barracks was built about a kilometre north of the existing barracks (Fig. 16.2). Likewise

Fig. 16.1 Cavalry barracks. *Longford*, map 12, 1830, by John Hill. Tullynally Castle, Co. Westmeath.

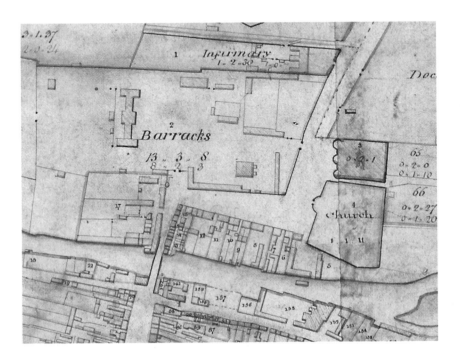

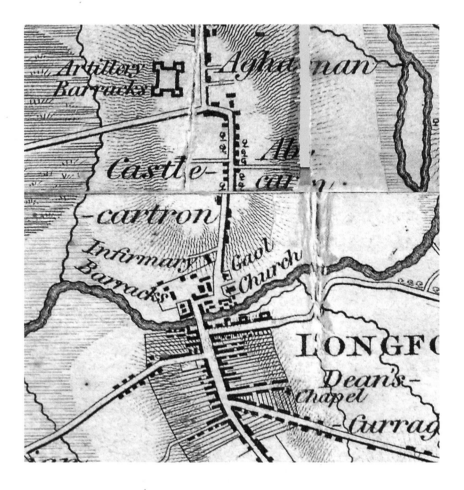

Fig. 16.2 Artillery barracks. *Longford*, map 11, 1813, by William Edgeworth, extract.

in Limerick, its older barrack buildings built in 1694 and 1726 were consolidated and then mostly replaced in 1798 and 1807 when two new and bigger barracks were built.

Towards the end of the century, much larger buildings were being constructed to accommodate more adequately the increasing numbers of soldiers in the army. For example, in Belfast the new barracks built in 1796 was six times larger than the older, 1715 building. In some cases older barracks continued in use, but in general these sites tended to be sold and found alternative uses as breweries, factories, hospitals and schools, as the fascicles highlight. Over the century the number of barrack locations declined as outlying and remote places were increasingly considered inadequate for both strategic and economic reasons.[19]

LOCATION

A number of factors determined the location of barracks including the existence of older fortifications, defence and topography.

(a) Existing fortifications

The king's castles, fortifications and garrisons that had long dominated the landscape, such as those at Dublin, Limerick and Athlone, were normally the preferred sites for the construction of new barracks in the first two decades after the 1689–91 war. Important centres in their own right and usually with town walls, these places were obvious for both strategic and economic reasons. Limerick was probably the first completed, in 1694, when a building was constructed within the medieval king's castle (Fig. 16.3). That the relationship with the existing fortifications was important was again emphasised when additional barracks, built in Limerick in the 1710s, were located directly to the east of the castle, with a line of communication between both, which in time would form a parade ground for drilling. Another example is Carrickfergus Castle, which seems to have provided accommodation for soldiers up to the nineteenth century. It had a barracks built within its walls in 1715 with room for one cavalry troop and five infantry companies.[20] Other examples include Athlone, Bray and Trim, where barracks were built in the shadow of medieval castles. Even in

Fig. 16.3 Barracks and castle. *Limerick*, map 15, 1752, by William Eyres. British Library, Maps, K Top 54 21, extract.

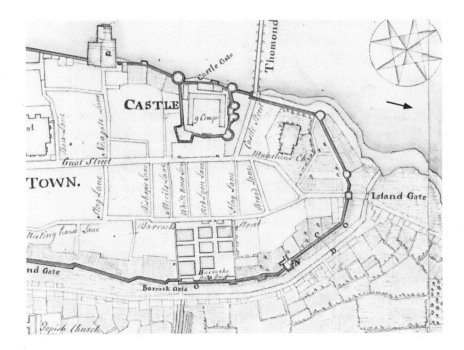

relatively new towns, such as Derry, the state preferred to build on government property. When a barracks was established there in the 1690s, it was located near the site of the late fifteenth-century castle and fort, around which the town had been built in the seventeenth century. In choosing such locations, the government was conscious of the continuing military importance of these areas as well as the expense that purchasing or leasing new ground would have entailed.

(b) Defence

As the first barracks were often built in close proximity to or within existing fortifications, they might be seen to be fulfilling or continuing a defensive function. Athlone, Carrickfergus, Derry, Limerick, Sligo and Trim fall into this category. But it is also clear that defensive or strategic desires were not always paramount or indeed necessary for the location of barracks. Indeed, the buildings themselves had little defensive architecture. The first barracks established in Bandon and Belfast, for example, were both located outside town walls. Dublin's already congested centre could hardly be expected to provide a space for the largest barracks in the country — in any event its walls had long been considered as having little or no defensive capacity. In cases where barracks were built in locations where there were no existing fortifications, it would seem that the suburbs of towns and cities were preferred. Certainly, the barracks built in the period from the 1770s onwards suggest that defensive needs were not necessarily a significant determinant for location. In any event the notion of a 'walled town' was considered obsolete. By then, large open spaces in the vicinity of towns were desired so that ever larger buildings could be provided for. Limerick's new barrack buildings, built in 1798, are a case in point, where there was obviously very little or no defensive purpose to them.

Strategic concerns were considered when choosing the towns in which barracks were located. It has already been mentioned that redoubts or smaller cantonments were built in places were bandits were active in the first decades of the century. Similarly, demands from the revenue for assistance in supporting tax collection occasionally prompted consideration of locations in isolated places. For example, in the 1750s a barracks in 'Eyre Connaught' in Galway had been established to support the revenue officers.[21] There seem to be few distinguishing factors determining the respective locations of cavalry and foot barracks. The larger cities could accommodate both, while smaller locations tended to be exclusive either for cavalry or for foot, though by mid-century the midlands (and Leinster in particular) had a greater proportion of cavalry accommodation. From the 1760s the defence of the kingdom from external invasion was given increasing attention, which influenced the location of new buildings and the development of existing barracks.[22] During the 1790s and 1800s when both internal and external threats became ever more obvious, efforts were again made, as they had been at the beginning of the eighteenth century, to control particular areas more effectively by the building of barracks such as those proposed along the new military road through the Wicklow mountains.[23] In other places defensive strategies to defeat an invading force determined the location or enhancement of barracks.[24]

(c) Topography

One important, practical factor for the location of barracks was proximity to water. A regular and large supply of water for men and horses was a necessity for consumption, washing and lavatories. While in smaller locations an excavated well might have sufficed, in other cases a location alongside a river was desired. Rivers may also have acted as a means of communication to the barracks, which is suggested by the location of a 'barrack slip' on the River Shannon at Athlone, and at Bandon where there seems to have been a quay that led directly to the barracks. Kilkenny's barracks was within yards of the River Nore. In Dublin, it is hard not to conclude that the proximity of the Liffey was at least one factor in its location in Oxmantown (Fig. 16.4). The duke of Ormonde owned the

Fig. 16.4 Royal Barracks. *Dublin, part II*, map 12, 1728. From Charles Brooking, *A map of the city and suburbs of Dublin.* Royal Irish Academy © RIA.

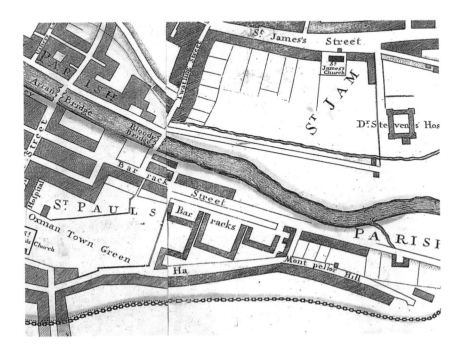

property and was lord lieutenant when the barracks was built there in 1708, which was probably the decisive factor in its location.

The role of political influence in determining the location of barracks in particular areas was important.[25] There was much to be gained. Individuals and landowners hoped that the presence of large numbers of officers, soldiers and their animals would bring significant economic and perhaps social advantages to a place. Finding evidence of political influence requires a close examination of estate papers and official correspondence. Throughout the eighteenth century those responsible for the building and maintenance of barracks, the commissioners and overseers of barracks (generally known as the Barrack Board or Barrack Office), generally sought proposals for the building of barracks in specific locations, which they often announced in the newspapers.[26]

The necessity to train and drill men and horses was also a consideration. While the barrack yard provided space for drilling, more large-scale manoeuvres and reviews required open and usually green spaces. In this instance, the barracks at Armagh seemed to be best placed to take advantage of the commons located to the east of the town, which also acted as a racecourse. The Phoenix Park in Dublin provided a review and training ground for the large Oxmantown or Royal Barracks, while the open space outside Limerick's town walls on the King's Island provided a similar setting.

INFLUENCE ON THE URBAN LANDSCAPE

The term 'garrison town' is commonly used to describe any town with a barracks, but this is misleading. The term should be used only for those locations that had a permanent military establishment, headed by a governor, such as Cork, Limerick and Kinsale. The vast majority of barracks did not have such an establishment. Yet the term is evocative, as it often implies a place that has been shaped by the presence of soldiers, and is indicative of the influence that barracks had in the places that accommodated soldiers.

The maps and images in the fascicles provide useful evidence for the layout or plan of the barracks and occasionally its architecture. Edward McParland's study of public architecture argued that the typical model for a barracks was a large block with two projecting wings, forming one half of a quadrangle. Examples are to be found in Athlone, Belfast, Downpatrick, Dublin, Kilkenny, Limerick and Sligo (Fig. 16.5). But there were other designs. In Limerick the first barracks, built in 1694, was distinctly domestic in style, with one five-bay, two-storey building and another of three storeys, with three bays. Presumably one of these buildings provided accommodation for the garrison's governor. Not far off, the barracks built some time around 1710 consisted of eight blocks built in a grid pattern (Fig. 16.3). Longford, too, had a slight variation of the typical plan, with one possibly square building along with a long L-shaped structure partly surrounding it. This latter building is likely to have been stabling for horses. In general barrack buildings were newly built, though in some cases existing buildings were converted, such as the former home of the King family at Boyle, Co. Roscommon and the seat of Lord Longford at Tulsk, also in Roscommon.[27]

These large buildings could form imposing features within towns and cities. Dublin's barracks of three squares was among the first substantial public building that travellers came upon when entering the metropolis from the west. Contemporaries boasted that this barracks was the 'finest of its kind in Europe'.[28] Likewise, in Kilkenny, the impressive features of its barracks can be easily discerned over the roofs of smaller buildings in its vicinity in Thomas Mitchell's painting of the town of about 1760 (Fig. 13.2).[29] Even barracks in smaller towns could be striking edifices. If the 1762 map of Bray in Co. Wicklow is to be read literally, the barracks there may have been three storeys high and would have sat prominently in the streetscape.[30] Barracks in rural locations such as Lurganboy in Leitrim, Cullen in Limerick and Ross Castle in Kerry seem to have left less of an impression, despite the ambitions of landowners who hoped that building barracks would give impetus for further growth and stimulate the local economy.[31] These places have not been covered by fascicles and are not likely to be owing to their size, though we should not neglect them.

One of the real strengths of the atlas is its identification of streets and their changing toponyms. It seems that locals and others were quick to identify and name streets, lanes and hills where barracks were located — evidence again that these became important points in the topography once built. Maps of Downpatrick dated 1705 and 1720 show Barrack Quarter as a distinct district, which was named within a decade of the barracks being built. Of the eighteen fascicles, fifteen record early references to either a Barrack Street or a Barrack Lane. For example, in Mullingar, though the location of the barracks is unknown, a Barrack Hill and a Barrack Street offer strong evidence to suggest where it might have been. Athlone, a town dominated by its barracks, had a Barrack Lane, Barrack Square and Barrack Street, all identified in the eighteenth century. Even where lanes and streets had long pre-dated the building of barracks, locals

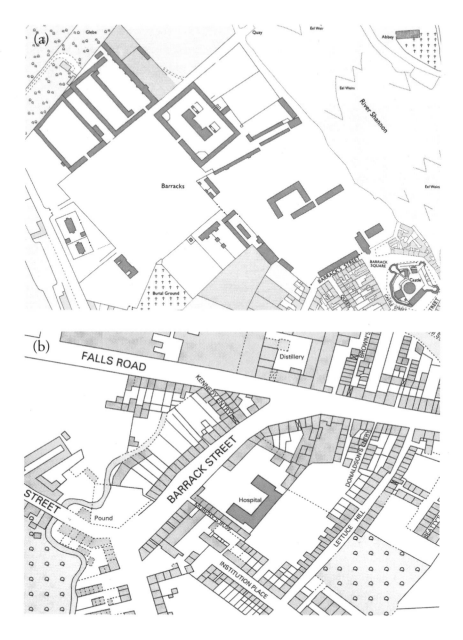

Fig. 16.5 Barrack buildings as depicted on map 2 in (a) Athlone (1837–8), (b) Belfast (c. 1830), (c) Downpatrick (c. 1833) and (d) Sligo (1837). The eighteenth-century barracks had become a hospital/infirmary in Belfast and Downpatrick by the 1830s.

seem to have altered the toponyms to reflect the new building in their midst. The case of Limerick is indicative. Abbey Street, which had been documented since the 1590s, was renamed Barrack Street by at least 1719, shortly after the building had been erected. What emerges then is very strong evidence for the influence that barracks had for the places where they were located.

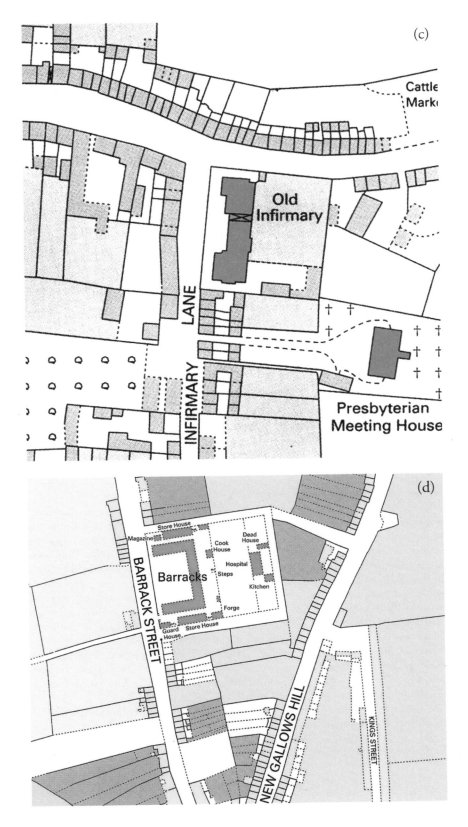

(c)

Cattle
Market

Old
Infirmary

LANE

INFIRMARY

Presbyterian
Meeting House

(d)

Store House

Magazine

Cook
House

Dead
House

BARRACK STREET

Barracks

Hospital

Steps

Kitchen

Forge

Guard
House

Store House

NEW GALLOWS HILL

KINGS STREET

The building of a network of barracks across Ireland expanded the reach of the state into areas that had until then a sometimes infrequent relationship with its agents. While the influence of the state was also facilitated by the building of customhouses and the expansion of the revenue service in the eighteenth century, the greater number of barracks and their dispersal around the country, as well as the number of soldiers and animals that they could accommodate, ensured that their presence was far more conspicuous. Their establishment often altered the political, economic and social characteristics of a town by adding a further layer of relationships. In other instances where the state had a long military presence, such as Athlone, Cork, Dublin and Waterford, the building of barracks significantly increased the capacity of these places to cater for soldiers, which likewise had economic and social consequences. As well as the location and identification of barracks discussed in this essay, future studies must assess the variety of experiences that emerged in the wake of this wide-scale programme of barrack building. Only then shall we have a better understanding of the role of the military and barracks during war and peacetime.

Notes

[1] C.I. McGrath, *Ireland and empire, 1692–1770* (London, 2012), p. 69.

[2] A.J. Guy, *Oeconomy and discipline, officership and administration in the British army, 1714–63* (Manchester, 1985), pp 9–10.

[3] 10 William III, c. 1 (1699).

[4] Thomas Bartlett, 'The augmentation of the army in Ireland 1767–1769', in *English Historical Review*, xcvi (1981), pp 540–59.

[5] For the nineteenth century, see Jacinta Prunty, 'Military barracks and mapping in the nineteenth century: sources and issues for Irish urban history', in H.B. Clarke, Jacinta Prunty and Mark Hennessy (eds), *Surveying Ireland's past: multidisciplinary essays in honour of Anngret Simms* (Dublin, 2004), pp 477–534; Stephen Mac Eoin, 'Drawn out of the archives: the maps, plans and drawings collection of military barracks in Ireland', in *Irish Archives*, xix (2012), pp 42–8; Judith Hill, 'Barracks, asylum and model school: public architecture in Limerick from the late-eighteenth to the mid-nineteenth century', in Liam Irwin, Gearóid Ó Tuathaigh and Matthew Potter (eds), *Limerick history and society* (Dublin, 2009), pp 277–306; Virginia Crossman, 'Irish barracks in the 1820s and 1830s: a political perspective', in *Irish Sword*, xvii (1989), pp 210–13.

[6] Harman Murtagh, 'Defence', in H.B. Clarke and Sarah Gearty (eds), *Maps and texts: exploring the Irish Historic Towns Atlas* (Dublin, 2013), pp 140–51. See also Harman Murtagh, 'The town walls of Athlone', in Harman Murtagh (ed.), *Irish midland studies: essays in commemoration of N.W. English* (Athlone, 1980), pp 89–106.

[7] McGrath, *Ireland and empire*; A.J. Guy, 'The Irish military establishment, 1660–1776', in Thomas Bartlett and Keith Jeffery (eds), *A military history of Ireland* (Cambridge, 1996), pp 211–30; S.J. Connolly, 'The defence of Protestant Ireland, 1660–1760', in Bartlett and Jeffery, *A military history of Ireland*, pp 231–46.

[8] T.G.F. Paterson, 'The Black Bank and Fews barracks', in *UJA*, 3rd ser., i (1938), pp 108–12; D.J. Butler, 'Controlling insurrection: garrisons, police barracks and bridewells in south Tipperary, *c.* 1750–*c.* 1840', in *Irish Sword*, xxiv (2005), pp 290–305; P.M. Kerrigan, 'Garrisons and barracks in the Irish midlands, 1704–1828', in *Journal of the Old Athlone Society*, vi (1985), pp 100–8; H.P.E. Pereira, 'Barracks in Ireland, 1729, 1769', in *Irish Sword*, i (1951), pp 142–4.

[9] D.A. Fleming, *Politics and provincial people: Sligo and Limerick, 1691–1761* (Manchester, 2010), chapter 6. For the architecture of eighteenth-century barracks, see Edward McParland, *Public architecture in Ireland, 1680–1760* (New Haven and London, 2001), chapter 5.

[10] 'Army barracks of eighteenth-century Ireland', https://barracks18c.ucd.ie/ (last accessed 5 June 2017).

[11] See, for example, Herman Moll, 'A new map of Ireland', 1714 (TNA: PRO, WO 78/419/16) and Thomas Jeffreys, 'Map of Ireland', 1759, in J.H. Andrews, *Shapes of Ireland: maps and their makers, 1564–1839* (Dublin, 1997), p. 189.

[12] For a local example of attempts to subdue bandits by building redoubts, see D.J. Butler, *South Tipperary, 1570–1841: religion, land and rivalry* (Dublin, 2006), pp 102–4.

[13] See, for example, 'Present quarters of the army in Ireland', 26 Mar. 1713 (BL, WO, Add. MS 38,713), f. 44; *Commons' jn. Ire.*

[14] 'Present quarters of the army in Ireland', f. 48; William Petty, *A geographical description of the kingdom of Ireland* (London, 1720); 'A list of the several barracks that is in each province in the kingdom of Ireland with the number of troops and companies each barrack will contain', 4 Mar. 1725; 'Scheme for the quarters of the army', 1726 (BL, Tyrawley Papers, Add. MS 23,636), ff 17–18, 33; *Quarters of the army in Ireland for anno 1733* (Dublin, 1733); *Quarters of the army in Ireland* (Dublin, 1752); 'Scheme for new quarters May 1784' (NLI, Kilmainham Papers, MS 1,007), f. 27.

[15] For a collection of deeds relating to barracks in Ulster, see PRONI, Treasury Solicitor papers, TSD/1.

[16] The database can be assessed at http://www.dia.ie/ (last accessed 2 Feb. 2017).

[17] A location may contain a number of separate barracks establishments. For a map of these locations see Fleming, *Politics and provincial people*, pp 192–3.

[18] Armagh, Athlone, Bandon, Belfast, Bray, Carlingford, Carrickfergus, Derry-Londonderry, Downpatrick, Dublin, Dundalk, Limerick, Longford, Kilkenny, Mullingar, Sligo, Trim and Tuam.

[19] Later sales of barracks and land were advertised in newspapers. See, for example, *Dublin Journal*, 24 Dec. 1816. Lifford's barracks in Donegal was converted into a hospital (D.A. Beaufort, 'Journal of a tour through part of Ireland begun 26 Aug. 1787' (PRONI, MIC 250/1)).

[20] T.E. McNeill, *Carrickfergus Castle* (Belfast, 1981), pp 13, 15; *Excavations on the Grand Battery at Carrickfergus Castle* (Belfast, 2011), pp 19, 29, 43–7; 'A list of the several barracks that is in each province in the kingdom of Ireland', ff 17–18.

[21] Thomas Eyre to Rt Hon. Richard Rigby, 9 Feb. 1758 (IAA, Eyre letterbook), p. 63.

[22] Lord Townshend to [Marquess of Granby], 24 June 1768; Thomas Hyde Page to [–], 4 Sept. 1768, in *The manuscripts of his grace the duke of Rutland* (3 vols, London, 1888–94), ii, pp 306, 307. See also various miscellaneous papers in NLI, MS 655.

[23] *Dublin Journal*, 24 Feb. 1803.

[24] General John Knox to marquess of Abercorn, 3 Oct. 1797 (PRONI, Abercorn Papers, D623/A/156/35); P.M. Kerrigan, 'The defences of the Shannon: Portumna to Athlone, 1793–1815', in Murtagh, *Irish midland studies*, pp 168–92.

[25] The role of political influence in the location of barracks was openly acknowledged in parliament in 1813. See *Dublin Journal*, 29 June 1813. For one example, see John James

Bourgoyne to marquis of Abercorn, 16 Apr. 1808 (PRONI, Abercorn Papers, T2541/IA/4/3/26).

[26] See, for example, *Dublin Journal*, 23 Feb. 1741, 28 July 1750, 7 Aug. 1781, 31 May 1787, 17 Mar. 1801, 1 July 1802, 19 Feb. 1803, 1 Nov. 1808, 3 Jan. 1809, 23 Jan. 1810.

[27] For Tulsk, see Beaufort, 'Journal of a tour through part of Ireland'.

[28] *Dublin Journal*, 30 Aug. 1788. Known (from at least 1801) as the Royal Barracks, they were renamed Collins Barracks after 1922 and now form part of the National Museum of Ireland.

[29] Bradley, IHTA, no. 10, *Kilkenny*, plate 2.

[30] Davies, IHTA, no. 9, *Bray*, map 4.

[31] For Lurganboy, see 'Estimate' from Thomas Burgh, engineer and surveyor general [no date] (PRONI, Wynne Papers, D429/222); 'A list of barracks which have been built since the year 1714', [*c.* 1730] (BL, Add. MS 23,636), f. 39.

17. Valuation maps

Hélène Bradley-Davies and Marie Taylor

Nineteenth-century Ireland was characterised by a significant increase in the regulatory role and power of the state and its ability to influence, shape and monitor the social and economic life of its citizens. This necessitated an expansion in its 'official repositories', resulting in an extensive 'documentary trail of data and knowledge' for the historical geographer. The *General valuation of tenements in Ireland* (1846–64) was part of this sustained attempt by the state to reduce the landscape of Ireland to a measurable and 'calculable space'.[1] This valuation, also known as the primary or Griffith's valuation, was an island-wide survey of 'tenement' value and has been utilised by the IHTA — in the production of valuation maps in its various fascicles.

The significance of the tenement valuation for the study of land value and building quality in nineteenth-century Ireland cannot be overstated. According to Prunty, the 'valuation mapping of Ireland was a milestone in the cartographical history of Ireland, a country-wide map-based property record which could at last supersede the Down Survey'.[2] Duffy, in turn, described this valuation as 'one of the most important sources for exploring the building fabric of Irish towns and villages' and 'potentially the most useful source for settlement studies and for profiling change at the local level into the twentieth century'.[3] For these reasons, the mapping of this very important source can enrich our understanding of the changing social and economic geography of the Irish town and aid in the reconstruction of the landscape in the mid-nineteenth century. A comparative investigation of these valuation maps can broaden our understanding of how land and buildings were valued and the resulting spatial patterns.

This essay will explore, firstly, the origins and contents of the tenement valuation and, secondly, how this source has been deployed in the atlas. In doing so, it will undertake an investigation of the factors and processes that determined building value in the mid-nineteenth century and the spatial patterns identified in the various fascicles.

Overview of the source

The tenement valuation was commenced in 1846 and was completed in 1864. Previously, two parallel systems had been in operation, namely the townland valuation from 1830 and the poor law guardians' valuation from 1838. In 1844, a government select committee agreed to move forward with one new system for all local taxation. The ensuing legislation was enacted in 1846. A further act in 1852 (15 & 16 Vict., c. 63) formally authorised the new valuation. In order to ensure consistency in how land and buildings were valued, Richard Griffith[4] issued detailed instructions to all surveyors in 1853.[5] Their compliance with these instructions ensured a 'transparent and reasonably fair system'[6] of land valuation across the island.

This new valuation contained manuscript field books (town books in urban areas), printed listings, town plans and field maps.[7] The field books recorded a wealth of information, including the dimensions of the building, an assigned quality letter, the number of measures, rate per measure, valuator's estimate of value, yearly rent and any qualitative observations that could impact on rateable value (Table 17.1). In Carrickfergus, for instance, these details led Robinson to conclude that 'the dwellings with the highest valuations were in most cases three storey dwellings without front gardens or yards'.[8] On examining the manuscript town books for Maynooth, Horner observed that 'rack rents' were prevalent in the poor districts of the town.[9] For the most part, however, the town books represent an under-utilised source in the IHTA fascicles, despite their obvious reference to urban morphology and building fabric.

TABLE 17.1 CLASSIFICATION OF BUILDINGS WITH REFERENCE TO THEIR SOLIDITY AND QUALITY[10]

Solidity

Roof type	Tenement type	Building material
Slated	House or office (1st class) Basements to ditto (4th) House or office (2nd)	Built with stone or brick and lime mortar
Thatched	House or office (3rd)	Stone walls with mud mortar Dry stone walls pointed Good mud walls
	Offices (5th)	Dry stone walls

Quality

Age of tenement	Quality letter	Tenement description
New	A + A A -	Built or ornamented with cut stone, or of superior solidity and finish Very substantial building, and finished without cut stone ornament Ordinary building and finish, or either of the above, when built twenty years
Medium	B + B B -	Not new, but in sound order and good repair Slightly decayed, but in good repair Deteriorated by age and not in perfect repair
Old	C + C C -	Old, but in repair Old, out of repair Old, dilapidated, scarcely habitable

The printed listing records the name of the occupier, the immediate lessor, a description of the property, area of tenement and the annual rateable valuation. The tenement entry was preceded by a number, which was also recorded on the relevant field map or town plan. These printed listings and the associated maps have been employed in the production of the valuation map in the various fascicles. There are, however, temporal variations in the surveying of individual towns. Bray, Fethard, Kilkenny and Maynooth have the earliest valuations dating to 1850, while Armagh was surveyed as late as 1864. This sequencing of data collection allows for a degree of longitudinal analysis.

The instructions to the surveyors contained a detailed description of what constituted a 'tenement' and the rationale behind how value was apportioned. A tenement was described as 'any rateable hereditament that may be holden or possessed for any term, tenure or arrangement, not less than from year to year'.[11] Such hereditaments included all lands, forms of communication (canals, railways and tramways) and residential, industrial and commercial units. Where a tenement appeared subdivided on visual inspection, the surveyors were instructed to treat the various units as one tenement unless the divisions were clearly defined and of 'simple character'. The obvious intention of the valuation was to ensure that the most unproblematic method of rate collection was facilitated rather than the accurate recording of the micro-geography of land or house tenure. This can cause considerable problems in many of the poorer districts of cities and towns where multi-occupancy was the norm, with many people occupying a house or a room in a house with tenure of less than one year. Despite this reservation, the system of placing value on land within an urban environment is very useful when evaluating the socio-spatial geography of the nineteenth-century town.

The rationale behind ascribing value to an individual tenement was well defined. In urban areas, the majority of buildings were described as either house or office. However, in some cases a further functional description (e.g. forge, factory) was provided. Each building was then valued according to its absolute value. The key determinant of absolute value was the rent achievable for a tenement once all necessary expenses had been deducted. Other factors, which the surveyors were told to consider, included the amount spent on its construction, solidity of the structure, age of the structure, state of repair and the cubic capacity. Additional factors taken into consideration by the surveyor, included the measurement of frontage, the presence of gateways, yards and gardens and a property's comparative value. Consequently, where large and small houses were located on the same street, the assigned value of the small house increased owing to its proximity to the larger house. It was also considered advantageous if the tenement contained gardens and yards — the bigger the garden or yard the more valuable the tenement. Commercial functions also added value: 'in towns, a shop for the sale of goods is always the most valuable part of a house; and any house that has much front, and affords room for two or three shops, is much more valuable than the same bulk of house with only one shop'.[12] A comparable pattern existed for stores. The value of a store increased if it adjoined a market or was located in close proximity to a quay. In the case of stores on a commercial street, the presence of a gateway was deemed to be advantageous as it permitted entry into the rear of the property and therefore added value.

The building valuation maps in the atlas

Twenty-three of the twenty-five towns published to date by the IHTA contain valuation maps. These thematic maps 'provide scope to utilise the available source material and to illustrate patterns that emerge from the draft topographical information'.[13] Variations, nonetheless, exist in the manner in which these maps have been labelled. In the majority of cases, residential buildings (described as either house or private dwelling) over a certain value have been mapped, although in the cases of Belfast, Derry, Dundalk and Limerick the more generic term 'building' was used. According to the tenement valuation, a building could include all structures used permanently as residential dwellings, all public buildings such as churches or courthouses and all 'offices' such as factories, mills, stores or stables.

Inconsistencies are also apparent in the classification system employed as there is a lack of uniformity in the value increments utilised. This, as has been acknowledged by Prunty and Clarke,[14] makes a comparison across the full series difficult on initial viewing. In Athlone, Bandon, Carrickfergus and Mullingar, properties valued under £10 were not classified, while in later atlases a £5 to £9 19s group was differentiated. Similar irregularity can be found in the upper ranges employed. In Armagh, for example, the upper limit of the classification scheme was £40+, while in Belfast the upper limit was £60+. This could direct a researcher to conclude that there was an absence of properties in Armagh valued over £60. This is not the case, a detail that only becomes apparent when one reverts to the original source. There is, therefore, a case for introducing a standard classification system across all fascicles, one that is truly representative of the range of valuations present.

A further difficulty, which may be inevitable owing to the sheer volume of data contained within the tenement valuation, is that the very act of categorising is also an act of generalisation. As Prunty and Clarke have remarked: 'A map is always selective, since it can represent only certain aspects of the real world ... . Selectivity is the secret behind the usefulness of maps; otherwise we would be overwhelmed by all the information'.[15] Researchers, nevertheless, need to ensure that important micro-details are not concealed in the classification system employed. As Horner notes:

Fig. 17.1 *Youghal*, fig. 7, valuation of residential buildings, 1853.

> Much greater attention could be given across the atlas to the cottages, courts, lanes and tenement housing in which so many people lived. A criticism of elitism seems valid when the valuation maps, currently produced in monochrome and using inexpressive symbols, treat valuations under £5 as a single category. If this grouping was split into even three categories (perhaps £1 and under, £1–3, and £3+), a greater interrogation would be possible of where, and perhaps how, the majority of the population lived.[16]

This criticism has been partly addressed in the Belfast, Youghal and Galway atlases by the inclusion of an under £5 category, but the repeated treatment of the under £5s as a single class (the single exception being the valuation map of Belfast in 1837[17]) ensures that the living conditions of the 'underclass and the marginalised' remain hidden from view. In Youghal, for example, 60% of all houses recorded were valued at under £5 (15% were valued £1 and under, 36% at £1–3 and 9% at £3+) and only 1% of buildings were valued £40 plus (Fig. 17.1). The properties valued over £20 were concentrated on the main street, while the majority of properties under £5 were located on the side streets and lanes and along the quays, where they were interspersed among higher-value store buildings. This pattern is duplicated in many towns across the IHTA series.

READING THE MAPS — MAPS AS TEXTS

In the nineteenth century, the experience of living in an urban environment differed according to an individual's location and/or social class. Landscapes of the wealthy urban dweller were characterised, for the most part, by spacious and airy residential streets and elegant architecture. The situation was entirely different for the urban poor; their worlds were dominated by overcrowded and run-down houses on unsanitary side lanes

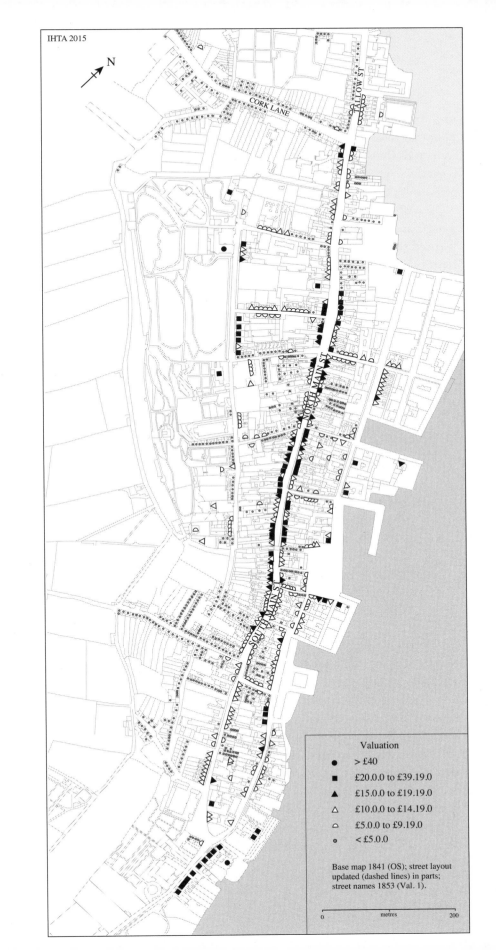

IHTA 2015

N

CORK LANE

TALLOW ST

NORTH MAIN ST

SOUTH MAIN ST

Valuation

●   > £40

■   £20.0.0 to £39.19.0

▲   £15.0.0 to £19.19.0

△   £10.0.0 to £14.19.0

⌂   £5.0.0 to £9.19.0

•   < £5.0.0

Base map 1841 (OS); street layout
updated (dashed lines) in parts;
street names 1853 (Val. 1).

0   metres   200

or in multiple occupancy tenement building on main streets. While the poor may have lived in close proximity to their wealthy neighbours, they were 'socially worlds apart, in a generally-accepted process of social segregation'.[18] The urban environment can, therefore, reveal stark contrasts between splendour and squalor, wealth and poverty.

Traveller accounts of the mid-nineteenth century undoubtedly indicate a disparity in wealth and living conditions in many towns. Inglis summarised the situation in Limerick in the early decades of the nineteenth century when he stated that he was unaware of any other town in Ireland 'in which so distinct a line is drawn between its good and bad quarters as in Limerick'. Elsewhere he remarks that Newtown Pery was 'unquestionably superior to anything out of Dublin … [its] principal street straight, regular, and modern looking; and contains an abundance of good private houses and of excellent shops'.[19] This was in direct contrast to the old town where he recalled that:

> Some of the abodes I visited were garrets, some were cellars, some were hovels on the ground floor, situated in the narrow yards or alleys. I will not speak of the filth of the places … In at least three-quarters of the hovels which I entered, there were no furniture of any description save an iron pot … two, three or four little bundles of straw, with, perhaps, one or two scanty and ragged mats … Rolled up in the corners … In a cellar which I entered, and which was almost quite dark and slippery with damp, I found a man sitting on a little sawdust. He was naked, this man was a living skeleton, the bones all but protruded through the skin.[20]

O'Flaherty has described such areas in Limerick as being 'typically occupied by rows of single-storey cottages with small back yards, served by a common conduit running down the middle of the lane, giving way to three- or four-storey tenements, with cellars and basements on the main streets'.[21] The tenement valuation of 1850 bears testimony to the social and economic divisions within the city at mid-century (Fig. 17.2).

Differences in building quality were also apparent in early nineteenth-century maps. Sherrard, Brassington and Greene's survey of Kells in 1817 (Fig. 17.3) and of Maynooth in 1821 reflect clear spatial inequalities in the quality of the built environment. A similar pattern is noticeable in James Frain's survey of building types in Carlingford in 1833. With regard to Kells, 'The well-established areas of the town centre extending

Fig. 17.2 *Limerick*, map 24, buildings valued at £5 or more, 1850.

SEXTON STREET

BROWNS QUAY

THOMOND GATE

DOMINICK STREET

CASTLE STREET

ABBEY STREET

ATHLUNKARD STREET

River Shannon

Abbey River

NORTH STRAND

NEWGATE QUAY

SIR HARRYS MALL

GEORGES QUAY

CLARE STREET

NELSON STREET

CHARLOTTE'S QUAY

BANK PLACE

CUSTOM HOUSE QUAY

WEST WATER

LITTLE CURRY'S LANE

OLD

CURRY'S LANE

HONAN'S QUAY

ARTHUR'S QUAY

FRANCIS STREET

PATRICK STREET

MICHAEL STREET

QUAY LANE

WHITE BOY LANE

MARY STREET

JOHN STREET

BRUNSWICK STREET

HOWLEY'S QUAY

BEDFORD ROW

CATTLE MARKET LANE

CARR STREET

OLD FRANCIS STREET

CURRY'S LANE

WILLIAM STREET

ROBERT STREET

MUNGRET STREET

JOHN'S SQUARE

SHANNON STREET

THOMAS STREET

UPPER WILLIAM STREET

O'NEILL'S QUAY

CECIL STREET LOWER

ROCHE'S STREET

HENRY STREET

CECIL STREET

CORNWALLIS STREET

NICHOLAS STREET

GEORGE'S STREET

SHEPHERD'S ROW

SEXTON STREET

NEWTOWNMAHON

MALLOW STREET LOWER

GLENTWORTH STREET UPPER

CATHERINE STREET

DOMINICK STREET

HARTSTONGE STREET LOWER

MALLOW STREET UPPER

QUEEN STREET

MULGRAVE STREET

NEWENHAM STREET

RICHMOND PLACE

HARTSTONGE STREET UPPER

BOHERBUOY

QUINLAN STREET

BARRINGTON STREET

WELLESLEY PLACE

CHARLES STREET

HENRY STREET BOHERBUOY

MILITARY ROAD

EDWARD STREET

CAREYS ROAD

COLLOONEY STREET

BARRACK LANE

PROSPECT ROW

Valuation

• > £40
■ £20.0.0 to £39.19.0
▲ £15.0.0 to £19.19.0
△ £10.0.0 to £14.19.0
▽ £5.0.0 to £9.19.0

Base map OS 1840; street layout updated
in parts to 1900 (shown as dashed lines);
scale approximately 1:3525.

Street names 1850 (Val. 2).

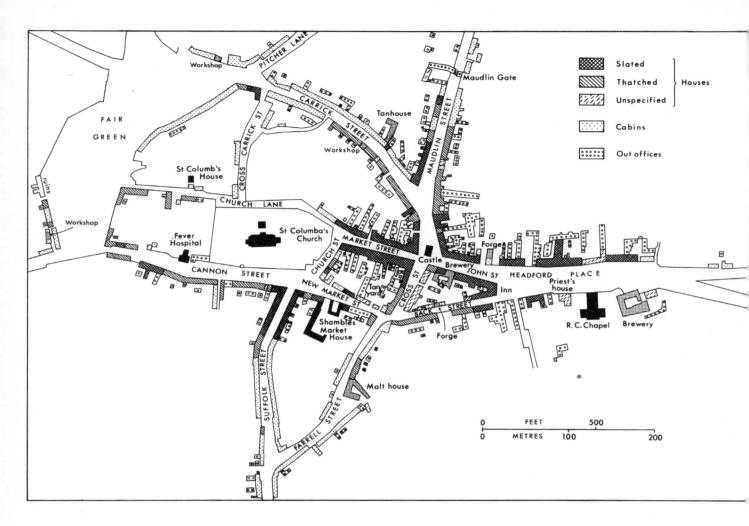

Fig. 17.3 *Kells*, house types, fig. 3, house types in Sherrard, Brassington and Greene's survey, 1817.

into Headfort Place for which substantial houses are recorded with slated roofs, stables and gardens, contrasted markedly with the more peripheral sections around Fair Green, Suffolk Street and Farrell Street, where thatched cabins straddled along the approach roads in untidy ribbons'.[22]

Additionally, the 1851 and 1861 censuses of population are useful sources, as they record numbers and classes of houses. Across the urban landscape variations were evident in the percentage of houses in each category (Table 17.2). The percentages in the first-class category were, on the whole low, averaging at about 11% in 1851 and 1861. However, they were more prolific in the cities of Limerick and Derry-Londonderry and in the larger market towns of Armagh and Mullingar. The majority of the housing stock was second-class, with percentages as high as 79% in Belfast in 1861. The combined figures for the third- and fourth-class housing suggest that 'inferior housing', nonetheless, dominated the urban landscape in some towns, a situation alluded to by Gearty, Morris and O'Ferrall in their study of Longford.[23] Much of this inferior housing in Longford was in 'buildings developed behind the streetscape and being away from the main street

Fig. 17.4 *Tuam*, fig. 3, valuation of
residential buildings, 1855.

frontage attracted the poor because of the lower rents' or on the periphery
of towns such as Tuam and Kells (Figs 17.4, 17.5).

The situation in Tuam was especially serious. In 1841, 825 cabins of
poor quality were located 'around Tierboy Barracks, along a 300-yard
stretch of Tirboy Road, Chapel Lane, a 950-yard stretch of the Galway
Road and a 1,000-yard stretch of Bishop Street beyond St Jarlath's "Old"
College'.[24] In 1851, 68% of all properties in the town were classified as
third- or fourth-class in quality, climbing to 72% by 1861. By the time of
the tenement valuation in 1855, thirty-three of the thirty-four properties
located on Tirboy Road were valued under £2 and of these twenty-three
were valued under £1. A comparable situation existed on Ballygaddy
Road, on the northern periphery of the town; here the valuation recorded

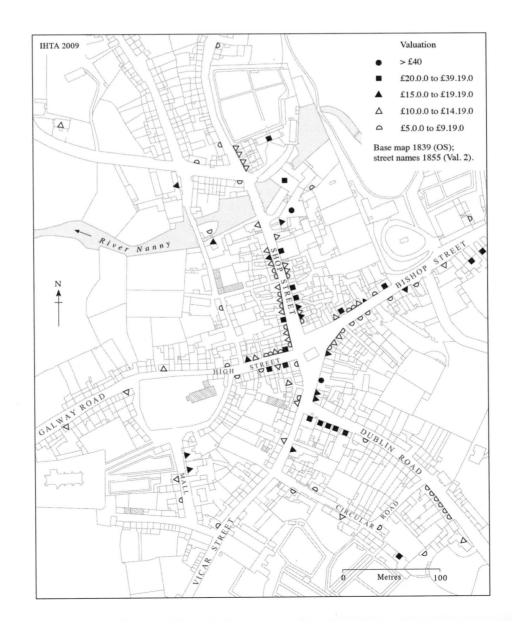

TABLE 17.2 PERCENTAGE OF HOUSES BY CLASS CATEGORY IN THE CENSUSES OF
1851 AND 1861 IN TOWNS AND CITIES COVERED BY THE IHTA

Town/city	1st class			2nd class			3rd and 4th class			Unoccupied %		
	1851	1861	change	1851	1861	change	1851	1861	change	1851	1861	change
Armagh	15	17	+2	50	58	+8	20	28	+8	15	7	-8
Athlone	9	8	-1	61	66	+5	26	31	+5	4	3	-1
Bandon	18	21	+3	50	57	+7	18	25	+7	14	6	-8
Belfast	10	9	-1	78	79	+1	5	6	+1	8	8	0
Bray	6	11	+5	31	36	+5	48	53	+5	15	14	-1
Carlingford	6	8	+2	38	45	+7	26	32	+6	30	25	-5
Carrickfergus	10	9	-1	41	49	+8	37	46	+9	12	8	-4
Derry-Londonderry	14	17	+3	49	54	+5	25	30	+5	12	0	-12
Downpatrick	15	17	+2	60	64	+4	14	18	+4	12	5	-7
Dundalk	10	10	0	41	47	+6	39	45	+6	10	4	-6
Ennis	11	9	-2	26	30	+4	53	57	+4	10	5	-5
Fethard	ND	4	ND	ND	27	ND	ND	27	ND	ND	11	ND
Kells	10	12	+2	31	35	+4	49	54	+5	9	7	-2
Kilkenny	8	13	+5	33	41	+8	45	53	+8	14	6	-8
Limerick	17	18	+1	49	58	+9	20	29	+9	14	8	-6
Longford	10	10	0	45	49	+4	32	36	+4	13	5	-8
Maynooth	12	9	-3	63	67	+4	17	21	+4	8	3	-5
Mullingar	13	14	+1	24	30	+6	63	69	+6	ND	ND	ND
Sligo	9	9	0	41	48	+7	36	44	+8	15	6	-9
Trim	10	11	+1	30	30	0	55	55	0	5	10	+5
Tuam	7	7	0	18	23	+5	68	72	+4	8	4	-4
Youghal	17	20	+3	53	55	+2	18	20	+2	12	14	+2

Fig. 17.5 *Kells*, view from the south, 1820, by George Petrie. From Thomas Cromwell, *Excursions through Ireland.*

sixty-nine properties and all bar six were valued under £5 (thirty properties were valued under £1, twenty-eight properties valued between £1 and £2 and five properties valued between £2 and £3). Regrettably, the building valuation map recorded none of the complexities of this distribution as properties valued under £5 were not considered (Fig. 17.4).

It is often left to photographs and illustrations of the period to 'capture the characteristic atmosphere of an Irish streetscape',[25] as is demonstrated in George Petrie's illustration of Pitcher Lane in Kells in 1820 (Fig. 17.5).[26] The tenement valuation bears testimony to the poor living conditions, in particular on the northern and eastern periphery of the town. On Pitcher Lane, for example, all properties recorded were valued under £3 and of these eight were valued under £1. An analysis of the information relating to solidity and quality of these houses, contained within the manuscript town books, can help the researcher to understand why valuations were so low in this area (Tables 17.1, 17.3). A similar situation existed on Maudlin Road, where fifteen of the twenty-one properties recorded were valued under £2 and subsequently eighteen of these properties were classified as third-class dwellings in 1901.

The question that needs to be asked is: how effective are the valuation maps in demonstrating these patterns? As Horner has suggested, and

TABLE 17.3 PITCHER LANE, KELLS FROM THE TENEMENT VALUATION[27]

Tenement number	Name of occupier	Total annual valuation	Quality letter
1	Mary Henry	10s	2C+
2	Elizabeth Tevlin	10s	2C+
3	Bridget Carpenter	10s	2C+
4	John Smith	£1 5s	2B-
5	Mary McDonnell	£1	2B
6	Bridget Carpenter	8s	Garden
7	Vacant	£1	2C
8	Ruins	–	–
9	Bridget Carpenter	£1	Garden
10	John Murtagh	£2 5s	–
11	Edward Martin	£2 5s	2B-
12	Thomas Horan	£1 5s	3B-
13	John McGuinness	£1 5s	3B-
14	John Hanratty	10s	3B-
15	Michael Brady	10s	3B-
16	Waste	–	–
17	John Johnson	15s	3C
18	Patrick Browne	£1 15s	2B
19	William Flood	£1 10s	2B
20	Matthew Fitzsimons	15s	2C+

indeed it is our contention, the atlas needs to ensure that the 'underclass and the marginalised' are represented on these maps. At present, the vast majority of valuation maps[28] treat the under £5 valuations, often the more numerous, as a single entity, and do not represent them cartographically on the map. In Athlone, for example, only 16% of all properties in the town were valued at over £10 and therefore mapped. On the east side of Athlone, 70% of properties were valued at below £5 and of those 47% were below £2. In the case of Fethard, nearly 50% of properties on Main Street were valued at below £5, while nearly 95% of properties on Barrack Street were below £5, with the average value being about £2.

In Armagh, there is a clear distinction between the area to the east of the town, which contained the commercial core and some of the high-value middle to upper class suburbs, and the west of the town, which contained some of the lowest-value buildings. In Callan Street, for example, large stretches were valued at £3 or less and were described as 'unoccupied' or 'dilapidated'. The situation worsens on some of the side lanes and courts off Callan Street. On Callan Street Lane, for example, the only building mapped is the Armagh Gas Light Company, valued at £220. A similar situation existed on Primrose Street and Charter School Lane. Low valuations were not, however, limited to the west of the town. Many of the lanes and courts off Scotch Street and Lower English Street were also valued under £5 and are therefore absent from the valuation map. On McElroys Row, off Lower English Street, five of the six buildings were valued under £1. Because of the classification scheme being employed, the narrative of these streets and lanes and of the people who lived on them is not being told (Fig. 17.6).

The valuation map for the city of Limerick tells a similar story. The most obvious pattern visible is the concentration of high-value properties along George's Street, identified by O'Flaherty as the 'principal axis of the city'.[29] The majority of properties on this and adjacent streets were valued at £40 or above. These streets formed part of Newtown Pery, which had replaced Englishtown as the social and business core of the city by the early nineteenth century. The St Michael's parish rate books (1810–47) record a gradual increase in the number of rateable properties in this area from 1810 to 1840. The improved living conditions and quality of the built environment persuaded the gentry and merchants to relocate there from Englishtown. By 1824, 64% of all business and residential listings in Pigot's directory were in Newtown Pery and this had increased to 72% in 1838. Social disparities subsequently emerged, as is evidenced by the low valuations in Englishtown and Irishtown. Indeed by 1841 the average rent on George's Street was four times higher than in Englishtown and Irishtown.

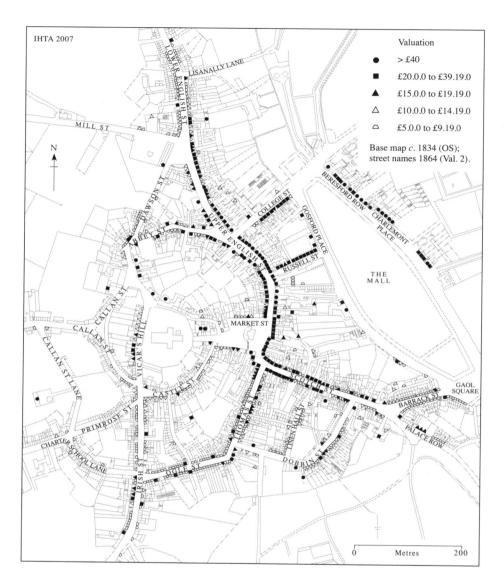

Valuation

● > £40

■ £20.0.0 to £39.19.0

▲ £15.0.0 to £19.19.0

△ £10.0.0 to £14.19.0

⬠ £5.0.0 to £9.19.0

Base map *c.* 1834 (OS);
street names 1864 (Val. 2).

N

0   Metres   200

Fig. 17.6 *Armagh,* fig. 6, valuation of residential buildings, 1864.

Off the main axes, most properties are valued under £5, indeed many under £1 (Fig. 17.2). These areas also saw high concentrations of lodging houses, slaughter houses, animal markets and graveyards, the presence of which may have reduced further the value of these buildings. The mapping of these streets and lanes, while absent from the Limerick fascicle, has recently been undertaken by Ruth Guiry.[30] Guiry concluded that the city of Limerick was spatially divided along east–west lines, with the eastern section dominated by poverty, poor housing and low rateable valuations.

One of the crucial factors in determining the economic value of an individual building was its functionality. Variations existed, though, in the range of functions evident across urban landscapes. The size of a particular town played a key role in determining the range and type of functions recorded. In general, the higher the population the greater the range of functions, in particular higher-order ones. A recurring pattern in the valuation maps is the clustering of high-value properties in the central business district of a given town. Proximity to the central business district ensured a competitive rental market, which in turn increased the potential rateable valuation of a property.

In cities, classified by the tenement valuation as locations with populations over 19,000, a greater concentration of higher-order functions ensured an increased demand and competition for prime sites in the centre of towns. This resulted in an increase in potential rent achievable. In Derry~Londonderry, the valuation map 'shows the continual dominance of the original main streets of the plantation town where values of over £20 were common'.[31] Ship Quay Street, with an average valuation of £67, was one of the primary commercial streets of the city where, in addition to standard shops, banks, attorneys, newspaper offices, consuls and surgeons were located. On Pump Street all valuations recorded were in excess of £13, with the average valuation being £29. Here the upper echelons of the medical profession, together with members of the gentry, dominated this high-value residential street. A rival to the commercial and residential dominance of the old town was nonetheless starting to emerge in the form of Foyle Street alongside the river and the new northern suburb of Edenballymore. However, proximity to the old market centre was still a key determinant of property value on Foyle Street (Fig. 17.7, Table 17.4).

The range and character of functions changed, however, as one moved from the high-value market core to lower-value peripheral streets. Cow Bog and Rossville Streets, to the east of the city wall, had average valuations of £12 and were dominated, in 1856, by industrial and lower-order functions such as shirt manufacturers, nail makers, coopers, tanners, cutters, clothes brokers, grocers, spirit and porter dealers and pawnbrokers.

A comparable pattern is found in the large market town of Armagh. By the mid-nineteenth century, Armagh had acquired the appearance and character of a regional capital with a growing mercantile class. As Duffy[33] has shown, commercial life was dynamic with a vast array of industries, workshops and manufacturing that paralleled the industrialisation of east Ulster. Armagh had a clustering of property values from £15 to >£40 on the main streets of the town. The rateable value of property on these streets was inflated by the presence of commercial and high-end residential use. Commercial trade directories record a concentration of higher-order professional services such as auctioneers, architects, doctors,

TABLE 17.4 COMMERCIAL ACTIVITY ON SHIP QUAY STREET/PLACE AND FOYLE STREET, DERRY, 1856[32]

Type	Ship Quay Street/Place	Foyle Street	Type	Ship Quay Street/Place	
Nobility, gentry, clergy	3	–	Engineers	–	
Agents	11	4	Flax spinners	–	
Attorneys	2	–	Grocers	10	
Apothecaries	1	–	Haberdashers and drapers	2	
Banks	3	–	Hairdressers	–	
Booksellers	2	–	Hotels	1	
Butchers	2	–	Ironmongers	2	
Bleachers	–	1	Leather cutters and tanners	–	
Braziers	–	1	Lime burners	–	
Cabinet makers	1	–	Masters extraordinary in chancery	1	
Coachbuilders	–	2	Merchants	8	
Contractors	–	1	Millers		
Consuls	3	–	Milliners, dressmakers and tailors	2	
Coopers	–	1	Newspapers	1	
Cutlers	–	1	Oil and Colourmen	2	

Foyle Street	Type	Ship Quay Street/Place	Foyle Street
5	Painters and glaziers	1	–
2	Printers	2	1
9	Rope and sail makers	3	–
–	Ship brokers	3	–
1	Ship owners	1	4
1	Ship stores dealers	2	–
–	Spirit and porter dealers	9	5
2	Steam package companies	–	1
1	Surgeons	2	–
–	Tobacco and snuff manufacturing	1	1
14	Toy warehouse	1	–
4	Watch and cloth makers	2	–
–	Woollen drapers	1	–
–	Wine and spirit manufacturing	–	1

Valuation

- ● > £40
- ■ £20.0.0 to £39.19.0
- ▲ £15.0.0 to £19.19.0
- △ £10.0.0 to £14.19.0
- ▽ £5.0.0 to £9.19.0

Base map *c.* 1831; street layout updated in parts to 1904–5 (shown as dashed lines); scale approximately 1:3625.

Street names 1858 (Val. 2).

CLARENDON ST

QUEEN ST

PATRICK ST

EDWARD ST→

FRANCIS ST

LOWER ROAD

GREAT JAMES'S ST

STRAND RD

CREGGAN ST

SACKVILLE ST

WILLIAM ST WITHOUT

STABLE LANE

BOG SIDE

FREDERICK ST

ABBEY ST

VIRGIN'S ROW

UNION ST

WILLIAM ST WITHIN

WATERLOO PLACE

SHIPQUAY PASSAGE

SHIPQUAY PLACE

SHIPQUAY

CASEY'S OR STABLE LANE

FAHAN ST

ANNE ST

THOMAS ST

ROSSVILLE ST

CORBETT ST

GREENSLEAD'S CLOSE

COW BOG

MAGAZINE ST

BANK PLACE

ADAM ST

SHIPQUAY ST

BUTCHER ST

THE DIAMOND

SOCIETY ST

CHAPEL LANE

BISHOP ST

TAILOR'S ROW

WELLS

ST COLUMB'S ROW

ORCHARD LANE

ORCHARD ST

SOAPHOUSE LANE

FERRYQUAY ST

PUMP ST

ARTILLERY LANE

MARKET ST

ST COLUMB'S COURT

MURRAY'S LANE

FOYLE ST

BRIDGE ST

SKINNER'S ALLEY

ANN ST S

STABLE LANE

CUNNINGHAM'S ROW

CHURCH LANE

CHURCH WALL

FOUNTAIN ST

GILMOUR'S OR HAGAN'S LANE

FISHBOAT QUAY OR FANNY'S LANE

PRIEST'S LANE

LONG

HENRIETTA ST

BISHOP ST WITHOUT

BARRACK ST

DARK LANE

FOUNTAIN PLACE

MAJOR'S ROW

WAPPING LANE

ADAM'S ROW

VICTORIA PLACE

BARRACK ROW

FOYLE ROAD

LECKY ROAD

ST COLUMB'S

FERGUSON'S LANE

COCHRAN'S ROW

WATERSIDE

FOUNTAIN HILL

River Foyle

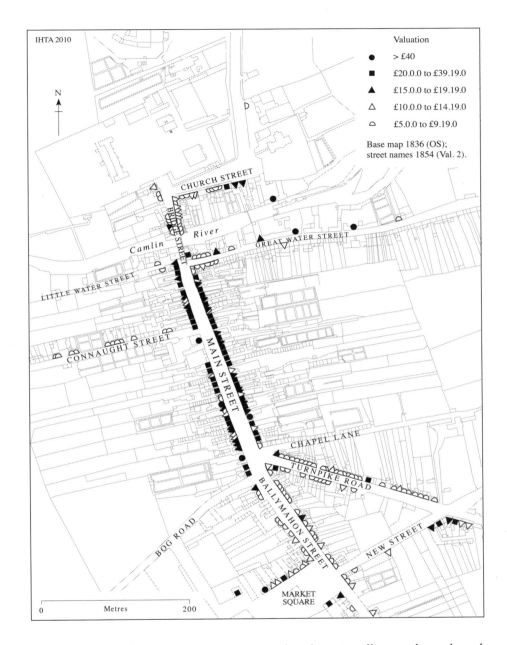

Valuation

● > £40
■ £20.0.0 to £39.19.0
▲ £15.0.0 to £19.19.0
△ £10.0.0 to £14.19.0
⬡ £5.0.0 to £9.19.0

Base map 1836 (OS);
street names 1854 (Val. 2).

IHTA 2010

Opposite: Fig. 17.7
Derry-Londonderry, map 20, buildings
valued at £5 or more, 1858.

Fig. 17.8 *Longford*, fig. 4, valuation
of residential buildings, 1854.

dentists, solicitors, surgeons, vets, undertakers, jewellers, and watch and
umbrella makers together with a proliferation of grocers, publicans and
spirit dealers on these high-value streets (Fig. 17.6).

While the town of Longford exhibits similar patterns, the range and
types of function recorded differ slightly. Here the wholesale and retail
trades dominated, in particular on Main Street (Figs 17.8, 17.9). The
growing regional importance of Longford in the early nineteenth century

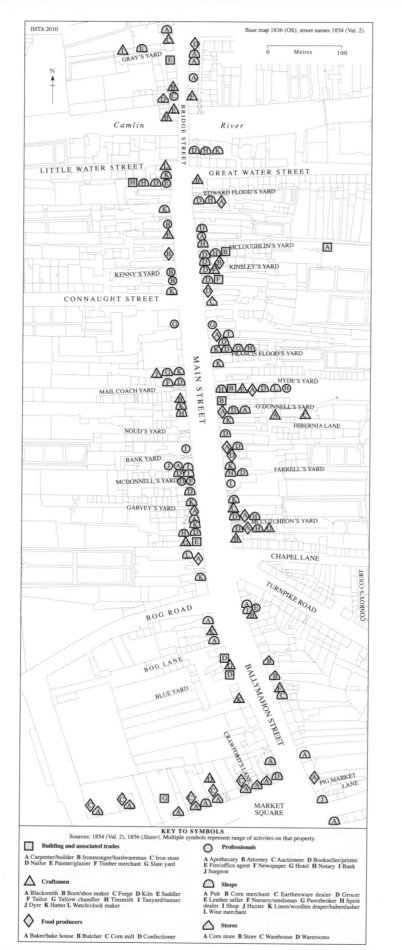

IHTA 2010

Base map 1836 (OS); street names 1854 (Val. 2).

0   Metres   100

Camlin   *River*

BRIDGE STREET

LITTLE WATER STREET

GREAT WATER STREET

EDWARD FLOOD'S YARD

MCLOUGHLIN'S YARD

KINSLEY'S YARD

KENNY'S YARD

CONNAUGHT STREET

FRANCIS FLOOD'S YARD

HYDE'S YARD

MAIL COACH YARD

MAIN STREET

O'DONNELL'S YARD

HIBERNIA LANE

NOUD'S YARD

BANK YARD

FARRELL'S YARD

MCDONNELL'S YARD

GARVEY'S YARD

MCCUTCHEON'S YARD

CHAPEL LANE

CONROY'S COURT

TURNPIKE ROAD

BOG ROAD

BALLYMAHON STREET

BOG LANE

BLUE YARD

CRAWFORD'S LANE

PIG MARKET LANE

MARKET SQUARE

KEY TO SYMBOLS

Sources: 1854 (Val. 2), 1856 (*Slater*). Multiple symbols represent range of activities on that property.

▢ **Building and associated trades**

A Carpenter/builder B Ironmonger/hardwareman C Iron store
D Nailor E Painter/glazier F Timber merchant G Slate yard

◯ **Professionals**

A Apothecary B Attorney C Auctioneer D Bookseller/printer
E Fire/office agent F Newspaper G Hotel H Notary I Bank
J Surgeon

△ **Craftsmen**

A Blacksmith B Boot/shoe maker C Forge D Kiln E Saddler
F Tailor G Tallow chandler H Tinsmith I Tanyard/tanner
J Dyer K Hatter L Watch/clock maker

⌂ **Shops**

A Pub B Corn merchant C Earthenware dealer D Grocer
E Leather seller F Nursery/seedsman G Pawnbroker H Spirit
dealer I Shop J Huxter K Linen/woollen draper/haberdasher
L Wine merchant

◇ **Food producers**

A Baker/bake house B Butcher C Corn mill D Confectioner

△ **Stores**

A Corn store B Store C Warehouse D Warerooms

had also attracted numerous banks and a hotel to Main Street. The location of such businesses added to the overall attractiveness of the town as
a place to conduct business, hence the high valuations evident on Main
Street. Beyond the façade, however, all was not well, as highlighted by
Fraser in 1854:

> Fraser's impression of the housing situation points to a dis-
> tinctive aspect of Longford in the nineteenth century and
> beyond: the prevalence of yards where the poorer people
> of the town lived. The laying out of the Newtown in the
> seventeenth century in large plots approximately 42 perches
> (883 feet) long encouraged the town to expand along an
> east–west axis as much as a north–south one. Buildings
> developed behind the streetscape and being away from the
> Main Street frontage they attracted the poor because of the
> lower rents. They generally had small outhouses that were
> intended for animals and machinery; however, most were
> rented to tenants. In 1854 there were no fewer than fifteen
> yards in Longford, and inevitably there were other areas of
> bad housing. Most of these yards were hidden behind the
> mix of banks, hotels and smaller higher-valued buildings
> that fronted onto Main Street hosting a variety of commer-
> cial and professional activities.[34]

The key conclusion to be drawn here is that the range and number of
economic functions in a town clearly impacted on the potential rent and
rateable value of a given building; however, this varied according to the
size and location of the urban settlement being investigated. The current
format of the IHTA valuation maps allows the researcher to identify
the business and commercial cores of individual town and cities and to
undertake a comparative analysis of towns of varying size and functions
in connection with contemporary trade directories.

CONCLUSION

The intention of the IHTA series is to 'trace the topographical development of Irish towns and cities'.[35] Central to this is the notion that, if
we undertake a comparative geographical analysis, we can increase our
understanding of the key driving forces behind morphological change.
The inclusion of valuation maps in twenty-three of the twenty-five towns,
published to date, facilitates this comparative analysis and a greater
understanding of the generic and localised factors impacting on property

valuation. As this essay has suggested, some changes should be considered regarding the format and content of the maps themselves.

A map is an 'abstraction and simplification of geographic reality', and if constructed correctly can be a very efficient means of communication, identifying patterns, trends and relationships within the data.[36] It is therefore imperative for the success of a map that the full extent of the data be represented. This has not always been the case in relation to the valuation maps in the IHTA. There is a clear need to ensure, into the future, that the voices and experiences of the urban poor are not marginalised or indeed absent from the analysis. There is a compelling case for the inclusion of a second valuation map in future atlases that plots property values under £5, along the lines advocated by Horner. This would add further value to what is, already, an excellent teaching and research aid, and provide a catalyst for further investigations into the factors impacting on property value in the mid-nineteenth century.

Notes

[1] Patrick Duffy, 'Nearly all that geography can require — the state and the construction of a geographical archive in nineteenth-century Ireland', in Patrick Duffy and William Nolan (eds), *At the anvil: essays in honour of Willian J. Smyth* (Dublin, 2012), pp 372, 374.

[2] Jacinta Prunty, *Maps and map-making in local history* (Dublin, 2004), p. 153.

[3] Patrick Duffy, *Exploring the history and heritage of Irish landscapes* (Dublin, 2007), p. 154.

[4] Richard Griffith had been appointed as the commissioner of the general survey and valuation of rateable property in the Valuation Office in 1827.

[5] These instructions were later reprinted in the parliamentary papers for 1882. Copies of the instructions issued by the late Sir Richard Griffith in the year 1853, under the provision of 15 & 16 Vict., c. 63, to the valuators and surveyors acting under him in making the tenement valuation of Ireland (*Return relating to tenement valuation* (Ireland), HC 1882 (144), lv).

[6] Prunty, *Maps and map-making in local history*, p. 148.

[7] Copies of these are available in the National Archives of Ireland and the Public Record Office of Northern Ireland.

[8] Robinson, IHTA, no. 2, *Carrickfergus*, p. 6.

[9] Horner, IHTA, no. 7, *Maynooth*, p. 5.

[10] *Return relating to tenement valuation* (Ireland), HC 1882 (144), lv, parg. 180, p. 31.

[11] *Return relating to tenement valuation* (Ireland), HC 1882 (144), lv, parg. 10, p. 9.

[12] Ibid., parg. 218, p. 34.

[13] H.B. Clarke and Sarah Gearty, 'Multi-dimensionality', in H.B. Clarke and Sarah Gearty (eds), *Maps and texts: exploring the Irish Historic Towns Atlas* (Dublin, 2013), p. 13.

[14] Jacinta Prunty and H.B. Clarke, *Reading the maps: a guide to the Irish Historic Towns Atlas* (Dublin, 2011), p. 221.

[15] Ibid., p. 16.

[16] Arnold Horner, 'Of Irish atlases and Irish towns', in *Studia Hibernica*, no. 39 (2013), p. 179.

[17] Gillespie and Royle, IHTA, no. 12, *Belfast, part 1, to 1840*, p. 9, fig. 6.

[18] Ruth McManus, 'Windows on a hidden world: urban and social evolution as seen from the mews', in *Irish Geography*, xxxvii (2004), p. 45.

[19] H.D. Inglis, *A journey throughout Ireland during the spring, summer, autumn of 1834* (2 vols, London, 1834), i, pp 295–6.

[20] Ibid., pp 303, 305.

[21] O'Flaherty, IHTA, no. 21, *Limerick*, p. 9.

[22] Simms with Simms, IHTA, no. 4, *Kells*, p. 4, fig. 3.

[23] Gearty, Morris and O'Ferrall, IHTA, no. 22, *Longford*, p. 6.

[24] Claffey, IHTA, no. 20, *Tuam*, 2009, p. 7.

[25] J.H. Andrews, 'Foreword: the first ten years', in Clarke and Gearty, *Maps and texts*, p. xviii.

[26] Simms with Simms, *Kells*, cover illustration.

[27] Tenement Valuation House Books: Pitcher Lane, parish of Kells, barony of Upper Kells, 1854, NAI, MFGS 46/115, VO/5.3155, pp 18–19.

[28] The exception to this is the valuation map of Belfast where properties under £5 are subdivided into three categories. This presents a far more balanced picture of the streets and lanes where the vast majority of people in Belfast lived (Gillespie and Royle, *Belfast, part 1*, p. 9, fig. 6).

[29] O'Flaherty, *Limerick*, p. 9.

[30] Ruth Guiry, 'Public health and housing in Limerick city 1850–1935: a geographical analysis' (Mary Immaculate College, University of Limerick, M.A. thesis, 2013).

[31] Thomas, IHTA, no. 15, *Derry-Londonderry*, p. 7.

[32] From Derry section in *Slater*, 1856.

[33] Patrick Duffy, 'Armagh and Kells', in Clarke and Gearty, *Maps and texts*, p. 24.

[34] James Fraser, *Handbook for travellers in Ireland* (Dublin, 1854), p. 436; Gearty, Morris and O'Ferrall, *Longford*, p. 6.

[35] Clarke and Gearty, 'Multi-dimensionality', p. 6.

[36] C.P. van Elzakker, 'The use of maps in the exploration of geographic data', in *Proceedings of the 21st international cartographic conference* (Durban, 2003), p. 1945.

18. The railway and the urban landscape: assessing the impact in Dublin, Belfast, Dundalk and Bray

Frank Cullen

Far beyond improving overland transportation methods in the nine-teenth century, the coming of the railway is better understood as a great multi-faceted phenomenon, the magnitude of which took Victorian society by storm. Leaving aside its direct physical impact, which was spectacular to say the least, the railway's wider, more indirect influence reverberated across many strands of daily life, affecting business practice, econom-ics, politics, literature and culture in a variety of ways that ultimately changed the urban landscape. Not all warmed to the new technology in the early years and the railway was not without its critics. Yet by the end of the 1840s only the very stubborn remained critical. Charles Dickens's delightful observation from his 1848 novel, *Dombey and son*, captures brilliantly this important change in attitude as the railway became rapidly assimilated into contemporary society. Speaking of the 'neighbourhood which had hesitated to acknowledge the railroad in its straggling days' but then 'boasted of its powerful and prosperous relation', Dickens tells his readers that there were now:

> Railway patterns in its drapers' shops, and railway journals in the windows of its newsmen. There were railway hotels, coffee-houses, lodging-houses, boarding-houses; railway plans, maps, views, wrappers, bottles, sandwich-boxes, and time tables; railway hackney-coach and cab-stands; railway omnibuses, railway streets and buildings, railway hangers-on and parasites, and flatterers out of all calculation.

In fact, he goes on to say that 'there was even railway time observed in clocks, as if the sun itself had given in'.[1] In less than two decades the remarkable influence of the railway had become so engrained into the national consciousness that, for many, it appeared as if the new technology had always been around and memories of life before the steam locomotive were dissolving rapidly.

During the construction process the railway's need for minimum gradients and subtle curves ensured large-scale bridging, tunnelling, embankment and excavation work to overcome the topographical features of the landscape. Outside the towns, rivers and valleys were bridged and hills and rocks tunnelled through, while within each town the tracks carefully negotiated the urban landscape, avoiding or obliterating existing streets and buildings as was necessary. For the promoters of these schemes, the railway company was a business venture first and foremost and provided a convenient outlet for investing surplus capital. Merchants, bankers and landowners were major investors in the new railway technology since they viewed it as an important stimulant for new business ventures such as hotels, eating houses, taverns, Turkish baths, carriage factories, engineering and steel works, and other associated businesses (many of which are listed in the relevant sections of the IHTA topographical information). In order to be sanctioned, every railway required a private act of parliament, the passing of which followed a complex parliamentary process where arguments for and against the railway scheme were heard before a select committee in Westminster. These political proceedings were often published in local newspapers, prompting further political debate. Through the new genre of railway literature a lively public discourse developed around the railway with pamphlets, newspapers, magazines and novels, in addition to railway guides, maps and timetables, abounding in the period between 1834 and 1850. More remarkable than all of this, however, was the railway's 'annihilation of space by time', to coin a contemporary phrase used to describe the dramatic speed of the new locomotives.[2] Considering that horse-drawn transport averaged speeds of between five and ten miles an hour, railway speed reached heights of up to twenty-five miles an hour and produced shockwaves throughout society. Prior to the railway's arrival, local towns had kept their own time. Galway, for example, was eleven and a half minutes behind Dublin, but considering it took over twelve hours to travel between the two cities, such time difference was hardly noticeable. With the advent of the railway, time needed to be co-ordinated in order for passengers to catch their trains. Through the facility of the electric telegraph, railway timetables nurtured a new awareness of time, which prompted the standardisation in 1848 of all localities to Greenwich mean time. This, perhaps, is the railway's most enduring legacy.

This essay sets out to explore the railway's impact on four Irish towns using the fascicles of the IHTA series as a research guide. The four towns under examination — Dublin, Belfast, Dundalk and Bray — each played a strategic role in the establishment of the early rail network along the east coast of Ireland. As the capital of the industrial north, Belfast businessmen viewed their town as rivalling, and in many ways, exceeding the importance of Dublin. Belfast's growing confidence during the nineteenth century was matched by a growing population. As Table 18.1 shows, Dublin at the beginning of the railway age was by far the largest of the four centres under review, yet by 1901 it had been eclipsed by its northern rival, which experienced a massive population explosion in the second half of the nineteenth century. The rivalry between the two is evident on close examination of the early rail networks in both cities. While all the main towns and cities in the south and west, including Cork, Galway, Limerick, Sligo, Waterford and Wexford, were each connected to Dublin via rail, northern equivalents such as Armagh, Derry, Lisburn and Portadown looked instead to Belfast. By 1849 there were two rail networks in Ireland, one radiating from Dublin, the other from Belfast, but with no connection between the two. Nevertheless a rail link between the two cities had always been contemplated and the smaller town of Dundalk was looked upon as playing a crucial role in this long-term objective.[3] Dundalk's strategic location on the east coast of Ireland, roughly half way between Belfast and Dublin, in addition to its early nineteenth-century harbour improvements, ensured its status as an important railway hub with lines from north, south and west converging on the town. By 1854 the coastal network had extended as far south of Dublin as the seaside town of Bray. By far the smallest of the four towns, Bray is deserving of attention since, more than any other town in Ireland, it was the product of the railway era, owing its impressive growth in population and its early planning wholly to the existence of the railway. Throughout this essay maps from each of the four IHTA fascicles are referred to, but owing to limitations of space not all are reproduced here and the reader is advised to consult the relevant fascicles for further examination.

TABLE 18.1: POPULATION IN DUBLIN, BELFAST, DUNDALK AND BRAY, 1831–1901[4]

	Dublin	Belfast	Dundalk	Bray
1831	204,155	58,445	10,078	2,590
1841	232,726	71,447	10,782	3,209
1851	258,369	87,062	9,995	3,178
1861	254,808	121,602	10,428	4,182
1871	246,326	172,412	11,616	6,087
1881	249,602	208,094	11,913	6,535
1891	245,001	225,924	12,449	6,888
1901	290,638	349,180	13,067	7,424

SOURCES

Sources for studying the railway phenomenon in Ireland are rich and varied, and from an urban topographical perspective the primary sources are particularly strong.[5] Because an act of parliament was required to incorporate all railways, much of the important primary source material for these schemes is housed in the parliamentary archive in London. This major collection includes maps, plans, accompanying books of reference, lists of shareholders and books of evidence. The cartographical material is exceptional and includes plans and cross-sections covering the entire route of each railway. Smaller annotated maps in addition to drawings of bridges, tunnels, terminus buildings and minor stations further enhance the coverage. Private landholdings and properties are also depicted on these maps together with a corresponding list of property owners in the accompanying books of reference. Since the required capital for each scheme was raised through shares, lists of shareholders show the names, occupations and addresses of all investors along with the value of their respective shares. Books of evidence show unpublished manuscript transcripts of the evidence presented in both houses of parliament by parties proposing and opposing each particular railway. As with railways, all other improvement schemes such as harbour works, inland navigation, reclamation and drainage schemes also required parliamentary approval and are similarly recorded in the parliamentary collection. While the occasional loose map or document can sometimes be found in the local libraries and archives of the towns where the works were carried out, the major boon to the parliamentary archive is that all the relevant material associated with each act, whether cartographical or otherwise, is accounted for in a particular file and available for consultation under one roof. Although not all of this material relates to the specific enquiry of the IHTA, the cartographical material does shed much light on various aspects of urban topography in nineteenth-century Ireland.

Company records for all the early Irish railways including directors' and shareholders' correspondence and minute books are housed in the Irish Rail Archive in Heuston Station, Dublin. While this material reveals the decision-making process at board level for the various private companies, issues relating to topography often arise in the minutes along with the occasional progress report containing accompanying maps and drawings. In response to the frenzied bout of railway construction in Britain and Ireland during the 1830s the railway department of the Board of Trade was established in 1840.[6] As one of few government regulators of railways, the records of this department constitute an important, yet underused source. While the bulk of this material is held in The National Archives, Kew, the Board of Trade records in the National Archives of Ireland comprise about 10,000 maps and plans and are divided into two separate series: the black series and the green series. Works in the black series were in all cases carried out, while those in the green series in many cases never passed the planning stage, thus revealing a fascinating alternative picture of what might have been in Ireland's towns and cities. Among the vast collections of published primary sources for railway history in

Ireland, specialised contemporary journals such as the *Irish Railway Gazette*, *Railway Times* and *Herepaths Railway Journal* are most revealing. In relation to the impact of the railway at the local level, however, by far the most informative journal is the *Irish Builder*. This specialised magazine, focusing mostly on local works of an architectural and engineering nature, contains a wealth of written and visual information on Ireland's urban railway heritage. Local newspapers also feature largely in the IHTA fascicles and carry much important information relating to the railway and the local topography. The National Library of Ireland's impressive pamphlet collection contains an array of material examining various aspects of railway construction, among which are many of the original company handbooks.

DUBLIN

IHTA, *Dublin, part III* is impressive in scale and vast in its coverage of the multifarious topographical issues associated with much of the eighteenth- and nineteenth-century city.[7] With so much happening in so large a city during such an expansive period, it would be impractical to devote too much attention to one aspect of urban topography and, considering the pace at which the city developed between 1756 and 1847, the construction of the early rail network receives brief, but adequate attention. At the beginning of the railway era Dublin, with a population of 204,155, dwarfed all other Irish towns, including Belfast, which by comparison lagged well behind at 58,445. The city's first railway, the Dublin and Kingstown, received parliamentary consent in 1831 and opened for business three years later. Its success inspired further schemes and by 1850 Dublin had four separate railway companies, each one operating from its own separate terminus. In order to minimise land costs and avoid objections from a multitude of small property owners, the fascicle tells us that these companies located their termini on the edge of the built-up district. Since the early network served Cork, Drogheda, Galway and Wicklow, these grandiose buildings stood in splendid isolation from one another at the north-eastern, north-western, western and south-eastern extremities of the city. This is shown clearly on map 4 in IHTA, *Dublin, part III*, which is a reconstruction of the Ordnance Survey, 1847, 1:1056 town plan of the city. The location of the termini became the cause of great disturbance within the city as passengers and goods had to be ferried through the streets in order to connect from one terminus to another. The absence of a direct link between the railway system and the docks further exacerbated

Fig. 18.1 Westland Row railway terminus. *Dublin, part III*, map 4, 1847, extract.

an already problematic situation. In response to these problems, Dublin's initial phase of railway development in the 1830s and 1840s was followed by a second, more ameliorative phase, the objective of which was to unite the existing disconnected system, while also providing a direct link with the docks. This second phase, which commenced in 1862, falls outside the time frame for the most recent Dublin fascicle.

Since *Dublin, part III* concludes in 1847 it necessarily focuses on the first phase of railway construction in the city and we must await the publication of *Dublin, part IV* in order to follow the progress of the railway through the remainder of the nineteenth century. The essay includes some important points about the railway's physical impact on the city and the accompanying maps serve as an effective means of demonstrating these. Here we are told that the railways, like the canals before them, 'divided communities through the construction of embankments'. Extracts from map 4 show the Dublin and Kingstown and the Dublin and Drogheda Railways approaching their Westland Row and Amiens Street termini across the underdeveloped North and South Lotts in the eastern part of

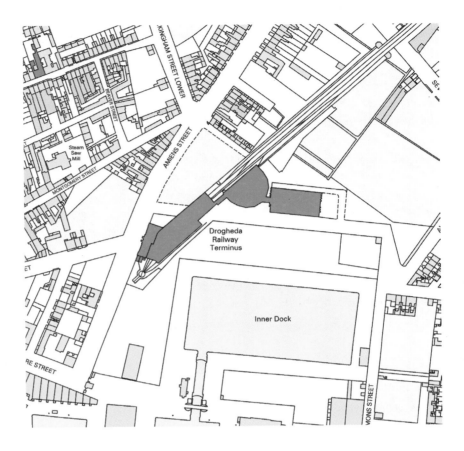

Fig. 18.2 Amiens Street terminus. *Dublin, part III*, map 4, 1847, extract.

the city (Figs 18.1, 18.2). Since this land had been reclaimed from the sea in the previous century, it was necessary to raise the lines upon two large embankments. In the case of the Drogheda line the choice of route across the barren North Lotts district was obvious since it meant far fewer property owners to contend with and, with few streets to cross, there were fewer bridges to build. By bridging only two streets, however, the physical presence of the railway embankment served to divide the future communities that grew up on either side of its tracks. With an already existing grid of streets on the opposite side of the river, the Kingstown line was required to build nine railway bridges and, according to section **17** of the topographical information, it completed this task in one year. Unlike with the Drogheda line, these bridges served to maintain existing communication links on both sides of the track.

Map 4, which includes the limits of the city beyond the two canals, shows the four termini located on what was then the edge of the city and, when compared alongside *Cooke's royal map of Dublin* published in 1822 (map 20), we are given a glimpse of what the planners saw as they sought out appropriate approach routes into the city. On first impressions it would appear that the Dublin and Kingstown line caused more interference to the existing street plan than any of the other three railways. By contrast, the Midland Great Western line encountered minimal topographical resistance on its approach to the Broadstone terminus in the north-western suburb of Phibsborough. By comparing the two maps it can also be shown how quickly the railway stamped its mark on the city with railway works and carriage factories springing up in the vicinity of the termini, helping to create what would become distinct railway districts. Referring back to Cooke's map, the Coal Gaslight Station west of Spencer Dock had by 1847 been replaced by the railway carriage factory of the Dublin and Drogheda Company. Similarly, what had been a vacant plot east of the Grand Canal Dock in 1822 had by 1847 become the site of the Dublin and Kingstown Company's railway engine and coach factory. As the century progressed, the addition of coal yards, steel works, cattle pens and timber yards further indentified these districts with the railway.

BELFAST

Belfast, we are told by the IHTA, was a 'very untypical Irish town' with an 'untypical history'.[8] Unlike the other two major urban centres, Dublin and Cork, which were medieval settlements and evolved slowly, Belfast was the product of early seventeenth-century landlord planning and remained exclusively under the control of the Chichester family until the passing of the Encumbered Estates Act of 1849. The lessening of control by the Chichesters in the early nineteenth century allowed the new leaseholders, mainly wealthy merchants, to develop the city by laying out new streets and squares from the 1830s on. This urban expansion and development coincided with the arrival of the railway in the city between 1839 and 1848. The Ulster Railway was the first to open, providing a link between Belfast and Lisburn in 1839. Nine years passed before the city acquired its other two main railways, the Belfast and County Down and the Belfast Northern Counties Railway. The Belfast and Cavehill Railway had also been under construction since 1833 and opened in 1840. This latter, however, was not a passenger railway and was used solely to transport quarry stone from Cavehill mountain to the docks.

Like Dublin in the south, Belfast was the centre point of the northern system of railways. Similarly to Dublin, Belfast required further post-1860 extensions to link the separate lines and connect with the docks. The essays in both Belfast fascicles are surprisingly quiet with regard to the railway's impact in the city.[9] In *Belfast, part II* the essay contributes only

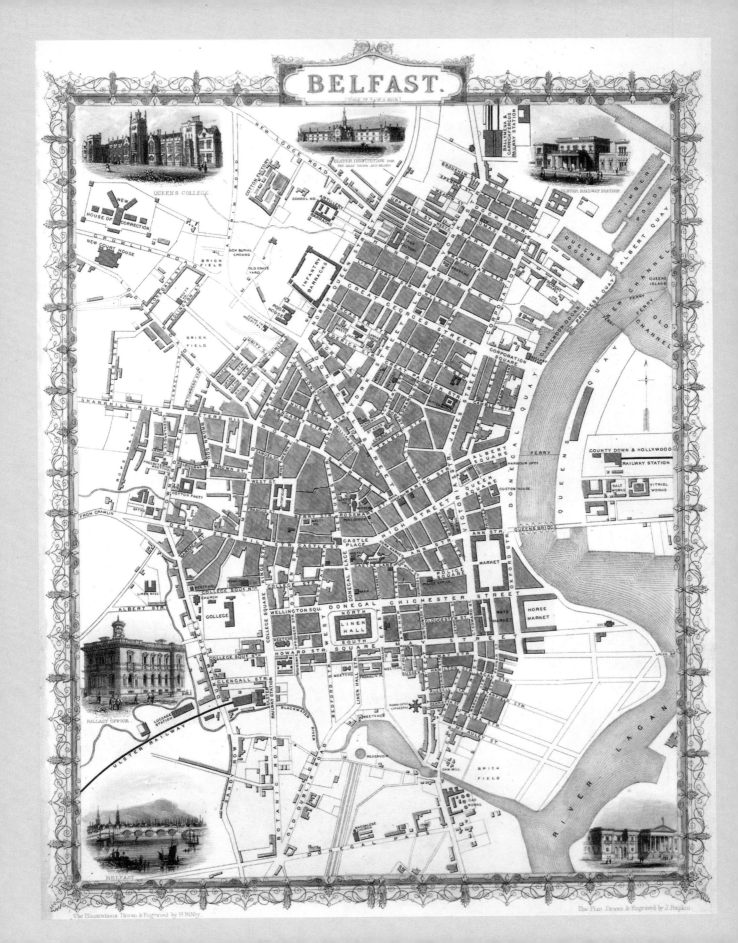

BELFAST.

[SCALE OF ¼ OF A MILE]

QUEEN'S COLLEGE.

ULSTER INSTITUTION FOR THE DEAF DUMB AND BLIND

BALLYMENA & CARRICKFERGUS RAILWAY STATION

ULSTER RAILWAY STATION.

BALLAST OFFICE.

BELFAST.

The Illustrations Drawn & Engraved by H Bibby.

The Plan Drawn & Engraved by J. Rapkin.

MAP OF BELFAS[T]

SPECIALLY PREPARED FOR

The Belfast & Province of Ulster Post Office Dir[ectory]

By MARCUS WARD & CO., Limited, BELFA[ST]

· 1884 ·

Scale - NINE INCHES TO A MILE - Divided into Quarter Mile Sq[uares]

[316]

two sentences to the question of urban railways and tends to focus more on the intra-city tramway system. Since the IHTA is concerned primarily with topographical developments within, rather than between towns, this lack of emphasis towards the early inter-city railway system is partially understandable, but mention might have been made of the later Belfast Central Railway established in 1864 to link the three main lines within the city. That said, where the essay devotes minimal attention to the railway question, the topographical index and maps compensate. Maps 6, 7 and 11 from *Belfast, part II* provide a useful comparative perspective on the railway's impact on the city. Maps 6 and 7, James O'Hagan's and John Rapkin's of 1848 and 1851 respectively, depict the newly-established railways, all three located on undeveloped lands at the edge of the built-up district to the north, east and south-west of the city (Fig. 18.3). What is already evident from these two mid-nineteenth-century maps is the necessity, later to become urgent, of uniting the three isolated railway lines and connecting them with the docks. Map 11, Marcus Ward's post office directory map of 1884, shows the solution to this problem in the form of the Belfast Central Railway (Fig. 18.4). Here we see the new railway branching east from the Ulster Railway line about a mile south of the Great Victoria Street terminus. From here it runs in an eastward direction acting as a barrier to the southward expansion of the city, before turning north-eastwards under East Bridge Street and crossing the Lagan into Ballymacarrett to link up with the Queen's Bridge terminus of the County Down Railway. A lighter docklands tramway links up with the Central Railway near Chichester Street and skirts the edge of the Lagan along Donegall Quay as far as Princes Dock, before turning north-west towards the York Street terminus at the northern end of the city.

In Rapkin's map the Ulster Railway is represented by a single line of railway entering the main terminus in Great Victoria Street, with a separate large building marked 'luggage station' situated west of the main building. By 1884 the same district had changed significantly as a result of the railway. Another large unmarked building had appeared north of the luggage station with two new tracks running into it and a third terminating close by. Also new are the adjacent cattle platform and goods platform, each connected to separate lines branching off the main line. The district, by 1884, had become so marked by the railway that a new street located south of the luggage station had been given the name Railway Street. The same map also shows the Railway Coke Works, on Middle Path, south of the County Down line in the eastern part of the city. All the main docks along Donegall and Albert Quays are linked to the railway, as is the

Abercorn Basin on the eastern side of the river. By comparing the later and earlier maps it can be seen how a rudimentary disconnected railway system grew during the course of the century to become a complex well-connected network providing access for all three lines to the busy docks.

Looking beyond the permanent features of the railway such as the track, terminus, carriage sheds, engine houses, railway arches and bridges, we must also recognise the railway's indirect impact on the city by considering the ancillary business that it attracted. A careful examination of the topographical information for *Belfast, part II* reveals some important and less noticeable aspects of the new railway culture. Bernard Hughes, owner of a bakery located in Donegall Street, recognised from the outset the unique marketing opportunity presented by the coming of the railway when naming his business. Reminiscent of Dickens's Old Established Ham and Beef Shop, which had subsequently become the Railway Eating House, Hughes's bakery in 1843 became the Railway Bakery.[10] So too in Derry the Tirkeeran Arms Hotel by 1847 had become the Railway Hotel. As the railway brought more visitors to the city, demand for hotel accommodation rose in accordance. Measuring the expansion of the city's hotel trade in the years following the railway provides an interesting means of gauging its impact. In Belfast there is a dramatic increase in the number of hotels in the city after 1840. From a total of 125 hotels listed in the topographical information for *Belfast, part II, 1840–1900*, fifty-four appear during the 1840s and 1850s. A large number of these new hotels are located in the vicinity of the three termini, including the Ulster Railway Hotel (1839), Dublin and Armagh Hotel (1846) and Downshire Hotel (1860), all in Great Victoria Street; the Victoria Temperance Hotel (1841), Albion Hotel (1860) and Station Hotel (1863), all in York Street; and the Vine Hotel (1852), Cumberland Hotel (1856) and Commercial Hotel (1863), all in Queen's Square. Belfast was not the only place in which hotel standards improved in response to the railway. The Athlone fascicle observes a similar rise, which it puts down to 'competition from new establishments such as Madam de Ruyter's refreshment rooms and hotel at the Great Southern and Western Railway station'.[11]

DUNDALK

The Dundalk fascicle of the IHTA successfully demonstrates the importance of the railway to the expansion of the town, particularly the south-western district in the later nineteenth century.[12] The essay feeds nicely from the topographical information and both components are communicated with clarity in the accompanying maps. Located on the east coast of the country mid-way between the two cities of Dublin and Belfast, Dundalk became an important railway hub in nineteenth-century Ireland. Unlike Belfast and Bray, the populations of which increased significantly during the period under examination, Dundalk's population hovered around the ten thousand mark until 1861, then rose steadily to reach the figure of 13,067 by 1901. At the beginning of the railway era Robert Jocelyn, the sixth earl of Roden, was the landlord of the town and oversaw numerous improvement schemes in the 1830s, 1840s and 1850s, including the extensive harbour works of the period. The improvement of the harbour provided the stimulus for Dundalk's first railway initiative, the Dundalk and Enniskillen Railway, which after a false start in 1837 was eventually opened in 1845 to link the north-western counties of Ireland with the port of Dundalk. The line reached Castleblayney in 1849, Ballybay in 1854 and Clones and Enniskillen in 1859. In 1845 the Dublin and Belfast Junction Railway had also been incorporated, the objective of which was to provide a rail link between Dublin and Belfast via the town of Dundalk. The 63-mile line was finally opened in 1855 and, as the Ordnance Survey one-inch hachured map at 1:50,000 shows, by 1874 Dundalk had become an important transport hub linking much of Ulster with the south, and via its port with Britain also. This map also shows the Dundalk and Enniskillen line crossing the Great Northern Railway on an east–west axis before looping northwards through the town at Barrack Street and Quay Street, and finally east towards Newry and Greenore.

Turning attention to the earlier maps, the reconstruction of the Ordnance Survey 1835 town plan at a scale of 1:2500 shows the town before the railway. The most conspicuous topographical feature of this map is the wide expanse of undeveloped land to the south of the town, which today is taken up with housing estates, factories and other buildings. This map explains the route of the Dundalk and Enniskillen Railway, the main objective of which was to connect with the new harbour works at Barrack Street and Quay Street. The map also depicts Lord Limerick's demesne to the west of the town, the future site of the main north–south railway line from Dublin to Belfast. If we compare this with map 17, the growth map that uses the Ordnance Survey, 1907–8, 1:2500 map as a base, it can be shown how the Enniskillen railway delicately approached its Barrack Street station with minimal interference to existing infrastructure (Fig. 18.5). Surprisingly, many of the houses had survived the demolition process involved in urban railway construction, as had the Corn Store House and customhouse, which is less surprising. A main platform with attached cattle pens is shown south of the Barrack Street goods station. The line then continues north towards Quay Street station, passing a large coal

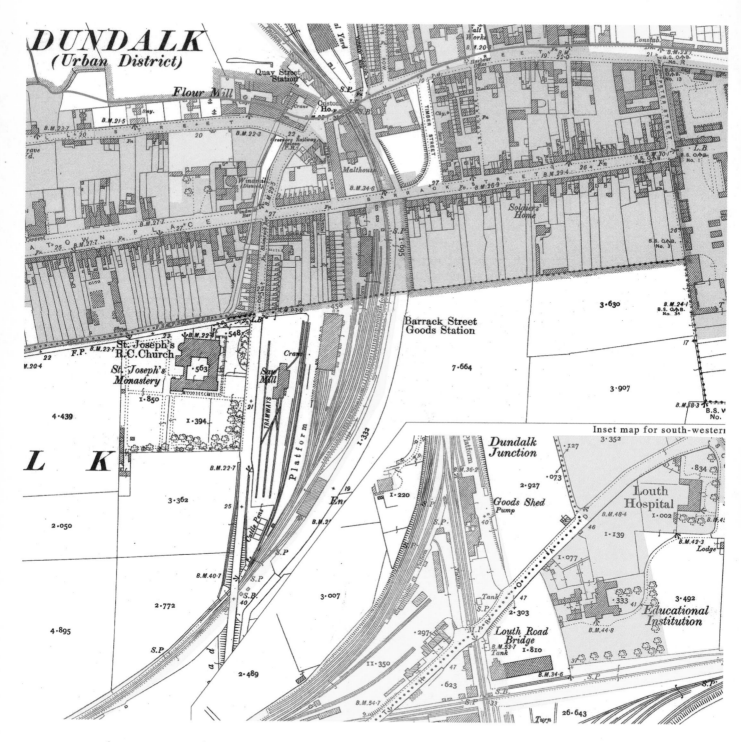

yard en route towards Newry. Some smaller branch lines are also shown serving George's Quay and the cattle pens east of Steam Packet Quay.

In 1876 the Great Northern Railway was established through the amalgamation of the Dublin and Drogheda, Dundalk and Belfast Junction and Ulster Railways. The company's decision to concentrate all

Fig. 18.5 *Dundalk*, map 17, growth to 1900, extract. Yellow shading shows development from *c.* 1835 to *c.* 1865.

its engineering works in Dundalk ensured that the strategically-located town became a major railway and industrial centre into the twentieth century. The railway works were located in the south-western part of the town at the point where the Great Northern and Enniskillen lines intersected. Spur lines were built at the intersection, enabling communication between the western counties and the north, while also connecting the southern counties with the harbours at Dundalk and Greenore. The latter had become an important harbour after the opening in 1876 of the Dundalk, Newry and Greenore Railway. The growth map shows the indelible mark left by the railway in the south-western suburb of the town with the G.N.R. Locomotive, Carriage and Wagon Works most conspicuous. The brewing industry had also been an important aspect of the town's economy going back to the seventeenth century. With the coming of the railway the industry grew rapidly as companies like Macardles began shipping large quantities of their produce to the busy markets in Belfast and Liverpool. The industry had become so lucrative by the close of the nineteenth century that the railway company even opened its own brewery in 1898. The Great Northern Brewery is also shown on the growth map at St Dominick's Place, east of the main station.

BRAY

The IHTA's fascicle on the small town of Bray is most informative on issues relating to the railway.[13] By far the smallest of the four towns discussed in this essay, Bray, with a population of 2,590 in 1831, was little more than a large village. The town is also unique in that it is a seaside resort on the model of the English and Welsh resorts of the nineteenth century and owes its new-found status entirely to the railway. The Dublin and Kingstown Railway had, since 1834, begun a period of rapid suburban development along the south coast of Dublin towards Kingstown and Bray. Villas and terraces sprang up along the coastal route and day trippers from the city descended on the small seaside village. William Dargan, the great railway contractor of the day, was the man chiefly responsible for bringing the railway to Bray, not only through his supervision of the works, but also by providing much-needed capital to complete them. Dargan's contribution to Bray went beyond the railway since he also became the chief architect of the town and was responsible for laying out the esplanade that became the focal point of Victorian Bray.

The most important factor that would determine the layout of the new town was the choice of route for the railway. A cheaper, less troublesome inland line could have been built west of the main street through the earl of Meath's Kilruddery estate and the fascicle alludes to the possibility that in order to avoid this option, the earl 'gave the site of the route around the headland free of charge'.[14] The coastal route, while picturesque, did present far greater topographical challenges for the construction process. Map 2, the Ordnance Survey 1837–8 at a scale of 1:2500, shows the River Dargle flowing across a wide expanse of shingle before entering the sea north of the town. In order to overcome this topographical hurdle a 130 metre-long embankment had to be built across the shingle at the Martello Tower. The railway company also had to negotiate the grid of new roads planned for the seafront area. This was achieved by elevating the line south towards Bray Head onto an embankment, so that it passed by means of a series of five low bridges over the new east–west street plan leading from the old town to the seafront. Map 8, the growth map, shows these embankments on both sides of the river north of the town and also farther south where the track crosses over Sidmonton Avenue. Tunnels and cuttings were then necessary to overcome the major obstacle presented by the cliffs around Bray Head.

John Quin jr, owner of Quin's Hotel in 1852 and one of Bray's most important businessmen, had much to do with the town's development in relation to the railway. Quin's Hotel at the northern end of Main Street was connected to the sea by a long gravel walkway known as Quin's Walk (see map 2). The IHTA states that Quin, as owner of the lands between his hotel and the coast, gave consent to the railway company to site its station at the far end of his walkway.[15] He did this on condition that the company lay out a new road running parallel to the walk to be known as Quinsborough Road. This was a pivotal step in the development of the new town since Quinsborough Road became, and remains, the main artery linking the old town with the seafront. Map 7, *Heffernan's illustrated plan of Bray*, shows the new road lined with terraced housing, extending eastwards from Quin's Hotel to the Royal Marine Hotel at the seafront. Although we know from the IHTA fascicle that Bray's status as a resort town pre-dates the arrival of the railway, it was in the decades following the arrival of the railway that the town really developed as a resort. Many new hotels, including the International, Kennedy's, the Bray Head, Breslin's and the Wicklow and Wexford, were established in the period between 1850 and 1870 to accommodate the growing numbers of visitors arriving by train. Breslin's, which opened in 1855, was sold to the railway and renamed the Station Hotel in 1900. The International was opened to great acclaim in 1862 as the largest hotel in Ireland and, according to the fascicle, was built specifically for Dargan. The exception

Fig. 18.6 *Bray*, map 8, growth *c.* 1838–1909. Pink shading shows the urban area in *c.* 1838; blue expansion to 1870; and yellow expansion to 1909, extract.

was Quin's Hotel which pre-dates the railway by about eighty years, having been in existence under various names including the Meath Arms since 1776. In addition to the new hotels springing up after 1855, the post-railway town also acquired a number of bathhouses including the Railway Baths, Kelly's and Naylor's, all built in the 1860s and 1870s, and the Turkish baths on Quinsborough Road built by Dargan in 1855. This wonderfully elaborate building emblazoned with eastern-style minarets and tower is shown inset on Heffernan's plan. Other post-railway amenities added to the town were the masonic lodge, the Bray Club House and the new Carlisle pleasure grounds, all located on Quinsborough Road, and most importantly of all, the Esplanade presented to the town by William Dargan. In addition to the Railway Baths, the railway company also encouraged sea bathing by erecting bathing boxes along the strand (Fig. 18.6).

CONCLUSION

An important conclusion to be drawn from the IHTA's coverage of the railway story is that each town was unique in terms of its geography, economy, administration and business interests and it was these crucial factors that determined the impact of the railway at the local level. In some towns this impact was felt more than in others. In Kildare, Bandon and Maynooth for example, the IHTA suggests that the railway did little to stimulate business and its impact was minimal. In Downpatrick it even had a negative impact on local business since it provided easy access to the larger shops in Belfast. Taking the four towns examined in this essay, two large and two small, the railway impact was greater in the latter. Not only did the railway leave a larger physical footprint on the two smaller towns, it also became indispensible to both towns' economies as the century progressed. Geography was another vital factor in attracting the railway. Dundalk, a coastal town located half way between Dublin and Belfast, became an important junction town for the northern and southern capitals, while its excellent harbour facilities encouraged the construction of other lines connecting with the western counties of Ulster. Bray's location, also on the coast, but within reach of the Wicklow mountains and the capital city, made it an ideal location for day trippers. To this end the railway single-handedly drove the town's economy, shuttling countless thousands of passengers from city to seaside during the second half of the century. The railway's location at the seafront also shaped the future development of the resort. By contrast the larger cities tended to swallow up the railway, making its physical impact, at least in the early years, not so pronounced.

This essay has also shown that the IHTA's combined use of maps and texts is a particularly effective means of conveying the impact of the railway on Irish towns. Map 2, a reconstruction of the early Ordnance Survey town plan, available in every fascicle, provides an excellent comparative tool for evaluating the railway's impact across all the relevant towns, capturing the early morphology and topography that dictated the routes through these towns. Map 1, the later Ordnance Survey one-inch map, surveyed mostly in the 1860s, provides a similar comparative purpose while placing the town and its railways in a regional setting. By using these maps alongside other local maps such as James O'Hagan's mid-nineteenth-century maps of Dundalk and Belfast, or later directory and post office maps, a fuller understanding of the relationship between railway and town can be deduced. Much of the visual information gleaned from these rare maps is then complemented by the textual information in the essay and topographical index, and where this is most apparent, as in the case of the Dundalk and Bray fascicles, the IHTA is particularly informative. With regard to the human side of the railway story, with the exception of the Bray fascicle which highlights the involvement of William Dargan and John Quin Jr, the atlas is less informative and in order to glimpse this aspect within the IHTA fascicles one must be willing to interpret the many clues that lie hidden in the maps and accompanying lists of businesses, trades and services associated with each town.

Notes

[1] Charles Dickens, *Dealings with the firm of Dombey and son, wholesale, retail and for exportation* (London, 1848), p. 155.

[2] The phrase, 'the annihilation of space by time' was taken from Karl Marx, *Grundrisse: foundations of the critique of political economy* (London, 1973), pp 538–9. Although Marx was referring to the processes of capitalism, the phrase was quickly adopted to describe the effects of railway speed. See also Wolfgang Schivelbusch, 'Railroad space and railroad time', in *New German Critique*, xiv (1978), p. 31.

[3] Dublin and Drogheda Railway minute book, 25 May 1835 (Irish Rail Archive, Heuston Station).

[4] Taken from section **8** Population in the relevant atlas fascicles.

[5] Some important secondary sources include Ralf Roth and Marie-Noëlle Polino, *The city and the railway in Europe* (London, 2003); David Smith, 'The railway mapping of British towns', in *The Cartographic Journal,* xxv, no. 2 (1998), pp 141–54; H.C. Casserley, *Outline of Irish railway history* (North Pomfret Vermont, 1974); J.R. Kellett, *The impact of railways on Victorian cities* (London, 1969); Joseph Lee, 'An economic history of early Irish railways 1830–1853' (University College Dublin, M.A. thesis, 1965).

[6] Railway Regulation Act, 1840 (3 & 4 Vict., c. 97).

[7] Goodbody, IHTA, no. 26, *Dublin, part III, 1756 to 1847.*

[8] Gillespie and Royle, *Belfast, part 1, to 1840*, p. 1.

[9] Essays in Gillespie and Royle, IHTA, no. 12, *Belfast, part I, to 1840* and Royle, IHTA, no. 17, *Belfast, part II, 1840 to 1900.*

[10] Dickens, *Dombey and son,* p. 46.

[11] Murtagh, IHTA, no. 6, *Athlone*, p. 5.

[12] O'Sullivan, IHTA, no. 16, *Dundalk.*

[13] Davies, IHTA, no. 9, *Bray.*

[14] Ibid., p. 4.

[15] This statement appears to conflict with map 6 (1853) from the Kilruddery estate collection, which depicts much of these lands as being under lease from the earl of Meath to Thomas [Tisdall].

19. From Georgian to Victorian: Dublin 1756 to 1847

Rob Goodbody

The mid-eighteenth century was a time when information was becoming more widely available and hence the sources for a study of Dublin at this time are many. The first of the Dublin street directories appeared in the 1750s and were soon being published annually; the information they contained became more detailed and in the 1830s they began to list individual properties, street by street. Newspapers were also increasing in numbers, though most of the information initially related to world affairs rather than to Dublin. Manuscript maps were produced by certain public bodies in substantial numbers in this period, while mapping of landed estates in the city was also becoming popular. The published maps of John Rocque appeared in the 1750s and were not surpassed in quality for almost a century, when the Ordnance Survey began the production of maps at various scales. In all, there are more than 1,500 surviving maps of Dublin, or parts of Dublin, for the period between the mid-eighteenth and mid-nineteenth century, though many of these show single plots or small areas. Meanwhile, the directories began to include maps of the city with each annual edition. These were intended as street maps, were small in scale and not entirely reliable. Other maps were published at larger scales but not sufficiently detailed to show individual buildings. There were also printed guidebooks and histories and these became more frequent and informative in the nineteenth century. Public records such as those in the Registry of Deeds and the Valuation Office noted topographical information, while parliamentary papers provided a useful record, particularly in the nineteenth century, though with a somewhat uneven coverage of topic.

IMPROVING DUBLIN: WIDE STREETS COMMISSIONERS

In 1756 Dublin was a thriving place and one of the largest cities in Europe. It was the seat of the Irish parliament, had its own administration Dublin Corporation, and its population was expanding. This growth had occurred in all directions in the earlier part of the eighteenth century and subsequently included grand projects such as the earl of Kildare's mansion on the eastern fringe of the city, now known as Leinster House, and Luke Gardiner's developments at Henrietta Street and Sackville Street. Public buildings of recent date were few in number but of major significance: the Royal Barracks, now Collins Barracks, at the beginning of the century; the parliament house, completed in the early 1730s; and the new front of Trinity College, which was under construction in the 1750s.

Dublin was on the brink of major change, however, and the spark that ignited a significant element of this change was the decision to rebuild Essex Bridge in the early 1750s. This bridge was relatively narrow and inconvenient but, more significantly, it was in extremely poor condition. George Semple, the engineer and architect engaged to rebuild the bridge, had the vision to expand the project by creating new access to Dublin Castle and connect it with the grand avenue of Capel Street. Semple's proposal included a new street to be driven through to the castle, finishing at a substantial square.[1] Parliament reacted to this by passing an act nominating commissioners and giving them the power to lay out the new street.[2] This act did not provide for the building of the square adjacent to the castle but it did contain a provision for the commissioners to engage on future works to streets in the city.

John Rocque's large-scale map of Dublin, published in 1756, notes the work of the Wide Streets Commissioners by depicting their new street

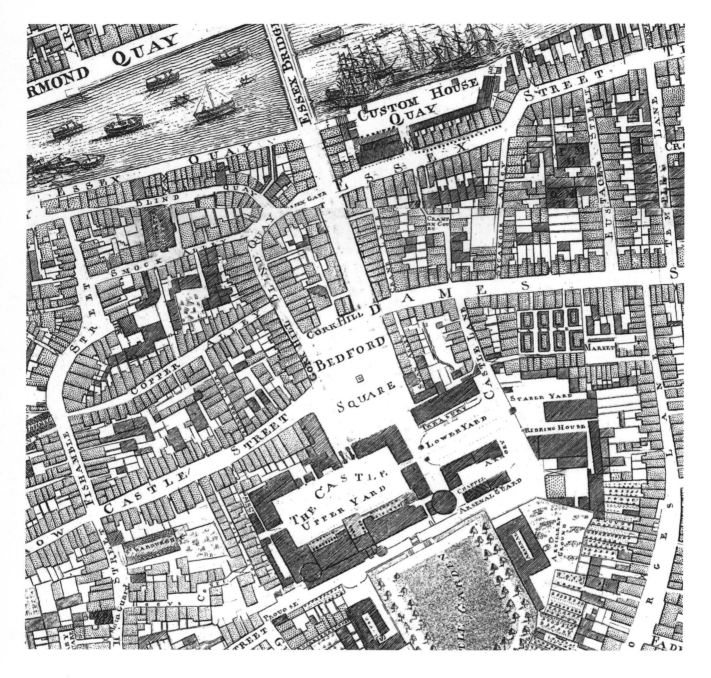

on a revised edition of the map — though he presumed, wrongly, that Bedford Square would also be laid out (Fig. 19.1).[3] This initial project marked the beginning of a series of major improvements to the city under-taken over a century by the Wide Streets Commissioners, empowered and funded by almost thirty acts of parliament. This involved significant work to existing streets, such as the widening and straightening of Dame Street with the provision of subsidiary streets such as Dame Lane and Dame Court — the commissioners' second great project — and the provision of designs for buildings to be erected along the new frontages.

Fig. 19.1 Bedford Square and Parliament Street. *Dublin, part III*, map 12, 1756–70, by John Rocque. Trinity College Dublin, extract.

Fig. 19.2 Wide Streets
Commissioners' proposal for
Westmoreland Street and D'Olier
Street overlaid on earlier street layout.
Dublin, part III, map 9, *c.* 1790.
Dublin City Library & Archive,
WSC maps, 196.

The greatest concentration of new streets laid out by the commissioners was designed to facilitate the eastern expansion of the city following the erection of the customhouse and the suggestion that a new bridge should be built to the east of the old city. The outcome was Carlisle Bridge, built in 1791, but the scheme as a whole included the extension of Drogheda Street to the new bridge, to form the present O'Connell Street Lower, and the provision of two new streets on the southern side of the river, leading from the bridge. Development went slowly in the 1790s, but Westmoreland Street was laid out at the end of the decade and D'Olier Street a little later (Fig. 19.2). Associated works included the widening of Fleet Street and College Street. Two new streets were provided running

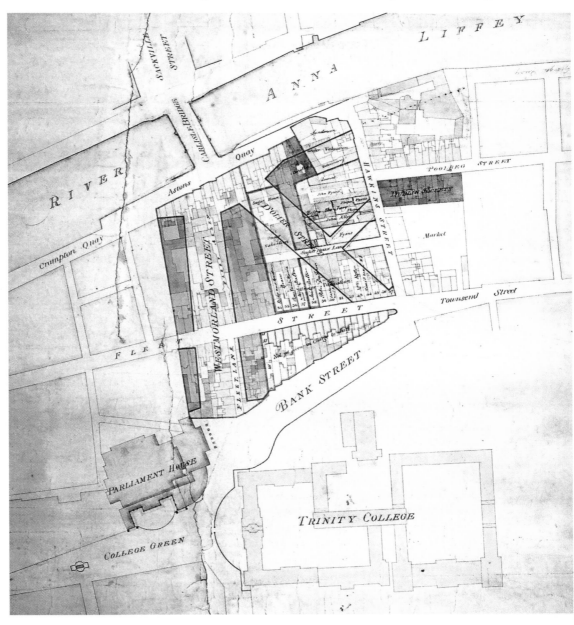

eastwards on the north and south sides of the river. The first, now Lower Abbey Street, connected with the new customhouse. This was part of a complex of streets, including Eden Quay, Old Abbey Street and the extension of Marlborough Street to the river. A proposed thoroughfare called Blenheim Street was not laid out, except for one short stretch, now known as Northumberland Square. The second on the southern side of the Liffey, now Pearse Street, connected through to the new Grand Canal Dock.

The Wide Streets Commissioners also created new quays — Eden Quay, Burgh Quay and Wellington Quay — to allow for a continuous line of quayside. In addition, small improvements were made, such as the widening of Skinners Row (now Christchurch Place) and Winetavern Street. A later power given to the commissioners was the oversight of new projects and under this provision the various developers submitted plans for new streets for approval.[4] To date no book has been produced to tell the story of the Wide Streets Commissioners, though a number of publications contain significant information, such as those by Edward McParland, Michael Gough and Edel Sheridan.[5] The papers of the commissioners are held in Dublin City Library and Archive and provide a useful primary source of information, with fifty minute books covering the period 1758 to 1851 and about nine hundred maps, more than six hundred of which may be viewed online.[6]

OTHER EIGHTEENTH-CENTURY IMPROVEMENTS

The Wide Streets Commission was not the only ad hoc body established to carry out works in the city. Arising from allegations of mismanagement by Dublin Corporation, some of the routine functions of the city were removed into the hands of bodies under central government control, including the paving, lighting and cleaning of the streets, policing and responsibility for Dublin port. A scheme was proposed in 1763 to provide a ring road around the city was given to commissioners rather than to the city authorities.[7] The project moved slowly, but was rejuvenated by a new act of parliament fifteen years later, which resulted in the construction of the north and south circular roads as turnpike roads.[8] Development along these roads came slowly, largely because they were well beyond the built-up area of the city along most of their length, though this must also have been affected by the presence of tolls. Their primary purpose, however, was traffic circulation not development.

Commissioners were established in the early 1770s to look after the paving, lighting and drainage in and around Sackville Street and another body was appointed to do likewise in Marlborough Street.[9] Twenty years later a new set of commissioners was established to enclose and lay out the ground at Merrion Square.[10] In each of these cases the commissioners were made up of local residents and the work was to be funded by money raised from the occupiers of the houses. Owing to the localised nature of these projects, records have not survived.

In 1774 the Dublin Paving Board was established to take over the paving and cleansing of the city, though in this instance the initiative came from the corporation itself.[11] The Paving Board had the power to remove obstructions from the streets, including bow windows on shops, and it exercised this authority diligently. The board was not without its problems and was reconstituted a number of times.[12]

While the establishment of these various bodies implies that Dublin Corporation was doing nothing for the city, this would not be entirely true. From time to time the city fathers implemented various projects to improve the city, including the laying out of new streets and the removal of obstructions to traffic. An example is the decision in October 1757 to widen Temple Bar and to lay out a new quay, Crampton Quay.[13] At the same time, the corporation stipulated in new leases for land along Aston Quay that the quay should be widened to 12.2 metres. In 1773 John Rocque's successor in business, Bernard Scalé, published a map of Dublin that was printed from the same plates as Rocque's map of 1756, but with alterations to bring it up to date.[14] A comparison of these two maps shows the appearance of Crampton Quay and Asdill's Row in the period between their publication. The corporation carried out another development near the top of Grafton Street in 1773, when an area was redeveloped to provide Chatham Street, Harry Street and the streets between.[15]

The corporation also took dramatic steps to secure a better supply of water for the growing city. The arrival of the Grand Canal led the corporation to enter into a contract with the canal company in 1765 for the supply of water to the city basin at James's Street. The company ran into difficulties, however, and faced with the urgent need for water Dublin Corporation decided to invest up to £20,000 to assist in the completion of the canal and a further £2,000 to keep the project going, pending the passing of an act of parliament to raise the necessary funds to finish the project.[16] The canal was duly opened to its terminus near James's Street and in the 1790s it was connected by a new line around the south of the city to the canal company's Grand Canal Dock, which opened in 1796.[17] While this was under way the Royal Canal was under construction across the northern side of the city, opening a dock at Broadstone and a connection to the River Liffey at North Wall by the end of the century.[18]

The best source of information about the activities of Dublin Corporation at this time, and indeed for the period from the twelfth century through to 1841, is the *Calendar of ancient records of Dublin*. The project to prepare this nineteen-volume work was commenced by Sir John Gilbert, who edited the first seven volumes. After his death his widow, Lady Rosa Mulholland Gilbert, continued the work and edited the other twelve volumes. Various maps have been produced over the years for the city, over and above those of the Wide Streets Commissioners, and the collection of maps of the city surveyors is held in the Dublin City Library and Archive, which has a catalogue of the maps. Many books have been written and published on the history of Dublin, most of which are concerned with specific aspects, though some have been general works. Of most use to the *Dublin, part III* atlas were Walter Harris's *The history and antiquities of the city of Dublin* published in 1766, Gilbert's three-volume *A history of the city of Dublin* of 1854–9, and the extremely detailed two-volume *History of the city of Dublin* by Warburton, Whitelaw and Walsh published in 1818. The second volume of this last-named work contains detailed information on Dublin as it was in the second decade of the nineteenth century.

PARLIAMENT AND THE PUBLIC SECTOR

During the latter half of the eighteenth century the number of acts of parliament passed in relation to Dublin increased significantly. Some of these related to financial matters, such as subsidising grain prices in the city, while others facilitated the various projects already mentioned. About 170 acts relating to Dublin were passed by the Irish parliament between 1757 and 1800. The number of acts passed in each decade increased after 1770, though it must be emphasised that this was part of a national trend and was not specific to Dublin. Some were for the support of charities such as the lying-in hospital and the female orphan house, and institutions such as the Hibernian Marine School and the foundling hospital.

It was in the opening years of the nineteenth century, however, that the provision of public institutions accelerated and their names mark the succession of lords lieutenant of the day — the Hardwicke Fever Hospital (1803), Bedford Asylum (1806), Richmond Lunatic Asylum (1810), Richmond Female Penitentiary (1812), Richmond Bridewell (1813), Richmond Surgical Hospital (1817), two Whitworth Hospitals (1817) and the Talbot Dispensary (*c.* 1818).[19]

Such institutions were concentrated in two locations. The bigger concentration was in the north city, where the house of industry was founded on Brunswick Street, now North King Street, in 1772. The availability of land nearby and, particularly, open farmland to the north allowed for sister institutions to be opened in the immediate vicinity, expanding northwards when larger premises were built. On the southern side of the river was the City Workhouse, which had been established in the early eighteenth century and by the end of the century was the location for the foundling hospital and a bridewell, as well as housing lunatics. These two locations became the focus for the two union workhouses established in the 1830s as part of the national programme. The South Dublin Union off James's Street replaced the old workhouse and foundling hospital, while the North Dublin Union north of Brunswick Street took over from the house of industry. By 1847 the area between North King Street and Grangegorman was the location for the North Dublin Union, Richmond Female Penitentiary, Richmond Lunatic Asylum, Richmond Surgical Hospital, Hardwicke Fever Hospital, Whitworth Hospital, a second lunatic asylum, a dispensary and a house of refuge.

The best summary of the Irish parliament and its workings from the late seventeenth century to the abolition of the parliament in 1800 is Edith Johnston-Liik's six-volume study, *History of the Irish parliament 1692–1800, commons, constituencies and statutes*, published by the Ulster Historical Foundation in 2002. This work includes a table of all of the statutes passed in that time. The statutes themselves are to be found in a twenty-volume set, *The statutes at large passed by the parliament in Ireland*. A second set entitled *Statutes passed in the parliaments held in Ireland* is not so useful, since the twelve volumes were published in the later eighteenth century and included only those acts, or parts of acts, that were still in force. Statutes of the United Kingdom parliament were also published in volumes and from 1801 a new volume was published for each year. Indexes were published periodically, including, in the mid-1830s, an index to statutes relating to Ireland, which was followed for a number of years by annual supplements.[20]

The various hospitals and other institutions are mentioned in directories over the years and also in statutes, particularly when parliament was voting money for their upkeep. Warburton, Whitelaw and Walsh, volume 2, contains a great deal of information about those institutions and charities that were in existence in 1818. In many cases, the history of individual institutions has been published in book form or in articles or papers. The most comprehensive set of articles on Dublin is to be found in the well over two hundred issues of the *Dublin Historical Record* that have appeared since its first volume in 1938.

Private development

Thus far we have looked at developments undertaken by various state agencies, with some input from charitable organisations. The lion's share of the expansion of housing in the city was, however, the result of private enterprise including ground landlords, large-scale developers such as the Gardiners and small builders or speculators who were carrying out work on sites made available by developers. Parts of this story are well known, particularly as regards the two large estates: the Fitzwilliam estate, which was land owned by one family since medieval times; and the contrasting Gardiner estate, which was the result of piecemeal, though substantial, land acquisition over a long period. While the Gardiners were constrained by the need to acquire land, they were not hindered by historic land-ownership and hence they could move in any direction that they wished. The major project on this estate was the creation of the longest Georgian street in the city, running over some 1,200 metres. This began at the cus-tomhouse where the twin streets of Gardiner Street and Store Street are aligned symmetrically on the north portico, though the view up Store Street is so short that its significance has been ignored. A look at a wider area on the 1843 Ordnance Survey six-inch map suggests that Amiens Street is closely aligned on Store Street but turns away from it rather than meeting it.[21] This meeting appears to have been the original intention and is shown on the street map in *Wilson's Dublin directory* of 1791, though by 1794 the proposal had failed to materialise.

Gardiner Street commenced at the oval feature that is Beresford Place and ran in a straight line to Mountjoy Square before turning slightly to meet Dorset Street. Crossing over Dorset Street, it entered a new focus of streets that converged on another oval feature at Royal Circus, which was similar in scale to Beresford Place. At the other end of Royal Circus, Blessington Street was laid out to continue the line of Sackville Street, via the Wide Streets Commissioners' North Frederick Street, to form the (asymmetrical) mirror image (to coin an oxymoron!) of the Gardiner Street line. This design managed to incorporate the pre-existing Eccles Street and all combined to produce a new architectural set-piece.

Generations of architectural historians have argued over whether Royal Circus ever existed, generally concluding that, despite leases being granted subject to strict conditions regarding the design and materials of the houses, the project never left the drawing board (Fig. 19.3). Nevertheless, the constituent streets still managed to be shown on maps and to be listed in directories for more than thirty years. In fact, Royal Circus *was* laid out. The Wide Streets Commissioners approved the layout on 13 July 1792

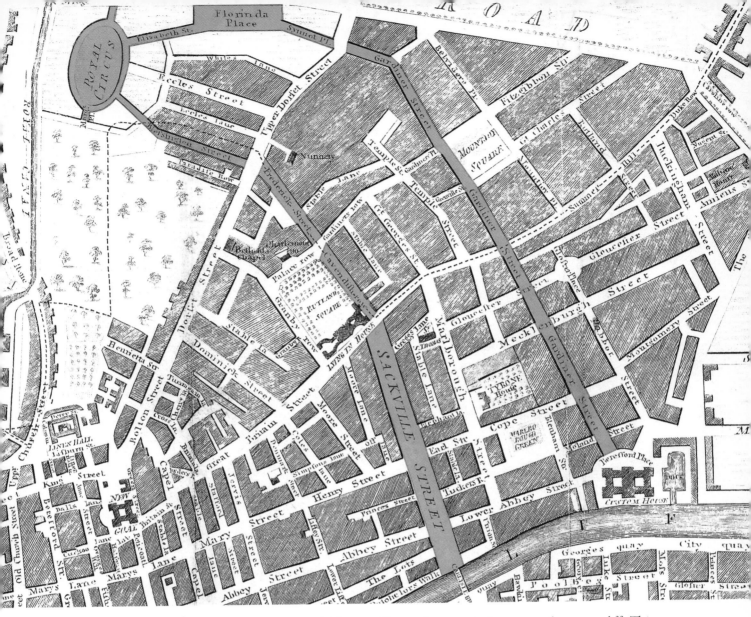

Fig. 19.3 Gardiner's grand design for the area around Gardiner Street, Royal Circus and Sackville Street. Base map from *Wilson's Dublin directory*, 1801.

and instructed Thomas Sherrard to mark it out on the ground.[22] This happened and the commissioners later noted that the grounds for Royal Circus had been laid out.[23] While directories and associated maps may anticipate development, the appearance of the remnants of the assemblage of streets on the Ordnance Survey maps of the 1840s, fifty-five years after being laid out, is proof that the project existed on the ground in some form, though it is clear that no houses were ever built on Royal Circus, Elizabeth Street or Florinda Place — the streets that connected Royal Circus, via Sinnott Place, with Gardiner Street (Fig. 19.4).

The two major developers of Georgian Dublin tend to hog the limelight and draw attention away from the smaller players, some of whom were influential. Notable in this regard was the development of Eccles Street and North Great George's Street, to the north of the city, and

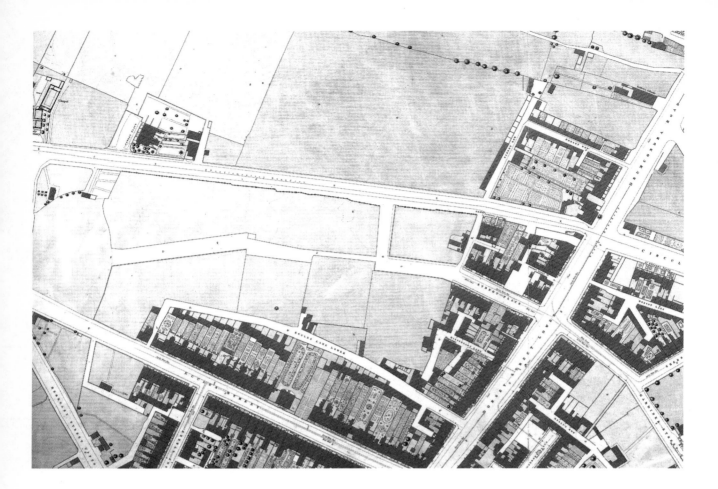

Fig. 19.4 Remnants of Royal Circus, Elizabeth Street and Florinda Place from OS printed town plan, Dublin city, sheet 3, 1847. National Library of Ireland, extract.

Hatch Street and Harcourt Street to the south. Some of these have date-stones but in most cases the streets and their names existed before dates were assigned on stones. For instance, a plaque in Sherrard Street gives a date of 1825, while the street is shown with that name on Campbell's map of 1811. Lower Mount Street is more extreme with a plaque bearing the date 1825, though the street is listed in the Registry of Deeds in 1780 and in the street directories by the 1790s.[24]

Various papers relating to the private estates in the city survive, though the coverage is uneven. There is a substantial collection of papers belonging to the Fitzwilliam estate, later known as the Pembroke estate, and these are held in the National Archives of Ireland. These records include leases, letters and maps. The papers of the Gardiner estate are held in the National Library of Ireland, as are those of the Domvile estate. This library also holds the Longfield Collection, which are the maps prepared by a firm of surveyors in the late eighteenth and, more particularly, early nineteenth century; these include more than three hundred maps relating to Dublin city, though many of these are of individual plots or small areas. Among the secondary sources, many Dublin-related books mention the urban estates. One enduring work has been Maurice Craig's *Dublin 1660–1860*, published in 1952 and republished several times since, including a facsimile edition in 1980 with notes by the author. An extremely comprehensive work relating to buildings and with a great deal of ancillary information is Christine Casey's *The buildings of Dublin: the city within the Grand Canal and the Royal Canal and the Circular Road with the Phoenix Park*, 2005. Since the publication of the *Dublin, part III* fascicle, David Dickson's *Dublin: the making of a capital city* has been published.

Apart from the manuscript maps mentioned above, printed maps show a progression, as more and more streets were added to the city. The city directories had maps bound with them from the latter half of the eighteenth century though, as has been mentioned, they are not always accurate since they tended to use the same plate for a number of years, often without updating.[25] Apart from Rocque's and Scalé's maps, a very useful map was published by Thomas Campbell in 1811 at a smaller but nonetheless useful scale. Those of Faden, in 1797, and Cooke, in 1822 are useful, but of a smaller scale. The Ordnance Survey produced a map of the city at a scale of six inches to the mile in 1837. It was updated and published in 1843. It should not be referred to as an 1837 map as this can cause confusion; for instance, Earlsfort Terrace is shown on the map but it was not laid out until the early 1840s. There are earlier manuscript Ordnance Survey maps at six inches to the mile and at the larger-scale of five-foot to the mile, prepared in 1838 and updated to 1843. The five-foot maps were issued in 1847 by the Ordnance Survey in thirty-three sheets and are of an exceptionally high standard.[26]

The Dublin directories provide another means of observing the growth of the city. *Wilson's Dublin directory*, published from the mid-eighteenth century, carried lists of streets with various other lists that can be used to trace streets, buildings and individuals, though not all people were listed. In the mid 1830s Pettigrew and Oulton began to publish a Dublin directory and for the first time this included listings by street with the names of the occupiers. In the 1840s Thom began a similar exercise and the two directories ran in parallel briefly before Thom became the sole publisher of the Dublin directories.

POPULATION

The various population figures that have been produced for the eighteenth and early nineteenth century need to be treated with caution. The first question mark must always be over the basis for the figure, as some are nothing more than estimates or guesses, while others are based on some rational statistic such as numbers of houses. An example is the population figures produced by Daniel Beaufort around 1790, which underestimated the number of people per house in the city.[27] The second point that is often overlooked is the geographical extent that is covered by population statistics and this is particularly significant when considering Dublin. While these population figures cannot be compared with the accuracy of the later census-derived numbers, they can still be instructive, provided their inadequacies are not forgotten.

A graph of the various figures shows a steady upwards trend but there is a distinct reversal in this growth around the year 1800 (Fig. 19.5). This is significant, since it coincides with the union between Ireland and Great Britain. This is a time when popular belief has it that Dublin began a steady decline. Given the need for extreme caution with the figures, already noted, how reliable is this non-aligned figure showing a contraction of population? This downturn figure relates to the year 1804 and has a good pedigree, originating with the Revd James Whitelaw, of St Catherine's Church of Ireland parish in Thomas Street. Whitelaw established himself as probably the most reliable statistician in eighteenth-century Dublin or, more correctly, the opening years of the nineteenth, since he gathered his data in 1798 and analysed it over the ensuing seven years. The story of how he carried out his census of the city in that strife-torn year of 1798 belongs elsewhere, but it must be noted that his methodology incorporated extremely rigorous checks and cross-checks of his data collection, with the

Fig. 19.5 Estimated population of Dublin, adjusted to correct Beaufort's error.

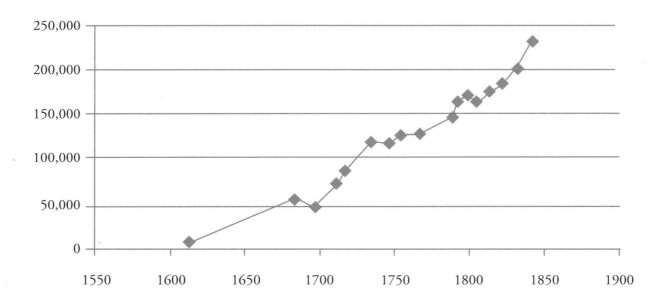

willingness to improve techniques where inadequacies were found.[28] In his analysis, he allowed for the problem arising from different definitions of the geographical area of the city by presenting his figures in a way that allowed them to be aggregated to accord with a variety of boundaries.

As a response to the Emmet rising of 1803 the government implemented certain measures in the city that included the enumeration of the population, district by district. Whitelaw found the data to be reliable and incorporated the results in his own publication. In so doing he examined the figures carefully and adjusted them to allow full comparison with his own figure of six years previously. The result is that Whitelaw has presented us with two figures for the population of the city, one taken at the time of the 1798 rebellion and the other four years after the union. The result, he found, was a fall in population of 4,200 over the six-year period. While this fits with the general perception of post-union Dublin, the subsequent population figures do not.

In 1813 the first official census of Ireland was carried out but, in general, it was a disaster. Out of forty local authorities charged with the task of carrying out the census, only ten managed it with any degree of success.[29] One of these was Dublin and the figure of 176,000 was recorded, representing an increase since 1804. The first full census of Ireland, carried out in 1821, is also not considered to be reliable and produced a figure of 186,000, representing an increase of 10,000 in six years. Subsequent censuses in 1831 and 1841 continued this trend, reaching 233,000 by the latter date. Whether or not we choose to believe the accuracy of the 1813 and 1821 censuses, their figures fit with the trend and show that the population of Dublin increased significantly after the union.

Towards the end of our period the boundaries of Dublin city were redrawn and an examination of the old and the new illustrate the problem of comparing population statistics depending on which boundary they relate to — the built-up area, the city, the city and the liberties or the area within the circular roads. The population statistics agree with what is seen on the ground, with development continuing in many parts of the city, particularly in the south-eastern sector. Virtually all of the development in Fitzwilliam Square and Fitzwilliam Street dates from after the union and the same applies to other streets nearby, such as Herbert Street and the two Mount Streets. This continued southwards into the area around Heytesbury Street and South Circular Road. Things were less vibrant on the Gardiner estate, where development fell off markedly, particularly in the area beyond Dorset Street.

CONCLUSION

Dublin in the late eighteenth century was a city of optimism. The independence from Westminster that the Irish parliament gained was part of this trend and represented the political aspect of this confidence, while the works of the Wide Streets Commissioners, the construction of great public buildings and the expansion of the city into salubrious Georgian squares and terraces reflected this in more tangible form. The political optimism was severely dented by the rebellion of 1798 and the schism caused by the Act of Union, followed by the Emmet rising, while the war with France, brought with it invasions and threats of invasions. Dublin after the Union was a changed city: it had become 'the deposed capital'.[30]

Development continued apace and the population increase was maintained, but the gloss was gone. What does not appear in the maps of development or in the population statistics is the continuing collapse of the traditional home-based textile industry of the city; this was blamed on the Union, but was more a result of Dublin's lack of natural resources while the industrial revolution was affecting other cities. With a city struggling to modernise, many of the middle classes chose to live outside the city boundaries from the second quarter of the century onward. As the nearby residential areas of Rathmines, Rathgar, Pembroke, Blackrock and Kingstown became the home for increasing numbers of the well-to-do, the city's struggle with its finances worsened. Development continued, but with the sizes of new houses decreasing, while more and more of the larger houses were built outside the city boundary. On the wealthy Fitzwilliam/Pembroke estate the first large development following the redrafting of the city boundaries was at Waterloo Road and Wellington Road, outside the new city limits.

In the meantime, the Gardiner estate, on the northern side of the city, was badly managed in the nineteenth century and without the guiding hand of a strong head landlord it descended into chaos, with many of the Georgian buildings sublet into multiple occupation, ultimately becoming one of the worst slum areas of the city. At the end of the period came the disaster of the Great Famine, bringing large numbers of refugees into the city and swelling the numbers living in poverty. While little of this is visible in map form, the more positive changes in the city are more in evidence, including the canals and the improvements in the port, the arrival of the railways, the expansion of the breweries and distilleries and increasing numbers of banks and other commercial enterprises. The Ordnance Survey's five-foot to the mile maps even show the street lighting, the water mains and the sewers. The map-based picture of the city is also augmented by the other sources that were becoming increasingly common during the period, including newspapers, census records, administrative records and, in particular, the street directories. In 1847, at the end of our period, Dublin was continuing to expand, though a significant amount of development was by now taking place beyond the canals, which brought new problems to the city — but consideration of this would involve straying outside our geographical area and our time zone.

NOTES

[1] Lennon, IHTA, no. 19, *Dublin, part II, 1610 to 1756*, map 15.

[2] 31 Geo. II, c. 19.

[3] John Rocque, *An exact survey of the city and suburbs of Dublin* (4 sheets, Dublin, 1756, with some later alterations to 1770); Lennon, *Dublin, part II, 1610 to 1756*, map 16.

[4] 30 Geo. III, c. 19.

[5] Edward McParland, 'The Wide Streets Commissioners: their importance for Dublin architecture in the late 18th–early 19th century', in *Quarterly Bulletin of the Irish Georgian Society*, xv, no. 1 (1972), pp 1–32; Michael Gough, 'The Dublin Wide Streets Commissioners (1758–1851): an early modern planning authority', in *Pleanáil*, no. 11 (1992–3), pp 126–55; Edel Sheridan, 'Designing the capital city: Dublin, *c.* 1660–1810', in Joseph Brady and Anngret Simms (eds), *Dublin through space and time* (Dublin, 2001), pp 66–135.

[6] Wide Streets Commission maps and minute books, Dublin City Library and Archive, Pearse Street, Dublin, http://www.dublincity.ie/library-galleries1/167 (last accessed 24 Feb. 2017).

[7] 3 Geo. III, c. 36.

[8] 17 & 18 Geo. III, c. 10.

[9] 11 & 12 Geo. III, c. 13.

[10] 31 Geo. III, c. 45.

[11] *Calendar of ancient records of Dublin in the possession of the municipal corporation*, ed. J.T. Gilbert and R.M. Gilbert (19 vols, Dublin, 1889–1944), xii, p. 308; 13 & 14 Geo. III, c. 22.

[12] Finnian Ó Cionnaith, *Exercise of authority: surveyor Thomas Owen and the paving, cleansing and lighting of Georgian Dublin* (Dublin, 2016).

[13] *Calendar of ancient records of Dublin*, x, p. 290.

[14] Bernard Scalé, *An accurate survey of the city and suburbs of Dublin by Mr Rocque with additions and improvements*, 4 sheets with 2 additional strips (London, 1773); Goodbody, IHTA, no. 26, *Dublin, part III, 1756 to 1847*, map 7.

[15] *Calendar of ancient records of Dublin*, xii, pp 285–8.

[16] Ibid., pp 134–6; 11 & 12 Geo. III, c. 31.

[17] Ruth Delany, *The Grand Canal of Ireland* (Dublin, 1995).

[18] Peter Clarke, *The Royal Canal: the complete story* (Dublin, 1992); Ruth Delany and Ian Bath, *Ireland's Royal Canal, 1789–2009* (Dublin, 2010).

[19] See John Warburton, James Whitelaw and Robert Walsh, *History of the city of Dublin* (2 vols, Dublin, 1818).

[20] Andrew Newton Oulton, *Index to the statutes at present in force in, or affecting, Ireland from the year 1310 to 1838, inclusive* (2nd edn, Dublin, 1839).

[21] This may be seen on map 4 of Goodbody, *Dublin, part III, 1756 to 1847*.

[22] Wide Streets Commission minute books, xi, 13 July 1792.

[23] Ibid., xii, 10 Mar. 1794.

[24] RD 333/301/224307; *Wilson's Dublin directory*, 1791, p. 7.

[25] Andrew Bonar Law and Charlotte Bonar Law, *A contribution towards a catalogue of the prints and maps of Dublin city and county, volume 2: maps* (Dublin, 2005), p. 361.

[26] See Frank Cullen, *Dublin 1847: city of the Ordnance Survey* (Dublin, 2015).

[27] D.A. Beaufort, *Memoir of a map of Ireland* (London, 1792), p. 44.

[28] James Whitelaw, *An essay on the population of Dublin, 1798* (Dublin, 1805).

[29] *Abstract of the answers and returns made pursuant to an act of the United Parliament*, HC 1824 (577), vii.

[30] M.E. Daly, *Dublin, the deposed capital: a social and economic history 1860–1914* (Cork, 1984).

Index

Page numbers in italic refer to illustrations.

H

Hamiltons, the (of Cos Down and
    Louth) 245–6, 247, 251
Hill, John 262, 269
Honorable the Irish Society 88, 200,
    202, 207, 209, 212, 214, 215
Horner, Arnold 282, 286, 293, 304

I

Iona 43, 70, 78, 93, 94, 95

J

James I 7, 88, 207
John, king of England 5, 6

K

Kells 9, 42, 43, 45, 50, 52, 57–8, 68,
    69, 72, 73, 75, 77, 79, 82, 83, 97,
    116, 122–3, *123*, 125, 126, 128,
    165, 167, 232, 288, *290*, 291, 292,
    293, 293–4
    Augustinian abbey of St Mary 122,
        123
    castle 123, 175
    Columban monastery 43, 84
    Fair Green 123, 290
    Headfort 58, 250, 251
    Headfort Place 9, 290
    market cross 230, 232
    parish church 123, 250
    round tower 122, 225
Kildare 17, 19, 42, 43, 45, 52, 57, 68,
    69, 75, *80*, 116–17, *117*, 125, 126,
    129, 165, 167, 324
    castle 116, *117*, 175
Kilkenny 8, 15, 32, 42, 43–4, 45, 52, 59,
    68, 72, 75, 82, 116, 118, *119, 120,*
    121, 122, 125, 126, 128, 129, 135,
    137, 138, 142, 143, 145, 223–4,
    225, 227, *231*, 241, 284, 292

barracks 273, 274, 275
church of St Mary 224, 226
Dominican priory 122, 228
Franciscan friary 122, 224, 226
Green's Bridge 44, 122
Hightown (or Englishtown) 44, 120,
    122, 142, 223
Irishtown 44, 120, 122, 138, 167, 223
James's Street 138, 139
Kilkenny Castle 44, 118, 120, 136,
    137, 138, 145, 175, 223
market cross 230, 231
market place 227, 230
parish church 118, 122
round tower 44, 118, 223
St Canice's Cathedral 44, 118, 120,
    223, 224, 226
St Mary's Church 227, 228
tholsel 227–8, 229
town wall 122, 129
Killaloe 256, 258
Kinsale 20, 243, 274

L

Lagan, River 34, 193, 317
Laois, Co. 7, 199, 255
Larkin, William 260, *261*
Lecale barony 188, 189
Leinster 8, 43, 120, 272
Leixlip 254, 259
Liffey, River 37, 46, 54, 152, 154, 159,
    273, 331
Limerick 10, 16, 17, 18, 20, 46, *47*, 48,
    50, 52, 60, 79, 84, 103–11, *104,*
    107, 108, 109, 110, 135, 147, 148,
    149, 150, 151, 152, *153*, 153–4,
    154, 155, 156, 157–8, 159–60,
    171, 221, 243, 246, 250, 255,
    256–9, *257*, 264, 270, *271*, 274,
    276, 285, 288, *289*, 290, 292,
    295–6, 308
    Athlunkard 46, 61, 103
    Baal's Bridge 105, 109, 110, 258
    barracks 270, 271, 272, 274
    Charlotte's Quay 158, 258
    Englishtown 8, 48, 106, 107, 154,
        158, 258, 295
    Irishtown 8, 48, 106, 107, 157, 158,
        167, 258, 295